Vietnam – Politics and Economics

edited by
Prof. Dr. Quang Minh Pham
PD Dr. Detlef Briesen
Dr. Thi Thuy Trang Nguyen

Volume 9

Vu Thi Anh Thu | Nguyen Thi Thuy Trang [eds.]

The Indo-Pacific Region

Insights into a Geopolitical Construct between Great Power Politics and New Forms of Regional Cooperation

USSH
TRƯỜNG ĐẠI HỌC KHOA HỌC XÃ HỘI VÀ NHÂN VĂN
VNU UNIVERSITY OF SOCIAL SCIENCES AND HUMANITIES

Nomos

© Coverpicture: https://de.wikipedia.org/wiki/Vietnam#/media/Datei:North_West_Skyline_of_Hanoi_(8719994394).jpg

The Deutsche Nationalbibliothek lists this publication in the Deutsche Nationalbibliografie; detailed bibliographic data are available on the Internet at http://dnb.d-nb.de

ISBN 978-3-7560-3359-1 (Print)
978-3-7489-6322-6 (ePDF)

Onlineversion
Inlibra

1st Edition 2026

Foreword

It is with great pride and anticipation that I present this significant volume, *The Indo Pacific Region: Insights into a Geopolitical Construct between Great Power Politics and New Forms of Regional Cooperation.* This book represents a pivotal contribution to the growing body of scholarship on a region whose strategic, economic, and political importance has never been more relevant to the international community.

In recent years, the Indo-Pacific has become a critical arena where the evolving architecture of global order is most visibly contested and constructed. As the world experiences a transformation in international relations – from bipolar rivalries to a fluid and multi-nodal system – the need to comprehend the region's complex dynamics has become urgent. This publication answers that need with intellectual rigor and rich interdisciplinary insight.

Produced through the collaborative efforts of scholars from both within and outside the Indo-Pacific, this book is especially notable for its emphasis on diverse perspectives. Of particular importance is the contribution of Vietnamese academics, who bring a distinct and balanced view shaped by Vietnam's strategic non-alignment and nuanced engagement in global affairs. Their work highlights the region's internal agency and the potential for cooperative solutions in an increasingly polarized world. The chapters reflect deep scholarly engagement, born out of the international conference *Opportunities and Challenges for the Stability and Development of the Indo-Pacific Region*, hosted by VNU – University of Social Sciences and Humanities, Hanoi. From theoretical explorations to practical ease studies, the book captures the dynamic interplay between global powers and regional actors, offering critical insights into both strategic competition and emerging avenues for multilateral cooperation.

Importantly, this volume will also serve as a key resource for the teaching of the International Studies major, supporting the development of globally attuned, analytically equipped students ready to engage with complex regional and international issues.

This volume will be of great value not only to policymakers and scholars but to all who seek to understand the challenges and opportunities shaping the Indo-Pacific's future. It is a testament to the VNU – University of Social

Sciences and Humanities, Hanoi's enduring commitment to academic excellence, international dialogue, and the pursuit of peace through informed research.

Prof. Dr. Hoang Anh Tuan
Rector
VNU – University of Social Sciences and Humanities, Hanoi

Table of Contents

II. Great Powers from Outside the Indo-Pacific Region: Imaginations, Interests and Strategies

III. The Indo-Pacific from the Inside: The Risks and Benefits of a Geopolitical Imaginary for the Countries Concerned

Editorial

This is already the ninth volume in our Vietnam – Politics and Economics book series, which has been published since 2020. The overall project is clear evidence of the very fruitful cooperation between two academic institutions: the University of Social Sciences and Humanities, Vietnam National University, Hanoi (USSH), and Justus Liebig University Giessen. The publication of this anthology is based on financial support from the USSH. We would like to express our special thanks to the rector, Prof. Hoang Anh Tuan. Another indispensable part of the book's creation is the support of the German co-editor of the book series, Detlef Briesen, through the DAAD (German Academic Exchange Service) in his capacity as an Advisor for Higher Education in Vietnam. We would also like to take this opportunity to express our sincere thanks to all those involved in this project, in particular the two editors responsible for the content, Dr Vu Thi Anh Thu and Dr Nguyen Thi Thuy Trang. This also applies, of course, to the authors of the individual essays, whose outstanding quality is further proof of the high standard of social and cultural research in Vietnam today.

The volume *The Indo-Pacific Region: Insights into a Geopolitical Construct between Great Power Politics and New Forms of Regional Cooperation* focuses on the issue of geopolitics in and for the so-called Indo-Pacific region, a topic that some of the contributors have already worked from 2020 to 2023 on as part of a project funded by the Konrad-Adenauer-Stiftung, Hanoi (KAS) – *Nguyen Thi Thuy Trang/Detlef Briesen: The EU Approach to Cooperation in the Indo-Pacific: From Strategy to Practice.*

The individual academic articles published as part of this partnership had already highlighted the diverse problems associated with the geopolitical concept of an *Indo-Pacific Region.* The present volume attempts to focus on these issues in three ways, in greater detail than was possible at the time: the first part is more theory-based, the second section looks at the involvement of major powers from outside the region, and the third presents the perspective of countries that can be classified as *Indo-Pacific* in the narrower geographical sense. The numerous innovative research findings presented here show one thing above all: that the era of bi- or even unipolar world orders from 1945 to 2001 is finally over and that the international system is beginning to develop globally and in respective regional interactions towards a new kind of complexity. The actual and thoroughly successful aim of this book is to examine more precisely this new complexity in a significant part of planet Earth.

Giessen and Hanoi, in Summer 2025
Detlef Briesen for the board of editors

Introduction

Vu Thi Anh Thu

The Indo-Pacific region spans a considerable expanse between the Atlantic and Pacific Oceans, possessing substantial strategic importance in economic and geopolitical contexts. This region, comprising 60 per cent of the global population and over half of the world's megacities, serves as the epicentre of international engagement. The Indo-Pacific region is at the intersection of strategic interests, emerging as a central area for both cooperation and contention among major powers. Many historical, economic, and geopolitical considerations impact interactions in this complicated region, as states struggle to cooperate while navigating old rivalries. Thus, knowing these intricate relationships is crucial to understanding modern international politics, especially given rising tensions and shifting alliances. It can be observed that traditional superpowers, particularly the United States, are trying to establish new orders in the international system with the help of new geopolitical imaginings, first and foremost the geopolitical construct of the *Indo-Pacific region*. Besides, China, Japan, India, and ASEAN countries are among the fastest-growing economies in the region. This presents avenues for trade, investment, and development; however, the geopolitical competition among the powers is notably intricate, and there is a clear desire to avoid destabilizing the region.

The region also faces transnational concerns regarding environmental degradation, climate change, pandemics, marine security and safety, etc. These issues could lead to regional conflicts or crises. Many multilateral and sub-multilateral cooperation mechanisms have been established in this region over the past decades to help countries resolve disagreements and build cooperative opportunities to address complexities and uncertainties to create a stable and sustainable future.

The research outcomes presented in this book emerged from comprehensive and candid conversations during the international conference titled *Opportunities and Challenges for the Stability and Development of the Indo-Pacific Region*, held at VNU – University of Social Sciences and Humanities, Hanoi, on September 17, 2024. *The in total 19 chapters* in the book are classified into three main parts.

Part I. The Strategic Landscape of the Indo - Pacific Region from Theoretical Perspectives

This section comprises four chapters that examine the concept of the *Indo-Pacific region*, the characteristics of the system and its associated uncertainties. The Indo-Pacific is examined from three different theoretical angles: firstly, from a systems theory perspective, i.e. from the viewpoint of so-called complex systems; secondly, based on Anthony Giddens' structuration theory; and thirdly, from a more geographical approach that examines the role of the imaginative in geopolitical projections such as that of the Indo-Pacific. Another chapter highlights the development of the *Cooperation and Conflict Index in the Indo-Pacific*, aimed at delivering a systematic evaluation of the region's stability using aggregated data.

Part II. Great Powers from Outside the Indo-Pacific Region: Imaginations, Interests and Strategies

This section has eight studies that examine the viewpoints and policies of the US, EU, and Russia on the Indo-Pacific region.

Chapters 5 and 6 elucidate the Indo-Pacific strategy adopted by US Presidents Donald Trump and Joe Biden, designed to contain China and recalibrate their approach from 2017 to the present. This strategy has resulted in the establishment of numerous new mechanisms in the region and engendered various evolvements that may influence the area's security and development. The US Indo-Pacific strategy is regarded as being in the preliminary phases of execution, with some outcomes not yet distinctly apparent. Concurrently, China is implementing initiatives to garner support from regional nations. Consequently, the topic of whether the United States would effectively limit China in the Indo-Pacific region remains unresolved and necessitates further time for a definitive answer.

It is fascinating to have chapters 7, 8, 9, and 10 by Vietnamese scholars analysing the *EU Connectivity Strategy* with the Indo-Pacific region. The authors discuss connectivity in terms of economic, security, and EU's value-based diplomacy with the Indo-Pacific region. Comments on the EU Connectivity Strategy from the perspective of those outside the EU but within the Indo-Pacific region can provide EU readers with a broader and more nuanced understanding of the interactions and connections in the strategies of the countries.

Chapter 11 provides a comprehensive analysis of the parallels and differences between the two strategies and their effects on international relations in the Indo-Pacific. The recent tariff policies enacted by President Donald Trump on many nations, including the EU, and direct disagreement with the EU about the resolution of the Russia-Ukraine war, will undoubtedly elicit a strategic reaction from the EU and other nations. The author anticipates that President Donald Trump may implement new modifications, enhancements, and ramifications for the Indo-Pacific region and the European Union's Indo-Pacific strategy.

Chapter 12 examines how geopolitical theory, neoliberal institutionalism, and soft power theory offer a conceptual framework for comprehending Russia's engagement in the region. Russia possesses a historical rapport with the Mekong nations and the capability to tackle issues concerning climate change, water resource management, and renewable energy technology, facilitating the formulation of a regional strategy that aligns with developmental objectives advantageous to both Russia and the Mekong Subregion.

Part III. The Indo-Pacific from the Inside: the Risks and Benefits of a Geopolitical Imaginary for the Countries Concerned

This section contains of seven studies that analyse the strategies and responses of various countries in the region, including India, China, Japan, Vietnam, and ASEAN. The competition between the US and China, coupled with their efforts to garner support from regional countries, has resulted in a degree of instability in the area while simultaneously creating numerous development opportunities. Japan, India, and China each engage in distinct strategic assessments, with ASEAN positioned as a focal point in their pursuit of support opportunities. The analysis of the similarities and differences in those strategies reveals the competitive dynamics in the region while also offering strategic advantages for ASEAN countries, including Vietnam, contingent upon the implementation of suitable and effective corresponding strategies.

Contribution of the Book

Firstly, the book explores novel theoretical frameworks and methodologies regarding the structure-unit connection within international relations theories and practices of the Indo-Pacific regional system, developing metrics to evaluate the interplay between cooperation and conflict in the region. The investigations aim to elucidate the interactions in this region by evaluating the internal structures and patterns that bolster cooperative frameworks while addressing potential disputes of the region. This indicator is significant not only for its capacity to improve diplomatic initiatives but also as a mechanism for forecasting alterations in regional stability and security dynamics.

Secondly, the book examines the strategies and policies of several big and medium-sized nations, including the US, China, Russia, Japan, South Korea, and the European Union, regarding the Indo-Pacific region. Collaborative opportunities and responses to problems aimed at ensuring stability and development in the Indo-Pacific area.

Thirdly, the book examines Vietnam's relationship, as an emerging middle power, with Indo-Pacific countries concerning collaboration, competitiveness, and conflict management in the region. The studies presented in the book will offer recommendations for Vietnam's response to the turbulent geopolitical landscape, consequently serving as a reference for the formulation of more suitable and successful foreign and security policies for the country.

Acknowledgements

The assistance of numerous institutions and individuals was indispensable in the composition of this book. We owe VNU – University of Social Sciences and Humanities, Hanoi a special note of thanks for awarding a grand under project number *7181/HĐ-XHNV-XBQT*. We also must thank the authors of the book, the editorial team of Faculty of International Studies who has work extremely hard to make the book a success, and we are deeply grateful for the excellent editing by Prof. Dr. Detlef Briesen from Justus-Liebig Universität Giessen, DAAD Counselor for Higher Education and the Nomos Publishing House, Germany.

I.
The Strategic Landscape of the Indo-Pacific from Theoretical Perspectives

Chapter 1: Navigating the Indo-Pacific Complex System

Philippe Le Prestre

The discourse around the Indo-Pacific Region (IPR) offers a good opportunity to examine how thinking in complex systems (CS) can help apprehend turbulence, integrate the dynamics of the system into the definition of foreign policy problems, and delineate the contours of foreign policymaking in the context of uncertainty. The IPR is an attempt at self-organisation in the context of a larger Indo-Pacific complex system, the properties of which have implications for how one approaches the definition of appropriate national strategies, questioning much received wisdom and common practices in the process. These aspects are examined through a discussion of the nature of the system and the attendant uncertainty problématique, a re-examination of the concept of power, and the identification of the contours of a method of foreign policy-making that a CS perspective entails.

1. Introduction

Foreign policymaking begins with framing, that is, defining the nature of the foreign policy problem, selecting principal and secondary issues, and identifying the roles that the country should play and the range of policy options it should consider. Framing reflects beliefs, culture, theory, and various interests. A shared definition of the foreign policy problem legitimises a particular order and distribution of values and benefits. Foreign policy debates are debates about the nature of the frame deemed appropriate at a particular time and in a particular context.

In the context of its instrumental function promoted chiefly by the United States (US) as well as Japan, the political discourse around the Indo-Pacific Region (IPR) has been dominated by the neo-realist dichotomy of balancing vs bandwagoning with China. Despite an occasional nod to neo-institutionalism arguments usually dismissed as obsolete wishful thinking, the scholarly literature has tended to follow suit. Yet, the discourse around the IPR offers a good opportunity to examine how thinking in complex systems (CS) can help apprehend turbulence, integrate the dynamics of the IPR into the definition of foreign policy problems, and delineate the contours of foreign policymaking in the context of uncertainty. Following a brief reminder of the nature of CS, including the challenge of defining the system (section 1), the subsequent sections draw a few implications from the properties of CS regarding the sources of uncertainty and the nature of foreign policymaking in a complex system (section 2), including revisiting one of the basic dimensions of foreign policy, that of power (section 3).

2. The Nature of Complex Systems

Identifying complex systems

A complex system perspective is slowly pervading scholarship. It has been seeping through the literature through overt calls (Katzenstein 2022a, Scartozzi 2018; Kavalski 2015; Bousquet/Curtis 2011; Harrison 2006; Jervis 1997; Rosenau 1990), the use of some of its central concepts by numerous scholars, and, indirectly, through the development of research programs that gradually make up the scaffolding of a coherent approach to International Relations (IR) as a complex system. The construction of a paradigm both analytically fruitful and politically enlightening has met with significant challenges, however. The International Relations (IR) literature typically focuses on a few properties of these systems, provides a truncated account of their nature, and overlooks their potential interactions. In addition, whereas some properties are well understood and have been part of IR analyses for decades (such as feedback loops) or recur in the scholarly and public discourse (such as tipping points), the meaning, application, and implications for IR of most properties (such as self-organisation, emergence, adaptation, or stability) are often muddled. Finally, policymakers have bemoaned the apparent inability of complex systems theorists to provide them with a clear intellectual frame and specific policy guidelines.

Bousquet and Curtis (2011, 51) provide a definition of CS that has the merit of not confusing attributes and behaviour:

> "Complex systems are open systems composed of multiple actors operating at a variety of spatial or functional scales, that engage in interactions according to nonlinear and networked patterns."

A complex system, therefore, is a set of interacting units which has distinct properties and behaves differently from the individual units that form it

(Jervis 1997, 6). Most international systems are not merely complicated, but complex. In a complicated system, if we know the inputs, we can predict the outputs. But the world is not a clock; rather, it is largely unpredictable and indeterministic.

Table 1 lists the constitutive and dynamic properties of complex systems. Constitutive properties refer to the basic attributes of a system that define it as complex. Such a system is associated with potential or actual dynamics that must inform the definition of the problem, the range of policy options, and the identification of possible scenarios. These properties are also interlinked in various ways. Finally, the list remains open; new dynamics will emerge or be discovered, and the nature of current properties deepened.

Table 1: Constitutive and dynamic properties of complex systems

Constitutive properties	Dynamic properties
Multiple elements	Path-dependence
Connections	Self-organisation
Non-linearity	Tipping points
Feedback loops	Emergence
Multiscalarity	Stability
Openness	Adaptation

Source: The author

Adopting a complex systems perspective holds several advantages, notably:

- it emphasizes the co-construction of the units and of the system, thus transcending the perennial agent-structure problem;
- it is not limited to relations among states but includes a variety of interdependent actors;
- it does not neglect but draws on existing paradigms (particularly on institutionalism and constructivism) while also bringing various strands of current research and partial theories under a coherent umbrella (such as transnational neo-pluralism, polycentric governance, agent-structure models, regime complexes, network theory, multiscalar governance, research on status and hierarchies, practice theory, or relational theory);

- it questions received ideas that stem from a positivist, linear, and deterministic perspective, and presents new conceptions of world politics (Scartozzi 2018);
- it focuses on those dynamics that stabilize or destabilize the system, hinder or foster the pursuit of collective goals;
- and in so doing, it leads to new ways of approaching or understanding basic concepts, such as power, multilateralism, governance, or stability.

Given the focus of most of the book's contributors on imagined IPRs and on national policies toward the region, this chapter focuses on the implications of a complex system perspective for foreign policymaking rather than regional governance. The question of stability, therefore, will be left aside. Instead of examining properties sequentially, their nature and implications will be clarified through a discussion of the uncertainty problématique and the fundaments of foreign policymaking. First, however, we need to distinguish between the Indo-Pacific Region (IPR) and the Indo-Pacific System (IPS).

Identifying the boundaries of the system

In International Relations, the notions of system and system structure have been understood differently and often conflated. Schematically, neorealists classify systems according to their organizing principle, the type and number of units (states in modern history), and the distribution of power among them. Classical realists add internal variables, such as the distribution of regime types, thus distinguishing between homogeneous and heterogeneous systems; with some authors also including the goals of the dominant units (for example, conservative, reformist, or revolutionary). The English school, for its part, focuses not only on states but also on the basic rules (or *institutions*) that govern their relations, such as sovereignty, international law, diplomacy, and war.

Liberals expand the number and type of indicators, adding the number and strength of interconnections, consider various types of agents, and insist on the importance of the flow of information and the diffusion of norms. Finally, while giving pride of place to norms, constructivists also emphasize ideas, culture, and identity, to which critical theorists add material capabilities and institutions. Note that geography nowhere features explicitly in the definition of an international system. Rather, it is about relations which geography, but also communication and culture, may or may not reinforce.

The IPR is a performative political construct that seeks to build a community of geopolitical interests from India to the western rim of the Pacific Ocean. Its meaning, boundaries, and scope remain contested, and its nature mostly articulated around states and interstate arrangements. Initially rooted in the protection of sea lanes, the various political overtones of the notion of Indo-Pacific imply no universal and coherent answer to the question of its scope. Some countries limit its geographical area to the Indo-Chinese civilisational areas and the western Pacific, while others enlarge it to the western reaches of the Indian Ocean, the Russian far east, and even the eastern shores of the Pacific. Its functional scope is also understood differently. In the political discourse, the concept of IPR focuses on cooperation mainly to overcome security issues, whereas the term *Asia-Pacific* is rooted in the desire to create intergovernmental regimes to promote trade and investment among ASEAN, China, and other economies.

The IPS, on the other hand, includes relations among a large set of actors (or agents) of different types, whose interests, legitimacies, and understanding of the nature and boundaries of the IPR may not coincide. The *Indo-Pacific Region* and the *Asia-Pacific* are imagined communities of states and societies, whereas the IPS embodies an existing set of political, social, economic, and ecological relations among a variety of units.

Following Wendt (1999), Tang (2014) urges a clear distinction between structure and system, with the notion of system going beyond the distribution of capabilities or the nature of the agents, to encompass the volume and nature of interactions, emergent properties, intersubjective understandings, as well as interactions with the biophysical world. Environmental change (biodiversity loss, climate change, pollution) affects relations (such as competition over fisheries) and increases uncertainties (see Briand, 2022). The IPS, therefore, is a set of dynamic relations among a variety of agents that compose various subsystems (political, economic, social, ecological) of shifting geographical scope, while the IPR is a contested socio-political construct that attempts to build a common worldview driving actors' subsequent behaviour in their interrelations and towards China.

Since they are inherently open, the composition and boundaries of complex systems are constantly shifting with

> (i) the number and variety of agents, (ii) the nature of the formal arrangements, norms, and rules that govern their interactions, (iii) the

perceptions that actors hold of the system, (iv) the existence of more or less self-organised complex sub-systems, and (iv) the ecological spaces they share.

The system is both an intersubjective construct and an ensemble of objective relations. The challenge is to understand how one should approach foreign policymaking in the context of the uncertainty generated by the properties of such systems.

3. Foreign Policymaking in a Complex System

The uncertainty problématique

Uncertainty lies at the heart of complexity and foreign policymaking. Often conflated, risk and uncertainty are distinct concepts. Risk (*known unknowns* or operational uncertainty) refers to instances where decision-makers, while not completely certain of the situation they face, have enough information (based on prior experience or other sources) to attribute probabilities to certain outcomes. On the other hand, *epistemic uncertainty* (or *unknown unknowns*) describes unfathomable situations or impacts given current knowledge and expectations (see Katzenstein 2022; Knight 1921 cited in Rathbun 2007; see also Jervis 2017, 178).

The notion of turbulence, first proposed by organization theorists in the 1960s, already touched on this problématique. Emery and Trist (1965) defined a turbulent environment as a highly dynamic environment over which organisations have very little control, resulting in extreme uncertainty regarding their access to the resources on which they depend. It goes beyond the risk attached to the behaviour of other actors; the ground itself (the system) is in motion. The problem is to recognise the nature of this environment and its impact on the organisation and then identify adaptation strategies designed to reduce vulnerabilities. Rosenau (1990) later made turbulence a central feature of his model of world politics characterised by the multiplication of actors, the emergence of new authority structures linking macro collectivities to citizens, and the latter's capacity to mobilise.

Rathbun (2007) has usefully analysed how IR paradigms understand differently the nature of uncertainty, its sources, and how to manage it. Uncertainty in realism is experienced as fear regarding the future behaviour of other states, a diffidence that no accumulation of information can improve. Concerns about relative gains preclude meaningful cooperation. For liberal neo-institutionalism, however, uncertainty is all about ignorance, not anxiety.

> "States cope with uncertainty by attempting to accumulate information about intentions" through signalling and institutions (Rathbun 2007, 553).

Both approaches eschew the problem of cognition, i.e. the importance of beliefs and misperceptions in the appraisal of any situation (including the nature and dimensions of uncertainty), the interpretation of the behaviour of other actors, and the selection of policy paths (Idem). As societies and the international system have become more complex, so have operational and epistemic uncertainties. Their sources may be intrinsic, that is attached to the properties of the system, extrinsic because of the openness of the system, or epistemic (such as lack of information or inappropriate models). Uncertainty applies not only to the nature of the situation or the behaviour of other actors, but also to the nature of national roles and interests, to the consequences of one's actions, and to the evolution of the system. Examining how several properties of complex systems contribute to these uncertainties will help uncover their various manifestations as well as clarify their nature.

To begin with, the absence of proportional relationship between inputs and outputs (non-linearity) means that system outcomes cannot be deduced from what takes place at the unit level. Local instabilities may spread throughout the system (as in *the springtime of the peoples* of 1848 or the *Arab Spring* of 2011). Surprises follow decisions and are both normal and inevitable. So are perverse effects, when actions are encouraging behaviour or situations that go against initial objectives.

In the IPS, particular attention is paid to *known unknowns*, such as nuclear proliferation, the impacts of local economic disturbances through supply chains, civil wars, ethnic unrest and migration spreading to other countries or inviting outside intervention, and to chain reactions stemming from bilateral defence treaties. By definition, *unknown unknowns* lay outside political calculations and are often rooted in unrecognized feedback loops.

Long familiar to students of IR, feedback loops may or may not increase uncertainties. For example, on the one hand, negative feedback loops (that is, countervailing forces fostering a return to equilibrium, as illustrated by the balance of power) might reduce uncertainties and foster stability; but on the other hand, they may hinder adaptation. Likewise, positive feedback loops are usually seen negatively since they induce spiral effects and a movement farther from equilibrium, as illustrated by the security dilemma, the domino theory, or global warming; but they may also help achieve collective goals.

Trade illustrates both situations. In a protectionist context, positive feedback loops have negative consequences; free trade, on the other hand, relies on positive feedback loops to expand. The response of ASEAN member states to China's Belt and Road Initiative (BRI) provides an example of encouraging positive feedback loops to enhance collective goals. ASEAN members endeavoured to link the BRI to the *Master Plan on ASEAN Connectivity* (Hanoi Master Plan) that identified the building of physical infrastructure as its highest priority with the hope that non-ASEAN countries would finance this large-scale scheme, thus indirectly also strengthening the integration of supply chains (see Shoji 2019). The challenge, therefore, is to identify or create those positive and negative feedback loops that may hinder or foster the probability of reaching individual or collective goals *in a given context.*

The openness of complex systems which exchange information with their environment (be it political, economic, social, ideational, or ecological) also reinforces uncertainty. As Katzenstein (2022b, 308) pointed out:

> "It is the closed system assumption that makes the classical model of world politics gloss over uncertainty. Complexity theory thus affirms what Newtonianism denies: the existence of uncertainty that also marks the broader Quantum context in which the Newtonian world exists."

With the notion of complex systems, emergentism is again at the forefront of thinking in IR (Katzenstein 2022a; Wendt 2015). Complex systems have the potential to give rise to unexpected arrangements that are not explainable by the behaviour of individual components of the system or do not represent the sum of the components acting as individuals (Wendt 1999; Jervis 1997). Emergence is the ultimate source of uncertainty. Examples are the taste of sugar, insect colonies, consciousness, democratic peace, polycentric governance, the works of Adam Smith's invisible hand, globalisation, and harmony. The whole is not just greater but different from the sum of its parts (Jervis 1997). The sum of foreign policies will not predict the state of the international system. The future of the Indo-Pacific system, therefore, cannot be deduced from the characteristics or behaviour of its individual units. The system changes the preferences and behaviour of agents, and conditions the impact of their actions. International hierarchical orders emerge from diplomatic practices (Pouliot 2016). What emerges is thus both rooted in what takes place at the level below and sometimes totally new.

Some authors have merged the notions of externality and emergence (e.g. He/Feng 2025); yet not all externalities are emergent phenomena. Foreseeability and intentionality matter. Some economic externalities are anticipated effects that are not factored into economic decisions (such as pollution from a factory); they are not emergent but simply neglected. Others, on the other hand, may be unknown or unexpected and are, therefore, potentially emergent, such as the cumulative impact of chlorofluorocarbons on the ozone layer, the effects of social media platforms on democracy, the transformation of ecosystems by invasive alien species, or the social consequences of the adoption of new technologies.

For the IPR, the literature identifies four possible futures: an American-led order (in support of regional containment leaders), a Chinese-led order, a bipolar order (with balancers, such as India-France, ASEAN), and a multipolar order US-Japan, China (with Russia, at least in the short term), India (with France). This reduction to models centred around the distribution of power among a few key states is surprising. A complex systems approach would include many more actors, pay attention to networks, and point to the development of polycentric governance and complex interdependence along different and overlapping security, economic, ideational, and cultural orders; that is, examine how the system and subsystems self-organise.

Indeed, complex systems are not chaotic. In the absence of external control, a certain order emerges naturally from unpredictable non-linear interactions among actors. This order can be new and unexpected (that is, emergent) or it can arise

> "From the coevolution of rules of behaviour among adaptive agents as an evolutionary response to the complexity of the system. (Scartozzi 2018, 128)

It is a response to uncertainty and reflects the ability of the system to change its internal structure to interact with its environment (Wells 2009). Instances at different scales are regimes, concerts and clubs, security systems, the development of networks, free trade agreements, value chains, or private governance of which the IPR and IPS provide numerous examples. Thus, pockets of order (local self-organisation) can exist within a generally unpredictable system. Some of the main challenges of global governance are to identify the more stable or orderly parts and the less stable or more disorderly parts of a system, the robustness or stability of the former, how both coexist, and to what extent those pockets of order hinder or promote the resilience and adaptation of the system (see Harrison/Geyer 2022)

This might be somewhat reassuring were it not that, in a complex system, self-organisation dynamics tend towards criticality, that is toward a tipping point that represents a bifurcation of the system towards a new state which may be more or less stable, predictable, or desirable, as illustrated by market failures or, in IR, by Modelski's cyclical model (1987). This implies that if one wishes to conserve, one should not leave things as they are. How then should one approach this endogenous and pervasive uncertainty?

The traditional way is first to minimize its importance (by overlooking non-linearity and other properties of complex systems), then try and reduce it. Realists insist on the accumulation and centralisation of power and identify balancing and bandwagoning as key strategies. Liberals emphasise information, enmeshment, and the diffusion of common values; while constructivists promote better knowledge of cause-effects relations, leading to convergent definitions of the problem, and to the adoption of appropriate norms and solutions, as illustrated by ASEAN's strategy of promoting specific procedural and behavioural norms (Yoshimatsu 2022).

From a complex perspective, uncertainty in the form of surprises is both normal and inevitable. It cannot be eliminated; rather, it must be factored in. Katzenstein's (2022) and Wendt's (2015) quantum approach to International Relations, for example, places uncertainty and relations at the centre of their model. Jervis (2017, 176–77, 186) identified the issue clearly in the context of intelligence studies:

> ...we may think that the role of intelligence, in both the sense of intelligence services and the sense of our ability to understand the world, is to reduce uncertainty... This thought is incorrect, however, because the world itself often is uncertain; reducing uncertainty would amount to denying reality. Intelligence should give an estimate that follows from information about the case combined with analysts beliefs concerning relevant generalizations that they think are applicable, even if the result is to increase uncertainty by showing the decision-maker that the evidence is not as clear-cut as it may seem at first glance, that alternative explanations for what others are doing are possible, and that the world he...is confronting contains a multitude of potential threats and opportunities, just as the quantum world does...[I]n international politics, uncertainties

> (of both scholars and actors) reflect not only lack of knowledge that in principle could be gained, but multiple possibilities that have yet to be realized.

"The past is not prologue," (Katzenstein/Seybert 2018a, 89) in the sense that it cannot be the basis for knowing future probability distributions. At the same time, the past enables and constrains the evolution of the system. For example, based on past actions, we cannot infer when the camel's back or the pile of sand will collapse under the last straw or with the last grain, but it surely will at some point.

Addressing these uncertainties cannot simply rely on the accumulation of information, which may increase uncertainty, or on better knowledge of cause-effects relations (that is, *how the world works*), for, in a complex system, knowledge is undetermined (multiple paths may lead to similar outcomes and, conversely, a given cause may not always have the same effects). Rather, complex system theorists emphasize fostering learning, maximizing options, developing interconnections (diversity fosters system stability and adaptation, as in the case of supply chains), encouraging experimentation at the sub-system level, decentralizing power and authority, and defining problems from a contextual perspective. As articulated by observers of the foreign policy of several south-east Asian nations, *hedging* exemplifies some of these strategies (see, for example, Viet/Dieu 2024).

Fundaments of foreign policymaking in a complex system

From this perspective, foreign policymaking first means adopting an approach that is neither reductionist (reducing knowledge about foreign policy to knowledge about the agents of the system) nor structural (subordinating the foreign policy problématique to structural variables). The domestic and the international are not separate arenas of action. Agents and structures are co-constructed and co-evolve, as exemplified by globalisation.

Second, relations among the units of the system matter more than the latter's intrinsic nature (for example, their material capabilities or the type of political system). Going beyond power relations among states, a CS perspective is concerned with relations among a variety of interdependent actors that (i) act more or less independently according to different rules, (ii) claim specific legitimacies, and (iii) form coalitions and networks, thus creating various authority structures. The Indo-Pacific system is more than a system of states; it includes intergovernmental organisations

(IGOs), sub-state actors (e.g. provinces, cities, armed rebellions, ethnic groups, crime syndicates...), non-governmental organisations (NGOs), corporations, networks, individuals, and the natural environment. New actors always emerge, often suddenly, as exemplified by the role of social media in security issues in China (Hayes/Yi/Diamond 2015, 4), one instance of developments that, according to some authors, form a "relational revolution." (Kurki 2020)

The first question one should ask, then, is *What is related to what, and how?* How might changes in one part of the system trigger changes in other parts of the system, affect other actors' outlook and behaviour, or induce the evolution of the system? What other problems might be generated by efforts to address a particular one? How should goals, received ideas, and current political strategies be re-examined in light of a shifting political, social, and economic context? Indeed, we can never hold the system constant. For example, many observers predicted that the fall of the Soviet Union in 1991 would represent the dawn of new and ambitious arms control agreements; but this event did not just remove a perceived impediment toward disarmament, the system also changed, and so did the nature of the issue and the strategies of actors, after a certain time lag. Some dynamics (such as specific feedback loops or types of self-organisation) considered to be adaptive in one context may prove counterproductive in another.

It also implies granting due consideration not only to trade-offs, but also to perverse effects, non-linearity, and networks (Qin 2018; Cerny 2014). International relations increasingly involve the interplay of agents and networks, leading to the formation of hybrid policy networks and coalitions. Networks also play key roles in linking various governance levels and regions. One should then ask how network form, how they are enabled by information technology, how they are affecting security and other issue-areas, and how they can impede or further national objectives.

A second implication of the focus on relations points to the importance of hierarchies (Zarakol 2010; Lake 2009) and status (Lebow 2010) as drivers of national roles and interest formation. The complex international system is multiscalar, that is, the product of sub-systems (or strata) that are, in turn, affected by it. The Indo-Pacific is composed of geographical, security, political, economic, cultural, and ecological subregions and subsystems. Multiscalarity means that at any level of analysis, order is driven by what takes place at a lower level of aggregation, rather than explained by causal drivers at the same level of analysis. For example, internal developments (in China, Taiwan, or the US), the diversification of supply chains (such as

Japanese and Chinese chains in ASEAN), security cooperation in the form of bilateral or trilateral security agreements and assorted arrangements, ASEAN's adaptation, Russia-China cooperation (with the potential for greater involvement of Russia in the Indo-Pacific region), all will affect the nature and dynamics of the system.

This implies that no action is strictly local; it has systemic impacts. Thus, one cannot act at only one level or place in the system or rely on a single set of policy measures limited to one target (Jervis 1997). One must act at several governance levels or in different areas simultaneously. The global level is no substitute for the local level, or the global-local link for the national-local one. What is *true* at one level may not be at other levels: local truths can be global errors, and conversely. When the immunological system rejects a heart transplant, this local truth becomes a global error since death ensues (Morin 2013). Conversely, the need to fight global terrorism can lead to interventions that may encourage its local occurrence, as in Irak (Ibid.).

Like the international system, the Indo-Pacific system is hierarchical, in the sense that agents do not have the same status (see Goh 2007) or have access to similar resources, which affects resilience and adaptation. At the international level, not all actors of the same level are equal. States may not be recognized by the U.N.; only some transnational non-governmental organizations can operate in specific countries; not all NGOs enjoy a consultative status with ECOSOC. Actors that are equal *de jure* may not be so *de facto*. If all states enjoy a formal equality of legal status conferred by the principle of sovereignty, their capacity to influence and resist the system differs (see Lake 2009). Some sort of authority relationship can also exist between actors, insofar as some enable others to operate. For example, business firms and NGOs are subject to laws adopted by states, beginning with the right of association.

Neorealism already insisted on the centrality of status (as opposed to power maximisation) in the definition of the national interest (Waltz 1979, 126). Globalisation, the aftermath of the end of the cold war, and power transitions have renewed interest in the importance of status in world politics (Paul/Larson/Wohlforth 2014), particularly regarding conflict (Renshon 2017; Wohlforth 2014; Lebow 2010), the definition of national roles (Clunan 2014; Le Prestre 1997), responsibilities (Hansen-Magnusson/Vetterlein 2021), and interests (Larson/Shevchenko 2019; Murray 2019). Decision-makers care about status because it confers privileges, strengthens self-esteem, and helps build identity (Götz 2021). It also comes with responsibilities that may engender new misunderstandings. The quest for middle-power status of several members of ASEAN testifies to the importance of this variable.

In this context, the concept of role appears particularly fruitful. Role theory posits that individuals often act more as role players than self-interested utility maximisers. A foreign policy role refers to the intersubjective understanding of appropriate behaviour orientations in the international arena. The articulation of a national role betrays preferences, operationalises an image of the world, triggers expectations, and influences the definition of the situation and of the available options. Roles define obligations and expectations that can be prescribed by external actors, derive from an actor's location in the system, or stem from the policymakers' own definitions. A role reflects a claim on the international system, recognition by international actors, and a conception of national identity. It gives meaning and purpose to foreign policy and helps define interests. Roles are learned and enacted through interactions with other actors and often come before interests since states do not always know what they want. One of the political dimensions of the discourse over the nature of the Indo-Pacific region is precisely how international social pressure attributes certain roles to specific countries, and how the latter accept them or claim different ones (such as middle-level power, balancer, allied, mediator, etc.; see Thies, 2014).

The concept of role interfaces with the individual, society, and the system. Its usefulness for the analysis of foreign policy in complex systems is three-fold. First, it reconciles different levels of analysis and provides a means of assessing the interplay between individual (cognitive), internal (domestic), and external (systemic) variables. Second, by bridging multiple levels of analysis, role theory helps illuminate foreign policy continuities as well as change and, more generally, the interplay among a variety of international actors interacting across levels in a complex governance system. And third, examining the evolution, origins, and contents of different roles that collective actors play on the international stage helps assess the possibility of cooperation in the maintenance of international order. Studies can help identify the risks of conflicts rooted in clashing role conceptions masquerading as interests, or in the contradictions between the internal conceptions and the external expectations of the role that a given state should play. This is also one of the ways path dependence enters into play, for states can be caught in role traps (Le Prestre 2017).

Path dependence means that the state of the system at time t is both a function of its state at time t-1 and of the order of succession of prior states. It refers to the future steps that previous behaviour enables, imposes, or facilitates. Classic examples are ecosystems successions, the layout of computer keyboards, institutions, organisations, production standards, or the adoption of consumer items rooted in positive feedback loops. Path dependence can also be the product of negative feedback loops as when the inertia of institutions perpetuates deleterious behaviour (Dryzeck/Pickering 2019). Policies endure despite their limited impact. Decisions create vested interests that make it politically easier to follow the same path than switch direction. In general, actors keep to a specific strategy unless they face strong negative consequences, even in the absence of positive data linking the strategy and observed results.

It is in this context that the nature and interplay of current institutions are likely to shape future governance. Institutions embody norms, rely on techniques, and represent political relations that prevailed at the time of their creation, and which thereafter inform their behaviour, membership, human resources, and decision-making processes as they adapt to their environment.

> "History is path dependent in the sense that the character of current institutions depends not only on current conditions but also on the historical path of institutional development." (March/Olsen 1998, 959; see also David 1994)

Consequently, foreign policy change often implies or even requires privileging different institutions or founding new ones, as illustrated by the Asia Infrastructure Investment Bank, the New Development Bank, or the Shanghai Cooperation Organization in the IPS. Path dependence may not always promote inertia. It can be used to force the system to evolve, as in the notion of spillover in neo-functionalist integration theory (Lindberg 1963). On the other hand, a series of partial decisions, each of them sound and apparently inconsequential for the system, may lead to an unexpected end-state. The progressive reduction of the private sphere, the self-organisation of global supply-chains, or the enlargements of the EU and NATO illustrate those dynamics. Such *surprises* follow a series of separate and logical decisions. Thus, path dependence points to the importance of reflexivity, that is the learning capacity of institutions and their ability to question their basic objectives and the fundamental premises of their actions (Dryzeck/Pickering 2019), which points to adaptive capacity.

In complex systems, foreign policy is about adaptation to uncertainty. Complex systems are sometimes defined as complex adaptive systems, as if adaptation were an intrinsic feature of such systems. Rather, it is their potential to adapt that matters, adaptation being dependent on a host of factors, including the specific structure and dynamics of the system. For example, the adaptive capacity of regimes is linked to their architecture.

In the natural sciences, adaptation starts at the unit level. The system per se does not adapt, it evolves. At the unit level and borrowing from organisation theory, adaptation can be defined as the capacity to harness resources on which a given actor depends to pursue its fundamental objectives. Actors devise strategies designed to enhance learning and reduce uncertainties. Since adaptability is an essential attribute for the actors' survival, the success of an actor derives from its ability to cope with the complexity of the system, process information, and develop rules of behaviour that maximise fitness, and not merely on a combination of material power and guile (Scartozzi 2018).

These strategies fall into two categories. Coping strategies are designed to protect the agent from the impact of systemic change, whereas transforming strategies are directed at the source of systemic change (Le Prestre 1999). Through coping strategies, the actor seeks to reduce vulnerabilities or attempts to modify its behaviour. Examples include information collection, robustness (the capacity to protect itself against unexpected change), coalition formation, specialisation (using existing resources better), diversification, and harmonisation (that is, adopting new values and behaviour in line with the expectations of the external environment). The objective is to maintain essential goals and structures by reducing vulnerabilities. *Hedging*, for example, is a type of coping strategy that combines diversification and coalition (see Yoshimatsu 2023; Kuik 2016).

On the other hand, the aim of transforming strategies is to eliminate or mitigate the threat either through direct influence on the source of the threat or, indirectly, by shaping the conditions that give rise to it. Examples include bargaining (cooperation in reducing uncertainties without any party losing autonomy), institutionalisation (building international institutions, notably regimes, such as ASEAN's strategy of *impartial enmeshment*, which implies role socialisation), coercion, positive inducements, persuasion (such as the promotion of specific norms of behaviour, of which ASEAN's attempts to articulate and promote an *Asean Way* might constitute an example), and system change (that is, altering the nature of other actors or their interrelations, rather than focusing only on the relations between the unit and the system).

Reducing uncertainty is only one of the alternatives of the adaptation dilemma. Although an actor's capacity to maintain its essential structures and pursue its essential goals depends on minimizing uncertainties, certain adaptation strategies entail a loss of autonomy or reduce future options. Without autonomy there cannot be purposeful adaptation either. Unit adaptation in a complex system, therefore, means minimizing the trade-off between reducing uncertainty and maintaining autonomy. Some actors emphasise uncertainty reduction, others autonomy; most attempt a delicate balance between the two and use a mixed strategy.

The systemic outcome of this process may or may not be adaptive, depending, for example, on the congruence between the types of relationships that have evolved and the definition of the common good, or the structure and dynamics of the socio-environmental system. Likewise, these strategies may or may not lead to a form of co-evolution that makes the system more resilient and allows for the pursuit of a common goal. In International Relations, actors may co-evolve through various mechanisms, such as institutional and policy diffusion, interdependence, private governance, participation, policy networks, interactions among regions, or the evolution of regime complexes. In a complex system,

> "[t]he internal attributes and rules of behaviour of an adaptive agent constantly change through interaction with the environment and with other agents." (Scartozzi 2018, 123)

Finally, adaptation involves all actors, not just states. Civil society organisations have a major role to play in tandem or in opposition to states and corporations (see Hayes/Yi 2015). For example, linking environmental and security civil society networks to those of local governments may foster resilience in the region and lend capacity to solving global problems in spite of their complexity (Hayes/Tanter 2015). Networked civil society organisations working closely with city governments can precipitate a new, emergent pattern of decentralised, networked governance that supplements and supersedes, but in no way substitutes for the role of states in the region.

4. Revisiting Power

Thinking in complex systems also implies revisiting basic concepts, such as that of power. Like stability, power is a generic term that refers to a variety of situations: the capacity to resist, the ability to coerce or reward using material sanctions or status recognition, the imposition of the discursive and intellectual parameters of a debate or of a specific situation, or the ability to define the rules of the system.

An actor's basic resources give an incomplete and flawed notion of its power. In a complex system, power has three other bases: the actor's environment (its relations with other actors, the nature of the rules of the system, and the dominant intellectual order), an actor's location in the system, and its capacity to learn and innovate. First, power is contextual. In a cards game, a good hand depends on the nature of the game; rules matter (Baldwin 2002). In international relations, power is not simply the capacity to impose one's preferences in a given situation, but also to structure the rules of the system and the intellectual environment that preside over the definition of problems and appropriate solutions, that is, framing (see Haas 1997). The aim is to construct an intersubjective understanding of the system (agents, connections, boundaries and rules). In this context, power is also rooted in the capacity to form coalitions; not only to increase one's ability to act, but also to legitimise the use of power resources. The distinction between power as resources and power as relations has represented an important evolution in thinking about power (Katzenstein/Seybert 2018a; Baldwin 2002; Lasswell/Kaplan 1950).

The second and often overlooked manifestation of the relational basis of power in a complex system is the importance of the actor's relative position in the system, notably its status and its nodal position, which affects the assessment of its power and the definition of its role and interests (Zhao 2019; Lake 2009). The importance of status was underscored previously in the context of multiscalarity. The transnational and pluralistic structure of complex systems (Cerny 2010) also tends to generate asymmetric networked structures with nodal points, that is, points that have many more connections with other parts of the system and constitute unavoidable hubs. Thus, power rests more on whether a given actor enjoys or can control a nodal position than on its intrinsic material capacities, although the latter may impact the former (Pattberg/Wideberg 2020). States that control key hubs (in information, finance, trade, etc.) enjoy a privileged position from which to exercise coercive power, as evidenced by the weaponisation of the international financial system by the United States (see Farrell/Newman 2023). It also opens more options, which increases negotiating power. For example, in the case of financial and even political crises, the margin of manoeuvre of an actor (a state, a large bank) depends on its position in the system. The more important it is, the more its weakness becomes an asset if the overall objective is to maintain the stability of the system. In short, the notion of empire itself expands. Contrary to a vertical model, empire becomes the ability to control cultural and economic networks, forge intersubjective understandings, and be at the centre of a web of interrelations (Bayly 2021).

From this perspective, three scenarios arise in the context of the Indo-Pacific. The multilateral scenario starts from ASEAN's special position as the geographical centre of the Indo-Pacific, and emphasises efforts to articulate a role, promote an ideational construct, frame problems, and set the agenda, starting with the establishment of the East Asia Summit and the ASEAN Defence Ministers Meeting-Plus (Yoshimatsu 2023; Aimsiranun/Poranaond 2023). But, although the various conceptions of Indo-Pacific recognise ASEAN centrality, the challenge remains for ASEAN to play a coordinating role. The second scenario is the development of a hub-and-spoke system resting on a series of bilateral arrangements with China, which would grant it network centrality, preserve power asymmetry, and limit the agency of smaller partners (Ng 2024, 279). A third scenario is for specific countries to strive to become key nodes in specific networks, and, in addition to power as control, develop what Katzenstein and Seybert (2018a) have called *protean power* which emphasises the capacity to learn, improvise, and innovate in the face of an unpredictable system.

5. Conclusion

Although it aspires to become a paradigm, complexity theory is first a method, a way of thinking about the world with, it is hoped, practical implications. From a foreign policy perspective, it often requires questioning received wisdom and practices. In particular, the properties of complex systems suggest that:

- rather than a source of chaos, the very diversity of actors strengthens stability and adaptation. Foreign policy must seek ways to harness the various legitimacies and authorities they represent, as illustrated by Canada's strategy of alliance with civil society to promote the 1997 Ottawa treaty.

This approach also warns us against assuming that actors share the same notion of how the world works;

- since a complex system is defined by the relations that hold among agents, one must first ask *What is related to what and how?* and keep in mind the role of networks as constraints to, and opportunities for action;
- non-linearity invites us to plan for surprises, accept the potential for accidents, guard against perverse effects, and recognise that a problem is never solved, but merely displaced;
- feedback loops abound, may foster or hinder adaptation, and generate stability or instability. The challenge is to identify potential feedback loops and devise ways to associate them with future scenarios regarding the evolution of the system, that is, find ways to use the complexity of the system to one's advantage instead of trying to simplify and control it. For example, although globalisation can be a straitjacket, it also opens new opportunities for action and new sources of power;
- lower levels matter in a multiscalar system. One cannot act only at one level. This perspective also calls for greater emphasis on modes of regional governance from the bottom up;
- the openness of complex systems points to the importance of context, not only in defining a situation but also in the functional or dysfunctional character of the dynamics at play;
- because of path dependence, one should pay attention to how past decisions constrain future options. A sound policy is one that increases future options or, at least, does not limit them;
- self-organisation, along with the multiplicity of legitimate actors, underscores the benefit, if not the necessity, of polycentric rather than centralized governance. The trend towards criticality also reminds us that stability requires change;
- emergent properties may be the unintended consequence of the development of new connections or of individualistic strategies of adaptation (including the exercise of power); but they may also be the product of wilful action;
- adaptation lies at the heart of foreign policy and rests upon learning, experimentation, and a mix of coping and transforming strategies, while managing various trade-offs, notably with autonomy.

The IPR is an attempt at self-organisation in the context of a larger Indo-Pacific complex system, the properties of which have implications for how one approaches the definition of appropriate national strategies, questioning much received wisdom and dominant practices in the process.

6. References

Aimsiranun, U./Porananond, P. (2023): Perceptions et réceptions de l'ASEAN autour de l'Indo-Pacifique. In: Revue internationale et stratégique, (120), 105–113.

Baldwin, D. A. (2002): Power and International Relations. In: Carlsnaes, W./ Risse, T./ Simmons, B. A. (eds.): Handbook of international relations. Sage. 177–191.

Bayly, M. J. (2021): Imperialism: Beyond the re-turn to empire in International Relations. In de Carvalho, B. (et al.) (eds.): Routledge handbook of historical international relations. Routledge. 355–367.

Bousquet, A./Curtis, S. (2011): Beyond models and metaphors: complexity theory, systems thinking and international relations. In: Cambridge Review of International Affairs 24(1), 43–62.

Briand, Y. (2022): La France et l'Indopacifique. In: Revue Défense Nationale, (853), 30–35.

Cerny, P. G. (2010): Rethinking world politics: A theory of transnational pluralism. Oxford University Press.

Cerny, P. G. (2014): Transnational neopluralism and the process of governance. In: Payne, A./ Phillips, N. (eds.): Handbook of the international political economy of governance. Edward Elgar. 48–68.

Clunan, A. L. (2014): Why Status Matters in World Politics. In: Paul, T. V./Larson, D. W./Wohlforth, W. C. (eds.): Status in World Politics. Cambridge University Press. 273–296.

David, P. A. (1994): Why Are Institutions the carriers of history? Path Dependence and the Evolution of Conventions, Organizations and Institutions. Structural Change and Economic Dynamics 5(2), 205–220. https://doi-org/10.1016/0954-349X(94)90002-7.

Emery, F. E./Trist, E. L. (1965): The causal texture of organizational environments. In: Human Relations, 18(1), 21–32. https://doi-org/10.1177/001872676501800103.

Farrell, H./Newman, A. (2023): Underground empire: How America weaponized the world economy. Henry Holt and Co.

Goh, E. (2007): Great Powers and Hierarchical Order in Southeast Asia: Analyzing Regional Security Strategies. In: International Security, 32(3), 113–157. https://www.jstor.org/stable/30130520.

Götz, E. (2021): Status Matters in World Politics. In: International Studies Review 23, 228–247.

Haas, P. M. (ed.) (1997): Knowledge, power and international policy coordination. University of South Carolina Press.

Hansen-Magnusson, H./Vetterlein, A. (eds.) (2021): Handbook on responsibility in international relations. Routledge. https://doi-org/10.4324/9780429266317.

Harrison, N. E. (ed.). (2006): Complexity in world politics: concepts and methods of a new paradigm. State University of New York Press.

Harrison, N. E./Geyer, R. (2022): Governing Complexity in the 21st Century. Routledge.

Hayes, P., K./Yi. K./Diamond, J. (2015): Introduction. In: Hayes, P./Yi, K. (eds.): Complexity, Security and Civil Society in East Asia: Foreign Policies and the Korean Peninsula. Open Books Publishers. 2–11. https://www.jstor.org/stable/j.ctt16gzg36.6.

Hayes, P./Tanter, R. (2015): Global Problems, Complexity, and Civil Society in East Asia. In: Hayes, P./Yi, K. (eds.): Complexity, Security and Civil Society in East Asia: Foreign Policies and the Korean Peninsula. Open Book Publishers. 13–84. https://www.jstor.org/stable/j.ctt16gzg36.6.

He, K./Feng, H. (2025): The positive externalities of US–China institutional balancing in the Indo-Pacific. International Affairs, 101(1), 35–52.

Jervis, R. (1997): System effects: Complexity in political and social Life. Princeton University Press.

Jervis, R. (2017): One World or Many? In: Critical Review, 29(2), 170–188. https://doi-org/10.1080/08913811.2017.1315920.

Katzenstein, P. J. (2022b): Of Gardens, Forests, and Parks. In: Katzenstein, P. J. (ed.): Uncertainty and its discontents: Worldviews in world politics. Cambridge University Press. 279–352.

Katzenstein, P. J. (ed.) (2022a): Uncertainty and its discontent: Worldviews in world politics. Cambridge University Press.

Katzenstein, P. J./Seybert, L. A. (2018a): Protean Power and Uncertainty: Exploring the Unexpected in World Politics. In: International Studies Quarterly 62, 80–93.

Kavalski, E. (ed.) (2015): World politics at the edge of chaos. Reflections on complexity and global Life. State University of New York Press.

Knight, F. H. (1921): Risk, uncertainty and profit. Houghton Mifflin.

Kuik, C.-C. (2016): How Do Weaker States Hedge? Unpacking ASEAN states' alignment behaviour towards China. In: Journal of Contemporary China, 25(100), 500–514.

Kurki, M. (2020): International Relations in a relational Universe. Oxford University Press.

Lake, D. A. (2009): Hierarchy in international relations. Cornell University Press.

Larson, D. W./Shevchenko, A. (2019): Quest for status: Chinese and Russian foreign policy. Yale University Press.

Lasswell, H. D./Kaplan, A. (1950): Power and society: A framework for political inquiry. Yale University Press.

Le Prestre, P. (1999): Adapting to Environmental Insecurities: A Conceptual Model. In: Lonergan, S. (ed.): Environmental Change, Adaptation and Security. Kluwer Academic Publishers. 57–74.

Le Prestre, P. (2017): Global Ecopolitics Revisited: Toward a Complex Governance of Global Environmental Problems. Routledge.

Le Prestre, P. (ed.) (1997): Role quests in the post-cold war era: Foreign policies in transition. Mc.Gill-Queens University Press.

Lebow, R. N. (2010): Why nations fight: Past and future motives for war. Cambridge, Cambridge University Press.

Lindberg, L. N. (1963): The political dynamics of European economic integration. Stanford, Stanford University Press

March, J. G./Olsen, J. P. (1998): The Institutional Dynamics of International Political Orders. In: International Organization, 52(4), 943–969.

Modelski, G. (1987): Long cycles in world politics. Palgrave Macmillan.

Morin, E. (2013): Complexité restreinte, complexité générale. In: Le Moigne, J./Morin, E. (eds.): Intelligence de la complexité: Épistémologie et pragmatique. Hermann. 28–64.

Murray, M. (2019): The struggle for recognition in international relations: Status, revisionism, and rising powers. Oxford University Press.

Ng, J. (2024): The BRICS Plus Challenge and Emerging Hierarchical Multilateralism. In: Global Governance, 30, 270–287.

Pattberg, P./Widerberg, O. (2020): Studying Global Governance as a Complex System: A Network Perspective. In: International Studies Review, 22(4), 1019–1022.

Paul, T. V./Larson, D./Wohlforth, W. (eds.) (2014): Status in world politics. Cambridge University Press.

Pouliot, V. (2016): International Pecking Orders. The Politics and Practice of Multilateral Diplomacy. Cambridge University Press.

Qin, Y. (2018): A Relational Theory of World Politics. Cambridge University Press.

Rathbun, B. C. (2007): Uncertain about Uncertainty: Understanding the Multiple Meanings of a Crucial Concept in International Relations Theory. In: International Studies Quarterly, 51, 533–557.

Renshon, J. (2017): Fighting for Status: Hierarchy and Conflict in World Politics. Princeton University Press

Rosenau, J. N. (1990): Turbulence in World Politics: A Theory of Change and Continuity. Princeton University Press.

Scartozzi, C. M. (2018): A New Taxonomy for International Relations: Rethinking the International System as a Complex Adaptive System. In: Journal on Policy and Complex Systems 4(1), 109–133.

Shoji, T. (2019): Belt and Road vs. Free and Open Indo-Pacific: Competition Over Regional Order and ASEAN. NIDS Commentary No. 88, National Institute for Defense Studies, Tokyo. https://www.nids.mod.go.jp/english/publication/commentary/pdf/commentary088e.pdf.

Tang, S. (2014): International System, not International Structure: Against the Agent–Structure Problématique in IR. In: The Chinese Journal of International Politics 7(4), 483–506.

Thies, C. G. (2014): The United States, Israel and the search for international order: Socializing states. Routledge

Waltz, K. N. (1979): Theory of international politics. Addison-Wesley.

Wells, J. L. (2009): Complexity and climate change: An epistemological study of trans-disciplinary complexity theories and their contribution to socio-ecological phenomena. (Publication No. 3410845) [Doctoral Dissertation, University of California, Berkeley]. ProQuest Dissertations & Theses.

Wendt, A. (1999): Social theory of international relations. Cambridge University Press.

Wendt, A. (2015): Quantum mind and social science: Unifying physical and social ontology. Cambridge University Press.

Wohlforth, W. C. (2014): Status Dilemmas and Interstate Conflict. In: Paul, T.V./Larson, D. W./Wohlforth, W. C. (eds.): Status in World Politics. Cambridge University Press. 115–140.

Yoshimatsu, H. (2023): ASEAN and Great Power Rivalry in Regionalism: From East Asia to the Indo-Pacific. In: Journal of Current Southeast Asian Affairs, 42(1), 25–44.

Zarakol, A. (ed.) (2010): Hierarchies in world politics. Cambridge University Press.

Zhao, S. (2019): Projection of China's Soft Power in the New Century: Reconstruction of the Traditional Chinese World Order. In: Edney, K./Rosen, S./Zhu, Y. (eds.): Soft Power with Chinese Characteristics: China's Campaign for Hearts and Minds. Routledge. 25–44.

Chapter 2: The Agent-Structure Relationship in the Indo-Pacific Region from a Structurationist Perspective

Vu Van Anh

The agent-structure problem is supposed to be a dilemma in international relations theory shown in the two most influential theories – neorealism and world-system theory. Structuration theory is expected to be the solution and to provide a more balanced analytical tool to examine the relationship between agency and structure. Accordingly, the duality of structure makes agency and structure shape and change each other. With the aim at clarifying the mutually constitutive relationship between structure and agency in the Indo-Pacific since the beginning of the 21st century, this chapter focuses on (i) clarifying key concepts of agency, power, and structure, demonstrated as elements of the theory, (ii) introducing the structuration theory, inspired by Anthony Giddens (1984), and a conceptual framework based on considering its specific adoption in international relations, and finally (iii) shedding light on the actual relationship between agencies and structure in the context of the Indo-Pacific region since 2001.

1. Introduction

Along with growing attention on Sino-American power struggle in the 21st century, the Indo-Pacific is also an object of interest in many studies because it serves as a focal point of intense competition between the two giants. By perceiving the Indo-Pacific region as an international system at the regional level, many studies scrutinise regional dynamics from the perspectives of neorealism and world system theory. In studies oriented by neorealism, the rise of China, which has led to a state of balance of power in the region is supposedly a key factor in determining how China and the United States dealt with the other, and how other states interact with the two great powers as well as with each other (Chan 2012; Fong 2024; Devi/Singh 2024). In other words, the distribution of capabilities across the most powerful state agents in the region has shaped the structure of the Indo-Pacific system. Following this neorealist interpretation, this structural state of a balance-of-power system, in return, has put constraints upon states' actions. Accordingly, states in the Indo-Pacific adopted strategies within the balance-of-power spectrum such as balancing, band-wagoning, or hedging to respond and adapt to this situation (Roy 2005; Kuik 2008; Lim/Cooper 2015; Marston 2023). Few studies use the lens of world system theory to investigate the core-periphery relationships in the region (Liu/Wang 2018).

Theoretically, both approaches – neorealism and world system are shown to be reductionist and unable to solve the agent-structure problem as Alexander E. Wendt (1987) argued. By treating the system structure characterized by relationships among core, semi-peripheral, and peripheral states as given or the ontologically primitive unit, world system theorists, or structuralists were unable to explain the properties of the structure itself. They focused on explaining the actions of state agents under the determination of the structure. Similarly, neorealists made a reductionist conceptualisation of structure as the distribution of capabilities across state actors, leading to the focus on how the structure is shaped by state agencies and how the structure constrains preexisting states. This shows that neorealists, who can be also called individualists in this sense, in contrast to world system theorists put state agents into the primitive unit. It, therefore, did not discuss the properties of state agents (Wendt 1987, 342). The problem that makes the two approaches problematic is their perception of agent and structure as separate rather than mutually constitutive. Structuration theory could give a solution, as Wendt suggested:

> "Structuration theory attempts to preserve the generative and relational aspects of structuralism while taking explicit conceptual and methodological steps to prevent the analytical separation of generative structures from the self-understandings and practices of human agents to prevent structural reification." (Wendt 1987, 355)

Despite critics seeing structuration theory as eclecticism, by acknowledging that state agencies and structure are co-determined, the agent-structure relationship can be analysed in a greater balance. It, therefore, provides an analytical tool to understand the relationship between agencies and structure in international relations. With the aim at clarifying the mutually constitutive relationship between structure and agency in the Indo-Pacific since the beginning of the 21st century, this chapter focuses on

- clarifying key concepts of agency, power, and structure, demonstrated as elements of the theory,
- introducing the structuration theory, inspired by Anthony Giddens (1984), and a conceptual framework based on considering its specific adoption in international relations, and finally
- shedding light on the actual relationship between agencies and structure in the context of the Indo-Pacific region since 2001.

2. The Agent-Structure Relationship in the Structuration Theory

Key concepts

In the work *The Constitution of Society: Outline of the Theory of Structuration*, Anthony Giddens (1984) introduced his idea of structuration, comprising of key concepts of agency, power, and structure. These concepts were also discussed in many studies in the field of international relations, showing that there are both differences and similarities between Gidden's approach and that of many other IR theorists.

Regarding the concepts of agent and agency, Giddens (1984) perceives agents as actors with "moral conscience" and agency as a property of an agent. Specifically, while many have commonly defined agency by the intentions of agents, Giddens distinguished reflexive monitoring or rationalization of actions from motivations, agency from intentions by giving cases to illustrate. To define agency as actually doing rather than being intending in doing something is not to eliminate the intentionality of what is done. Giddens concluded:

> "Agency refers not to the intentions people have in doing things but to their capability of doing those things in the first place... Agency concerns events of which an individual is the perpetrator, in the sense that the individual could, at any phase in a given sequence of conduct, have acted differently. Whatever happened would not have happened if that individual had not intervened." (Giddens 1984, 9)

This definition also implies the connection between agency and power characterized by what Giddens (1984, 16) called the dialectic of control that agency should not include all types of actions but actions which help agents produce an effect or exert power. In international relations, actors can be divided into two groups: state and non-state actors such as international organisations, transnational corporations, and even influential individuals. Although transnationalism highly values the role of non-state actors, especially TNCs, this type of actor should not be treated as equivalent to a state actor in a level of analysis when studying its relationship with the structure. State agents with sovereignty and comprehensive capabilities are always the protagonists in the international arena. Actions of state agents considered the "agency" include planned actions or foreign policy behaviours because power frequently represents both a means and an end of foreign policy of states (Holsti 1964, 179).

The concept of structure poses difficulties in grasping due to its ontological abstractness. Although Waltz's concept of structure in international politics is supposed to be reductionist to individualism, his concept of political structure in general should be considered. Waltz (1979) shows three core elements of it, including: ordering principles, functional differentiation across interacting units, and distribution of capabilities (Waltz 1979, 81–82) The *problematic* lies in his realist thought based interpretation of international structure. Waltz pointed out that there are two types of ordering principles:

(i) the state of being ordered or organized like domestic political structures where interactions among units were constrained by governmental institutions, and
(ii) the state of anarchy reflected in international politics when there is no supranational agent able to command or require state agents to obey (Waltz 1979, 88–89).

Order in anarchy is formed as a result of the aggregate of individual decisions and unilateral actions of political units. In addition, political units are often functionally differentiated as a consequence of the ordering principles. Accordingly, in international relations, the state of being anarchic leads to coordination relationships between/among state actors in the system, which shows the similarity in their functions (Donnelly 2000, 84; Waltz 1979, 93). State agents are supposed to articulate policies to ensure their survival in the self-help system, then act indifferently. These arguments lead to the conclusion that in the international structure, the distribution of capabilities is the only determinant. Giddens conceptualises structure as "rules and resources, or set of transformation relations, organized as properties of social systems" (Giddens 1984, 25). He defines rules with signification and legitimation, and resources with power or domination arising out of relationships and capabilities coming from the resource allocation

(Giddens 1984, 31). By acknowledging that functional differentiation across units is coming from the ordering principles, Giddens and Waltz (referring to his concept of political structure) share some common understandings of the properties of structures.

It is obvious that there is no central government in the international system like in a domestic one: but rules including both regulative and constitutive aspects and resources exist in both cases. That means that they should be considered when an analysis of the international system is conducted. The difference between the two approaches to the concept of structure is that while Waltz perceives structure as external to individuals, Giddens sees it as more *internal.* According to Giddens, the agent-structure relationship is mutually constitutive, expressed in his understanding of the duality of structure.

The duality of structure in international relations

By defining structuration as

> "Conditions governing the continuity of transmutation of structures, and therefore the reproduction of social systems" and arguing "the constitution of agents and structures are not two independently given sets of phenomena, a dualism, but represent a duality," (Giddens 1984, 25)

the duality of structure becomes the core idea of the structuration theory. Giddens's use of this term shows his effort to clarify his view in which agency and structure are not the two separate entities or units, and their relationship exists as the two dimensions in the properties of a structure. This idea is different from a neorealist point of view, seeing agents and structure the two separate levels of analysis in which structure exists externally to agents and places constraints upon agents. In contrast to Waltz's individualist view of structure in which agents work within constraints from the structure, Giddens stated:

> "Structure is not to be equated with constraints but is always both constraining and enabling. This, of course, does not prevent the structured properties of social systems from stretching away, in time and space, beyond the control of any individual actors. Nor does it compromise the possibility that actors' own theories of the social systems which they help to constitute and reconstitute in their activities may reify those systems." (Giddens 1984, 25)

Accordingly, the duality of structure shows the co-determined relationship between agency and structure, in which structure is shaped and maintained by actions of agents, and conversely structure enables agents to take actions that they would not otherwise take. In international relations, the mutually constitutive relationship between agency and structure is reflected in many phenomena. The norm of non-proliferation of nuclear weapons, for instance, was formed due to the increase of interstate cooperation in the field of nuclear technology in diverse fields including the military one in the 1950s within the context of the Cold War. Although the idea of non-proliferation can be traced back to the *Atoms for Peace* program initiated by the US President Eisenhower in 1953 with the aim at promoting peaceful uses of nuclear technology, the program's implementation by sharing nuclear technology with other nations caused the supposedly unintended consequence – the spread of dual-use technology. Non-proliferation became a norm when state agents perceived the extent of insecurity caused by uncontrolled proliferation of this technology and took cooperative actions by joining the *Non-proliferation Treaty (NPT)* established in 1968. Indeed, there would have been no norm of non-proliferation if states had not accepted and committed to it. Conversely, joining the NPT and becoming a part of the structure have provided state agents with opportunities to make a difference or produce an effect. Through the transparency principles of the NPT, some states can seek accountability or access to examine and control others' uses of nuclear technology, which would have not been easily attained if the NPT had not existed.

The duality of structure also shows the continuities in system reproduction, which is characterized by the operation of reflexive self-regulation and homeostatic causal loops. While causal loops show the possibilities that "unintended consequences of action feedback to reconstitute the initiating circumstances," (Giddens 1984, 27) reflexive self-regulation through feedback is intended and selective. In the history of international relations from a systemic approach, the evolution of the international structure since the establishment of the Westphalian system is a result of a long-lasting turbulent and chaotic historical era. It is characterized by the Thirty Years' War (1618–1648) and the Eighty Years' War (1568–1648) and demonstrates a process of system reproduction in both aspects of self-regulation and causal loops. In each period of the system, there were always self-regulation operations in the sense that great powers as the most powerful agents negotiated and cooperated to adjust and modify the rules to meet their national interests. There were also unintended consequences of actions causing the decline of the structure and then paving the way for agents to reconstitute it. Like every large-scale war, the two World Wars, for example, led to a variety of unintended consequences including economic recession, environmental decay, and other post-war problems, which were not originally foreseen by those initiating the war. These consequences posed challenges to state agents, showed limitations of the structure and required solutions, which then served the ground for intended actions of agents with efforts to fix the structure.

To sum up, considering dimensions of the structuration theory with the core idea of the duality of the structure, this theory provides an analytical tool to examine the relationship between agency and structure in international relations besides neorealist and structuralist approaches. The analytical framework is illustrated in Figure 1, in which the mutually constitutive relationship between agency and structure in international relations is represented. The international structure including both aspects of rules and resources is shaped by various types of agencies coming from states. By communicating and coordinating, assumptions and values of one or a group of states, giving meaning to some actions and experiences are diffused and guide how other agents think, behave and interact with others (interpretive schemes as modality of the signification property of rules).

Similarly, by cooperating and sanctioning, norms are initiated and disseminated, in most cases, they are institutionalised to become regulations with binding effects, reflecting the legitimation aspect in the international structure. Regarding the aspect of resources in structure, theorists focused on capabilities and power, which are the two different approaches to power in international relations which Baldwin calls the power-as-resources approach and the relational approach respectively. However, to examine the agent-structure relationship, a structural approach to power should be employed. Accordingly, power in the structure is determined by the degree of contribution to the system an agent has made as Keohane suggests a classification of state actors based on their influence in the system (Keohane 1969, 295–6). Therefore, by contributing to the system, agents shape the distribution of power in the international structure. International structure, conversely, enables as well as limits state agents with opportunities and preferences of actions through affecting mechanisms similar to the other way round.

Figure 1: Agent-structure relationship in IR from a structurationist perspective

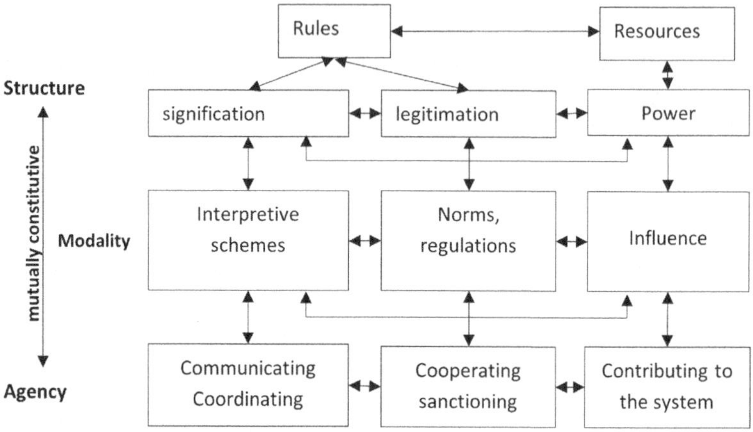

Source: The author

3. *The Agent-Structure Relationship in the Indo-Pacific since the Beginning of the 21st Century*

The Indo-Pacific region is a geo-political term, which focuses on maritime region spanning the Indian and Pacific oceans. The debate may arise when it comes to determining which states can be labelled as Indo-Pacificians. Regarding the *structure* of the Indo-Pacific, agents should not be necessarily Indo-Pacificians but those who participate in the regional system in the sense that they produce a particular effect. Moreover, as theoretically analysed above, state agents are examined in their relationship with the international structure. In the following analysis, the European Union (EU) is also considered as an agent due to its participation in the Indo-Pacific. Finally, the agent-structure relationship in the Indo-Pacific is analysed from the two dimensions:

(i) the bottom-up dimension from state agents to the regional structure, and
(ii) the top-down dimension from the regional structure to the agents' actions.

From state agents to the regional structure

> Firstly, state agents have contributed to the regional structure at different degrees, which has been shaping a multi-layered power hierarchy in the Indo-Pacific.

Instead of using the term of polarity concerning the power of only great powers to depict the distribution of power in the Indo-Pacific system, a multi-layered approach should be adopted. Different degrees of contribution to the system have been shaping five layers in power distribution, arranged in descending order as follows:

> (i) system-determining, (ii) system-influencing, (iii) system-coordinating, (iv) system-committing, and (v) system-participating.

System-determining actors, including the US and China – the two great powers with comprehensive pre-eminence in term of capabilities are on top of the regional power hierarchy. In addition to the domain of national capabilities, the United States and China have also possessed a wide network of relationships in which they play the role as influencers. By competing through diverse types of actions in their interaction with other states in the region – coordination, cooperation, and even sanction – the two giants have created preeminent regional interaction patterns. Therefore, the United States and China are considered the two great powers with the highest potential to create a bipolar order, dominating international interactions not only in the region but also in the world (Maher 2018; Cooper 2020; Kupchan 2021)

Following the system-determining actors in the hierarchy of the Indo-Pacific, the *system-influencing* group of actors includes India, Russia, and the EU who have been actively involved in regional interactions. Although these actors also possess great capabilities in comparison to other states in the region, the power gap between them and the two system-determinants is obvious. Because they are geographically distant from the centre of the region, the Indo-Pacific would not be placed as the top strategic priority in their foreign policies like South Asia in India's, Europe in the EU's, and Eastern Europe in Russia's strategy. These actors become important partners that other states in the region must take into account in their balance-of-power based alignment strategy. The presence of these powerful actors has led to the growing perception of a multipolar order in the region (Lukin 2018; Tourangbam 2021; Bomassi 2025).

The third tier called *system-coordinating* is made up of traditional middle powers who have enough capabilities to be seen as major states and produce visible effects in shaping and maintaining rules in the regional system. These actors are usually developed countries, including Japan, South Korea, and Australia with stronger economic, military and scientific and technological capabilities than others in the following tiers (Nagy 2022). Differing from the actors in the second tier, the system-coordinating states have favourable geographical locations in the region as well as traditional relationships to build a network for influencing other states in the region. The coordination of these states with the great powers through alignment and alliance acts has a considerable influence on the power distribution of the entire Indo-Pacific system.

Following the system-coordinating, the *system-committing* tier includes other middle powers who has been actively contributing to the maintenance and stability of the regional system by taking part in a wide range of regional forums. Therefore, New Zealand, Pakistan, Indonesia, Singapore, Malaysia, Thailand, Vietnam and the Philippines can be labelled as system-committing (Emmers 2018; Erskine 2022; Gilley 2024).

Finally, the fifth tier is made up of small states that are largely *participants* whose policies are heavily influenced by the regional system such as Laos, Cambodia, Myanmar, Brunei, Bangladesh, Nepal, Bhutan, Sri Lanka and the Pacific Island States.

Figure 2: The multi-layered power hierarchy in the Indo-Pacific

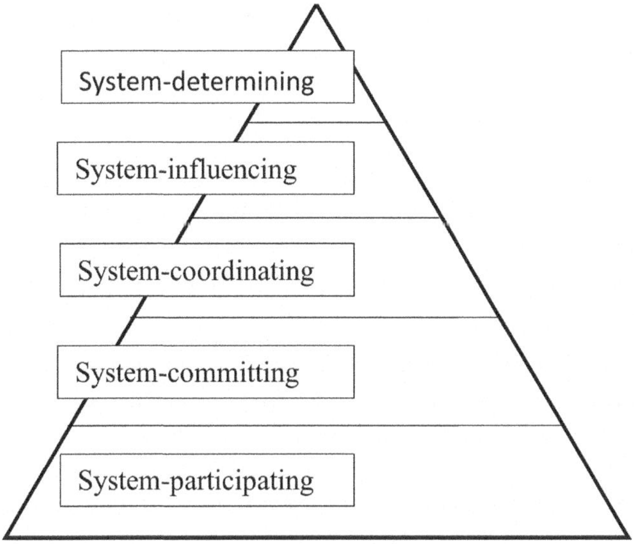

Source: The author

> Secondly, the United States and China have been making efforts to persuade others with their competing visions for the Indo-Pacific, which leaves the signification aspect of the structure in the process of being shaped.

Both the United States and China have their own interpretations of what the regional system should become. The *rules-based order* and the *Community of Common Destiny* are among two notable discourses of the United States and China respectively. While the discourse of rules-based order originated from the term of liberal international order refers to the US-led order built upon a liberal, rules-based trade system, alliance and security relationships, multilateralism, and the spread of liberal norms and values (Mazarr et al. 2016, 45), China's discourse of the *Community of Common Destiny* rooted in the *harmonious world* implies a more pluralist view of the world. According to China, the world should be an "open, inclusive, clean, and beautiful world" where the values of "peace, universal security and common prosperity" should be enjoyed by all humans. (Xinhua 2020) In the surface, both discourses seem not to be conflicting, but their interpretations of their role and challenges posed to such an order reflect a fierce competition.

Since the presidency of Barack Obama, the United States has been seeing China as a revisionist threatening the rules-based order. In order to promote the Trans-Pacific Partnership (TPP) as a US-initiated mechanism of trade liberalization, US President Barack Obama implied China as a challenger to the rules of the international system. He stated:

> "America should write the rules. America should call the shots. Other countries should play by the rules that America and our partners set, and not the other way around... The world has changed. The rules are changing with it. The United States, not countries like China, should write them." (Obama 2016)

Under Donald Trump administration (2017–2021), in the 2017 National Security Strategy (NSS), China coming along with Russia is portrayed as "revisionist powers" with the intention to "shape a world antithetical to U.S. values and interests" (White House 2017, 25). This perception of threat from China has continued under the Joe Biden administration but represented in another way in which China was seen as

> "The only competitor with both the intent to reshape the international order and, increasingly, the economic, diplomatic, military, and technological power to do it." (White House 2022, 23)

In response, China has directly criticised the US's rules-based order as well as the US hegemony. At the opening session of bilateral talks in Anchorage, Alaska, on March 18, Yang Jiechi as the director of the Chinese Communist Party's Central Foreign Affairs Commission stated:

> "What China and the international community follow or uphold is the United Nations-centred international system and the international order underpinned by international law, not what is advocated by a small number of countries of the so-called rules-based international order." (Nikkei Asia 2021)

This shows the ongoing competition between the two most powerful states in the signification domain to decide which way of interpretation to dominate, and then who to be the regional leader. Through this agency, the structure of the Indo-Pacific continues to evolve. However, as of 2024, it can be seen that the United States has had the advantage because the US rules-based order approach has been supported and promoted by the US regional allies who are system-coordinating powers as listed above. Australia, for instance, publicly supported the US leadership and rules-based order in its 2017 white paper, so did Japan in its 2022 Diplomatic Bluebook. Although China has been making efforts to incorporate its interpretation of common values into the joint statements on building a community of shared future with its regional partners, support from these remains limited.

> Thirdly, ASEAN representing cooperation among small states plays a central role in shaping the legitimation aspect of the regional structure.

Although there have been concerns about the possibly fading role of ASEAN in the context of growing great power competition, the reality is that ASEAN has not only been relevant but also become a normative power. Through its principles and practices, the *ASEAN way* characterised by non-interference, informality, minimal institutionalisation, consultation and consensus has been accepted and adopted by external partners. The expansion of ASEAN principles through ASEAN plus mechanisms like ASEAN+1, ASEAN+3, ASEAN+6, ASEAN Regional Forum, ADMM+, and East Asia Summit gives evidence to ASEAN's actual role.

By seeing the Indo-Pacific as a geo-political expansion of the Asia-Pacific, ASEAN tends to continue to have a crucial role in shaping the regional structure, which has been also recognised by other states. In the policy document entitled *A Free and Open Indo-Pacific: Advancing a Shared Vision* (known as FOIP) under the Trump administration, ASEAN is perceived to "sit at the geographical centre of the Indo-Pacific" and considered "central to the U.S. vision" (U.S. Department of State 2019, 6). The United States has seen ASEAN as a supporter of its vision of rules-based order:

> "A strong, rules-based architecture anchors the U.S. vision for the Indo-Pacific region. Representing ten countries, 650 million people, and a combined GDP of almost $3 trillion, ASEAN is central to this architecture... We see a clear convergence between the principles enshrined in ASEAN's Indo-Pacific Outlook – inclusivity, openness, good governance, and respect for international law – and the vision of the United States for a free and open Indo-Pacific, as well as the regional approaches of our allies, partners, and friends." (U.S. Department of State 2019, 7)

Japan in its New Plan for a Free and Open Indo-Pacific (FOIP), released in 2023, has also expressed the respects for ASEAN centrality and unity, and full support for the ASEAN Outlook of Indo-Pacific (Ministry of Foreign Affairs of Japan 2023, 8). The respect for ASEAN's centrality is also reaffirmed by many other states in the region, including China (ASEAN-China Centre 2025).

The success of ASEAN is a good indicator of how institutionalized interactions among small states not only help manage their relationships but also contribute to the formation of a larger structure – the Indo-Pacific regional structure.

From the regional structure to state agents' actions

> Firstly, the regional structure of the Indo-Pacific empowers small powers to navigate great powers relations by encouraging hedging and multi-alignment strategies of these states.

Although small states are independent decision-makers in the realm of foreign affairs, their strategic options are often more limited than those of great powers due to limited resources and considerations of many internal and external factors. However, from the perspective of structuration theory, the international structure enables states to take actions that would not be conducted without the existence of structures. This statement is true in the context of the Indo-Pacific. Differing from being neutral, a hedging policy which means maintaining a delicate balance in relationships with both competing great powers by deepening political security and defence ties with both. Small and middle powers cannot implement such policy unless the regional structure is characterized by a multi-layered situation with a balance of power between the two great powers at the top of the regional power hierarchy and relative interdependence by signification and norms within the structure. In the so called Yalta system during the Cold War, characterised by bipolarity, and fragmentation caused by hostilities between the two blocs, small and middle powers did not have opportunities to contribute to the system in the way that is possible today regarding the Indo-Pacific system. During the Cold War, many small and middle powers decided to align with one great power – the United States or the Soviet Union, others chose not to take sides and align in the sense that they did not have close security and defence ties with both great powers, which kept them relatively safe but underdeveloped.

Relative interdependence between the United States and China as well as among all states in the Indo-Pacific since the beginning of the 21st century has not divided the regional system into two sub-systems like what happened in the Yalta system, giving state agents the strategic options of hedging or being in-between. Moreover, because ASEAN has a central role in the regional architecture, major states in the first and second tiers have paid more attention to ASEAN states. In other words, ASEAN states have more opportunities to conduct such policy. Figure 3 in the appendix shows that bilateral relationships between ASEAN states and major powers have been significantly enhanced since 2001.

Especially since 2010 when the distribution of power between the United States and China came towards the state of balance of power, bilateral relationships between the two great powers and ASEAN states have been rapidly upgraded through different types of partnership. Not mentioning Singapore, who signed a high-quality comprehensive cooperative partnership towards the future with China in 2023, and Vietnam, who upgraded its relations with China to a comprehensive strategic partnership in 2008, eight out of ten Southeast Asian countries have upgraded their relations with China to the highest level since 2009.

Despite many concerns, Southeast Asian states also tend to participate and show a certain level of support for China's major initiatives and projects, especially the Belt and Road and the Community of Shared Future initiatives. Notably, seven out of ten ASEAN states have agreed to build a Community of Shared Future with China since 2019. Regarding the US partnership network, excepting Thailand and the Philippines as the two treaty allies of the United States, since 2010, four of the eight remaining Southeast Asian countries have upgraded their relations with the United States. Singapore has chosen to be a dialogue partner of the United States in many important areas such as national security, science and technology and aeronautics. In fact, only the Philippines under Bongbong Marcos administration is pursuing a balancing strategy, most of ASEAN states are choosing to be a hedger instead.

Besides hedging, multi-alignment is another active strategy that a multi-layered power hierarchy of the Indo-Pacific structure facilitates. Not only focusing on the two system-determining powers, small states also actively cooperate in depth and in width with the system-influencing, especially the EU and India. Cooperation and engagement tend to focus on areas of strength of the EU and India. The cooperation with India, which initially focused on trade and investment, has tended to expand to deeper cooperation in the field of defence and security since the implementation of the Act East policy (Palit 2016, 87). With the EU, the cooperative relationship tends to progress from the Comprehensive Partnership Agreement (PCA) to economic-trade cooperation and cooperation in the fields of development. This is also consistent with the EU's regional strategy focusing on development areas such as green transition, maritime governance, digital governance, and human security (EEAS 2024). However, due to many differences not only in distance but also in development models and political systems, the cooperation process still needs more time for states to negotiate and reach consensus. For Russia, the relationship between Southeast Asian countries and Russia mainly focuses on energy cooperation and arms trade in addition to maintaining the role of dialogue partners in regional forums (Grossman 2024).

> Secondly, the Indo-Pacific structure maintains both cooperation and competition aspects in Sino-American relations and constrains the two from direct confrontation.

There are three structural factors that keep the US and China from escalating into the conflict, including:

(i) the balance of power between the two,
(ii) the interdependence not only between the two rivals but also among the rest of the states, and
(iii) small states like ASEAN states who find interests in maintaining and stabilising the system for their security and development playing a central role in shaping the norms – the legitimation aspect of the regional structure.

4. Conclusion

Structuration theory, which can avoid individualist determinism of neorealists as well as structuralist determinism of world system theorists provides a useful analytical framework to examine the agent-structure relationship in international relations. By acknowledging the mutually constitutive relationship between agency and structure, the Indo-Pacific structure should not be analysed separately from state agents. In the case of the Indo-Pacific, it can be concluded that most aspects of the regional structure are still being shaped, in which the resource or power aspect is the most progressive one, forming a multi-layered power hierarchy on the regional structure. Followed by the signification aspect, the United States has had the advantage over China in their competition in this domain thanks to its allies and established power during the so-called unipolar moment after the Cold War ended. The final aspect of the structure-legitimation depends on whether ASEAN manages challenges to maintain its relevance and central role in the regional structure.

5. *References*

Australian Government (2017): 2017 Foreign Policy White Paper. https://www.dfat.gov.au/sites/default/files/2017-foreign-policy-white-paper.pdf.

ASEAN-China Centre (2025): The ACC Joint Executive Board Convenes the 1st Working Group Meeting in 2025. http://www.asean-china-center.org/english/2025-04/14930.html.

Baldwin, D. (2002): Power and international relations. In: Carlsnaes, W./Risse, T./Simmons, B. A. (eds.): Power and international relations. SAGE. 177–191.

Bomassi, L. (2025): The Geopolitics of Multipolarity: How to counter Europe's waning relevance in Southeast Asia. European Union Institute for Security Studies (EUISS).

Chan, S. (2012): Looking for Balance: China, the United States, and Power Balancing in East Asia (1st ed.). Stanford University Press.

Cooper, Z. (2020): The Future Indo-Pacific Order. Security Challenges, 16(3), 5–9.

Devi, P./Singh, J. (2024): China's Assertive Escalation in the Indo-Pacific Region and its Repercussions on India-US Relations. In: Journal of Strategic Security, 17(4), 1–22.

Donnelly, J. (2000): Realism and International Relations. Cambridge University Press.

EEAS (2024): EU-Indo Pacific Strategy. European Union External Action – The Diplomatic Service of the European Union. https://www.eeas.europa.eu/eeas/eu-Indo-Pacific-strategy_en.

Emmers, R. (2018): The Role of Middle Powers in Asian Multilateralism. In: Asia Policy, 13(4), 42–47.

Erskine, A. (2022): The Middle Power Dynamic in the Indo-Pacific: Unpacking How Vietnam and Indonesia Can Shape Regional Security and Economic Issues. In: Journal of Indo-Pacific Affairs, 1–16.

Gilley, B. (2024): Will Malaysia become an active middle power? In: Australian Journal of International Affairs, 79(1), 132–149.

Fong, B. C. H. (2024): US-China Rivalry: Great Power Competition in the Indo-Pacific (first edition). Edinburgh University Press.

Giddens, A. (1984): The Constitution of Society: Outline of the Theory of Structuration. Cambridge.

Grossman, D. (2024): Russia Is a Strategic Spoiler in the Indo-Pacific. In: Foreign Policy. https://foreignpolicy.com/2024/07/09/russia-india-putin-modi-Indo-Pacific-china-north-korea-geopolitics/.

Holsti, K. J. (1964): The Concept of Power in the Study of International Relations. In: Background, 7(4), 179–194.

Keohane, R. O. (1969): Lilliputians' Dilemmas: Small States in International Politics (Review of Alliances and the Third World; Alliances and American Foreign Policy; Alliances and Small Powers; The Inequality of States). In: Liska, G. et al.: International Organization, 23(2), 291–310.

Kuik, C. C. (2008): The Essence of Hedging: Malaysia and Singapore's Response to a Rising China. In: Contemporary Southeast Asia, 30, 159–185.

Kupchan, C. (2021): Bipolarity is Back: Why It Matters. In: The Washington Quarterly, 44(4), 123–139.

Lim, D. J./Cooper, Z. (2015): Reassessing Hedging: The Logic of Alignment in East Asia. In: Security Studies. 24(4), 696–727.

Lukin, A. (2018): Russia and the United States in the Asia Pacific: A Perspective of the English School. In: Asian Perspective, 42(3), 307–331.

Maher, R. (2018): Bipolarity and the Future of U.S.-China Relations. In: Political Science Quarterly, 133(3), 497–525.

Marston, H. S. (2023): Abandoning Hedging: Reconsidering Southeast Asian Alignment Choices. In: Contemporary Southeast Asia. 45(1), 55–81.

Mazarr, M. J. (et al.) (2016): Understanding the current international order. RAND Corporation.

Ministry of Foreign Affairs of Japan (2022): Diplomatic Bluebook 2022. https://www.mofa.go.jp/policy/other/bluebook/2022/pdf/en_index.html.

Ministry of Foreign Affairs of Japan (2023): New Plan for a Free and Open Indo-Pacific (FOIP). https://www.mofa.go.jp/files/100477660.pdf.

Nagy, S. R. (2022): Middle-Power Alignment in the Free and Open Indo-Pacific: Securing Agency through Neo-Middle-Power Diplomacy. Asia Policy, 17(3), 161–179.

Nikkei Asia (2021): How it happened: Transcript of the US-China opening remarks in Alaska. https://asia.nikkei.com/Politics/International-relations/US-China-tensions/How-it-happened-Transcript-of-the-US-China-opening-remarks-in-Alaska.

Roy, D. (2005): Southeast Asia and China: Balancing or Bandwagoning? In: Contemporary Southeast Asia, 27 (2), 305–322

Liu, C./Wang, Z. (2018): Peripheral development theory: world-systems and the development of Southeast Asia. In: Asian Review of Political Economy 1 (8) (2022).

Obama, B. (2016): Cross Post: President Obama: The TPP would let America, not China, lead the way on global trade. Office of the United States Trade Representative. https://ustr.gov/about-us/policy-offices/press-office/press-releases/2016/may/cross-post-president-obama-tpp-would.

Palit, A. (2016): India's Act East Policy and Implications for Southeast Asia. In: Southeast Asian Affairs, 81–92

Tourangbam, M. (2021): India and the New Geopolitics of the Indo-Pacific. Indian Foreign Affairs Journal, 16(1), 54–66.

U.S. Department of States (2019): A Free and Open Indo-Pacific: Advancing a Shared Vision. https://www.state.gov/wp-content/uploads/2019/11/Free-and-Open-Indo-Pacific-4Nov2019.pdf.

Xinhua (2020): Why President Xi strongly advocates building community with shared future. Qiushi: CPC Central Committee Bimonthly. http://en.qstheory.cn/2020-09/23/c_538500.htm.

Waltz, K. N. (1979): Theory of International Politics. Addison-Wesley.

Wendt, A. E. (1987): The Agent-Structure Problem in International Relations Theory. In: International Organization, 41(3), 335–370.

White House (2017): National Security Strategy of the United States of America. https://trumpwhitehouse.archives.gov/wp-content/uploads/2017/12/NSS-Final-12-18-2017-0905.pdf.

White House (2022): National Security Strategy. https://bidenwhitehouse.archives.gov/wp-content/uploads/2022/11/8-November-Combined PDF for Upload.pdf.

6. Appendix

Figure 3: Developments in bilateral relationships between system-determining, system-influencing and Southeast Asian nations

	The United States	**China**	**The European Union**	**India**	**Russia**
Brunei	1984: diplomatic ties 1994: MoU in defence **2002:** Trade & Investment Framework Agreements	1991: diplomatic ties **2013:** Strategic Partnership **2018:** Comprehensive Strategic Partnership	**2023:** Partnership Facility	1984: diplomatic ties **2021:** MoU in defence	1991: diplomatic ties
Cambodia	1950: diplomatic ties **2006:** Trade & Investment Framework Agreements **2011:** joint maritime exercise **2024:** restart joint exercise and training programs	1958: diplomatic ties **2010:** Comprehensive Strategic Partnership **2019:** 2019–23 Action Plan on building community of shared future **2023:** 2024–28 Action Plan on building community of common destiny	1997: Cooperation agreements	1952: diplomatic ties **2007:** 7 MoUs including MoU in defence **2018:** MoU in security	1956: diplomatic ties
Indonesia	1949: diplomatic ties 1996: Trade & Investment Framework Agreements **2010:** comprehensive partnership **2015:** Strategic Partnership	1950: diplomatic ties 1999: cooperative partnership **2005:** Strategic Partnership **2013:** Comprehensive Strategic Partnership **2015:** enhanced Comprehensive Strategic Partnership	**2014:** Partnership and Cooperation Agreement **2024:** CEPA	1949: diplomatic ties **2001:** MoU in defence **2005:** strategic partnership	1950: diplomatic ties Arms-trade
Laos	1950: diplomatic ties **2003:** trade agreement **2016:** comprehensive partnership	1961: diplomatic ties **2009:** Comprehensive Strategic Partnership **2019:** Action Plan on building Community of Shared Future	1997: Cooperation Agreement Cooperation on sustainable development	1956: diplomatic ties **2002:** MoUs in security and defence	1960: diplomatic ties 1991: Treaty of Friendship
Malaysia	1957: diplomatic ties **2004:** Trade & Investment Framework Agreements, joint naval exercise **2014:** comprehensive partnership	1974: diplomatic ties **2009:** Action Plan on Strategic Partnership **2013:** Comprehensive Strategic Partnership **2023:** agree to build Community of Shared Future	**2022:** Partnership and Cooperation Agreement	1957: diplomatic ties **2010:** strategic partnership **2015:** enhanced strategic partnership	1967: diplomatic ties Agreements on economic and technological cooperation

	The United States	China	The European Union	India	Russia
Myanmar	1947: diplomatic ties **2013:** Trade & Investment Framework Agreements	1950: diplomatic ties **2011:** Comprehensive Strategic Partnership **2020:** agree to build Community of Shared Future		1948: diplomatic ties 1951: Treaty of Friendship **2018:** Agreement on Land Border Crossing	1948: diplomatic ties Maintain cooperation in the field of economics, trade, non-traditional security, counterterrorism.
The Philippines	1946: diplomatic ties 1951: defence treaty 1989: Trade & Investment Framework Agreements 1998: Visiting Forces Agreement **2014:** Enhanced Defense Cooperation Agreement	1975: diplomatic ties 1996: cooperative partnership **2005:** Strategic Partnership **2018:** Comprehensive Strategic Partnership	**2011:** Partnership and Cooperation Agreement **2024:** restart FTA negotiation	1949: diplomatic ties 1952: Treaty of Friendship MoUs in sustainable development, health care, and climate change	1976: diplomatic ties Cooperation in the field of economics, agriculture, security, defence and space
Singapore	1966: diplomatic ties 1981: regular joint air and naval exercises **2003:** FTA **2005:** Strategic Framework Agreement in Defense and Security **2021:** Partnership for Growth and Innovation **2023:** Critical and Emerging Technology Dialogue	1990: diplomatic ties **2015:** All-Round Cooperative Partnership Progressing with the Times **2023:** All-Round High-Quality Future-Oriented Partnership	**2019:** ratify Partnership and Cooperation Agreement, FTA, Investment Protection Agreement **2024:** Global Gateway Dialogue	1965: diplomatic ties **2015:** Strategic Partnership **2024:** Comprehensive Strategic Partnership	1968: diplomatic ties Maintaining regular talks
Thailand	1882: diplomatic ties 1950: military assistance agreement 1966: Treaty of Amity and Economic Relations **2020:** Joint Vision Statement 2020 for the US-Thai Defense Alliance **2022:** Communiqué on Strategic Alliance and Partnership	1975: diplomatic ties **2001:** Strategic Partnership **2012:** Comprehensive Strategic Partnership **2023:** agree to build Community of Shared Future	**2022:** Partnership and Cooperation Agreement	1947: diplomatic ties **2012:** MoUs in defense	1941: diplomatic ties
Vietnam	1995: diplomatic ties **2001:** BTA **2007:** Trade & Investment Framework Agreements **2011:** MoU in defence	1950: diplomatic ties 1990: cooperative partnership **2008:** Comprehensive Strategic Partnership	**2016:** Partnership and Cooperation Agreement **2019:** Free trade agreement and Investment Protection Agreement	1972: diplomatic ties **2007:** Strategic Partnership **2016:** Comprehensive Strategic Partnership	1950: diplomatic ties **2001:** Strategic Partnership **2012:** Comprehensive Strategic Partnership

	The United States	China	The European Union	India	Russia
	2013: Comprehensive Partnership **2023:** Comprehensive Strategic Partnership	**2023:** agree to build Community of Shared Future		**2020:** Joint Vision Statement for Peace, Prosperity and People	

Source: The author compiling from official sources on the websites of the Ministries of Foreign Affairs of relevant countries

Chapter 3: Building a Composite Index of International Cooperation and Conflict: A Case Study of the Indo-Pacific Region

Nghiem Tuan Hung and Nguyen Thi Nhu Quynh

The Indo-Pacific is the geopolitical and economic centre of gravity in the 21st century, characterised by simultaneous cooperation and conflict among key regional actors. Existing analytical tools fail to capture this duality, relying on fragmented security, economic, and diplomatic indicators, leading to misaligned policy responses and strategic blind spots. This study argues for the development of an Indo-Pacific Index of Cooperation and Conflict (IPI) to provide a structured, data-driven assessment of regional stability. By integrating economic partnerships, military posturing, diplomatic engagements, and geopolitical risks, the index would serve as a predictive tool for conflict prevention, a benchmark for accountability, and a framework for guiding strategic policymaking. The research highlights the practical and theoretical imperatives of such an index, addressing data fragmentation, misallocated resources, and reactionary policymaking. Implementation challenges, including data inconsistencies, geopolitical sensitivities, and methodological standardisation, require a consensus-driven approach using Delphi-based weighting models and institutional partnerships. Future research should focus on AI-driven real-time monitoring, evolving regional frameworks, and crisis prevention applications. A composite index is essential for decoding Indo-Pacific dynamics, ensuring more precise, forward-thinking policies, and mitigating the risks of strategic miscalculations in an increasingly volatile region.

1. Introduction

The Indo-Pacific region, commanding over half the world's population and its vital trade arteries, teeters between unprecedented opportunity and perilous tension. Spanning from the eastern shores of Africa to the western coasts of the Americas, this vast expanse is not merely a geographic construct but a geopolitical crucible where the 21st century's fate is being forged. Home to over 4.7 billion people – or 60 per cent of global humanity (The United Nations, Economic and Social Commission for Asia and the Pacific 2023) – and channelling 60 per cent of the world's maritime trade through its waters as estimated by the United Nations Conference on Trade and Development (UNCTAD) (2024; 2024a; 2025), the Indo-Pacific is an economic juggernaut. Yet, beneath this veneer of prosperity lies a cauldron of rivalry: contested seas, militarised borders, and a tug-of-war between superpowers like China, the United States, and India. It is a region where the Regional Comprehensive Economic Partnership (RCEP) "covers nearly 30 per cent of global GDP and population, representing a combined GDP of USD 29 trillion and 2.3 billion people" (Kao Kim Hourn 2024), yet the South China Sea bristles with naval stand-offs, and the Himalayan frontier witnesses deadly skirmishes. This volatile interplay of cooperation and conflict defies simplistic analysis, rendering traditional tools inadequate for grasping its pulse. The Indo-Pacific is not just an economic lifeline but a strategic chessboard where the moves of today dictate the global order of tomorrow. It is the centre of gravity for global power. These paradoxes – economic arteries entwined with strategic chokeholds – reveal a region teetering on a knife-edge, where prosperity and peril are inseparable twins. In an era of escalating geopolitical tensions and deepening economic interdependence, constructing a composite index to assess the Indo-Pacific region's overall state – integrating cooperation and conflict – is indispensable for decoding its volatile dynamics, steering effective policies, and safeguarding regional stability.

The Indo-Pacific's future hangs in this precarious balance, where a misstep could unravel decades of progress. Creating a broad index that captures both when countries work together and when they clash, makes a lot of sense in the Indo-Pacific. Taking things further than just gathering numbers, this index could open up a window onto broader trends by merging stories of teamwork and rivalry. By looking into the nuts and bolts of country-to-country relations in the region, the index could very well guide policy decisions and diplomatic moves geared towards easing disputes and boosting collaboration. In most cases, these insights would show policy makers where potential partnerships lie – areas that might otherwise be overlooked – and offer a more blended approach to dealing with local challenges. A composite index, as proposed here, is not a luxury but a necessity – a compass to decode these volatile dynamics, steer policies with precision, and safeguard stability before the region slips into chaos.

We'd be looking at a tool that gives policymakers and researchers useful, if sometimes messy, snapshots of collaboration and conflict.

2. The Need for a Composite Index in the Indo-Pacific

International relations in the Indo-Pacific have grown messy, and there's a real need for an all-embracing index that breaks down the different ways nations work together – or clash – with one another. Despite this intricate interplay between conflict and cooperation, no composite index exists to quantify these dynamics holistically. Current assessments remain fragmented, relying on military-centric indices, economic datasets, and diplomatic reports that fail to capture the multifaceted nature of Indo-Pacific relations. The absence of a structured metric hinders strategic foresight, distorts policy responses, and perpetuates a cycle of reactionary decision-making. This part argues that establishing a composite index is both a practical and theoretical necessity.

Exposing and eradicating data gaps: the fallacy of scattered insights

The Indo-Pacific, a region of immense geopolitical significance, is currently analysed through a fragmented array of security, economic, and diplomatic metrics. Policymakers and analysts rely on disparate indices such as the Global Peace Index (GPI) for military tensions, the Uppsala Conflict Data Program (UCDP) for armed conflicts, and various trade datasets for economic relations. However, these indicators operate in silos, failing to capture the interwoven reality of conflict and cooperation (Minnich 2025). This disjointed approach creates severe blind spots, preventing policymakers from making informed, data-driven strategic decisions (Wiśniewski 2023).

One of the most glaring consequences of this data fragmentation is the inability to accurately assess the dual nature of state behaviour in the Indo-Pacific. China and the United States exemplify this contradiction: despite their escalating military rivalry in the Taiwan Strait and the South China Sea, bilateral trade reached over 583 billion US dollars in 2024 (Ma 2025). Similarly, India and China, despite enduring border skirmishes, continue to engage in substantial economic exchanges through BRICS and the Regional Comprehensive Economic Partnership (RCEP) (Lau/Zhou 2022). This paradox – where adversarial states remain economically interdependent –

defies simplistic categorisation as either conflict or cooperation. Without a composite index that integrates these dynamics, policymakers risk drawing flawed conclusions and miscalculating strategic priorities. The reliance on segmented data sources also results in policy misalignment, where governments prioritise narrow security considerations while neglecting economic and diplomatic trade-offs. In the absence of a structured metric that correlates economic, military, and diplomatic shifts, policymakers fail to anticipate how economic engagements influence security relationships and vice versa. A composite index would bridge this analytical gap, enabling governments to construct more nuanced, context-sensitive policies that reflect the multidimensional nature of Indo-Pacific relations.

Further exacerbating the problem is the lack of a unified data system that tracks both short-term fluctuations and long-term trends in Indo-Pacific security and cooperation. Current databases typically provide snapshots of specific issues, such as military incidents or trade volumes, but fail to contextualise them within broader strategic trends. For instance, while China's naval expansion in the South China Sea is well documented, its concurrent investments in Southeast Asian infrastructure via the Belt and Road Initiative (BRI) receive separate, unconnected analysis (Lau/Zhou 2022). This fragmented perspective prevents policymakers from recognising the full scope of Beijing's regional strategy, which blends economic incentives with coercive military tactics. A composite index would capture these interactions systematically, preventing misjudgements based on incomplete data. A further dimension of data fragmentation is the lack of real-time tracking, which reduces the effectiveness of early warning mechanisms. For example, diplomatic disputes often precede trade restrictions or military escalations, yet existing frameworks fail to quantify these pre-crisis indicators in a single analytical model (Minnich 2025). This deficiency means that escalations occur with little forewarning, forcing governments into reactive rather than proactive crisis management. A composite index would synthesise these indicators, allowing early detection of regional flashpoints and enhancing strategic foresight.

Thus, data fragmentation is not merely an academic limitation – it has direct, tangible consequences for regional stability. Without an integrated framework, strategic assessments remain incomplete, and governments struggle to balance economic cooperation with security deterrence. A composite index is essential for transforming Indo-Pacific policymaking from fragmented guesswork into structured, evidence-based strategy.

Empowering policy makers: precision over paralysis

In the absence of a composite index, policymakers operate in a landscape defined by contradiction and uncertainty. Government agencies, intelligence services, and multilateral organisations rely on vastly different datasets, often leading to conflicting interpretations of the same geopolitical events (Wiśniewski 2023). The Indo-Pacific is a rapidly evolving region, where alliances, trade partnerships, and military stances shift constantly. Without a structured analytical framework, policymakers lack the clarity needed to anticipate and adapt to these shifts.

One of the most serious consequences of this data incoherence is reactionary rather than strategic policymaking. In the absence of an index, leaders are forced into short-term crisis management, unable to develop long-term, forward-looking policies. Decisions are driven by immediate military concerns, while economic and diplomatic engagements are considered separately. This leads to a cycle of reactive, rather than proactive, governance. A composite index would break this cycle, allowing policymakers to synthesise military, economic, and diplomatic trends into a single strategic framework. Furthermore, the lack of an integrated analytical tool results in misallocated resources. Currently, governments prioritise military spending (McGerty 2024; Tian et al. 2024) based on security indices, while trade policies must be always crafted with geopolitical risk assessments (Tijaja/Dzakwan 2025). This disjointed approach leads to inefficient resource allocation, where nations either overinvest in deterrence at the expense of economic integration or vice versa. A composite index would allow policymakers to optimise national strategy, ensuring that security, trade, and diplomatic investments are harmonised rather than conflicting. Equally problematic is the failure to anticipate regional shifts before they materialise. Given that the Indo-Pacific operates under a system of alliances (Grossman 2024) and adversaries (Leben 2024), governments must be able to predict changes in regional power dynamics with accuracy. A composite index, by aggregating multiple dimensions of conflict and cooperation, would function as an early warning system, helping policymakers identify patterns and pre-empt strategic shifts before they escalate into crises.

Ultimately, precision in policy is impossible without structured analysis. The development of a composite index would transform chaotic, disjointed data into a coherent, actionable framework, ensuring that Indo-Pacific policymakers are equipped to navigate the complexities of the 21st-century geopolitical landscape.

Imposing accountability and catalysing action: transparency as a weapon

Transparency is a strategic asset in international politics. Yet, in the Indo-Pacific, governments and institutions operate in an environment of ambiguity, where policy contradictions and geopolitical manoeuvres remain largely unchecked (Wiśniewski 2023). A composite index would act as a force multiplier for accountability, compelling regional actors to align their policies with their public commitments.

One of the most persistent challenges in the Indo-Pacific is the strategic obfuscation of aggressive actions under the guise of economic engagement. China, for instance, presents itself as a champion of regional economic cooperation through the BRI and RCEP (Rana/2020; Yu 2024), yet simultaneously engages in militarisation of contested maritime zones (Chen et al. 2024; Helmus et al. 2024). Similarly, the United States advocates for a *Free and Open Indo-Pacific*, while pursuing inconsistent economic approaches which trouble regional trade integration (Kavanagh/Cuéllar 2024; Mishra 2024). A composite index would expose these contradictions, ensuring that states are held accountable for policies that undermine regional stability. Moreover, transparency is essential for sustaining multilateral trust and cooperation. The Indo-Pacific is home to competing security frameworks, including Quad, AUKUS, and ASEAN-centric mechanisms. A composite index would provide a neutral, data-driven benchmark against which nations can measure their strategic alignments. By quantifying both cooperation and aggression, it would serve as a deterrent against escalatory actions, while rewarding constructive engagement.

Thus, the creation of a composite index is not just an analytical necessity – it is a diplomatic imperative. It would not only inform better policymaking but also enforce higher standards of accountability and regional stability.

Grasping systemic complexity: beyond reductionism

The Indo-Pacific, a region marked by intricate geopolitical relationships, cannot be reduced to simplistic dichotomies of conflict or cooperation. Traditional international relations frameworks tend to segment military, economic, and diplomatic dimensions into discrete categories, thereby oversimplifying the complex web of interactions that define the region (Medcalf 2020). Reducing these relationships to binary oppositions – either cooperation or conflict – fails to capture the interdependent realities that shape the region's dynamics. The Indo-Pacific is characterised by simultaneous cooperation and competition across multiple fronts, where military alliances and economic interdependence coexist, often within the same state-to-state interactions.

The theoretical concept of complex interdependence, as articulated by Keohane and Nye (Keohane/Nye 2012), offers a more comprehensive lens through which to understand Indo-Pacific relations. This theory suggests that economic, diplomatic, and security relationships are deeply interwoven, and actions in one domain often have profound implications in the others. A composite index of conflict and cooperation would align with this framework, providing an empirical measure that integrates the various facets of regional interactions. By doing so, it would offer a clearer, data-driven understanding of how these dimensions interact and influence each other. For instance, Japan's participation in Quad's security initiatives – a clear commitment to regional security and countering China's military expansion – does not preclude its economic cooperation with China through mechanisms like the RCEP (Oxford Analytica 2021; Oba 2022). This simultaneous engagement in security competition and economic cooperation illustrates the limitations of reductionist approaches that treat these two spheres as mutually exclusive. Similarly, ASEAN nations demonstrate strategic complexity by relying on US military guarantees for security while benefiting from China's economic relations (The Asia Foundation 2024). A composite index would provide a structured framework for capturing these dynamic and often paradoxical relationships, enabling more accurate assessments of the region's evolving power dynamics.

In this context, complex interdependence theory highlights the need for analytical tools that can account for the fluidity and overlap between military, economic, and diplomatic actions. A composite index would integrate these dimensions into a single analytical model, offering policymakers a multidimensional perspective on regional stability. Such a tool would enable them to navigate the intricacies of Indo-Pacific geopolitics with a much clearer understanding of the forces at play.

Reconciling the cooperation-conflict duality: a theoretical synthesis

A pervasive fallacy in Indo-Pacific studies is the assumption that conflict and cooperation are mutually exclusive. This dualistic thinking often leads to binary policy prescriptions – states are either allies or adversaries, depending on the prevailing context. However, as the Indo-Pacific's dynamics consistently demonstrate, conflict and cooperation can exist simultaneously within the same relationship. This cooperation-conflict duality challenges conventional international relations paradigms, where cooperation is typically seen as the antidote to conflict. In reality, economic interdependence often serves to dampen tensions, but it does not necessarily negate the possibility of conflict.

For example, India and China's long-standing border disputes continue to simmer despite the robust economic interdependence between the two nations (Balázs 2024). Both countries have extensive trade ties, and their engagement in multilateral forums like BRICS and the Shanghai Cooperation Organisation suggests a cooperative dimension. However, their military confrontations along the LAC (Line of Actual Control) demonstrate that economic cooperation does not preclude military rivalry. A composite index would capture this paradox, allowing for the quantification of the degree to which economic cooperation tempers military rivalry, thus providing policymakers with a more accurate picture of the state of bilateral relations. Similarly, Japan's post-war pacifism – as enshrined in its Constitutional Article 9 – is evolving towards a more assertive security posture, especially through its participation in Quad and the US-Japan security alliance (Liow/Chong 2023; Pajon 2024; Baldauff 2024). Despite this shift, Japan remains deeply economically integrated with its regional neighbours, particularly China, South Korea, and ASEAN nations. The shift from pacifism to assertiveness does not negate Japan's economic dependence on its regional partners; rather, it underscores the complex interplay between security concerns and economic necessities in the Indo-Pacific. A composite index would assess the impact of such evolving dynamics, allowing analysts to track the extent to which security escalations undermine or complement economic relations.

This blending of cooperation and conflict underscores the need for an index that can quantify these simultaneous dimensions. A composite index would offer a robust tool for reconciling these dualities, enabling more accurate geopolitical forecasting. By combining economic, diplomatic, and security indicators, the index would measure how security escalations affect trade relations and vice versa, providing a comprehensive assessment of regional stability.

Unlocking predictive and normative power: theory in action

Indices are not just descriptive tools – they also have the potential to shape policy norms and inform strategic foresight. The value of a composite index extends beyond its ability to map the complex interplay of conflict and cooperation; it can also predict future regional dynamics and shape normative frameworks for regional stability. Quantifying conflict and co-operation allow policymakers to anticipate potential flashpoints, thereby enabling early diplomatic interventions. A composite index would offer an early warning system, highlighting areas of growing tension and unrealised potential for cooperation.

One of the critical benefits of a composite index is its predictive power. By tracking historical trends in military, economic, and diplomatic interactions, an index could forecast future shifts in regional power dynamics. This is particularly crucial in the Indo-Pacific, where the region's fluid alliances and shifting geopolitical priorities make it difficult to discern long-term trends. For instance, a rising military competition between China and the United States may coincide with increased economic cooperation through multilateral trade agreements (Chivvis 2024). A composite index would allow policymakers to anticipate the thresholds at which economic tensions may escalate into security crises or where diplomatic initiatives could prevent military conflict. Moreover, a composite index would serve as a normative benchmark, encouraging states to align their actions with established regional norms. The Indo-Pacific's commitment to a *rules-based order* could be tracked and evaluated using a composite index. States that violated international norms – such as unilateral military actions in the South China Sea – could be held accountable through the data-driven transparency provided by the index. In this sense, the index would reinforce a regional rules-based order, encouraging states to act within a predictable, transparent framework. For example, the Center for Strategic and International Studies has had some success with its Asia Maritime Transparency Initiative when

> "AMTI aims to promote transparency in the Indo-Pacific to dissuade assertive behavior and conflict and generate opportunities for cooperation and confidence building." (Center for Strategic and International Studies n.d.)

In fact, Indo-Pacific policy is often shaped by subjective narratives rather than empirical analysis. By offering a data-driven approach, a composite index would reduce diplomatic ambiguities, clarify strategic miscalculations, and ensure that policies are grounded in evidence rather than assumptions. This would lead to more precise policy making, reducing the likelihood of unintended consequences and strategic missteps.

In short, both practical realities and theoretical necessities point unequivocally towards the need for a composite index. The cost of inaction is severe: policymaking remains reactive, accountability is undermined, and strategic clarity is sacrificed. The Indo-Pacific is the defining geopolitical arena of the 21st century. Yet, its stability is analysed through fragmented lenses, leading to analytical blind spots that fuel miscalculations. A composite index would transform Indo-Pacific assessment from conjecture to structured foresight, equipping policymakers with a precise, data-driven framework to navigate regional complexities. The failure to develop such an index is tantamount to strategic irresponsibility. As the Indo-Pacific grows more volatile, those who remain blind to its complexities will forfeit their ability to shape its future.

Construction of a composite index

In the realm of international relations, a composite index serves as a crucial tool for measuring complex dynamics such as cooperation and conflict. By synthesizing multiple quantitative and qualitative indicators, it offers a nuanced overview of interactions among nations, revealing patterns that individual metrics might obscure. The purpose of such an index is not merely descriptive; it aims to provide a framework for comparative analysis, facilitating both academic research and policy making. Summarily, a well-constructed composite index enhances understanding, aids in forecasting future trends, and fosters informed decision-making in complex international landscapes.

Identifying component indicators and data sources

International relations in the Indo-Pacific are messy and demand a careful, sometimes non-systematic look at both cooperation and conflict. A broad index – one that isn't just a list of numbers – might help policymakers sort through the overlapping issues of diplomacy, economics and security. Generally speaking, when we talk about cooperation, think of things like trade deals, joint military drills or even cultural exchanges; these aspects, measured properly, give insights into how deep and strong partnerships really are. At the same time, flagging signs of conflict – say, rising military buildups or simmering territorial disagreements – adds another layer, giving an overall, nuanced picture of the region's challenges (Bergin et al.).

The Cooperation Index (CoI) for the Indo-Pacific integrates five domains – Economic Cooperation (E), Political Cooperation (P), Security Cooperation (S), Environmental Cooperation (En), and Cultural-Social Cooperation (C) – each with specific metrics. These criteria are chosen to comprehensively capture the region's cooperative dynamics, reflecting its economic weight, geopolitical tensions, security imperatives, environmental vulnerabilities, and social ties.

- *Economic Cooperation (E): Trade Values, Agreements, FDI.* Trade values (e.g., ASEAN's 900 billion US dollars intra-regional trade) are sourced from the ASEAN Secretariat and World Bank trade databases, offering annual aggregates. Economic agreements (e.g., RCEP, Indo-Pacific Economic Framework [IPEF]) are tracked via official texts from ASEAN or national trade ministries. FDI data is extracted from the UNCTAD, detailing inflows like China's Belt and Road investments. These sources provide verified, comparable figures, essential for the region. Regular updates ensure timeliness, while institutional credibility minimises bias.
- *Political Cooperation (P): Summits, Agreements, Organisations.* Summit frequency (e.g., QUAD, ASEAN Summit) is compiled from official schedules published by hosting bodies (e.g., ASEAN Secretariat,) and news archives (e.g., Reuters). Bilateral agreements are sourced from foreign ministry records (e.g., Japan's MOFA), and participation in organisations like IPEF is tracked via signatory lists from US State Department reports. Primary sources ensure accuracy, while secondary verification (news) fills gaps. This captures the diplomatic pulse critical to a geopolitically tense region.
- *Security Cooperation (S): Exercises, Defence Pacts, Crime Collaboration.* Joint military exercises (e.g., Quad drills) are logged from the International Institute for Strategic Studies, supplemented by national defence ministry announcements. Defence agreements are sourced from bilateral treaties (e.g., US-Indonesia pacts via US DoD), and crime collaboration data comes from Interpol Asia-Pacific reports. IISS and governmental data offer precise counts, vital for tracking security alignments in contested zones like the South China Sea.

- *Environmental Cooperation (En): Climate Agreements, Renewables, Emissions.* Climate agreements are obtained from ASEAN Secretariat environmental frameworks. Renewable energy investments are sourced from the International Renewable Energy Agency, and emissions reductions from national pledges via UNFCCC submissions (e.g., China's NDC). These specialised agencies provide consistent metrics, crucial for a region facing 20 billion US dollars in annual climate losses.
- *Cultural-Social Cooperation (C): Exchanges, Aid, Community Projects.* Educational exchanges are tracked via UNESCO student mobility data, aid programmes (e.g., UNDP initiatives) from UNDP annual reports, and community projects from regional non-governmental organisations records or ASEAN socio-cultural updates. UNESCO and UNDP offer reliable, region-specific figures, capturing soft ties essential for social cohesion

The Indo-Pacific's complexity – economic might, security threats, environmental fragility, and cultural diversity – demands a multidimensional index. Economic and political cooperation drive integration, security counters instability, environmental efforts ensure sustainability, and cultural-social ties cement trust. Omitting any would yield a lopsided measure, failing to reflect the region's interdependent dynamics. Together, they form a holistic framework, empirically grounded in the region's strategic realities.

The Conflict Index (CI) for the Indo-Pacific incorporates five factors – Frequency and Intensity of Armed Conflict (F), Difference in Yearly Military Expenditure and Arms Transfers (M), Casualties and Displacement (D), Geopolitical Tensions and Proxy Conflict (G), and Economic and Social Impact (E) – to comprehensively assess conflict dynamics. These criteria are selected to capture the region's multifaceted conflict landscape, from overt violence to underlying tensions and their ripple effects, in a theatre marked by territorial disputes, militarisation, and economic stakes.

- *Frequency and Intensity of Armed Conflict (F): Violent Incidents.* Data is sourced from the UCDP, which logs incidents and casualties (e.g., Myanmar conflicts). Supplementary reports from regional think tanks (e.g., CSIS) verify events like South China Sea clashes. UCDP's global standard ensures comparability, while regional sources add context, critical for pinpointing violence hotspots.
- *Difference in Yearly Military Expenditure and Arms Transfers (M): Militarisation.* Defence spending and arms transfers are extracted from SIPRI, detailing budgets and deals. National defence reports (e.g., Chi-

na's MoD) supplement where available. SIPRI's comprehensive dataset tracks militarisation trends, vital for a region with escalating arms races.

- *Casualties and Displacement (D): Human Costs.* Casualty figures come from UCDP, while displacement data is sourced from UNHCR. National statistics (e.g., Myanmar Government) provide secondary checks. UCDP and UNHCR offer authoritative, real-time data, essential for assessing conflict's human toll in a populous region.
- *Geopolitical Tensions and Proxy Conflict (G): Disputes and Influence.* Territorial disputes (e.g., India-China, Senkaku) are documented via CSIS and national claims. Proxy conflict data is inferred from intelligence reports (e.g., CIA World Factbook) and academic analyses. Combining primary claims with expert analysis captures latent tensions, key in a region of strategic rivalry.
- *Economic and Social Impact (E): GDP, Unemployment, Unrest.* GDP declines and unemployment rates are sourced from World Bank and IMF country reports. Social unrest data is gathered from media archives (e.g., Reuters) and Global Database of Events. Economic institutions provide hard data, while event databases track unrest, linking conflict to its broader effects.

The Indo-Pacific's conflict profile - violent clashes, arms races, human crises, geopolitical rivalries, and economic fallout - demands a holistic index. F and D measure active conflict and its toll, M and G capture preparatory and latent threats, and E ties it to socioeconomic stability (Gleditsch et al. 2002). Together, they reflect the region's full conflict spectrum, ensuring the CI is neither narrow nor superficial but a robust tool for analysis and action.

The Indo-Pacific's complexity - economic dynamism, security threats, and data disparities - demands a mix of global datasets (UCDP, SIPRI, UNHCR), regional reports (ASEAN, CSIS), and national sources. This triangulation ensures reliability, fills gaps (e.g., small states' weak statistics), and aligns with the indices' goals - measuring cooperation and conflict holistically. Regular updates and cross-verification mitigate bias, making the data robust for policy use.

Formula and calculation method

Standardising Data

Each component indicator is standardised to a 0–1 scale based on the maximum and minimum values from real-world data:

$$X_{norm} = \frac{X - X_{min}}{X_{max} - X_{min}}$$

Where:

- X: Raw value of the indicator (e.g., trade volume).
- X_{min}, X_{max}: Minimum and maximum values in the reference dataset.

Weighting the Components:

Cooperation Index (CoI): Each of the five areas (E, P, S, En, C) is assigned a weight to reflect perspectives across all aspects:

CoI = we.E + wp.P + ws.S + wen.En + wc.C

In this context, we, wp, ws, wen, wc are the weights assigned to economic cooperation (E), political cooperation (P), security cooperation (S), environmental cooperation (En), and cultural-social cooperation (C), respectively, with the sum of the weights equal to 1:

$w_e + w_p + w_s + w_{en} + w_c = 1$

Conflict Index (CI): $CI = w_f.F + w_m.M + w_d.D + w_g.G + w_e.E$

Where w_f, w_m, w_d, w_g, w_e are the weights for armed conflict (F), difference in yearly military expenditure (M), casualties and displacement (D), geopolitical tensions (G), and socio-economic impact (E), with the sum:

$w_f + w_m + w_d + w_g + w_e = 1$

To determine the weights for each component, consulting expert opinions is a rational and necessary approach. Some methods we can employ to establish the weights (w) for each component are *Delphi Method, Direct Expert Survey, and Data-Driven Analysis.* Determining the optimal method for assigning weights requires evaluating their strengths and weaknesses against the goal of creating a robust composite index for the Indo-Pacific. Each method offers distinct advantages, but the choice hinges on objectivity, feasibility, and contextual fit. The Delphi Method emerges as the best approach due to its balance of expert input, iterative refinement, and capacity to mitigate bias in a region marked by complexity and competing interests.

The Delphi Method involves multiple rounds of surveys with a panel of experts, refining their assessments of component importance (e.g., economic cooperation, security, conflict) until consensus emerges. Its strength lies in its structured process, which reduces individual bias by anonymising responses and allowing experts to adjust their views based on group feedback (Linstone/Turoff 1975). In the Indo-Pacific, where economic giants like China and security-focused states like Australia coexist, this method ensures diverse perspectives – say, from ASEAN economists or Quad strategists – are harmonised into a balanced weighting scheme. Its iterative nature also counters initial subjectivity, delivering weights that reflect collective expertise rather than isolated opinions.

The Direct Expert Survey gathers rankings or weights from specialists in one round, leveraging their regional knowledge. It's faster and simpler than Delphi, ideal when time is constrained. For example, the Indian experts might prioritise economic factors, while the Japanese analysts emphasize security and conflict. However, its flaw is vulnerability to bias – experts' personal leanings or national agendas can skew results without a mechanism to reconcile differences. In a region rife with geopolitical tensions (e.g., US-China rivalry), this risks weights that favour one bloc over others, undermining the index's credibility and acceptance.

Data-Driven Analysis uses statistical tools like regression to derive weights from historical data promises empirical rigour. If data shows trade strongly correlates with regional stability – say, ASEAN's 769.9 billion US dollars intra-regional trade (ASEAN 2024) – it could justify a higher economic weight. Yet, this method falters in the Indo-Pacific due to inconsistent data quality. Small island states "lack of data and skills to devise evidence-based policy" (Everest-Phillips 2014, 14), forcing estimates that weaken precision. Moreover, historical data may not capture emerging dynamics, like recent Quad exercises, limiting its forward-looking relevance.

The Delphi Method excels for three reasons. First, it balances expertise with objectivity – its multi-round consensus filters out bias, crucial in a region where economic and security priorities clash. Unlike Direct Surveys, it avoids single-shot subjectivity; unlike Data-Driven Analysis, it doesn't hinge on patchy data. Second, it's adaptable – experts can weigh shifting factors like climate risks or Belt and Road impacts, ensuring relevance. Third, it fosters buy-in – consensus weights are more likely to gain acceptance across diverse Indo-Pacific stakeholders, enhancing the index's utility.

Integrating into the Composite Index (ICI)

The formula for the composite index combines the CoI and CI, but the ratio between cooperation and conflict can be adjusted if experts believe they should not each account for 50 per cent. Since conflict negatively impacts stability, the CI is inverted (1 - CI), and the result is scaled to a 0–10 range:

$$IPI = 10 \times [w_{CoI} \cdot CoI + w_{CI} \cdot (1 - CI)]$$

where $w_{CoI} + w_{CI} = 1$

3. *Potential Impacts of an Index*

Informing diplomatic strategies and negotiations

A composite index might be just the tool needed to steer diplomacy amid the mixed signals of cooperation and conflict that mark the Indo-Pacific. Rather than burying the point in technical jargon, think of it as a means to track everything from trade deals and security links to those pesky environmental partnerships. When considering the US-China tensions alongside maritime disputes, it becomes clear that a sharp focus on pinpointing risks can help countries like Indonesia devise plans that tie together regional teamwork with a bit of naval flair (Parasasti/Warka/Sutanto 2023, 691). Generally speaking, such an approach matters a great deal in times when uncertainty and rivalry run high.

Rolling out this kind of index could really mix up the diplomatic playbook across the region. Matching up bits of data on both collaborative moves and conflict signals might give stakeholders a better feel for what's coming next. In many cases, this deeper understanding might even lead to closer partnerships among nations with shared interests – think of South Korea's shifting Indo-Pacific strategy as it nudges itself closer to allies like the EU and the US (Ballbach 2023). This kind of strategic nudging highlights how collective efforts, whether against maritime or cyber security challenges, can be vital. In effect, the index wouldn't just crunch numbers but would also spark the creation of new frameworks to boost security and economic resilience.

Enhancing regional security and stability

Creating a full-scale record to track both cooperation and conflict across the Indo-Pacific might be the key to boosting regional security and stability. Instead of sticking to a neat checklist, this approach gets into the messy, real-world dynamics of how nations mix, clash or sometimes even do both at once. In most cases, having such a measure means catching early hints of tension spikes or sudden alliance shifts – which could, in turn, prompt speedy diplomatic moves. It also offers a peek at how well our current treaties are holding up, giving policymakers a chance to adjust their strategies when fresh challenges crop up. With rising geopolitical pressures, and assertive behaviours from countries such as China and Russia (Spiegeleire al. 2014; Kim et al. 2025), it's hard to overstate the need for a solid monitoring framework.

An index like this brings with it a host of possibilities – it might completely change the way nations relate in the Indo-Pacific. It can build transparency and trust by presenting a shared, no-nonsense yardstick for judging state actions, which in turn lowers the risk of costly misunderstandings spilling into conflict. Interestingly, it isn't only governments that stand to benefit; regional organisations and think tanks could also contribute their own insights to the security debate. By involving a broad mix of stakeholders, the whole process may encourage a more inclusive, sometimes even looser, approach to security – one that values cooperation over cut-throat competition and paves the road for long-term peace and prosperity in the region (Rudolf 2020). Generally speaking, it's this kind of dependable gauge that stands ready to counter the increasingly assertive moves on the global stage.

Fostering academic research and public discourse

International relations in the Indo-Pacific keep shifting, and we really need a broad index to sort out the messy mix of cooperation and conflict. It isn't just a dry store of data – it's more like a springboard for lively research and everyday debate. Researchers can pull together bits on security, economic links, and diplomatic chats, often spotting hidden trends that might otherwise slip by. This hands-on method helps policymakers make smarter choices while giving both scholars and locals a clearer picture of what's really happening. By looking at how different nations interact – say, comparing US-led moves with India's maritime pushes – such an index can, in many cases, boost regional stability and deepen academic insight (Sattar 2023).

Setting up this kind of tool has broad consequences that stretch well beyond academia, touching on real-world policy too. By offering a neatly lined-up, yet flexible, overview, the index sheds light on the tangled ties and underlying tensions among Indo-Pacific countries. For example, as nations like India and Japan work through the challenges driven by China's resurgence, the tool might reveal shared strategic aims and suggest spots where cooperation could thrive. This sort of clarity lets regional players engage in a more constructive way, helping to ease conflicts along the line. On top of that, the index doubles as a great educational resource, drawing in the public and sparking debate about international affairs – ultimately, this helps to strengthen democratic processes and build a more informed citizenry.

Challenges for the development of an index in the Indo-Pacific Region

The Indo-Pacific is a region of strategic significance, marked by complex economic interdependencies, geopolitical rivalries, and evolving security challenges. Developing a composite index that accurately captures both conflict and cooperation in the region is an ambitious yet necessary endeavour. However, numerous challenges hinder the feasibility of such an index, ranging from data fragmentation and geopolitical sensitivities to methodological inconsistencies and rapid regional change. Addressing these obstacles requires a multidisciplinary approach that balances empirical rigour with political pragmatism.

Diversity and indicator selection show the very first challenge. Indo-Pacific spans some of the world's largest economies – such as China, India, and Japan – alongside smaller island nations that face unique challenges related to security and economic resilience (Prabhu/Basu 2024). This diversity complicates the selection of indicators for a composite index, as what may be relevant to major economic powers might be of limited utility to smaller states. Economic growth and trade metrics may be prioritised by countries like Indonesia, while smaller Pacific nations might focus on environmental cooperation and security guarantees. Existing frameworks, such as the Global Peace Index or the UCDP, offer insights into specific dimensions of security and conflict. However, those tools fail to integrate the economic and diplomatic variables that shape state behaviour in the Indo-Pacific. The challenge is, therefore, to construct an index that captures the region's multifaceted realities without reducing them to a simplistic binary of peace versus conflict.

Next, a fundamental barrier to the development of a composite index is the uneven availability and reliability of data across the Indo-Pacific. While developed economies maintain extensive statistical records, smaller and conflict-prone nations often lack institutional capacity to provide consistent and accurate data (Minnich 2025). Many regional conflicts, including those in the South China Sea and along the India-China border, involve elements of information asymmetry, where states strategically manipulate or restrict data to shape international perceptions (Wiśniewski 2023, 186). Furthermore, reliance on international organisations and think tanks introduces biases depending on the sources consulted. Reports from the United Nations or ASEAN may present more diplomatic perspectives, whereas datasets from defence institutions such as the SIPRI may emphasise security dynamics over economic interdependence. Addressing these disparities requires a hybrid approach, incorporating both quantitative indicators (such as trade volumes and military expenditures) and qualitative assessments from regional experts.

One of the central theoretical dilemmas in designing a composite index is how to integrate cooperation and conflict into a single, meaningful metric. Traditional indices tend to focus either on economic integration or security threats but rarely both (Kapetas 2023). However, Indo-Pacific relations frequently defy simplistic categorisation. Countries like India and China engage in high-stakes border confrontations while maintaining substantial trade flows through BRICS and the Regional Comprehensive Economic Partnership (RCEP). Similarly, Japan participates in the Quad to counterbalance China's rise but remains economically interdependent with Beijing (Prabhu/Basu 2024). A well-designed composite index must reflect these paradoxes rather than forcing them into rigid categories. This requires adopting a dynamic weighting system, where economic and security variables are assigned importance based on their impact on regional stability at any given time. Such an approach aligns with complex interdependence theory, which posits that security and economic relationships are deeply intertwined (Keohane/Nye 2012).

Besides, geopolitical tensions in the Indo-Pacific further complicate the feasibility of a composite index. The region is home to strategic rivalries between the United States and China, territorial disputes in the South

China Sea, and competing regional frameworks such as the IPEF and China's BRI. The construction of an index that incorporates both cooperation and conflict runs the risk of being perceived as biased, particularly if certain countries feel misrepresented or unfairly assessed. For example, any attempt to quantify military assertiveness might be seen as targeting specific nations, leading to resistance from key stakeholders. Conversely, a focus on economic cooperation without addressing security concerns could undermine the index's credibility in forecasting geopolitical risks. Thus, ensuring neutrality in both methodology and presentation is critical for securing broad acceptance of such a tool. Moreover, many regional actors engage in strategic ambiguity – deliberately maintaining unclear or contradictory policies to balance competing interests (Wiśniewski 2023, 214). This further complicates efforts to create a clear-cut measurement framework, as states may signal commitment to regional stability while simultaneously engaging in coercive economic practices or military brinkmanship.

Otherwise, the Indo-Pacific is a highly volatile region where economic and security dynamics evolve rapidly. Any composite index must be designed to adapt to these shifts rather than becoming a static measurement tool that fails to capture emerging trends. The growing significance of minilateral frameworks such as AUKUS (Australia-UK-US alliance) and the evolution of Quad demonstrate the region's fluidity (Hoang Thi Ha 2022). Similarly, economic disruptions – whether due to US-China trade tensions, supply chain realignments, or energy security concerns – can rapidly alter the cooperative and competitive landscape. A rigidly structured index that fails to incorporate real-time data updates risks becoming obsolete. Instead, an effective index should integrate machine learning models or expert-driven adjustments to reflect changing geopolitical realities. A dynamic weighting system that recalibrates based on emerging trends, as seen in financial risk models, could offer a potential solution.

Finally, developing a composite index to measure cooperation and conflict in the Indo-Pacific carries significant risks of oversimplification. One of the primary risks lies in the potential for high cooperation scores to mask underlying tensions. Nations in the Indo-Pacific frequently engage in economic cooperation while simultaneously navigating deep-seated security rivalries (Beeson 2019; Rossiter/Cannon 2020). For instance, China's trade ties with ASEAN continue to expand, even as territorial disputes persist in the South China Sea. If a composite index fails to account for such dualities, it risks portraying an overly optimistic picture of regional stability. Conversely, high conflict scores may exaggerate tensions and overlook the role of diplomatic mechanisms and economic integration in mitigating hostilities. The use of broad aggregates in geopolitical indices is particularly problematic because it can lead to misinterpretation by policymakers, analysts, and the media. Many rely on such indices for quick assessments, but a simplified ranking system may encourage reactionary rather than strategic policymaking. A nation categorised as high-risk due to security concerns might still be a vital economic partner, but an oversimplified index could lead to policies that neglect the broader geopolitical picture. Moreover, indices can create unintended diplomatic consequences, shaping perceptions in ways that influence negotiations, alliances, and public opinion. If a country is ranked as a major security threat, it may be diplomatically isolated despite having avenues for cooperation. Similarly, states perceived as highly cooperative might avoid necessary scrutiny over their aggressive policies in specific domains.

In summary, while a composite index for the Indo-Pacific is both conceptually and practically necessary, its development faces significant challenges. The diversity of regional actors, the fragmented nature of available data, and the difficulty of balancing economic cooperation with security threats all present formidable obstacles. Political sensitivities further complicate the index's feasibility, as states may resist being quantified in ways that challenge their strategic narratives. Moreover, the rapid pace of geopolitical change demands an adaptive and flexible methodology that prevents obsolescence.

4. Conclusion

The Indo-Pacific is the defining geopolitical arena of the 21st century, where economic interdependence and security rivalries intertwine, shaping global stability. However, existing analytical tools fail to capture the full complexity of regional interactions, as they remain fragmented between military, economic, and diplomatic assessments. The absence of a composite index that quantifies both cooperation and conflict leaves policymakers operating in a landscape of uncertainty, strategic miscalculations, and reactionary decision-making.

This study underscores the urgent need for a composite Indo-Pacific Index of Cooperation and Conflict (IPI) – a structured framework that integrates economic ties, security concerns, diplomatic engagement, and geopolitical tensions. By offering a multidimensional assessment of regional stability, such an index would enable data-driven policy formulation, enhance strategic foresight, and promote greater accountability among regional actors. The index would provide real-time tracking of conflict-cooperation dynamics, helping governments anticipate potential flashpoints, identify underutilised areas of collaboration, and mitigate misaligned resource allocation.

The Indo-Pacific's volatility demands structured analysis. A composite index is not just a theoretical construct – it is a necessity for ensuring informed, proactive decision-making. Without such a tool, nations will continue to misread intentions, mistime interventions, and misallocate resources, risking regional instability and global repercussions. Future research should focus on refining methodologies, enhancing real-time capabilities, and ensuring broad acceptance among regional stakeholders. The Indo-Pacific's future depends on those who can accurately measure and anticipate its shifts – without a structured framework, strategic blindness will persist, jeopardising global stability. A composite index is the key to unlocking a more predictable, cooperative, and stable Indo-Pacific.

5. References

ASEAN (2024, May): Exploring Intra-ASEAN Merchandise Trade Dynamics. Retrieved from ASEANstats. https://www.aseanstats.org/wp-content/uploads/2024/05/ASB-202405-03.pdf.

Balázs, D. (2024, November 29): China-India pact a borderline solution. https://eastasiaforum.org/2024/11/29/china-india-pact-a-borderline-solution/.

Baldauff, N. (2024): Japan's Defense Engagement in the Indo-Pacific. Cham: Springer.

Ballbach, E. J. (2023, March): South Korea's Evolving Indo-Pacific Strategy: Opportunities and challenges for cooperation with the EU. In: SWP Research Paper (2).

Beeson, M. (2019): Rivalry and Cooperation in the Asia-Pacific: The Dynamics of a Region in Transition. Singapore: World Scientific Publishing Company.

Center for Strategic and International Studies (n.d.): About AMTI. https://amti.csis.org/about/.

Chen, W.-C. (et al.) (2024): China's gray zone actions in the East China Sea, Taiwan Strait, and South China Sea: A comparative study and impact on fisheries. In: Marine Policy, 167.

Chivvis, C. S. (2024): U.S.-China Relations for the 2030s: Toward a Realistic Scenario for Coexistence. Washington, DC: Carnegie Endowment for International Peace Publications Department.

Everest-Phillips, M. (2014): Small, So Simple? Complexity in Small Island Developing States. Singapore: UNDP Global Centre for Public Service Excellence.

Gleditsch, N. P. (et al.) (2002): Armed Conflict 1946–2001: A New Dataset. In: Journal of Peace Research, 39(5), 615–637.

Grossman, D. (2024, November 1): The State – and Fate – of America's Indo-Pacific Alliances. https://magazine.thediplomat.com/#/issues/-OA2mbifGT2SHfYyqDnN/read.

Helmus, T. C. (et al.) (2024): Understanding and Countering China's Maritime Gray Zone Operations. Santa Monica: RAND Corporation. https://www.rand.org/content/dam/rand/pubs/research_reports/RRA2900/RRA2954-1/RAND_RRA2954-1.pdf.

Hoang Thi Ha (2022): Understanding the Institutional Challenge of Indo-Pacific Minilaterals to ASEAN. In: Contemporary Southeast Asia, 44(1), 1–30.

Kao Kim Hourn (2024): RCEP High-Level Dialogue on Economic and Trade Cooperation. Association of Southeast Asian Nations. Retrieved from https://asean.org/wp-content/uploads/2024/09/SG-Dr.-Kao-Remarks-for-the-RCEP-High-Level-Dialogue-on-Economic-and-Trade-Cooperation-24-Sept-2024-As-Delivered.pdf.

Kapetas, A. (2023): China, climate and conflict in the Indo-Pacific. In: Strategic Insight (180). https://ad-aspi.s3.ap-southeast-2.amazonaws.com/2023-03/China%2C%20climate%20and%20conflict%20in%20the%20Indo-Pacific.pdf.

Kavanagh, J./Cuéllar, M.-F. (2024): U.S. Engagement in the Indo-Pacific: Don't Trade Away Trade. Washington D.C: Carnegie Endowment for International Peace Publications Department.

Keohane, R. O./Nye, J. S. (2012): Power and Interdependence: World Politics in Transition (4th edition). New York: Longman.

Kim, P. M. (et al.) (2025, March 6): China and Russia's strategic relationship amid a shifting geopolitical landscape. Brookings: https://www.brookings.edu/articles/china-and-russias-strategic-relationship-amid-a-shifting-geopolitical-landscape/.

Lau, S. Y./Zhou, P. (2022, March): Strengthening Pluralism in the Indo-Pacific and the Role of the ASEAN. In: Reitaku. Journal of Interdisciplinary Studies, 30, 10–19.

Leben, W. (2024): Escalation risks in the Indo-Pacific. A review for practitioners. Australian Strategic Policy Institute. https://ad-aspi.s3.ap-southeast-2.amazonaws.com/2024-02/SR201%20Escalation%20risks%20in%20the%20Indo-Pacific.pdf?VersionId=EclJMi.G8DGKlGvD_w6Qf3B.rEYCW393.

Linstone, H. A./Turoff, M. (1975): The Delphi Method: Techniques and Applications. Addison-Wesley.

Liow, J. C./Chong, W. (2023, May 5): Japan's Role in Regional Security: Recalibration and Regional Reactions. https://fulcrum.sg/japans-role-in-regional-security-recalibration-and-regional-reactions/.

Ma, Y. (2025, February 12): Total value of U.S. trade in goods (export and import) with China from 2014 to 2024. Statista: https://www.statista.com/statistics/277679/total-value-of-us-trade-in-goods-with-china-since-2006/#:~:text=In%202024%2C%20the%20total%20value,of%20295.4%20billion%20U.S.%20dollars.

McGerty, F. (2024, May 22): Asian defence spending grows, China's grows more. https://www.iiss.org/online-analysis/military-balance/2024/05/asian-defence-spending-grows-chinas-grows-more/.

Medcalf, R. (2020): Indo-Pacific empire: China, America and the contest for the world's pivotal region. Manchester: Manchester University Press.

Minnich, J. M. (2025): Finding Security in the Indo-Pacific Mosaic. In: Minnich, J. M. (ed.): The Indo-Pacific Mosaic: Comprehensive Security Cooperation in the Indo-Pacific. Honolulu: Daniel K. Inouye Asia-Pacific Center for Security Studies. 1–40.

Mishra, V. (2024, November 9): Trump 2.0 Could Recalibrate U.S. Indo-Pacific Engagements. https://www.stimson.org/2024/trump-2-0-could-recalibrate-u-s-indo-pacific-engagements/.

Oba, M. (2022): Japan and the Regional Comprehensive Economic Partnership (RCEP). ERIA Discussion Paper Series (461). https://www.eria.org/uploads/media/discussion-papers/FY22/Japan-and-the-Regional-Comprehensive-Economic-Partnership-(RCEP).pdf.

Oxford Analytica (2021, April 29): Japan and China will cooperate as well as compete. https://doi.org/10.1108/OXAN-ES261187.

Pajon, C. (2024, July 1): Japan's Enhanced Security Engagement with the Pacific Islands. https://thediplomat.com/2024/06/japans-enhanced-security-engagement-with-the-pacific-islands/.

Parasasti, M. A./Warka, I. W./Sutanto, R. (2023): The Role of Indonesian Naval Diplomacy in the Indo-Pacific Region as Indonesia's Maritime Strategy in Supporting National Defense. In: International Journal of Progressive Sciences and Technologies, 36(2), 682–294.

Prabhu, S./Basu, P. (2024, March): Navigating the Indo-Pacific: Development Cooperation as a Diplomatic Tool. Issue Brief (703). https://www.orfonline.org/public/uploads/posts/pdf/20240403111557.pdf.

Rana, P. B./Ji, X. (2020): China's Belt and Road Initiative: Impacts on Asia and Policy Agenda. Singapore: Palgrave Macmillan.

Rossiter, A./Cannon, B. J. (2020): Conflict and Cooperation in the Indo-Pacific: New Geopolitical Realities. New York: Routledge.

Rudolf, P. (2020): U.S. Geopolitics and Nuclear Deterrence in the Era of Great Power Competitions. In: Political Science Quarterly, 136(1), 129–153.

Sattar, I. (2023). Pakistan's Security Dilemma in the Era of Great Power Competition. Naval Post Graduate School. Calhoun, Institutional Archive of the Naval Postgraduate School. Retrieved from https://core.ac.uk/reader/610636840.

Spiegeleire, S. D. (et al.) (2014): Assessing Assertions of Assertiveness: The Chinese and Russian Cases. The Hague: The Hague Centre for Strategic Studies.

The Asia Foundation (2024): U.S.–China–Southeast Asia Relations: Challenges and Opportunities for Regional Cooperation. Bangkok: The Asia Foundation. https://asiafoundation.org/wp-content/uploads/2024/10/US-China-Southeast-Asia-Relations-Challenges-and-Opportunities-for-Regional-Cooperation.pdf.

The United Nations, Economic and Social Commission for Asia and the Pacific (2023): Asia-Pacific Population and Development Report 2023. Bangkok: United Nations Publication.

Tian, N. (et al.) (2024, April): Trends in World Military Expenditure, 2023. https://www.sipri.org/sites/default/files/2024-04/2404_fs_milex_2023.pdf.

Tijaja, J./Dzakwan, M. H. (2025, January 7): Preparing the ASEAN Economic Community for a Securitised World. https://fulcrum.sg/preparing-the-asean-economic-community-for-a-securitised-world/.

UNCTAD (2024): Global Trade Update (December 2024) (UNCTAD/DITC/INF/2024/3). United Nations. https://unctad.org/system/files/official-document/ditcinf2024d3.pdf.

UNCTAD (2024a): https://unctad.org/publication/review-maritime-transport-2024. United Nations. https://unctad.org/publication/review-maritime-transport-2024.

UNCTAD (2025). Handbook of Statistics 2024. New York: United Nations Publications. https://unctad.org/system/files/official-document/tdstat49_en.pdf.

Wang, W./Chen, X./Chang, Y. (2016, July 7): The South China Sea Won't Stop China-ASEAN Economic Ties. https://thediplomat.com/2016/07/the-south-china-sea-wont-stop-china-asean-economic-ties/.

Wiśniewski, R. (2023): Military power as an instrument of international politics in the Indo-Pacific. In: Kratiuk, B. J. (et al.) (eds.): Handbook of Indo-Pacific Studies. London: Routledge India. 175–204.

Yu, H. (2024): Understanding China's Belt and Road Initiative. In: Asia in Transition, 2024, 26.

Chapter 4: Imaginative Geographies and Mental Maps. Constructivist Approaches to the Analysis of Geopolitics in the Indo-Pacific

Detlef Briesen

This essay looks at the Indo-Pacific region from a more theoretical angle. The first part deals with the traditions of geopolitics and the political and historical roots of the term Indo-Pacific: it originally stemmed from the German geopolitical author Karl Haushofer who influenced the strategies of Japanese great power politics in the years leading up to 1945. In the second part, we clarify our understanding of geopolitics as a specific form of mental mapping, a process of creating geographical-political imaginaries. In doing so, we follow the constructivist turn in perception psychology and geography. The third part then demonstrates the fruitfulness of this theoretical and research approach in previous studies of the mental maps of geopolitics. Finally, we apply the insights gained in this manner to a brief, exemplary analysis of two contemporary geopolitical documents, the *US Free and Open Indo-Pacific (FOIP)* of 2019 and the *EU strategy for cooperation in the Indo-Pacific* of 2021.

To avoid any misunderstanding: geographical imaginaries form the basis of every human spatial comprehension. But imagination does not mean pure invention. The term imaginary refers more to an essential insight, that those constructs are meaningful whenever people deal with any kind of *space*: in everyday life as well as in scientific and political theory and practice. However, geographical imaginaries may contain spatial markers that are more or less empirically verifiable: they are more empirically based or more suggestive. As we will see, the differences between the US and EU concepts regarding the Indo-Pacific are particularly striking in this regard.

My paper is only a starting point for a more in-depth investigation of the mental maps for the Indo-Pacific region. Its main aim is to raise questions for future research.

1. On the Old and New Conjunctures of Geopolitics: Framing the Indo-Pacific

The *Indo-Pacific region* is as geopolitical concept, and geopolitics are controversial. One reason for this lies in its dual meaning. In the 19th century, geopolitics was originally a synonym for the spatially oriented foreign policy actions of major powers within the framework of their geostrategy. This, in turn, was understood to mean their targeted imperial actions aimed at gaining or exercising power, control or influence over large-scale regions. In addition, especially since the turn of the century, geopolitics has referred to the interpretation of geographical conditions, particularly from a political science perspective. Both meanings still exist today; geopolitics thus means:

- On the one hand, it is an academic discipline that examines the influence of geographical conditions and dynamics on the foreign and security policy of a country, especially a major power; and
- On the other hand, it is a practice-oriented method of security and defence policy decision-making and, based on this, concrete measures taken by governments, especially those of major powers, with scientists with a geopolitical focus often acting in an advisory capacity.

During its heydays between the 1890s and 1950s, geopolitics was stylised as a kind of master discipline for statesmanship, as it supposedly enabled rational insights to be gained for high politics based on objective geographical factors. The possibility of providing scientific support for the imperial expansion or at least consolidation of states was very tempting for scientific geography in the decades of imperial rivalry (and perhaps again today). From the turn of the century to the 1950s, there was hardly a geographer who did not also engage in geopolitics. Important protagonists and their most significant writings at that time were: Alfred Thayer Mahan (1898/99), Halford Mackinder (1902), Friedrich Ratzel (1903), Rudolf Kjellén (1924), Karl Haushofer (1935), and Carl Schmitt (1941). An important feature of these geopolitical schools was thinking in terms of so called *greater spatial units (Großräume)*, i.e. geographically extensive areas of the world over which certain states could claim a natural right to rule.

The term Indo-Pacific also stems from this tradition; more precisely, it was introduced into scientific and political debates by the German geopolitician General Karl Haushofer, one of the classics of this discipline. The Indo-Pacific is originally a term that comes from maritime ecology. As such, it makes perfect sense: In the relevant encyclopaedias, it is defined as a huge biogeographical region stretching from the coast of East Africa to the tropical Pacific. It is sometimes also referred to as the Indo-West Pacific or Indo-Pacific Asia, encompassing the tropical waters of the Indian Ocean, the western and central Pacific, and all the seas connecting these two oceans. The term is certainly useful for marine biology (Tardent 2005). From Madagascar to Japan, many marine habitats in this vast region are similar; these do not exist in the tropical waters of the Atlantic.

Image 1: The tropical waters of the Indo-Pacific

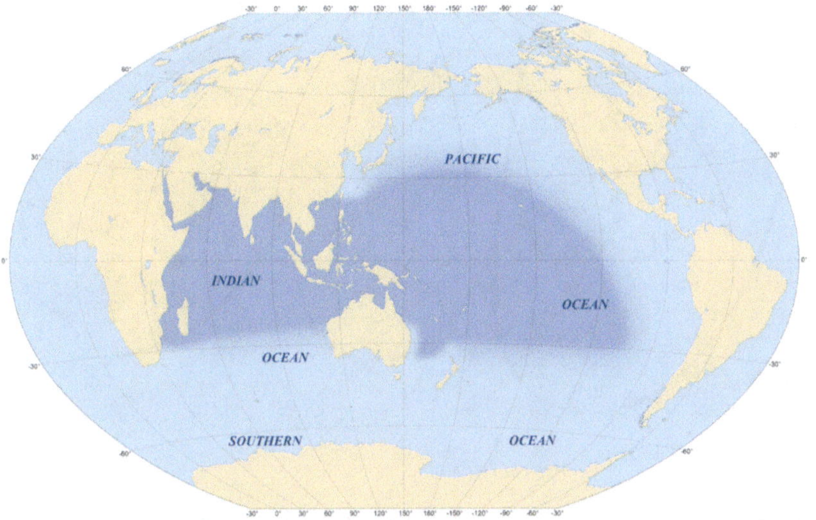

Source: Eric Gaba, public domain

However, Haushofer had something completely different in mind: In his numerous works on the Indo-Pacific concept he created (Haushofer 1924; 1925; 1932; 1937; 1939), he legitimised the idea of integrating the two oceans not with a focus on marine biology, but on ethnography and history. The actual function of his imaginative was to identify important anti-colonial forces in this vast space and mobilise them for Germany's resurgence after its defeat in the First World War. Especially in alliance with the anti-colonial liberation fighters in China and India, Germany could oppose the imperial powers (Great Britain, the USA and France) that dominated the Indo-Pacific after 1919. But above all, Haushofer had very close academic ties to Japan. Through Haushofer's publications, the Indo-Pacific region found its way into the geostrategy of the Empire of Japan in the interwar period and served as scientific grounding for its Greater East Asia Co-Prosperity Sphere. It is therefore somewhat surprising, but also not entirely unexpected, that it was Japan of all countries that was the first to revive this concept in 2007 (Li 2021).

Image 2: Karl Haushofer's Pan-Regions Theory

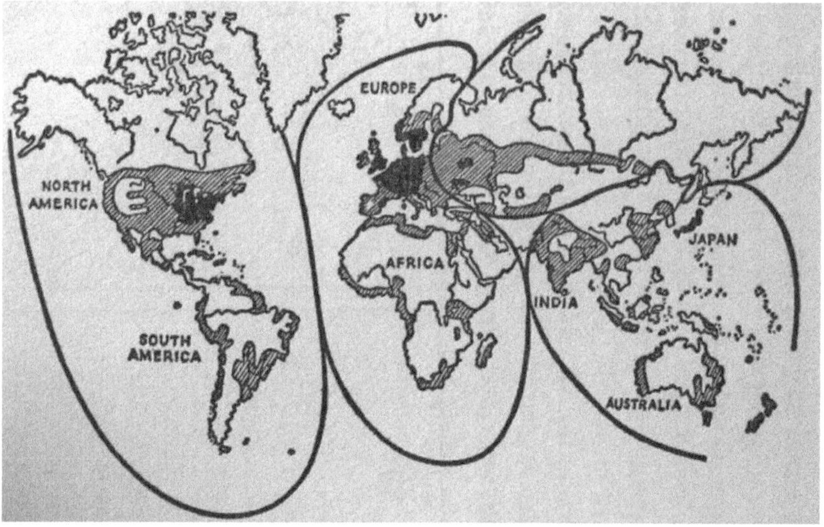

Source: Public Domain

The geopolitical boom in Western Europe subsided noticeably after 1945, as it was considered corrupted by National Socialism, imperialism or colonialism. An important criticism of geopolitics was that it has tended to serve the purpose of legitimising the imperial order or reorganisation of the world in the interests of a particular great power. Even geopolitical authors such as Yves Lacoste (2010) therefore emphasise that geopolitics is first and foremost an instrument of rule, and that geopolitical knowledge is political-strategic knowledge. Benno Werlen (2000) also highlights the geo-determinism of geopolitics in his relevant definition; in his view, it is based on the (wrong) assertion that human action is generally predetermined by space and nature. The core of practical geopolitics would be the recognition of this predetermination by those responsible in government; they had to recognise the *Raumschicksal* (spatial fate of a state) and act in accordance with an equally deterministic realism. These turns of phrase also point to the often explicitly normative character of geopolitics. The massive criticism of all this even gave rise to a separate geopolitical school in the 1980s, known as critical geopolitics (Dalby/O Tuathail 1996).

But geopolitics survived, especially in the United States where it served attempts to establish the position of the United States as a superpower on a *spatial science* basis – both as an academic discipline and as an explicit political advisory subject. The geopolitical school of Nicholas Spykman (1944) gained particular significance at that time. He followed in the footsteps of his academic teacher Halford Mackinder (who had emphasised the dominance of land power over sea power) and modernised many of his ideas. Mackinder's Eurasian *heartland* as the politically critical zone for world domination was replaced by the concept of European and Asian peripheral areas, which was more useful during the Cold War and the territorial realities of the time. Spykman referred to these as the *rimland.* From Mackinder, a direct line leads via Spykman to Zbigniew Brzeziński, the most influential geopolitical author since the 1970s. Concepts such as heartland and rimland had a decisive influence on US foreign policy in the post-World War II era:

> from the containment, roll-back and domino strategies of the 1940s and 1950s, the *transatlantic* political, military, economic and cultural partnership between North America and Western Europe, the Carter Doctrine of the 1980s and Kissinger's *world order*, to the current policy on Ukraine.

Transatlantic relations were probably at the core of US geostrategy. One could also argue that, from an American perspective, relations between the United States and Western Europe were always genuinely geopolitical designed until the collapse of the Eastern Bloc; from the perspective of the Federal Republic of Germany, for example, this was not the case. Here, at least before Donald Trump took office, the politicians and academics tended to think in categories of special relations with the United States or even a German American friendship.

Nevertheless, geopolitics has gained new momentum since the collapse of the Eastern Bloc and, above all, since the turn of the millennium. This is evidenced, on the one hand, by the wealth of academic works published in North America and Western Europe since then (here only a selection: Huntington 1996; Brzeziński 1997; Brill 2008; Lacoste 2010; Hoffmann 2012; Kaplan 2012; Kissinger 2014; Marshall 2015; Schlögel 2016; Paul 2022). On the other hand, there is hardly a state today, or with the EU a supranational community, that does not have one or several geopolitical strategies, now sometimes referred to as geostrategies. Especially in the numerous think tanks, some of which are financed from unclear sources, studies on this topic are being produced at an almost inflationary rate. Here again is just a selection: On the polar region (Braune 2020); on European geopolitics (Laïdi 2023); on US geostrategy (Bokhari 2025); on China (STRATEGIECS Team 2020); on Russian geostrategy (Meister 2024); on India (Kushre 2023), and so on.

An important reason for the new boom in geopolitics is probably that, following the collapse of the Soviet Union and the rise of countries such as China and India, the international system is undergoing a profound transformation, the end of which is not yet in sight. The Cold War brought about a historically almost unique reduction in the complexity of the international system: the West on one side, the East on the other, a rather, from power politics perspective irrelevant Global South, plus a newly emerging superpower, China. China's rise was largely promoted by the mastermind of US foreign policy, Henry Kissinger. However, the era of relatively straightforward bipolar world orders (or, in the decade from 1989 to 2001, even that of only one globally dominant power, the United States) is clearly over. For authors such as Herfried Münkler (2023), for example, there are signs of a return to a historically proven order of great powers, the pentarchy, which in future could perhaps be formed by the five powers of the United States, China, Europe, India and Russia. This puts geopolitics back on the international agenda, stronger than at any time since the end of the Second World War.

2. On the Scientific Investigation of Geopolitical Imaginations

But what makes geopolitics so appealing to academics and politicians? An obvious answer is that it is not just the power relations within the rapidly transforming international system. Geopolitics is about more than that: Geopolitical concepts are spatial imaginations, and such cognitive-spatial constructs are, as will be shown shortly, constitutive for human thought and action. An excellent starting point for an in-depth exploration is the constructivist turn in geography, the science that has made space its central research paradigm. The current state of knowledge is that even this academic discipline does not establish irrefutable truths but rather represents a way of summarising certain forms of socially produced knowledge. This calls into question traditional concepts that refer to the neutrality and objectivity of space and its imperatives, in geopolitics for example. Neither mountains nor straits are strategic per se; they only become so through human attribution. The space of geographers, and thus also of geopoliticians, is therefore full of symbols, attributions and covert or overt forms of articulation of interests (see Gieseking 2017 for a fundamental discussion of this).

The most important contributions to date in geography itself come from David Harvey and Derek Gregory. They are both influenced by theories of spatial cognition that originate from constructivism – more on this below. David Harvey's starting point was the concept of geographical imagination, or the notion of a spatial consciousness that actively decodes the organic, perceptible and symbolic spaces of everyday life (Harvey 1973). Academic spatial analysis also represents a specific form of active construction of space, albeit with scientific pretensions. Derek Gregory then went one step further (Gregory 1994; 2009). His achievement lies in pluralising this geographical imagination and making it group specific. People (and thus politicians from different countries) have diverse perceptions of space. These are characterised by a broad spectrum and are based on the active ordering and appropriation of their environment – from everyday pragmatic categories to culturally conditioned symbols and stereotypes. According to Gregory, geographers do not find *their* space ready-made; rather, geographical space is the product of acts of understanding and action that can be interpreted in terms of constructivist theories. The space of geography/geopolitics thus emerges through the diverse activities of a specific social group, for example scientifically oriented geographers or politicians. The nature of these construction processes is directly determined by cultural traditions. Gregory demonstrates this in his analysis of products from cartography, art, travel literature and scientific writings.

Gregory's concept of geographical imagination is influenced by the works of Benedict Anderson and Edward Said. In his 1983 publication, Benedict Anderson demonstrated the extent to which nations are based on imagination and are therefore *imagined communities*. According to Anderson, such imaginations are largely generated by the mass media, creating imaginative inclusion. This puts Anderson not far from a significant constructivist media theory known as *framing*. Edward Said dealt with the opposite, imaginative exclusion, in his works *Orientalism* (1978) and *Imaginative Geography and Its Representations: Orientalising the Oriental* (1979). Thus, geographical imagination can mobilise the citizens of a country for political purposes, both internally and externally, for internal unity or imperial expansion (see also Scheffler 2003).

In 1966, Peter L. Berger and Thomas Luckmann published their groundbreaking work (*The Social Construction of Reality*). In it, Berger and Luckmann applied insights from cognitive and constructivist learning theories to fundamental problems in sociology. Their social constructivism therefore assumes that social reality is indeed a constructed one. Its basis is that people interpret the reality around them and can only acquire knowledge or act accordingly based on these interpretations. According to social constructivism, knowledge therefore never exists in its *pure form*. It is always dependent on the mental models of the world of people who produce it. This gives social reality something dynamic and processual; it is constantly reproduced or changed by human actions. People decide how to act because of their everyday knowledge or more general interpretations that are *societally preformed*. General interpretations, values, etc. have a considerable influence on social interactions within a society and even on foreign policy relations between different states.

However, the most relevant findings from research into spatial imagination come from an area that has primarily worked with theories developed in perception psychology and geography, known as mental maps or, under a similar term, cognitive maps. The two termini are often used synonymously, as are comparable expressions such as (spatial) scripts, schemata or frames of reference. They all refer to very fundamental theoretical systems that have developed primarily from the study of human learning. The term cognitive map was first used by Tolman (1948). In his studies, Tolman found considerable shortcomings in the behaviourist learning theories and demonstrated that cognitive processing operations take place between environmental stimuli and learning. This cognitivism was followed by constructivism. The latter summarised the central insights even more precisely: as a learning theory (not as a general philosophical school of thought), constructivism postulates that human experience and learning are subject to cognitive activities. They are influenced by sensory-physiological, cognitive and social processes. The core principle of constructivism is that humans create individual, including spatial, representations of the world through their diverse learning processes.

Thus, cognitive or mental maps are terms related to fundamental constructivist theories of learning and society. The basic idea is that persons actively structure or construct their environment spatially for a wide variety of reasons. Cognitive maps and mental maps refer to forms of mental representation of human environments. They are used to organise personal information about every-day or large symbolic spatial environments and the relationships between their components. However, there is one important difference to note:

- A *cognitive map* is a spatial representation of the outside world. It is stored in the brain and can be retrieved, for example, for specific actions. For this reason, cognitive maps are primarily studied in psychology and neuroscience today.
- *Mental maps*, on the other hand, is a general term that is more oriented towards the context of social and cultural sciences. It refers not only to pragmatic action patterns, but more generally to cognitive, emotional and motivational aspects of human behaviour that can be expressed in spatial representations. Mental maps are not only characterised by pragmatic information, but also by numerous metaphors and symbols.

In the following, we will therefore refer to mental maps. This term has been used to describe the phenomenon of spatial orientation in humans, ranging from concrete, every-day, pragmatic to metaphorical and symbolic orientation. It has found its way into sciences beyond education, psychology and neuroscience, particularly in all fields interested in spatial analysis categories, such as geography, architecture, spatial planning and history. An important research finding was that the less pragmatic and everyday-life-related people's mental maps are, the greater the importance of general knowledge, supposed scientific findings or fundamental social values. This scaling from the everyday world through various stages to general levels of knowledge is easy to understand on a personal level. The mental map of my neighbourhood may still be shaped by every-day and practically significant spatial entries, i.e. by so-called real life; my ideas about cities, regions, landscapes, states or the Indo-Pacific, on the other hand, are largely shaped by prejudices, and mass media. Imaginaries of large spatial entities are subject to explicit or implicit values that can range from simple stereotypes to intentional projections, such as those of great power or grand geopolitical designs. This is why maps of large-scale areas (and thus, geopolitical imaginations) have such suggestive power, and they are anything but fantasies with no influence on reality. On the contrary, they emerge in societal discourses and influence the construction of realities.

A groundbreaking study on mental maps was Kevin Lynch's *The Image of the City*, published in 1960. Lynch (1960) demonstrated that even the mental representation of an urban area is not based solely on lasting pragmatic information but is mixed with many other concerns. Subsequent studies have repeatedly demonstrated the importance of values, metaphors and symbols for all levels of human spatial perception – from residential preferences and the choice of holiday destinations to the fundamentals of scientific research and the big cartography of the world. Excellent examples of these different spatial scales to which mental maps can refer, and of the increasing importance of social knowledge for mental maps that extend beyond the neighbourhood, have been provided by Gould (1966; Gould/White 1974), Downs/Stea (1977), and many follow-up studies.

Image 3: How China sees the world

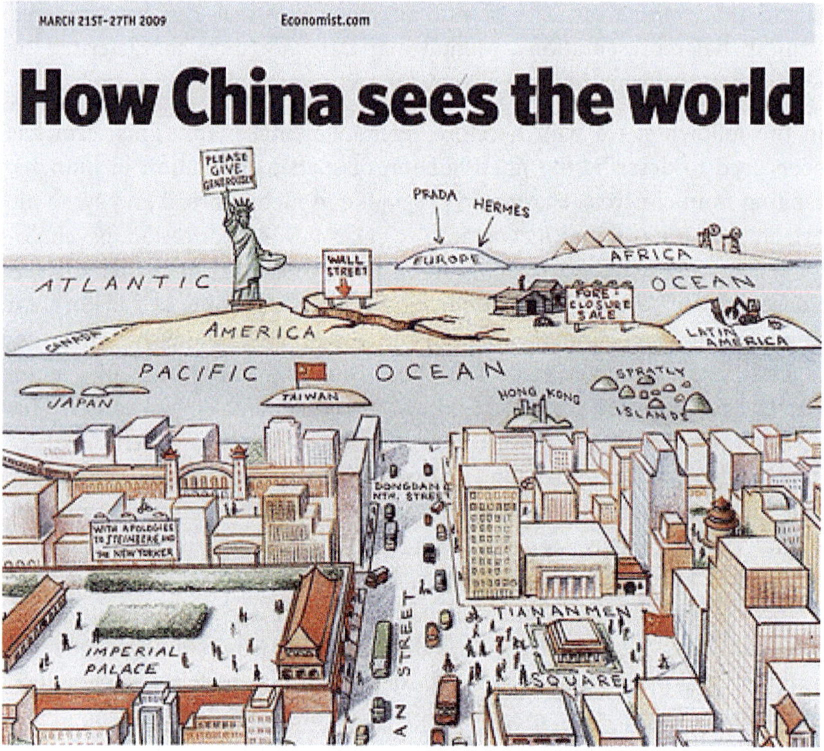

Source: The Economist 2009

3. On the Critical Exploration of Geopolitics and its Mental Maps

The concept of mental maps has played a significant role both in general perception geography and in research into the imaginative aspects of geopolitics. In German *perceptual geography*, the pioneering study was conducted by Briesen, who used the concept of mental maps as early as the beginning of the 1990s (Briesen 1994). His aim at the time was to identify regional awareness and its symbolic markers, such as history, landscape aesthetics and environmental quality, using the example of mining regions, and to contrast this with external perceptions and official regional marketing. The concept was systematically applied to the *analysis of geopolitical designs* in the pioneering work of Casey and Wright on the history of mental maps from 1939 to 1991 (Casey/Wright 2008; 2011; 2015). After the turn of the millennium, a German-language historical journal, *Geschichte und Gesellschaft* (History and Society), devoted an entire issue to this topic. The anthology, edited by Christoph Conrad (2002), aims at a kind of critical historical cartography that deconstructs historical-spatial imaginaries. The 2018 issue of the *Journal of Cultural Geography, Mental maps: geographical and historical perspectives* (Götz/Holmen 2018), can be placed in a similar context. Noteworthy in a more recent work by Holmen and Götz is, among other things, the essay by Ute Schneider on the mental maps of a German geographer, Heinrich Schiffer. Using an analysis of the corresponding cartographic illustrations in Schiffer's books, she shows how extensively he *re-mapped* his cartographies, i.e. adapted them to the prevailing societal norms (Schneider 2021). Schneider's findings are comparable to those of Casey and Wright.

In connection with the Critical Geopolitics school of thought, there has been a wealth of studies, particularly since the turn of the millennium and parallel to the new boom in geopolitics, which has critically applied the concept of mental maps to renewed spatial politics and research. Here, too, is just a selection:

- The literature review by da Vinha (2012) provides an excellent summary of the research conducted up to around 2010.
- The paper by Criekemans and Duran (2011) is an interesting basic analysis.
- Bilenky's (2012) essay on the role of romantically legitimised political imaginations and their impact on the mental maps of actors is insightful regarding the border regions of Russia and Ukraine.

- Schenk's topic is the mapping of Europe in the course of history (Schenk 2013).
- Erforth (2016) has examined mental maps as a basis for legitimising military interventions.
- Petri notes that the *expectations* of stakeholders with regard to marine areas can change rapidly and almost arbitrarily (Petri 2016).
- A fundamental contribution to the critical reflection on mental maps for foreign policy decision-making processes is provided by da Vinha (2019).

All these contributions reveal a wealth of findings:

- *Firstly*, geopolitical studies and governmental geostrategies are intentional constructions of space that are to some degree based on stereotypes, metaphors, prejudices, symbols, etc. Empirical content is usually present, but mostly intentionally moulded.
- *Second*, geopolitics have the same characteristics as other projections for large-scale mental maps. They are symbolic constructions that serve multiple purposes rather than just one. Geopolitically motivated mental maps of large regions are therefore just as inaccurate as projections developed for other non-everyday spatial imaginaries, such as for tourism or economic investments. In these areas, there may be many stereotypes about an ideal holiday destination or a perfect location for an investment that have no direct bearing on empirically verifiable reality.
- *Thirdly*, geopolitical mental maps have a suggestive power, and many of them continue to perpetuate the ideas of early geopolitics: that there are real characteristics of space that are immediately recognisable and practically applicable, or that make certain actions unavoidable.
- *Fourthly*, even the mental maps of renewed geopolitics all too often serve to suggestively formulate power interests. However vague they may be, they shape world views and influence foreign policy.

Fifthly, further interesting insights are provided by the study by Didelon-Loiseau, de Ruffray and Lambert (2021). They examined the characteristics of the large-scale units that are the focus of contemporary geostrategy. Examples include the Middle East, sub-Saharan Africa, the Transatlantic region, and Southeast Asia. Didelon-Loiseau, de Ruffray and Lambert have developed an important distinction here. In their terminology, there are *harder* and *softer* regions; firstly, those that can be more precisely defined by certain criteria; and secondly, those that remain so diffuse that their actual existence has little more than a suggestive or even manipulative function. There are therefore empirical criteria, albeit limited, for better or worse geopolitical concepts.

The terms *harder* and *softer* can also be defined more precisely based on classical geographical regional studies. Two criteria are commonly used to delimit regions:

- According to the *homogeneity criterion*, territorial units are grouped into homogeneous regions that are similar to each other in terms of certain characteristics. Examples of such homogeneity criteria are the same or similar climate, raw material deposits, industrial structure, income, language, culture, settlement density, etc.
- According to the *functionality criterion*, territorial units are grouped together if they are particularly closely linked or interdependent according to certain indicators, such as economic or political ties, transport systems or links in the field of ecology and nature.

Let's summarise: Geopolitics is also based on mental maps of large spatial units. It is a socio-cultural construct. But can geopolitics really construe arbitrary spaces? Or should it not, beyond all symbolism, retain a certain link to verifiable facts from the real world? Or: Although socio-spatial reality is constructed, it cannot be constructed arbitrarily. Societal truth is a *construct*, but not every construct is empirically *true*. This is precisely what makes our research approach so important for the critical analysis of the mental maps of geopolitics.

4. Indo-Pacific Geopolitics

In the following, the research approach developed here will be test-run on two geopolitical concepts for the Indo-Pacific:

- *The US Free and Open Indo-Pacific (FOIP) of 2019* (Department of State. United States of America 2019)
- And the concept of the European Union, *EU strategy for cooperation in the Indo-Pacific* (Council of the European Union 2021; European Commission 2021).

A brief historical background to these documents: since the end of the Second World War, a system of order has existed in the Pacific and in the maritime and island regions east of the former Soviet Union, China and Vietnam, in which the United States has dominated politically and, above all, militarily after 1990, but not more than for one decade. Given the circumstances at the time, the term *Asia-Pacific* was generally used as a geopolitical concept, particularly in the United States. The references to rimland theory are not coincidental. Since the turn of the millennium, this system has been increasingly challenged by China's economic, political and military rise. China has also begun to assert its own interests more strongly in the regional and international context, including through a comprehensive cooperation and investment programme known as the *Belt and Road Initiative (BRI)*. In response to this Chinese foreign policy, several states have developed counter-models under the label Indo-Pacific. Following Japan, the United States has been at the forefront of this response, showing remarkable continuity under Presidents Trump, Biden and now Trump again with geostrategic concepts such as the Free and Open Indo-Pacific (FOIP), which can be seen as a direct, primarily military-political counter-proposal to the Belt and Road Initiative (BRI). This was supplemented in 2022 by the Indo-Pacific Economic Framework for Prosperity (IPEF) (Executive Office of the President of the United States 2022).

In addition to the US, Japan, Australia, India and the Association of Southeast Asian Nations (ASEAN) have also published geostrategic plans for the Indo-Pacific, some of them even before the United States, but these differ significantly from the US ideas in some respects. Already during Trump's first term, the US increased pressure on individual EU member states and the EU as a whole to commit directly or indirectly to the Indo-Pacific concept. The EU finally did so with its policy paper *The EU strategy for cooperation in the Indo-Pacific* (Council of the European Union 2021; European Commission 2021).

From the above, we can conclude that geopolitical concepts such as the Indo-Pacific are socio-spatial constructs. They serve specific purposes, have at least some empirical groundings and are based on what systems theory refers to as the reduction of complexity, but through symbols and metaphors. Furthermore, we can assume that if a concept originally comes from an author such as Haushofer, it can generally be considered as a highly constructed piece of imagination. And indeed, an examination based on the homogeneity and functionality criteria developed above leads to a rather negative result. This is because:

- *The Indo-Pacific is not a region according to the criteria of homogeneity*: in terms of climate, natural resources, economic structure, income,

language, culture, population density, etc., there is nothing in common between Alaska and Somalia, to take two extreme examples.
- *Nor is the Indo-Pacific a region according to the functionality criteria*: there are no particularly close ties or interdependencies, no deeper economic, political or military links, no common transport systems or forms of cultural exchange – not from the Cape of Good Hope to the Bering Strait or from the Persian Gulf to New Zealand.

Even for Haushofer, the Indo-Pacific was largely a politically motivated spatial construct divorced from reality. In terms of classical foreign policy, it mainly expresses an imperial claim to power or the desire to resist an imperial power. This is probably the deeper meaning behind the discourse on the Indo-Pacific today, although, as we shall see, claims to power can be expressed in various ways and with different consequences.

Let us now turn to the two documents selected here, starting with the US Free and Open Indo-Pacific (FOIP) strategy. It serves to revitalise Haushofer-style foreign policy in a paradigmatic way – in the formulation of its goals, in the details of its programmes and in the graphic presentation of the concept. In view of the suggestive cartography of the US concept, a few longer quotations from the concept and a corresponding commentary are certainly useful.

First and foremost: The Indo-Pacific has always existed, and the US has always been part of it since its foundation. This is also referred to as geo-determinism:

> „The United States is and always will be an Indo-Pacific nation. From our first trading ships that departed for Canton just after the American Revolution to our first consular presence in Kolkata in 1794, U.S. engagement in the Indo-Pacific is a story of trade, exchange, shared sacrifice, and mutual benefit." (Department of State. United States of America 2019, 5)

The Indo-Pacific has been an economically emerging region of the world in recent decades (without mentioning China), and this is of course thanks to the USA:

> "In recent decades, the Indo-Pacific has undergone are markable transformation. As hundreds of millions of people climbed out of poverty, the region has become home to world-class companies and an important engine of global economic growth. This transformation was possible because a free and open regional order ensured stability and a level playing field on which countries could grow and prosper as sovereign,

> independent states." (Department of State. United States of America 2019, 5)

Today, this dynamic and highly advantageous order is under threat (from China, although this is not mentioned directly in this section of the text), and the United States is naturally stepping in to defend it. They are coming to the rescue:

> "Today, Indo-Pacific nations face unprecedented challenges to their sovereignty, prosperity, and peace. The U.S. National Security Strategy, released in December 2017, recognizes that the most consequential challenge to U.S. and partner interests is the growing competition between free and repressive visions of the future international order. Authoritarian revisionist powers seek to advance their parochial interests at others' expense." (Department of State. United States of America 2019, 5)

The political cartography constructed in this way is thus characterised by a dualism of positive and negative symbolism; on the one hand, the good USA and its partners, and on the other, the authoritarian powers that want to destroy the order established since the Second World War. All of this is very reminiscent of the dichotomous mental maps from the Cold War analysed by Casey and Wright (Casey/Wright 2008; 2011; 2015). A geopolitical suggestive narrative is constructed, which is then contrasted with the corresponding offers of assistance, also originating from the USA. The aim is to

> "We are committed to upholding a free and open Indo-Pacific in which all nations, large and small, are secure in their sovereignty and able to pursue economic growth consistent with international law and principles of fair competition. We will compete vigorously against attempts to limit the autonomy and freedom of choice of Indo-Pacific nations." (Department of State. United States of America 2019, 5)

The term *freedom of choice* used here is, of course, strongly reminiscent of the Truman Doctrine of 1947. What follows in the document is a list of classic foreign policy instruments that were also used particularly between 1947 and 1987:

> *Engaging Partners and Regional Institutions*, meaning a network of various states led by the US (Department of State. United States of America 2019, 7)

Enhancing Economic Prosperity in the sense of a radical market order (Department of State. United States of America 2019, 13)
Championing Good Governance in the sense of adopting the US political model (Department of State. United States of America 2019, 21)
Ensuring Peace and Security, very aptly illustrated with a picture of a US aircraft carrier (Department of State. United States of America 2019, 22)
Investing in Human Capital, emphasising the quality of US education (Department of State. United States of America 2019, 25)

Image 4: USS Carl Vinson (CVN 70) arrived in Da Nang, Vietnam

Source: Department of State. United States of America 2019, 22

The illustrations accompanying the concept speak for themselves: President Trump is depicted six times, former Secretary of State Mike Pompeo four times, and the images focus on Japan, India and Vietnam, which the administration at the time considered to be the most important potential partners for the United States. In summary, the US Free and Open Indo-Pacific (FOIP) is a mental map in the tradition of US geopolitics, with all the elements of selective and suggestive cartography that can be traced back to the deep-rooted US tradition of good-versus-evil schemas. All differentiating spatial markers are omitted.

Let us now turn to the EU strategy for cooperation in the Indo-Pacific and ask what distinguishes it from the US geopolitical concept. This strategy also makes use of geopolitical imagery in some places, particularly at the beginning, in the very vague description of the underlying area or region:

> "The Indo-Pacific – a vast region spanning from the east coast of Africa to the Pacific Island States – is increasingly strategically significant for Europe." (European Commission 2021, 1)

Unlike the Free and Open Indo-Pacific (FOIP), however, this region remains relatively undefined; in particular, the EU is not described as a historically significant player in the region – which it could have been, given its colonial past and the intensive partnerships that EU countries have had with various countries in the region since 1945. At least some relevant territorial landmarks are mentioned:

> "The region hosts major waterways that are of vital importance to EU trade, including the Malacca Straits, the South China Sea, and the Bab el-Mandeb Strait." (European Commission 2021, 2)

Unlike the United States, which appears to be focusing its attention on the Pacific, the EU defines the Indian Ocean as an area of particular interest and emphasises its historically good relations with the ASEAN countries:

> "The Indian Ocean is the principal passage for Europe to and from Indo-Pacific markets. Stability and freedom of navigation in this area are therefore vital." (European Commission 2021, 4)
> "The Association of Southeast Asian Nations (ASEAN), an increasingly important partner for the EU." (European Commission 2021, 1)

Image 5: Differences between the US and EU focus in the Indo-Pacific

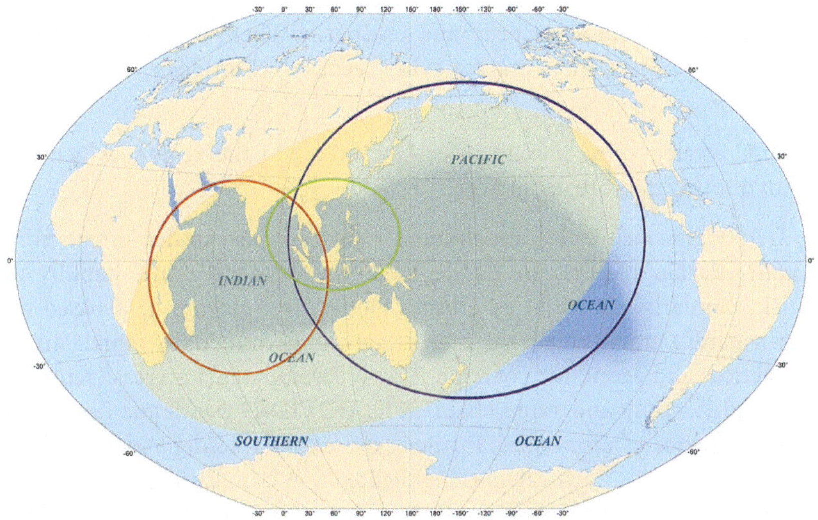

Source: https://www.asean.emb-japan.go.jp/files/000352880.pdf.

Overall, however, the EU is not defined as part of the region, but rather as its partner, particularly in the economic sphere.

> "The EU and the Indo-Pacific are natural partner regions in terms of trade and investment. The EU is the top investor, the leading provider of development cooperation, and one of the biggest trading partners in the Indo-Pacific region. Together, the Indo-Pacific and Europe account for over 70% of the global trade in goods and services, and over 60% of foreign direct investment flows. Trade exchanges between the Indo-Pacific and Europe are higher than between any other geographical regions in the world." (European Commission 2021, 1)

The EU strategy also mentions the security dimension and explicitly names China, but does not single it out as the only power driving the escalation in the region:

> „In recent years, geopolitical dynamics in the Indo-Pacific have given rise to intense competition, including tensions around contested territories and maritime zones. There has been a significant military build-up, including by China, with the Indo-Pacific's share of global military spending increasing from 20% of the world total in 2009 to 28% in 2019. The

> display of force and increasing tensions in regional hotspots such as in the South and East China Sea and in the Taiwan Strait may have a direct impact on European security and prosperity. There is also an increase in hybrid threats, including on cyber security." (European Commission 2021, 1)

The EU strategy also identifies further threats to the region, which are worth quoting in more detail here:

> "Democratic principles and human rights are also under threat from authoritarian regimes in the region, putting the region's stability at risk. Similarly, efforts to establish a global level playing field based on transparent trade rules are increasingly undermined by unfair trade practices and economic coercion. These developments increase tensions in trade, supply and value chains. The COVID-19 pandemic has tested the resilience of economies, further exposed the interdependence of EU and Indo-Pacific partners, and highlighted that both gain resilience from open, diversified and undistorted access to world markets. Finally, the ongoing crisis in Afghanistan also demonstrates the direct impact that events in the region have on Europe's security." (European Commission 2021, 1)

However, the following passages make it clear how little the concept can be interpreted as a classic geopolitical mental map. Above all, it lacks the imaginative element of a global political power offering protection. Instead, it focuses on cooperation, which the EU wants to concentrate on seven priority areas. This shows that the EU is not seeking a fundamentally new strategy for political leadership, but rather wants to strengthen activities in existing areas of cooperation:

- Sustainable and inclusive prosperity.
- Green transition.
- Ocean governance.
- Digital governance and partnerships.
- Connectivity.
- Security and defence.
- Human security. (European Commission 2021, 5)

The EU strategy for cooperation in the Indo-Pacific is therefore, in the true sense of the word, more of an attempt to label the programmes already implemented by the EU and its member states at the time the agenda was published with a geopolitical tag. In other words, the EU strategy is a mental map based on many single, pragmatic programme points, with a rather limited suggestive, surely not manipulative dimension. Essentially, the EU is concerned with intensifying its economic and environmental policy for the region. Finally, this can be illustrated in the catalogue of the most important concrete measures planned by the EU:

- to build more resilient and sustainable global value chains by diversifying trade and economic relations and developing technological standards and regulations.
- Completing EU trade negotiations.
- Concluding Partnership and Cooperation Agreements.
- Concluding Green Alliances and Partnerships.
- Strengthening ocean governance in the region.
- Expanding the network of digital partnerships.
- Stepping up implementation of the Connectivity Partnerships.
- Strengthen cooperation on research and innovation under *Horizon Europe*.
- Exploring ways to ensure enhanced naval deployments to ensure maritime security.
- Reinforcing support to healthcare systems and pandemic preparedness. (European Commission 2021, 17)

The EU approach also refrains from using the suggestive elements of the Free and Open Indo-Pacific (FOIP) in its presentation. There are no photos of politicians, flags or even aircraft carriers. It is based on the recognition that, in terms of the above-mentioned criteria of homogeneity and functionality, the Indo-Pacific has only one thing in common: that the EU in this region is aiming at reducing tensions and promoting a rules-based international order through cooperation with all partners.

7. Imaginative Geographies and Mental Maps for and in the Indo-Pacific

The analyses carried out here are only a first step towards exploring the mental maps that underpin United States and European geopolitics in the Indo-Pacific. Nevertheless, it is already rather promising to apply the research criteria identified above to the analysis of *The Free and Open Indo-Pacific (FOIP)* and *The EU Strategy for Cooperation in the Indo-Pacific*:

- Both approaches are explicit geostrategies that are (largely) based on stereotypes, metaphors, prejudices and symbols. An empirical content is recognisable in each case, but the intentional reshaping in the US concept is many times greater than in the European one.
- Both geostrategies are mental maps for large regions and both contain various target projections. However, the spatial imaginations in the US strategy are undoubtedly more focused on suggesting, even manipulating, the target audience, if only through the graphic design of the concept.
- The difference is most evident in relation to underlying geo-determinism. This is very pronounced in the US strategy (the US has always been part of the Indo-Pacific and acts in accordance with its territorial destiny), while the EU concept defines itself more in terms of facts and common interests in and with the region.
- The US geostrategy is a suggestive concept of claiming a position of military power, while the EU tends to formulate common interests and further develop policies that have already proven successful.
- Ultimately, the US concept leads its readers to believe that the Indo-Pacific exists despite the lack of *hard* facts and that the US is called upon to guarantee law and security in this region. The EU acts more as a moderator in a region with rather unclear borders where conflicts can be resolved through cooperation.

Let us return to our theoretical considerations at the beginning of this text: mental maps relating to large regions are imaginary, symbolic constructions of space which does not mean they are pure fantasy. They construct diverse realities for everyone who perceives such concepts; in the case of US geostrategy, they even use images of aircraft carriers to create threatening scenarios. By this alone, they influence US society and its foreign relations. However, it is also useful for their creators to check these constructs against empirical facts. If this is not done, they primarily express political claims to power. This seems to be the case with the United States and here we'll just leave a question mark. Given the size of this region and the fact that at least three other major powers are active here (China, India and Russia, as well as an increasingly independent European Union and middle-powers like Japan), this aspiration could prove somewhat excessive. Even during the era of the so-called transatlantic partnership, the United States was heavily reliant on cooperation with the European NATO states.

As historians, we might recall that the United States has suffered its greatest foreign policy disasters since 1945 in an area which is now called the Indo-Pacific region: in China, Korea, Vietnam, Iran and Afghanistan. It is to be hoped that no further defeats will be added to this list in the future. Perhaps those responsible in the United States should work on revising their mental maps: Namely that they cannot simply replace their previous transatlantic alignment with a transpacific one. For this reason alone, mental maps of the Indo-Pacific region remain a research task of enormous importance.

Image 6: Re-inventing the Indo-Pacific

https://www.economist.com/asia/2023/01/04/reinventing-the-indo-pacific

8. References

Anderson, Benedict (1983): Imagined communities: reflections on the origin and spread of nationalism. London.

Bilenky, Serhiy (2012): Romantic nationalism in Eastern Europe: Russian, Polish, and Ukrainian political imaginations. Stanford University Press.

Bokhari, Kamran (2025): The US Geostrategy and the Old World Order. In: GPF. Geopolitical Futures February 20, 2025. https://geopoliticalfutures.com/the-us-geostrategy-and-the-old-world-order.

Braune, Gerd (2020): Geopolitik in der Arktis (Geopolitics in the Arctic). In: Internationale Politik. Das Magazin für globales Denken. Nov. 1, 2020. https://internationalepolitik.de/de/geopolitik-der-arktis.

Briesen, Detlef (et al.) (1994): Regionalbewusstsein in Montanregionen im 19. und 20. Jahrhundert: Saarland – Siegerland – Ruhrgebiet (Regional awareness in mining regions in the 19th and 20th centuries: Saarland – Siegerland – Ruhr region). (= Mobilität und Normenwandel 10.) Bochum.

Brill, Heinz (2008): Geopolitische Analysen. Beiträge zur deutschen und internationalen Sicherheitspolitik (Geopolitical analyses. Contributions to German and international security policy) (1974–2008). Bissendorf.

Brzeziński, Zbigniew (1997): The Grand Chessboard: American Primacy and Its Geostrategic Imperatives. New York.

Casey, Steven/Wright, Jonathan (eds.) (2008): Mental maps in the era of two world wars. Basingstoke.

Casey, Steven/Wright, Jonathan (eds.) (2011): Mental maps in the era of the early cold war 1945-68. Basingstoke.

Casey, Steven/Wright, Jonathan (eds.) (2015): Mental maps in the era of detente and the end of the cold war 1968–91. Basingstoke.

Conrad, Christian (ed.) (2002): Mental maps. Geschichte und Gesellschaft, 28 (3), 339–514.

Council of the European Union, EU Strategy for Cooperation in the Indo-Pacific – Council Conclusions, April 16, 2021: https://data.consilium.europa.eu/doc/document/ST-7914-2021-INIT/en/pdf.

Criekemans, David/Duran, Manuel (2011): Mental maps, geopolitics and foreign policy analysis: basic analytical framework and application to sub-state diplomacy in the Mediterranean. Presentation August 2011. University of Porto.

da Vinha, Luis (2012): Charting Geographic Mental Maps in Foreign Policy Analysis: A Literature Review. In: Human Geographies – Journal of Studies and Research in Human Geography 6.1 (2012), 5–17.

da Vinha, Luis (2019): Maps of War and Peace: Rethinking Geography in International Affairs. In: Brown Journal of World Affairs. Spring/Summer 2019, xxv, Issue ii, 25, 73–89.

Dalby, Simon/O Tuathail, Gearoid (1996): Special Issue Critical Geopolitics. In: Political Geography, 15 (6–7): 451–665.

Department of State. United States of America (2019): A Free and Open Indo-Pacific. Advancing a Shared Vision. Washington. https://www.state.gov/wp-content/uploads/2019/11/Free-and-Open-Indo-Pacific-4Nov2019.pdf.

Didelon-Loiseau, Clarisse/de Ruffray, Sophie/Lambert, Nicolas (2021): Mental maps of global regions: identifying and characterizing hard and soft regions. In: Holmen, Janne/Götz, Norbert (eds.) (2021): Mental Maps. Geographical and Historical Perspectives. London. 55–75.

Downs, Roger/Stea, David (1977): Maps in Mind. New York.

Erforth, Benedikt (2016): Mental Maps and Foreign Policy Decision-Making: Eurafrique and the French Military Intervention in Mali. In: European Review of International Studies 3(1, 38–57.

European Commission, Joint Communication to the European Parliament and the Council: The EU Strategy for Cooperation in the Indo-Pacific, September 16, 2021: https://www.eeas.europa.eu/sites/default/files/jointcommunica-tion_2021_24_1_en.pdf.

Executive Office of the President of the United States (2022): Indo-Pacific Economic Framework for Prosperity (IPEF). https://ustr.gov/trade-agreements/agreements-under-negotiation/indo-pacific-economic-framework-prosperity-ipef.

Gieseking, Jen Jack (2017): Geographical Imagination. In: Richardson, E. (et al.): International Encyclopedia of Geography: People, the Earth, Environment, and Technology. New York.

Götz, Norbert/Holmen, Janne (2018): Introduction to the theme issue: Mental maps: geographical and historical perspectives. In: Journal of Cultural Geography, 2018 Vol. 35, No. 2, 157–161.

Gould, Peter (1966): On mental maps. Ann Arbor.

Gould, Peter/White, Rodney (1974): Mental maps. Harmondsworth.

Gregory, Derek (1994): Geographical Imaginations. Malden.

Gregory, Derek (2009): Geographical Imagination. In: Gregory, Derek Gregory (eds.): The Dictionary of Human Geography. Malden.

Harvey, David (1973): Social Justice and the City. Baltimore.

Haushofer, Karl (1924): Geographie des pazifischen Ozeaniens. Studie über die Wechselbeziehungen zwischen Geographie und Geschichte. Berlin.

Haushofer, Karl (1925): Geopolitik des Pazifischen Ozeans. Berlin 1925.

Haushofer, Karl (1935): Geopolitische Grundlagen. Berlin/Wien 1935.

Haushofer, Karl (1937) Weltmeere und Weltmächte. Berlin.

Haushofer, Karl (1939): Deutsche Kulturpolitik im indopazifischen Raum. Hamburg.

Haushofer, Karl (ed.) (1932): Macht und Erde. 2: Jenseits der Großmächte. Berlin.

Hoffmann, Nils (2012): Renaissance der Geopolitik? Die deutsche Sicherheitspolitik nach dem Kalten Krieg (Renaissance of geopolitics? German security policy after the Cold War). Wiesbaden.

Holmen, Janne/Götz, Norbert (eds.) (2021): Mental Maps. Geographical and Historical Perspectives. London.

Huntington, Samuel P. (1996): The Clash of Civilizations and the Remaking of World Order. New York

Kaplan, Robert D. (2012): The Revenge of Geography. What the Map Tells Us About Coming Conflicts and the Battle Against Fate. New York.

Kissinger, Henry (2014): World Order. London.

Kjellén, Rudolf (1924): Der Staat als Lebensform. Berlin.

Kushre, Lakhan Singh (2023): Geostrategic Importance of India – An Analytical Study, In: International Journal of Research in Social Sciences and Humanities. April 21, 2023. https://www.researchgate.net/publication/374061594_GEOSTRATEGIC_IMPORTANCE_OF_INDIA_-AN_ANALYTICAL_STUDY.

Lacoste, Yves (2010): La géopolitique et le géographie. Paris.

Laïdi, Zaki (2023): Was das geopolitische Europa bedeutet (What geopolitical Europe means). In: Internationale Politik. Das Magazin für globales Denken. März/April 2023. https://internationalepolitik.de/de/was-das-geopolitische-europa-bedeutet.

Li, Hansong (June 2021): The Indo-Pacific: Intellectual Origins and International Visions in Global Contexts. In: Modern Intellectual History. 19 (3): 807–833.

Lynch, Kevin (1960): The image of the city. Cambridge.

Mackinder, Halford John (1902): Britain and the British Seas. New York.

Mahan, Alfred Thayer (1898/99): Der Einfluß der Seemacht auf die Geschichte. Berlin 1898/99.

Marshall, Tim (2015): Prisoners of geography. Ten maps that tell you everything you need to know about global politics. London.

Meister, Stefan (2024): Russia's Geostrategic Shifts January 10, 2024. In: Internationale Politik Quaterly. https://ip-quarterly.com/en/russias-geostrategic-shifts.

Münkler, Herfried Münkler(2023): Welt in Aufruhr. Die Ordnung der Mächte im 21. Jahrhundert (World in turmoil. The order of powers in the 21st century. Berlin.

Paul, Michael (2022): Der Kampf um den Nordpol. Die Arktis, der Klimawandel und die Rivalität der Großmächte (The battle for the North Pole. The Arctic, climate change and the rivalry between the major powers). Freiburg.

Petri, Rolf (ed.) (2016): Maritime areas: spaces of changing expectations. In: Comparativ (Special Issue), 26 (5), 7–75.

Ratzel, Friedrich (1903): Politische Geographie oder die Geographie der Staaten, des Verkehres und des Krieges. München.

Said, Edward (1978): Orientalism. New York.

Said, Edward (1979): Imaginative Geography and Its Representations: Orientalizing the Oriental. New York.

Scheffler, Thomas (2003): Fertile Crescent, Orient, Middle East: the changing mental maps of Southwest Asia. In: European Review of History, 10 (2), 253–272.

Schenk, Frithjof Benjamin (2013): Mental maps: the cognitive mapping of the continent as an object of research of European history. European History Online (EGO). http://www.ieg-ego.eu/schenkf-2013-en.

Schlögel, Karl (2016): In Space We Read Time: On the History of Civilization and Geopolitics. Bard Graduate Center.

Schmitt, Carl (1941): Völkerrechtliche Großraumordnung mit Interventionsverbot für raumfremde Mächte. Ein Beitrag zum Reichsbegriff im Völkerrecht (A large-scale international order with a prohibition on intervention by foreign powers. A contribution to the concept of empire in international law). Berlin.

Schneider, Ute (2021): Dimensions of remapping: Heinrich Schiffers and his mental map of Africa. In: Holmen, Janne/Götz, Norbert (eds.) (2021): Mental Maps. Geographical and Historical Perspectives. London. 32–58.

Spykman, Nicholas (1944): The Geography of the Peace. New York.

STRATEGIECS Team (2020): China's Geostrategy: A Broad Overview. In: STRATEGIECS Think Tank. November 16, 2020. https://strategiecs.com/en/analyses/chinas-geostrategy-a-broad-overview.

Tardent, Pierre (2005): Meeresbiologie: Eine Einführung Marine (Biology: An Introduction). Stuttgart.

Tolman, Edward C. (1948): Cognitive maps in rats and men. In: Psychological Review, 55 (4), 189–208.

Werlen, Benno (2000): Sozialgeographie. Eine Einführung (Social geography. An introduction). Bern.

II.
Great Powers from Outside the Indo-Pacific Region: Imaginations, Interests and Strategies

Chapter 5: Implementing the US-American Indo-Pacific Strategy: New Developments and Prospects

Bui Thanh Nam

The Indo-Pacific strategy was issued by the administration of President Donald Trump in 2017. This strategy inherited measures implemented by previous US administrations to contain China's rise. However, given China's comprehensive and overall growth in key economic, political, and military sectors, along with its strong steps to reshape the international order with the values and institutions it seeks to establish, the United States has made several adjustments to the content and implementation of the Indo-Pacific strategy – not only to contain China but also to counterbalance its approach. The United States's increased engagement in the Indo-Pacific region has led to the formation of new mechanisms in the area, generating developments that could impact the development prospects of more than 50 per cent of the world's population. Whether the goal of containing China can be achieved remains an open question, subject to various scenarios that depend not only on regional dynamics but also on other factors in the global power landscape.

Nevertheless, strengthening and maintaining its economic power, enhancing connectivity, and creating economic and security benefits for countries in the Indo-Pacific region – while simultaneously curbing China's high-growth momentum by adjusting the regional production system – are considered viable options for the United States. Although these measures require time to implement, they appear more feasible given America's current power realities.

1. Introduction

The US Indo-Pacific Strategy has been implemented for nearly a decade, leading to a substantial body of research on this strategy. The studies cover a wide range of topics but primarily focus on two main aspects:

(a) The content and practical implementation of the strategy.
(b) The reactions of countries both within and outside the region.

Some notable works include:

- *The Free and Open Indo-Pacific and Implications for ASEAN* (Lee 2018), which highlights the significant impact of this strategy on the Association of Southeast Asian Nations (ASEAN). Given that the region falls within the scope of the strategy, ASEAN plays a crucial role in maintaining stability and economic development.
- *The Indo-Pacific: Trump, China, and the New Struggle for Global Mastery* (Heydarian 2020), which explores the geopolitical dynamics of the Indo-Pacific region, focusing on strategic interactions between the United States and China during the Trump administration.
- *Indo-Pacific Empire: China, America, and the Contest for the World's Pivotal Region* (Medcalf 2021), which explains why the concept of the Indo-Pacific holds strategic importance. The book concludes with a strategy designed to help the West engage with China's power in the region while avoiding conflict.
- *The U.S. Indo-Pacific Strategy & The Prospect of Forging a New Multipolar World* (Jin Ran 2023), which aims to explore and analyse key factors, issues, and mechanisms likely to influence relationships among major powers and entities in both Europe and the Indo-Pacific. It also examines the potential for key players in these two regions to collaboratively shape an alternative global order based on how they manage and engage in core issues identified in the study.

More recently, we have come across several new publications, including:

- *Lost Decade: The U.S. Pivot to Asia and the Rise of Chinese Power* (Blackwill/Fontaine 2024), in which the authors assess the outcomes of the US pivot to Asia strategy and its implications for China's growing influence.
- *World on the Brink: How America Can Beat China in the Race for the Twenty-First Century* (Alperovitch/Graff 2024), which discusses the geopolitical and economic challenges posed by China's rise and proposes strategies for the United States to maintain its global leadership position in the 21st century.

Thus, there have been ongoing developments in the content of the strategy itself due to the implementation and adjustments made by the United States. The involvement of relevant stakeholders has also contributed to these developments, particularly from China – the primary target of the strategy. Analysing these new dynamics helps assess the actual effectiveness of the US Indo-Pacific strategy, predict shifts in the regional order, and gain a deeper understanding of United States foreign policy toward Asia. At the same time, this study holds significance for regional countries in shaping their foreign policies and cooperation with the United States including Vietnam.

With this objective in mind, the study focuses on analysing the following key aspects:

- *The strategic context and motivations of the United States*, with a focus on answering why the United States has implemented this strategy and identifying its core interests in the region.
- *New developments in the strategy's implementation*, analysing specific policies inherited across United States administrations while also examining the reactions of regional countries, particularly China and India.
- *Future prospects*, assessing how the United States may strengthen this strategy and exploring possible scenarios for the regional landscape.

2. Regional Developments

China's rise: strengthened global position through economic growth, assertive claims, and strategic initiatives

After more than three decades of record-high economic growth, China surpassed Japan in 2010 to become the world's second-largest economy. It is now challenging the United States' economic superpower status, with many projections suggesting that if its current growth rate continues, China could surpass the United States to become the world's largest economy by the 2030s. Alongside its economic development, China has implemented a range of strategic policies to enhance its security. China has capitalized on tensions between Russia and the West to establish its closest-ever relationship with Russia. In addition to a steadily growing economic partnership, China and Russia have co-founded and led several multilateral platforms, such as the Shanghai Cooperation Organization (SCO) and BRICS. These initiatives aim to strengthen the collective influence of nations seeking to reduce Western dominance while safeguarding their security and economic interests in a more equitable manner.

On the geopolitical front, China has built a strategic security buffer by systematically pushing the United States out of key strategic areas that could pose security threats. One notable example is China's successful efforts to distance Pakistan from its alliance with the United States by providing extensive political, security, and economic support. These moves have helped China solidify domestic security, stabilize its land borders, and create a more advantageous position for expanding its international role. With an economy significantly larger than the next five largest economies combined (Germany, Japan, India, the UK, and France), China has taken decisive steps to assert its new status on the global stage and reshape the current world order, which has long been dominated by Western ideologies, values, and institutions. Chinese President Xi Jinping has dismissed the idea of the G8 – which would include China alongside the G7 nations – and instead proposed the possibility of a G2 framework in which the United States and China would jointly lead global development. President Xi has emphasized that

"The world is big enough for both China and the U.S. to succeed."

This bold and direct message openly challenges America's leadership in the global order, which it has largely controlled since the collapse of the post-World War II bipolar world system. Beyond seeking recognition from major powers, China has also reinforced its dominance over smaller nations by showcasing its superior hard power while expanding its soft power influence. In certain strategic areas, the traditional Chinese foreign policy approach of *befriending distant states while attacking nearby ones* appears to still resonate among some policymakers, emerging whenever opportunities arise – especially in regions where US influence remains significant, such as the Indo-Pacific, an area of critical security and economic interests.

China has asserted historical sovereignty over the South China Sea, demanding that regional nations recognize its *nine-dash line* territorial claims. Alongside these territorial assertions, China has significantly increased its naval presence, frequently clashing with the Philippine navy near the Scarborough Shoal. It has also deployed coast guard vessels and resource exploration rigs, threatened the livelihoods of local fishermen and infringed on the economic interests and sovereignty of affected countries. Additionally, China has expanded its military presence in the East China Sea, pressuring Japan to make concessions in the territorial dispute over the Diaoyu/Senkaku Islands.

China's expanding global presence and strategic initiatives: counterbalancing US-led global order

China's naval ambitions have extended beyond the Asia-Pacific region, where it has well-established naval bases with essential logistical support, reaching as far as West Africa. This expansion has created a maritime security belt for China while potentially threatening the security of the United States and its allies. The rapid expansion of the Chinese navy, second in scale only to the United States, is not merely for training, patrols, or live-fire exercises in the congested waters of the Yellow Sea or the South China Sea. Beyond its first overseas naval base in Djibouti, established in 2016, China plans to construct additional naval bases, forming a chain of military outposts to safeguard its trade and resource supply routes vital for its international production and commerce system.

China is also actively engaging in new geopolitical arenas where it has historically had little influence. According to an Aid Data report, Chinese companies spent 30 billion US dollars between 2000 and 2021 to construct and upgrade infrastructure at 78 international ports across 46 countries, evaluating their potential to host Chinese naval vessels. Among these, Hambantota (Sri Lanka), Bata (Equatorial Guinea), and Gwadar (Pakistan) are three of the eight locations where China is most likely to establish new naval bases. Additionally, ports such as Kribi (Cameroon), Nacala (Mozambique), Nouakchott (Mauritania), and Vanuatu (Pacific Islands) are reportedly under consideration by the Chinese military. Amid China's growing military presence in West Africa, United States national security officials have expressed concerns. The distance from Senegal – where China has established strong economic ties and hinted at military-defense cooperation – to New York is approximately 4,000 miles, well within the 5,000-mile strike range of China's advanced guided-missile destroyers.

Challenging the United States-led global order with alternative institutions and values

As a counterbalance to the global institutions and rules established and led by the United States, China has introduced a series of initiatives to assert itself as a global power while shaping new values and institutions aligned with its vision. In the early 21st century, China proposed the concept of the *Beijing Consensus* as an alternative to the *Washington Consensus* promoted by United States-led international and regional economic organizations. The latter's stringent economic reform and market liberalization requirements often placed heavy burdens on developing nations. China's approach to economic integration took a different path, starting with the Closer Economic Partnership Arrangement (CEPA) in 2003 – a simple, thirteen-page free trade agreement with Hong Kong. This laid the groundwork for China's future trade agreements, which omitted labour standards, environmental protections, and strict service market liberalization demands, making them more appealing to lower-income developing economies.

Following the launch of the trillion-dollar Belt and Road Initiative (BRI) in 2013 and the establishment of the Asian Infrastructure Investment Bank (AIIB) to support its implementation, China further solidified its global leadership ambitions by introducing the Global Development Initiative (GDI) in 2021. This initiative aims to enhance China's influence in developing nations while countering Western-led efforts such as the United States-backed *Build Back Better World* (B3W) initiative. GDI focuses on finance, sustainable development, technology, and global cooperation – key priorities for countries seeking rapid economic growth.

During this period, China also reinforced its role in regional economic integration by bridging the Indian and Pacific Oceans through the negotiation of the Regional Comprehensive Economic Partnership (RCEP). The goal was to incorporate South Asian nations into a new economic order led by China. Recognizing the absence of global coordination mechanisms for non-traditional security threats, China introduced the Global Security Initiative (GSI) in 2022. This initiative aims to create a security model that balances global influence with existing Western-led organizations, protects Beijing's interests, and garners support from developing countries amid intensifying United States-China competition. In 2023, China launched the Global Civilization Initiative (GCI) to further establish itself as a major cultural and ideological power. The initiative seeks to counter Western influence in ideology and values by promoting China's 5,000-year-old civilization as an attractive soft power tool. By positioning itself as a global cultural leader, China aims to sustain its long-term influence worldwide.

These initiatives are interconnected, reinforcing each other through complementary objectives. Collectively, they strive to build a multipolar world order independent of Western dominance, advancing China's vision of a *Community of Shared Future for Mankind* – a global framework that aligns with Beijing's strategic interests and leadership ambitions.

The imbalance of United States security and economic control in the region: challenges to existing mechanisms

The imbalance of United States security and economic control in the region has weakened the effectiveness of existing United States-led mechanisms such as APEC, which struggles to assert its role due to China's involvement and its current alliance with Russia. Similarly, newer initiatives like the Trans-Pacific Partnership (TPP) lack the influence to counterbalance China's Belt and Road Initiative (BRI). While the United States remained entangled in the war on terror launched in response to the 9/11 attacks – focusing on conflicts in Iraq and Afghanistan, China took advantage of this period to rise, leaving the United States relatively passive in the face of new developments in the Indo-Pacific. The balance of power, which has implications for both regional and global affairs, has visibly tilted in China's favour.

China has successfully broken free from the land-based containment strategy set up by the United States by forming alliances with neighbouring countries in Central and Southwest Asia. In particular, China has deepened its relationships with Russia and Mongolia, securing its longest land borders and enhancing its overall security posture. This shift allows China to proactively strengthen control over key maritime routes, potentially further unsettling the United States's security presence in the region. China's increasing assertiveness in territorial disputes, such as the Senkaku/Diaoyu Islands, despite existing United States-Japan security treaties, has raised concerns among American allies. If China gains the upper hand in its South China Sea territorial claims, the security of vital maritime trade routes linking the Indian and Pacific Oceans – integral to United States and allied economic and security interests – will face significant threats.

The limitations of US-led mechanisms in the region

Both old and new US-led mechanisms in the Indo-Pacific have shown inadequacies in containing China's rise. Established frameworks such as APEC cannot constrain China's role in the region, as China itself is an active member of the organization. Additionally, efforts to revitalize APEC through negotiations have stalled, leading to growing disillusionment among regional nations seeking greater economic benefits from regional integration (Hoang Thi Ha 2023). Newer initiatives, such as the Obama administration's TPP, have also failed to effectively counter BRI, as China has positioned itself as the leader in regional and global economic integration from the Asia-Pacific. In essence, in the strategic game of Go, the Obama administration failed to place its pieces in a way that could block or significantly disrupt China's expansion.

The rising strategic importance of the Indo-Pacific

Since the establishment of APEC, the Asia-Pacific region has evolved into the world's most dynamic economic hub, accounting for over 40 per cent of global GDP. Fuelled by effective economic cooperation initiatives, regional and bilateral free trade agreements, and the economic booms of China and ASEAN, the Asia-Pacific has overtaken Europe in key industries, particularly in manufacturing and consumption. The region's trade volume with the rest of the world now exceeds 50 per cent of total global trade. Even during the COVID-19 pandemic, the global economy experienced major disruptions as strict containment measures in the region led to supply chain breakdowns. The resulting inflationary crisis, although exacerbated by geopolitical tensions in Europe – particularly Russia's military campaign in Ukraine – was primarily triggered by supply chain disruptions, with the Indo-Pacific being the most critical link.

The integration of the Indian Ocean with the Asia-Pacific has created an economic super-region, home to over 50 per cent of the global population, two-thirds of global GDP, and over 60 per cent of world trade (White House 2022). Any negative developments in the region could send global shockwaves, reinforcing its crucial role in international stability. Consequently, ensuring the security of this region has become a matter of global concern, with major powers competing to shape its security architecture. Holding the key to regional security not only safeguards a nation's own interests but also elevates its global standing.

3. United States Response and Countermeasures

US policy responses to China's rise and regional influence

Amid China's rapid ascension, the United States Government has implemented policies aimed at curbing China's growing influence, which has significantly impacted America's regional standing. For years, United States presence has been seen as a crucial factor in maintaining stability and development in the region. Many nations in the Indo-Pacific have welcomed United States commitments, expecting its sustained presence to help preserve their security and prosperity. In response to the shifting landscape, the United States has continued a largely traditional approach – leveraging its existing military presence, strengthening alliances with Japan and South Korea, capitalizing on India's aspirations to become a global power, and deepening engagement with ASEAN countries to counterbalance China's values and mechanisms.

The Obama administration's Pivot to Asia strategy

In 2011, the Obama administration introduced its *Pivot to Asia* foreign policy strategy, making the Asia-Pacific a central focus for rebalancing United States power, containing China's influence, ensuring regional security, and maintaining America's leadership in the Indo-Pacific. Then-Secretary of State Hillary Clinton outlined this policy in an article on *Foreign Policy*, stating:

> "Open markets in Asia present unprecedented opportunities for the United States in terms of investment, trade, and access to advanced technologies... Strategically, maintaining peace and security across the Asia-Pacific is becoming increasingly essential for global progress – whether it's through defending freedom of navigation in the South China Sea, countering nuclear proliferation in North Korea, or ensuring transparency in the military activities of major regional players" (Foreign Policy 2011).

Militarily, the Obama administration restructured US naval deployment, shifting its focus to the Indo-Pacific. The administration increased the presence of US aircraft carrier strike groups in the region to account for 60 per cent of the US Navy's total force.

On a diplomatic and institutional level, the United States reinforced regional frameworks, placing ASEAN at the centre of its policies (East West Center 2024). Washington actively participated in ASEAN-led security dialogues such as the ASEAN Defence Ministers' Meeting-Plus (ADMM+), engaged in forums like the Shangri-La Dialogue, and initiated high-level United States-ASEAN discussions on regional security hotspots, including

South China Sea disputes. Additionally, the United States expanded existing mechanisms, such as the Lower Mekong Initiative (LMI) and the Quadrilateral Security Dialogue (QUAD). It also strengthened alliances with Japan, South Korea, and Australia, while enhancing cooperation with India and Taiwan and supporting Vietnam and the Philippines in South China Sea disputes. Economically, the Obama administration advanced the idea of a new regional free trade area, building upon the P4 group (Brunei, Chile, New Zealand, and Singapore). This led to negotiations for the Trans-Pacific Partnership (TPP), which culminated in a 2016 agreement between the United States and eleven other regional nations – excluding China. TPP was designed as a key instrument to reduce dependence on China in global supply chains.

China's expanding influence and the limits of US containment efforts

Despite these measures, China's regional dominance continued to grow, with no single framework strong enough to counterbalance its expansion. China has bolstered its influence by establishing and leading its own mechanisms and forums, promoting the concept of a *Community of Shared Destiny*, which has been reinforced since its introduction in 2017. As United States influence waned, regional nations recalibrated their foreign policies, increasingly considering China's economic and military strength. The current regional frameworks are largely led by either the United States or China, intensifying the strategic rivalry between the two powers. The diplomatic dilemma in the region is evident – even a major power like India pursues a dual strategy. While India is a founding member of Quad (which aims to contain China), it also remains a key player in BRICS, an organization committed to creating a multipolar world order that reduces reliance on the West and challenges US hegemony.

The Trump administration's escalation of China containment policies

The Trump administration inherited and significantly intensified China-containment policies with aggressive economic and technological measures. In 2018, Trump launched a trade war aimed at undermining China's manufacturing sector. His administration also spearheaded a coordinated effort – including persuading European allies – to counter China's high-tech enterprises, particularly targeting Huawei. Trump implemented strict policies to block Chinese firms from accessing high-tech industries, notably in semiconductors, 5G infrastructure, and advanced manufacturing – sectors critical to global industrial leadership.

The Free and Open Indo-Pacific (FOIP) Strategy

In 2017, Trump introduced the *Free and Open Indo-Pacific* (FOIP) strategy. Although FOIP's framework did not explicitly focus on China, its core objectives were clearly aimed at countering Beijing's initiatives, such as the BRI and China's claims in the South China Sea – particularly the controversial *nine-dash line*. FOIP included direct measures against China's aggressive actions, such as its disregard for international law in territorial disputes and its deployment of an armed coast guard beyond routine law enforcement operations. The Trump administration publicly supported other regional nations' rights to explore and utilize South China Sea resources, reiterated US positions on maritime security in regional forums, and conducted regular freedom of navigation operations (FONOPs) with US destroyers challenging China's illegal claims.

Regional economic integration and US policy under the Trump and Biden administrations

Regarding regional economic integration, the Trump administration's decision to withdraw the United States from the Trans-Pacific Partnership (TPP) was criticized by some economists, as it potentially deprived American businesses of broader market access to the eleven member countries under the agreement's open trade framework. However, this move was deemed effective by the Trump administration, as the Obama administration was believed to have sacrificed the economic interests of US businesses and consumer welfare by granting trade concessions – particularly in intellectual property – to expedite negotiations and curb China's leadership in regional economic integration. Meanwhile, China invested in negotiations to establish the Regional Comprehensive Economic Partnership (RCEP), which deviated from the Asia-Pacific axis and pulled South Asia into China's integration strategy. This approach by the Obama administration was seen as a misallocation of resources and an impractical attempt to counter

China's globalization ambitions. Even after the Democratic Party regained the White House in 2020, the Biden administration did not revive the idea of rejoining the TPP, despite calls from scholars and allied nations advocating for America's return to this trade initiative.

The Biden administration's National Security Strategy explicitly identifies China as "the only competitor with both the intent and capability to reshape the international order" (White House 2021). In response, Biden's administration has introduced clearer policy measures and enforcement tools to counter China's strategic initiatives, maintaining a focus on controlling its rise (South China Sea Studies 2023). In February 2022, the Biden administration unveiled a new Indo-Pacific Strategy, which expands beyond the Trump administration's Free and Open Indo-Pacific (FOIP) framework, which primarily emphasized security and maritime freedom. The new approach integrates economic cooperation and development under the evolving security landscape, potentially garnering greater engagement due to its comprehensive benefits.

Additionally, Biden established new mechanisms to enhance security assurances for US allies, focusing on strengthening deterrence capabilities – particularly against China – by leveraging the military strength of the United Kingdom and Australia through the AUKUS security pact (announced in 2021) and bolstering regional allies like Japan and the Philippines through more localized security arrangements, such as the JAPHUS trilateral alliance (announced in 2023). The United States has also allocated 800 million US dollars to upgrade military infrastructure on Tinian Island in the Northern Mariana Islands, reinforcing defence capabilities against potential Chinese threats. Biden has also successfully brought India and key ASEAN nations into a new economic cooperation framework, the Indo-Pacific Economic Framework for Prosperity (IPEF), launched in May 2022. Although IPEF lacks the extensive trade liberalization measures of the TPP (Japan MOFA 2024), it successfully secured India's participation, a nation historically focused on import-substituting industrialization and reluctant to engage in economic integration beyond its traditional South Asian sphere of influence. This strategy strengthens the US countermeasure against China's Belt and Road Initiative (BRI) by drawing India into an alternative economic framework.

Since World War II, the United States has promoted global trade liberalization. However, in executing the Indo-Pacific Strategy, the United States has shifted toward less trade-liberalized initiatives. India's decision to reject RCEP but join IPEF reflects the success of this approach and underscores

Washington's commitment to the Indo-Pacific strategy. The Biden administration has also proposed a more integrated alliance model, where in the near future, the QUAD security group may be linked with IPEF, replacing the dual security-economic model with a more comprehensive and unified strategy to counter China (China Daily 2022). Another key achievement of Biden's Indo-Pacific strategy is the widespread adoption of its principles and values among allied nations. Countries within the QUAD, ASEAN, and the EU have gradually outlined their own strategic visions for the region. Although these approaches vary – the EU emphasizes maritime security, sustainable development, and economic cooperation in the Indo-Pacific, while ASEAN prioritizes connectivity, regional stability, and economic recovery amid great-power competition – they nonetheless indicate broad recognition of the region's importance.

India, in particular, has pursued rapid economic and trade expansion to protect its national interests, secure maritime freedom, expand its regional influence, and counterbalance China, while also enhancing cooperation in regional security, economic growth, and sustainable development. However, these strategies remain less comprehensive than the US Indo-Pacific vision and reflect the dilemma between supporting United States security objectives and maintaining pragmatic relations with China.

Despite cautious responses, the fact that these countries have articulated Indo-Pacific strategies signals their acknowledgment of the region's geopolitical significance and a measured endorsement of US leadership, driven by realistic concerns about China's growing power. Countries like the Philippines clearly recognize the Indo-Pacific Strategy's importance for their national security and strategic interests. Given that this strategy is a core pillar of US national security, a United States withdrawal from the region remains unlikely. The Philippines and the United States have reaffirmed their alliance and shared regional interests through recent bilateral meetings, reinforcing Washington's continued commitment to Indo-Pacific engagement.

4. Emerging Issues: Prospects and Future Developments

International context and its impact on the Indo-Pacific Strategy

The international landscape is presenting multiple factors that could divert the focus of US policy and its allies from the Indo-Pacific strategy. The ongoing geopolitical crisis in Europe, with the Russia-Ukraine war surpassing three years without an end in sight, has already consumed approximately 300 billion US dollars from the United States and its European allies. In Africa and the Middle East, the recent developments in Syria, where the government of President Bashar al-Assad has been overthrown, have plunged the country into a state of fragmented control by various factions, creating new security chaos. Meanwhile, the conflict between Israel and Iran, along with Iran's proxy forces such as Hamas and Hezbollah in Palestine, has forced the United States to intervene, given the region's crucial role in the international energy market. In South Asia, recent instability in Bangladesh, where the government of Sheikh Hasina has collapsed due to widespread opposition to economic and social policies, could divert India's resources, potentially hindering its efforts to advance its Indo-Pacific strategy. For ASEAN, the ongoing military conflicts between autonomous regions in Myanmar have made it difficult for the organization to fully implement its Indo-Pacific vision.

Global initiatives challenging the Indo-Pacific Strategy

In addition to regional instability, new global initiatives are rapidly being implemented, including the expansion of BRICS and the Regional Comprehensive Economic Partnership (RCEP). These competing economic mechanisms clearly pose challenges to the Indo-Pacific strategy, as their dense agendas can distract many participating countries from US-led initiatives. This distraction is evident, as one of the objectives of these mechanisms is to establish a multilateral international order, thereby reducing US influence in the region and globally. Consequently, the United States is compelled to invest resources and strategies to counter these mechanisms.

China's strategic advantage and the Indo-Pacific Strategy's effectiveness

The Indo-Pacific Strategy was introduced to contain China, but in the geopolitical chess game for global leadership and a multipolar world order, China has made the first move ahead of the United States. Whether the containment strategy succeeds depends on several key factors:

(1) China's Strength and Resistance

Despite facing short-term and long-term economic challenges, including a real estate market crisis and the United States-China trade war, China maintains a dominant role in global supply chains, a massive economic footprint, and extensive international economic ties. This makes containing China extremely difficult. China has retaliated aggressively in the trade war with the United States, imposing reciprocal tariffs on American goods. Additionally, its trillion-dollar global initiatives continue at full pace, signalling its resilience against US containment efforts.

Furthermore, China recognizes the dilemma faced by smaller developing nations in the region. If China pressures them excessively, they may turn to US security guarantees, allowing Washington to expand its presence in the Indo-Pacific. Thus, China may shift from aggressive tactics to a more calculated, incremental approach, similar to its economic reform strategy of *crossing the river by feeling the stones*. If China adopts this strategy, regional uncertainty could persist for at least a decade, as immediate security threats diminish, and the United States finds fewer justifications to expand its military presence in the region.

(2) The Response of Affected Countries

The United States must rebuild trust and economic prosperity in Asia-Pacific to compete with China's influence. China's *Beijing Consensus* – which offers unconditional economic integration – has made its initiatives highly attractive. Meanwhile, many countries still view United States economic commitments as uncertain. The United States currently benefits from 1.75 trillion US dollars in bilateral trade and over 5 million jobs created in the region (White House 2022), but this is insufficient given the region's economic scale and development needs. Expanding the Indo-Pacific Economic Framework (IPEF) is the most viable path forward.

IPEF must provide substantial economic benefits so that economic ties with China become secondary for Indo-Pacific nations. As long as China's economic initiatives continue delivering tangible benefits, US-led containment efforts will remain ineffective. This is because security concerns are not the top priority for many developing nations in the region, where economic growth remains the primary focus.

Trump's second term and the US-China trade war

President Donald Trump has begun his second term by immediately implementing strong executive policies across various sectors, continuing his *America First* agenda. His foreign economic policy prioritizes tariffs, forcing other nations to share trade benefits and international responsibilities, a method that has proven both traditional and effective for Trump.

The US-China trade war, initiated in 2018, has not significantly reduced the US trade deficit with China, nor has it lowered the overall trade volume between the two nations. However, it has pushed China down to third place among the largest exporters to the United States. Within his first month in office, President Trump has resumed the trade war, imposing a 10 per cent tariff on most Chinese exports to the United States. According to The Conference Board, exports to the United States contribute 3 per cent to China's GDP (Vu Huy Hung 2023). A decline in exports to the United States due to tariff barriers could significantly impact China's economy. Beyond trade measures, the United States is also pressuring dependent nations to reduce their engagement in China's Belt and Road Initiative (BRI). Recently, Panama announced its withdrawal from the initiative, marking a notable setback for China's global strategy.

Based on President Trump's actions during his previous term, it is evident that the US administration was not particularly enthusiastic about multilateral cooperation initiatives. Trump withdrew the United States from the Trans-Pacific Partnership (TPP) and several other global organizations, such as the World Health Organization (WHO) and the Paris Agreement on climate change. However, the inherent pragmatism of American policy meant that the Trump administration still maintained and even strengthened certain multilateral mechanisms, such as the security cooperation framework QUAD, which was originally established in 2007 under the initiative of Japanese Prime Minister Shinzo Abe. Additionally, Trump introduced the Free and Open Indo-Pacific (FOIP) strategy, attracting participation from multiple countries. This suggests that in the upcoming Indo-Pacific strategy, the Trump administration will likely continue and even intensify this approach to contain China more effectively. As a result, the Indo-Pacific Economic Framework (IPEF), which currently focuses on areas such as supply chains, clean economy, and fair economy, is likely to be further promoted and refined. Beyond existing agreements on establishing regional business logistics networks, discussions on investment and trade cooperation could be the next step in efforts to shift production systems out of China, disrupt its manufacturing structure, and limit its international economic relations.

In addition to renewing alliances, President Trump has demonstrated a particular interest in influential nations within the Indo-Pacific region. During his previous term, the Trump administration acknowledged India's role as one of the key global powers. At the same time, Japan's national status improved significantly under Trump. Some Southeast Asian nations were also given greater importance by the administration in addressing security hotspots in Northeast Asia. This approach is likely to be maintained and expanded in the coming period. US actions over the past decade indicate a persistent commitment to the Indo-Pacific strategy, focusing on tightening existing containment measures and reinforcing new ones to exert pressure on China's development space from multiple directions. However, China has taken the lead in shaping globalization according to its own vision. Whether the balance of power can be achieved depends not only on the mechanisms established by the United States but also on other conditions in a world full of uncertainties, which challenge America's ability to intervene and maintain the international order it has built.

In reality, China's convincing rise is primarily driven by its economic boom over the past 40 years. Therefore, the ability to counter China will depend on the United States maintaining its economic strength over the next few decades. A strong economy is essential to project power and sustain the necessary investments in military superiority, ensuring security for the United States and its allies while maintaining its leadership role on the global stage. Given the current situation, simply maintaining the existing economic gap with China over the next two decades would already be considered a success for the United States.

5. Implications for Vietnam Regarding the US Indo-Pacific Strategy

The implementation of the US Indo-Pacific Strategy and policy adjustments by relevant countries present both opportunities and challenges for Vietnam. Vietnam plays a significant role in the US Indo-Pacific Strategy due to its strategic geographic location, rising economic potential, and independent foreign policy focused on diversification and multilateralism. Emerging security structures, development opportunities, and concerns over political tensions are crucial implications that Vietnam must consider when engaging in this strategy.

Opportunities

(1) Enhancing Economic, Trade, and Investment Cooperation

As analysed earlier, the United States aims to gather allies and partners in the Indo-Pacific Strategy to counter China. To achieve this, Washington must provide comprehensive security and economic benefits to target countries. The United States considers Vietnam a key partner in counterbalancing China's influence, ensuring maritime security, and restructuring supply chains.

The Indo-Pacific Economic Framework (IPEF) – a core economic pillar of the US Indo-Pacific Strategy – will likely expand both in terms of cooperation areas and membership. Deeper engagement in the IPEF or other economic structures within the Indo-Pacific Strategy could help Vietnam increase trade opportunities, attract investment, and enhance its competitiveness. Additionally, the supply chain shift away from China – one of the US objectives to weaken China's economic growth – is already underway. The United States is actively pursuing China de-risking policies, and Vietnam has emerged as a crucial destination in the new supply chain ecosystem. Many top US CEOs have visited Vietnam to explore investment opportunities. Major corporations such as Apple, Intel, and Google have already relocated part of their production to Vietnam. Furthermore, access to high technology presents a great opportunity for Vietnam to accelerate industrialization. US corporations have supported Vietnam in semiconductors, digital technology, and renewable energy, enhancing its production capacity and attracting high-tech investment. Recently, NVIDIA CEO Jensen Huang visited Vietnam, opening doors for AI and semiconductor industry growth.

Another key global development trend is the energy transition. Vietnam has actively participated in these initiatives, particularly through the Just Energy Transition Partnership (JETP), securing a 15.5 billion US dollars support package for renewable energy development. This initiative will help Vietnam achieve carbon neutrality by 2050.

(2) Strengthening Diplomatic Standing and Maritime Security Balance

United States President Joe Biden's visit to Vietnam and the upgrade of bilateral ties to a Comprehensive Strategic Partnership in September 2023 reaffirm Vietnam's central role in the region and elevate its diplomatic standing. Furthermore, United States-China strategic competition provides Vietnam with greater manoeuvrability in multilateral diplomacy, allowing it to strengthen relations with both nations while maintaining independence. By leveraging its relationships, Vietnam can maximize benefits from both sides without becoming overly dependent on any single power.

The United States prioritizes cooperation with key Indo-Pacific nations, such as Indonesia, the Philippines, and Vietnam, to counterbalance China and uphold a regional order favourable to Washington. In Southeast Asia, the United States has supported maritime security through the Maritime Security Initiative (MSI), enhancing the region's patrol and surveillance capabilities in the South China Sea. In Vietnam, the United States has provided patrol vessels, surveillance radars, and coast guard training to bolster law enforcement capabilities, protect fishermen, and safeguard Vietnam's Exclusive Economic Zone (EEZ).

Challenges and risks to consider

(1) Pressure from China

China perceives the US Indo-Pacific Strategy as a containment effort. If Vietnam deepens its involvement in this strategy, China may escalate pressure through various means.

Military pressure in the South China Sea

- China's advanced naval capabilities and geographic proximity enable it to maintain a long-term military presence and logistical support in the South China Sea.
- If Vietnam aligns more closely with the United States, China may increase military activities in disputed waters.

Economic retaliation

- China is Vietnam's largest trading partner, and it has historically used trade restrictions as a tool of economic pressure.
- Even minor diplomatic disagreements have led China to limit Vietnamese exports in the past.
- Should Vietnam lean too far toward the United States, China may implement stricter economic retaliation, such as controlling imports and investments.

(2) Uncertainty in US policy

The bipartisan political system in the United States has led to unprecedented foreign policy reversals, especially under former President Donald Trump.

- Trump's administration overturned several Democratic-led foreign policies, demonstrating the potential for abrupt shifts.
- If a future United States President reduces commitment to Asia, the Indo-Pacific Strategy could lose momentum, affecting Vietnam's long-term engagement.

Thus, Vietnam must be cautious in balancing its involvement to avoid over-reliance on shifting US policies.

Policy implications for Vietnam

Vietnam pursues a foreign policy of independence and self-reliance. Its engagement in the Indo-Pacific Strategy must maintain balance with other actors in the region, particularly China and ASEAN. To capitalize on the opportunities while avoiding entanglement in major power conflicts, Vietnam should adopt the following approaches:

(1) Maintaining an independent and balanced foreign policy

- Continue the *Four No's* defence policy:
- No military alliances.
- No aligning with one country against another.
- No foreign military bases in Vietnam.
- No using force or threatening to use force.
- Accept US support for maritime security and sovereignty protection but avoid military alliances targeting China.
- Leverage US relations while maintaining stable ties with China and other partners.

(2) Flexible economic engagement

- Participate in the IPEF selectively, focusing on supply chains, digital economy, and clean energy to maximize practical benefits.

- Expand exports to the United States while diversifying markets in China, EU, Japan, and South Korea to avoid overdependence.
- Attract high-tech investments from the United States in semiconductors, AI, and renewable energy.
- Develop renewable energy to reduce dependence on imported energy and meet international green standards.

The US Indo-Pacific Strategy offers Vietnam economic, security, and technological opportunities but also carries risks related to China's response and US policy unpredictability. To navigate this complex landscape, Vietnam must maintain a balanced, multilateral diplomatic approach – leveraging economic benefits without being drawn into United States-China rivalry, while enhancing domestic resilience for sustainable development.

6. Conclusion

The Indo-Pacific strategy has been increasingly implemented by the United States through various approaches aimed at encircling and containing China's growing influence. This strategy has garnered significant attention from many countries due to its promising security and economic benefits. Major powers participate in the strategy to expand their political influence and gain economic and trade advantages, while developing countries engage in search of development opportunities and, to some extent, security assurances against China's assertive actions in certain regions.

In response to the containment efforts orchestrated by the United States through the Indo-Pacific strategy, China has taken both strategic and short-term countermeasures. It has actively promoted the establishment of international mechanisms led by China to secure a stronger global position. China continues to strengthen its bilateral relations in economic and political domains, with some expansion into military cooperation with various countries. Additionally, China has collaborated with other major powers to create cooperation frameworks explicitly aimed at counterbalancing Western-imposed values and institutions. At the same time, China has focused on economic development with a high degree of self-sufficiency, gradually testing its economy's resilience against potential disconnection from the global economy as its power struggle with the United States intensifies.

Whether the US Indo-Pacific strategy will successfully contain China remains an open question, as the evolving execution of the strategy has yet to fully reveal the extent of support on both sides or the next moves that

China and the United States might take. Above all, both countries must prioritize economic growth – not only to outcompete their rival in power but also to mobilize sufficient support to achieve their ambitions. Given the current situation, the Indo-Pacific strategy should be seen as still in its early stages of implementation, with tangible outcomes likely to become apparent only in at least another decade.

7. References

Alperovitch, Dmitri/Graff, Garrett M. (2024): World on the Brink: How America Can Beat China in the Race for the Twenty-First Century. PublicAffairs.

ASEAN Secrectary, ASEAN Outlook on the Indo – Pacific. https://asean.org/wp-content/uploads/2021/01/ASEAN-Outlook-on-the-Indo-acific_FINAL_22062019.pdf.

Blackwill, Robert D./Fontaine, Richard (2024): Lost Decade: The U.S. Pivot to Asia and the Rise of Chinese Power. Oxford University Press.

East West Center (2024): U.S. Indo-Pacific Strategy after one year: Perspectives of Allies, Partners and across the Indo-Pacific. https://www.eastwestcenter.org/sites/default/files/2024-02/U.S.%20Indo-Pacific%20Strategy%20after%20One%20Year%E2%80%94Perspectives%20from%20Allies%2C%20Partners%2C%20and%20across%20the%20Indo-Pacific.pdf.

European Parliamentary Research Service (2023): Geopolitics in the Indo-Pacific: Major players' strategic perspectives. https://www.europarl.europa.eu/RegData/etudes/BRIE/2023/751398/EPRS_BRI(2023)751398_EN.pdf.

Foreign Policy (2011): American Pacific Century. https://foreignpolicy.com/2011/10/11/americas-pacific-century/

Heydarian, Richard Javad (2020): The Indo-Pacific: Trump, China, and the New Struggle for Global Mastery. Springer.

Hoàng Thị Hà (2023): Why Is China's Global Development Initiative Well Received in Southeast Asia? ISEAS. https://www.iseas.edu.sg/wp-content/uploads/2023/01/ISEAS_Perspective_2023_9.pdf.

Japan MOFA (2024): Agreement on the Indo-Pacific Economic Framework for Prosperity. https://www.mofa.go.jp/mofaj/files/100680386.pdf.

Lee, John Cheong Seong (2018): The Free and Open Indo-Pacific and Implications for ASEAN. ISEAS Yusof Ishak Institute.

Medcalf, Rory (2021): Indo-Pacific Empire: China, America and the Contest for the World's Pivotal Region. Manchester University Press.

NATO (2022): Regional Perspectives report on the Indo-Pacific. https://www.act.nato.int/wp-content/uploads/2023/05/regional-perspectives-2022-07-v2-2.pdf.

South China Sea Studies (2023): Overview of the Biden administration's Indo-Pacific policy documents in 2022. https://nghiencuubiendong.vn/tong-quan-cac-van-ban-chinh-sach-ve-an-do-duong-thai-binh-duong-cua-chinh-quyen-biden-nam-2022.56481.anews.

Ran, Jin (2023): The U.S. Indo-Pacific Strategy & The Prospect of Forging A New Multipolar World. Via tolino media.

The White House (2022): Indo-Pacific Strategy of the Unites States. Executive office of the President. https://www.whitehouse.gov/wp-content/uploads/2022/02/U.S.-Indo-Pacific-Strategy.pdf.

The White House (2021): The U.S. National Security Strategy. https://www.whitehouse.gov/wp-content/uploads/2021/03/NSS-1v2.pdf.

Vu Huy Hung (2023): US-China relations and impacts on Vietnam's trade, Ministry of Industry and Trade, Institute for Strategic Studies and Public Policy. https://vioit.org.vn/vn/chien-luoc-chinh-sach/quan-he--my---trung-va--nhung-tac-dong-toi-thuong-mai-viet-nam-5554.4050.html.

Chapter 6: The Evolution of the Indo-Pacific Strategy under President Joe Biden (2022–2024)

Pham Thi Thu Huyen

Since the early the 21st century, as the strategic significance of the Indo-Pacific region has continued to rise, the term Indo-Pacific has emerged, attracting attention and stimulating discussions within academic and strategic circles. The Indo-Pacific strategy was officially proposed and systematically developed under the Trump administration and subsequently inherited and further refined by the Biden administration, becoming the strategic compass guiding the United States' engagement in the Indo-Pacific region. As President Joe Biden's term in office approaches its end, his Indo-Pacific strategy has affirmed the United States' presence in the region. A comprehensive assessment of the implementation of President Joe Biden's Indo-Pacific strategy remains a relatively new area of inquiry and necessitates further research and publication. Therefore, this study focuses on examining the development of the Indo-Pacific strategy during the Biden Administration, emphasising the robust US presence in the Indo-Pacific region from 2022 to 2024. This paper employs event analysis and synthesis methods, along with international research methodologies, to elucidate the development of the Indo-Pacific Strategy under the Biden Administration. The research findings emphasise that the United States has focused on regional partnerships spanning from Northeast Asia and Southeast Asia to South Asia and Oceania, including the Pacific Islands, and has identified policy objectives and action plans tailored to specific regions and countries within the Indo-Pacific.

1. Introduction

The first person to officially use the concept of the Indo-Pacific was the late Japanese Prime Minister Shinzo Abe. In August 2007, Abe called for a broader Asia spanning the Pacific and Indian Oceans – free and prosperous, open and transparent to all nations – in his speech before the Indian Parliament (Cheng Enfu/Li Jing 2024). Although Abe did not explicitly mention the Indo-Pacific concept, he provided the initial inspiration for the United States' Indo-Pacific strategy. On November 10th, 2017, during the Asia-Pacific Economic Cooperation (APEC) Business Leaders' Summit in Vietnam, former US President Donald Trump officially proposed the vision of a free and open Indo-Pacific.

In June 2019, the United States Department of Defense released the Indo-Pacific Strategy Report, beginning with a statement on strategic competition among nations, defined by geopolitical rivalry and the goal of maintaining a free international order. The report demonstrated the United States' foremost concern for security in the Indo-Pacific and affirmed that the United States would achieve its regional objectives through preparedness, partnerships, and the promotion of a connected region. Subsequently, in February 2022, the Biden Administration released the United States Indo-Pacific strategy, emphasizing that the United States would focus on all areas of the region, from Northeast Asia and Southeast Asia to South Asia and Oceania, including the Pacific Islands, and would define policy objectives and action plans for specific regions and countries. The administration also introduced a more narrowly focused Indo-Pacific strategy, emphasising its regional approach (The White House 2022b). The primary objective of the Indo-Pacific strategy affirms the relative importance of the region, emphasising alliances and partnerships, maintaining a region free from coercion and open to trade, investment, and maritime security, while rebuilding the strength of the United States in seeking greater consensus with other countries in its approach to China (United States Studies Center 2022).

As the Biden administration entered its second year, its Indo-Pacific efforts became more pronounced. The content of President Joe Biden's Indo-Pacific strategy focuses on the following key points (U.S Embassy & Consulate in Vietnam 2023):

First, the strategy seeks to advance a free and open Indo-Pacific by investing in democratic institutions, a free press, and a vibrant civil society; strengthening fiscal transparency in the region to expose corruption and drive reform; ensuring that its waters and airspace are governed and utilized according to international law; and promoting common approaches to critical and emerging technologies, the internet, and cyberspace.

Second, the strategy focuses on strengthening connectivity to build collective capacity within and beyond the region by enhancing US treaty alliances with Australia, Japan, South Korea, the Philippines, and Thailand; deepening relations with key regional partners, including India, Indonesia,

Malaysia, Mongolia, New Zealand, Singapore, Taiwan, Vietnam, and Pacific Island nations; contributing to a more cohesive and influential ASEAN; reinforcing Quad and fulfilling its commitments; supporting India's continued rise and leadership role in the region; coordinating efforts to enhance the resilience of Pacific Island nations; fostering connectivity between the Indo-Pacific and the Euro-Atlantic regions; and expanding the diplomatic presence of the United States in the Indo-Pacific, particularly in Southeast Asia and the Pacific Islands.

Third, the strategy aims to promote prosperity in the Indo-Pacific region by proposing an Indo-Pacific economic framework; advancing free, fair, and open trade and investment through the Asia-Pacific Economic Cooperation forum, particularly in 2023 when the United States hosted APEC; and narrowing regional infrastructure gaps through the Build Back Better World Initiative in collaboration with G7 partners.

Fourth, the strategy seeks to enhance security in the Indo-Pacific region by strengthening integrated deterrence; tightening cooperation and enhancing coordination with allies and partners; maintaining peace and stability in the Taiwan Strait; innovating to operate effectively in rapidly evolving threat environments, including space, cyberspace, and critical and emerging technologies; expanding deterrence capabilities and coordination with allies such as South Korea and Japan while pursuing the complete denuclearization of the Korean Peninsula; advancing the objectives of the Australia-United Kingdom-United States security partnership; increasing the presence of the United States Coast Guard vessels and enhancing cooperation against transnational threats; and securing Congressional funding for the Pacific Deterrence Initiative and the Maritime Security Initiative.

Fifth, the strategy aims to strengthen the region's resilience to transnational threats by collaborating with allies and partners to develop goals, strategies, plans, and policies through 2030 and 2050, aligned with the objective of limiting global warming to 1.5 degrees Celsius; reducing the region's vulnerability to the impacts of climate change and environmental degradation; and ending the COVID-19 pandemic while enhancing global health security.

Thus, the Indo-Pacific Strategy during the Biden administration begins by emphasising the region's centrality to the core interests of the United States and the challenges posed by China. However, this strategy differs from that of the Trump administration in at least two notable aspects (United States Institute of Peace 2022). *First*, this strategy places greater emphasis on cooperation with regional allies and partners. *Second*, it highlights plans for the Indo-Pacific Economic Framework, underscoring a new approach to trade that meets high labour and environmental standards. Similar to the administrations of former Presidents George W. Bush, Barack Obama, and Donald Trump, the Biden administration has maintained a strong focus on supporting India's continued rise and reinforcing the United States' leadership role in the Indo-Pacific region.

2. Main Findings

Since the announcement of the Indo-Pacific strategy in February 2022, the United States has made historic progress in advancing a shared vision of an Indo-Pacific region that is free and open, connected, prosperous, secure, and resilient. The United States continues to demonstrate leadership and commitment to the Indo-Pacific, strengthening regional capabilities and resilience to address the challenges and opportunities of the 21st century. The United States Department of State plays a central role in reinforcing the diplomatic architecture and global engagement through the Indo-Pacific strategy. After two years of implementation, the strategy has yielded the following outcomes (Office of the Spokesperson 2024):

First, in advancing a free and open Indo-Pacific, the United States has strengthened global democratic innovation through the Summit for Democracy, as well as through direct and candid dialogues on human rights with China, North Korea, and Myanmar. In 2023, the United States launched multilateral dialogues, including the United States-ASEAN Dialogue on the Rights of Persons with Disabilities in October, the Australia-the United States Strategic Dialogue on Gender Equality in June, the Trilateral United States-Japan-Republic of Korea Meeting on Women's Economic Empowerment in August, and the United States-Japan Dialogue on Transnational Repression.

Furthermore, the United States has addressed humanitarian crises in Myanmar and among the Rohingya population. In Myanmar, over the three years since the military coup, the United States has delivered over 317 million US dollars in humanitarian aid to support the people of Myanmar and allocated 400 million US dollars to promote democracy, human rights, and justice. Additionally, the United States has sanctioned 91 individuals and 50 entities to deprive the military regime of the means to perpetuate violence. Regarding the Rohingya crisis, the United States remains the largest humanitarian assistance contributor, providing nearly 2.4 billion US dollars to support regional response efforts since the escalation of violence in August 2017. The United States assistance has reached nearly one million Rohingya refugees residing in Bangladesh and has contributed to maintaining regional stability (Office of the Spokesperson 2024).

As part of its efforts to promote a free and open Indo-Pacific, the United States remains committed to upholding international maritime law in the South China Sea. In collaboration with Quad partners, the United States launched the Indo-Pacific Partnership for Maritime Domain Awareness, enabling regional partners to better monitor their territorial waters. The United States signed an agreement with Palau to strengthen maritime domain awareness. Through the Southeast Asia Maritime Law Enforcement Initiative, the United States has provided training to over 850 maritime law enforcement officers. Furthermore, the United States has allocated 6.5 million US dollars to South Asia to build capacity in combating illegal fishing, including evidence processing and conducting simulated trials to enhance maritime security capacity and address maritime crimes (Office of the Spokesperson 2024).

Second, in building connections within and beyond the region (The White House 2022a), the United States has strengthened relationships with its allies and partners to an unprecedented level over the past two years. The evolution of US partnerships into flexible groupings and dialogues tailored to strategic objectives has become a crucial tool in diplomatic engagement. The United States has reinforced bilateral relations, strengthened regional structures, and mobilised collective strength with its partners and allies.

Regarding the advancement of bilateral partnerships, the South Pacific has gained additional strategic importance compared to other regions amid the transition from the Asia-Pacific to the Indo-Pacific framework, becoming a critical location for the implementation of the United States' Indo-Pacific strategy. In 2023, the United States expanded its diplomatic presence in the Indo-Pacific, establishing embassies in the Solomon Islands, Tonga, and the Maldives. That same year, the United States recognised the Cook Islands and Niue as sovereign and independent states and established diplomatic relations with them. Meanwhile, the United States appointed a special envoy to the Pacific Islands Forum to facilitate closer coordination on Pacific priorities. In May 2023, the United States committed 7.2 billion US dollars and introduced new programmes for the Pacific Islands region. The United States intends to open an embassy in Vanuatu in 2024 and is actively discussing the establishment of an embassy with the Government of Kiribati. One of the objectives of these measures in the South Pacific

Island nations is to counter the influence of China's 21st Century Maritime Silk Road Initiative. The United States has also fulfilled its commitment to open a USAID Regional Pacific Mission in Fiji and a National Representative Office in Papua New Guinea (The American Presidency Project 2023).

Pacific security has been a hallmark of the Biden administration, highlighted by the 2023 bilateral security agreement with Papua New Guinea and multiple agreements enabling Pacific maritime law enforcement officers to ride aboard US vessels as part of joint maritime security operations.

Additionally, the Biden administration's Indo-Pacific strategy identifies strengthening United States-India cooperation as a key effort. India has consistently welcomed the United States' deep engagement in the region, and this strategy aligns with India's strategic priorities. The strategy considers building on India's continued rise and regional leadership as one of the ten core directions essential for success. The focus on priority areas driven by India, such as its role in the Quad, creates multiple opportunities for cooperation across sectors including health, climate, high technology, and maritime security.

To strengthen the regional architecture and mobilise collective power with partners and allies, the United States reinforces its alliance system and builds partnerships to enhance its position in competition with China. The United States advances its alliances and expands the scope of cooperation; the Quadrilateral Security Dialogue, comprising the United States, Japan, India, and Australia, has been elevated to a summit-level security dialogue mechanism; the trilateral security partnership between Australia, the United Kingdom, and the United States has been established; progress has also been made in trilateral security cooperation among the United States-Japan-South Korea; the United States-Japan-Australia; and the United States-Japan-the Philippines; at the same time, the United States has strengthened bilateral relations with its five allies, including Australia, Japan, South Korea, the Philippines, and Thailand. Meanwhile, the United States continues to deepen its Indo-Pacific partnerships with India, Indonesia, Malaysia, Mongolia, New Zealand, Singapore, Pacific Island nations, and Taiwan (Nguyen Van Duong 2024). As a result, the US-centred multilateral security network has been further strengthened and expanded.

Furthermore, Japan, South Korea, Australia, and other US allies have responded positively to the Indo-Pacific strategy. Although India is not a US ally, the United States has intensified cooperation with India for strategic imperatives, particularly recognising India's role in balancing China, endorsing its regional leadership, and openly affirming that Southern Tibet is part of India. Currently, US-India relations are growing deeper and stronger, with little possibility of reversal. In August 2023, the leaders of the United States, Japan, and South Korea met at Camp David and reached a consensus on strengthening the trilateral consultation mechanism, enhancing security cooperation, promoting regional collaboration, and deepening economic and technological cooperation. The Quad mechanism, comprising the United States, Japan, India, and Australia, was first launched in 2007 but remained largely dormant for nearly a decade. In March 2021, the mechanism was elevated to the summit level. Since then, in-person summits have been held in Washington, D.C. (September 2021), Tokyo (May 2022), and Hiroshima (May 2023). Currently, Quad cooperation primarily focuses on science and technology, economic collaboration, and non-traditional security issues, including strategic technology, supply chain resilience, healthcare, maritime security, and counterterrorism. While officially promoting the provision of public goods for the region, in practice, this cooperation mechanism primarily aims to counter China's influence in the Indo-Pacific.

Regarding ASEAN, the Biden administration has hosted four US-ASEAN summits to better advance its Indo-Pacific strategy. At the US-ASEAN Leaders' Summit in November 2022, President Biden and ASEAN leaders elevated US-ASEAN relations to a Comprehensive Strategic Partnership, marking a significant breakthrough in bilateral cooperation.

Third, in promoting regional prosperity, the United States is also invigorating its partnerships with nations in the Blue Pacific. President Biden hosted summits at the White House in 2022 and 2023 with members of the Pacific Islands Forum, demonstrating the United States' long-term commitment to the region and its intention to uphold the sovereignty of Blue Pacific nations, particularly in the face of climate change and rising sea levels, which endanger low-lying island nations. The White House announced that the United States is investing over 810 million US dollars in expanded programmes to support Pacific Island nations (U.S. Department of State 2024).

Over the past two years, the Department of State and USAID have allocated approximately 4 billion US dollars in foreign assistance to the Indo-Pacific region. Foreign direct investment (FDI) from the United States into the region has nearly doubled over the past decade. In 2023, the United States concluded eight agreements related to the Compacts of Free Association, signed by the Federated States of Micronesia, the Republic of Palau, and the Republic of the Marshall Islands, to enhance economic prosperity and stability, including support for essential sectors such as healthcare, education, and infrastructure.

With the gradual implementation of the US Indo-Pacific strategy, the Regional Comprehensive Economic Partnership, the Comprehensive and Progressive Agreement for Trans-Pacific Partnership, and the Indo-Pacific Economic Framework have become key mechanisms for economic cooperation in the Indo-Pacific. The US Trade Representative is leading negotiations on the trade pillar, while the Secretary of Commerce oversees the remaining pillars. All participating partners have opted to engage in all four pillars of the Indo-Pacific Economic Framework, except for India, which chose not to join the first pillar. In November 2023, the Indo-Pacific Economic Framework partners signed the Pillar II Supply Chain Agreement and concluded negotiations on the Clean Economy Agreement and the Fair Economy Agreement.

*Fourth, regarding enhancing regional stability and resilience against 21st-century transnational threat*s, the United States continues to invest in regional security through advancements in force posture and expanded multinational military operations in the Indo-Pacific. This includes the announcement of four new Enhanced Defense Cooperation Sites in strategically significant areas of the Philippines to strengthen coordination in addressing Indo-Pacific challenges, including natural disasters and humanitarian crises. Additionally, the US collaborates with allies and partners in joint exercises such as the first-ever US-EU joint naval exercise off the coast of Oman, as well as RIMPAC (Rim of the Pacific), Cobra Gold, Super Garuda Shield, and Malabar.

The United States has also conducted cybersecurity dialogues with ASEAN, Japan, South Korea, and India, while continuing to provide cybersecurity policy training for ASEAN member states in collaboration with Singapore. it has supported strategic planning for Thailand's National Cybersecurity Agency through the Digital Connectivity and Cybersecurity Partnership. At the same time, the United States has worked closely with the governments of Timor-Leste, India, and the Philippines to enhance cybersecurity resilience.

Through the Quad Counterterrorism Working Group, Quad partners share best practices and expertise and coordinate counterterrorism policies. Together with its Quad partners, the United States has funded, produced, and distributed nearly 400 million doses of COVID-19 vaccines across the region and launched the Quad Health Security Partnership in 2023. In collaboration with APEC partners, the United States convened the first

Sustainable Future Forum to develop public-private solutions and address environmental challenges, laying the groundwork for the launch of the APEC Coastal Resilience Framework in 2024 to help coastal communities enhance adaptive capacity.

3. Limitations

The strategy lacks clear prioritisation between economic engagement, military deterrence, and normative leadership (The 2022 Indo-Pacific Strategy document offers broad aspirations, but scholars argue it reads more like a declaratory policy than a coherent strategy with actionable steps). In its Indo-Pacific strategy, the Biden administration aimed to rebuild US global leadership and strengthen national power, both of which had been weakened during the Trump administration. As a result, the areas of cooperation in the strategy appear more focused on building stronger alliances and partnerships with countries in the region than on a single, clear strategic priority.

The economic pillar remains weak: The US Indo-Pacific Economic Framework for Prosperity (IPEF) lacks market access provisions, making it unattractive to regional partners seeking tangible trade benefits. Some countries view the IPEF as symbolic. The Biden administration designed the IPEF as a flexible agreement, allowing partner countries to participate in any of its four pillars without being required to commit to all of them. This has raised questions about the framework's ability to secure concessions from partners, as well as the overall sustainability of the framework itself. This approach has deliberately avoided tariff liberalisation or enhanced market access. As a result, the framework does not constitute a traditional free trade agreement. It remains unclear which countries in the Indo-Pacific region will *endorse* the individual pillars of the framework, particularly since India has only joined as an observer. Therefore, the IPEF has yielded limited and uncertain outcomes in the Indo-Pacific region.

Regional actors – especially within ASEAN – are wary that the strategy implicitly aims to contain China, which could polarise the region. ASEAN is concerned about being sidelined or forced to choose sides. Given that China continues to play a central role in the Indo-Pacific region and seeks to strengthen cooperation with like-minded countries, the United States has not backed down from competing with China over strategic interests. In line with President Joe Biden's Indo-Pacific strategy, the United States supports a rules-based order in the region and rallies allies and partners – not only by reassuring them of US interests in the Indo-Pacific but also by openly expressing support for the national interests of countries confronting China.

As strategic competition between China and the United States intensifies across the Asia-Pacific, countries in the region are compelled to pursue independent foreign policies to navigate an increasingly challenging and contested environment. The long-term and multifaceted nature of US-China competition is expected to lead to regional divisions and strategic considerations in managing cooperation with countries across the Asia-Pacific.

4. Summary

Achievements of the Indo-Pacific strategy during the Biden administration

The Indo-Pacific strategy places US allies and partners at the forefront of its efforts in the Indo-Pacific region. Although this focus is not new, it has been incorporated into a more comprehensive strategic vision for the region, addressing challenges and objectives with greater clarity in US Indo-Pacific policy. This approach provides enhanced clarity to the US policy community abroad, while building collective capacity in a new geopolitical era. It also encourages the development of strategic relationships among US allies and partners in the Asia-Pacific region and Europe, particularly through initiatives such as the Quad, where the United States is a direct actor.

Specifically, the Indo-Pacific strategy emphasises the strategic importance of India. This is reflected in high-level bilateral meetings between India and Quad members, as well as regular engagements between the United States and India across multiple domains, including defence, technology, and drone procurement.

The bilateral and multilateral commitments within the strategy have enabled the United States to collaborate on key regional areas, such as climate resilience, public health, and data sharing, to help nations safeguard their economic interests. Therefore, countries see the shared benefits of partnering with the United States, contributing to the development of a more free and open vision.

Challenges in the implementation of the Indo-Pacific strategy (2022–2024)

First, potential security developments in the Indo-Pacific

Currently, competition among major powers in the region is intensifying, regional flashpoints are evolving in complexity, non-traditional security threats are escalating, security dilemmas are deepening, and the risk of conflict is rising. With the implementation of the US Indo-Pacific strategy, major powers increased their defence budgets. For Fiscal Year 2024, the official US defence budget was 886 billion US dollars, accounting for approximately 40 per cent of global military spending. This marked an increase of 28.1 billion US dollars compared to the 857.9 billion allocated in Fiscal Year 2023, reflecting a real growth rate of about 3.3 per cent. Additionally, the 2024 defence budget allocated 15.3 billion US dollars to the US Indo-Pacific Command – surpassing the budgets of other combatant commands and representing a nearly 4 billion US dollars increase from the previous fiscal year, a rise of over 26 per cent (Kieu Oanh 2024).

Besides, the Biden administration's commitments in the Asia-Pacific region have faced obstacles in securing funding for policy implementation in the region. The Compacts of Free Association agreements with the Republic of the Marshall Islands, the Republic of Palau, and the Federated States of Micronesia have been in place since the 1980s and 1990s, allowing the US military to maintain strategic ties with these nations in exchange for financial assistance and the right for their citizens to work in the United States. These agreements expired in 2023, but their renewal has been delayed as funding priorities have shifted toward conflicts in Ukraine, Israel, and Taiwan. Clearly, the ongoing wars in Ukraine and Gaza have strained US aid budgets, affecting the allocation of resources for the Biden administration's focus on the Asia-Pacific (Maguire 2024).

Overall, security mechanisms in the Indo-Pacific demonstrate inefficiencies in governance. Existing regional security organizations and mechanisms include the US-led Indo-Pacific Alliance, the ASEAN Regional Forum led by ASEAN, the Shanghai Cooperation Organisation, and several loosely structured dialogue platforms, such as the Shangri-La Dialogue and the Beijing Xiangshan Forum. However, a lack of mutual political trust among regional countries has led to competition between multiple security organisations and mechanisms, even resulting in an overload of overlapping mechanisms. Compared to the rapid progress in regional economic integration, there is a notable gap in security governance, as existing security frameworks remain insufficient to meet the region's actual security governance needs.

Second, economic development prospects in the Indo-Pacific

Unlike the Regional Comprehensive Economic Partnership and the Comprehensive and Progressive Agreement for Trans-Pacific Partnership, the Indo-Pacific Economic Framework is not a trade agreement but rather an initiative of the US executive branch aimed at negotiating standards and regulations in the Indo-Pacific, lacking key trade elements such as tariff concessions and market access. The Indo-Pacific Economic Framework seeks to expand US economic presence in the Indo-Pacific while aligning with US trade protectionism, which contradicts the priorities of regional nations that aim to enhance economic cooperation and achieve post-pandemic recovery. Meanwhile, the Indo-Pacific Economic Framework has not been approved by the United States Congress and is solely promoted through presidential executive orders, making it legally non-binding and susceptible to shifts in US political leadership. Should the United States government attempt to expand and institutionalise economic standards within the current framework, it is likely to face constraints due to US electoral and partisan politics. These factors raise concerns among participating nations regarding the sustainability, reliability, limitations, and potential benefits of the Indo-Pacific Economic Framework.

Third, the United States' containment strategy against China

As global powers, the strategic competition between China and the United States is undoubtedly a long-term, complex, and challenging endeavour, with the possibility of a prolonged and tense stalemate. The United States has advanced an integrated deterrence strategy against China across multiple fronts. It has accelerated the Pacific Deterrence Initiative (PDI) to enhance war preparedness and achieve comprehensive readiness for potential conflicts by strengthening US military defence capabilities in the Indo-Pacific and reinforcing regional partnerships. The United States has launched the Indo-Pacific Partnership for Maritime Domain Awareness, aimed at enhancing surveillance across the Indo-Pacific maritime domains. The United States has promoted NATO's involvement in Asia-Pacific affairs to construct an Asia-Pacific NATO equivalent. The United States has coordinated military exercises with allies and partners to enhance strategic military coordination in the region. The United States continues to escalate tensions in the Indo-Pacific in an effort to establish a comprehensive containment strategy against China, significantly undermining regional stability. While Biden's approach has provided a degree of stability in United States-China bilateral relations, his strategic competition framework has been economically and diplomatically effective, destabilising China's high-tech industry and diplomatic outreach. However, with Donald Trump winning the 2024 presidential election, his unpredictability and maximum pressure tactics will likely place China in an extremely difficult position in the region. As the US Indo-Pacific strategy progresses, major forces in the Indo-Pacific are undergoing political fragmentation and realignment, forcing regional nations into a dilemma of choosing sides. ASEAN member states are divided and influenced by the United States and its allies, further weakening ASEAN's centrality. Meanwhile, South Pacific nations are likely to align with either China or the United States based on their national interests.

Impact of the Indo-Pacific strategy under President Joe Biden on Vietnam:

Vietnam, as a nation in the Asia-Pacific region, has consistently expressed its interest in a rules-based regional order and has strengthened diplomatic, economic, and defence relations with the United States. Vietnam welcomes regional initiatives and joint efforts that contribute to regional peace and security, aiming to resolve South China Sea disputes through peaceful means (Trinh Viet Dung/Do Huy Hai 2024).

President Joe Biden has identified Vietnam as one of the key regional partners to strengthen ties in pursuit of a free and open Indo-Pacific Strategy.

In September 2023, the United States and Vietnam officially upgraded their relationship to a Comprehensive Strategic Partnership, deepening political and diplomatic relations, enhancing trade and investment cooperation, and strengthening defence ties.

In the economic sector, a key component of President Joe Biden's Indo-Pacific Economic Framework is its focus on the digital economy. The United States can collaborate with Vietnam to accelerate Vietnam's digital transformation and support its rapidly growing digital economy. This includes building secure digital infrastructure and developing rules and regulations to govern cross-border data flows. Vietnam's digital economy has been expanding rapidly. In 2011, only 35 per cent of Vietnam's population used the internet, but by 2020, this figure doubled to 70 per cent. A report projected that Vietnam's total gross merchandise value would reach 21 billion US dollars by 2021, when all sectors experienced growth (Tran Bich 2022).

Currently, during his second term, President Donald Trump has enforced tariff policies on various goods worldwide, imposing different tariff rates across multiple countries. Vietnam is not exempt from the impact of this policy implemented by the United States.

However, Vietnam's exports to the United States currently account for approximately 30 per cent of its total export value, making Vietnam particularly susceptible to shifts in United States trade policy (Nguyen Son 2025). Another major risk is the rising cost of raw materials resulting from disruptions in global supply chains, which could drive up production costs and diminish export competitiveness. Vietnam aims to maintain and strengthen a balanced, sustainable, and mutually beneficial economic and trade relationship with the United States. Accordingly, Vietnam asserts that it has no policies that would undermine the interests of American workers or jeopardise the national security of the United States.

Vietnam and the United States have mutually complementary economies. The trade imbalance between the two countries stems from their complementary economic structures, shaped by their export compositions and foreign trade patterns, rather than any other factors. Vietnamese exports to the United States primarily compete with third-country suppliers rather than directly competing with businesses based in the United States. Conversely, Vietnamese goods enhance market accessibility by providing American consumers with more affordable products.

Vietnam is an open economy, and as part of its global integration efforts, it pursues a free trade policy, with only a marginal tariff differential on imports from the United States. In the future, these tariff rates may continue to decline, as Vietnam remains committed to reducing tariffs on goods from World Trade Organization member countries across various sectors. As a result, certain highly competitive exports from the United States, such as automobiles, agricultural products, liquefied natural gas and ethanol, will benefit from this policy, while also stimulating positive import flows from the United States and contributing to an improved trade balance between the two nations.

Vietnam will facilitate the participation of investors from the United States in the formation and development of key industries within the country, particularly in strategic energy projects such as renewable energy, hydrogen and nuclear power. This will lay the groundwork for expanding imports of liquefied natural gas, fuel, machinery and technology from the

United States, thereby contributing to an improved trade balance between the two nations (Hương Giang 2025).

Currently, the two nations have established a policy dialogue mechanism under the Vietnam-United States Trade and Investment Framework Agreement. Therefore, any outstanding bilateral economic and trade issues, if they arise, will be proactively addressed through the Vietnam-United States Trade and Investment Council.

Under the impact of President Donald Trump's tariff policies in early 2025, US companies are actively seeking alternative suppliers, and Vietnam's strong manufacturing sector, particularly in electronics, textiles, footwear and furniture, positions Vietnam as a leading contender. Vietnam's trade agreements and cost-effective production capacity provide a competitive advantage in securing long-term contracts with US importers. To fully leverage these opportunities, Vietnamese enterprises must adhere to trade regulations of the United States, ensure transparency in product origin, and meet established quality standards. Investments in brand development, research and innovation, and advanced manufacturing technologies will further enhance Vietnam's competitiveness (Nguyen Son 2025).

Regarding traditional security cooperation, amid tensions over territorial disputes in the South China Sea, the United States has assisted Vietnam in improving its maritime law enforcement capabilities, including the transfer of patrol vessels to the Vietnam Coast Guard. Vietnam is one of seven countries to which the United States provides support and training under the Indo-Pacific Maritime Security Initiative. This initiative remains in effect until December 2025 and aims to strengthen maritime security and enhance maritime domain awareness for foreign nations along the South China Sea and South Asia.

Regarding energy security, Vietnam's economic growth has significantly increased its demand for electricity. Through the Vietnam Low Emission Energy Programme, the US Agency for International Development has allocated 36.25 million US dollars from 2020 to 2025 to support Vietnam's transition to a clean, secure, and market-oriented energy sector. This includes expanding the deployment of advanced energy systems, improving energy sector efficiency, promoting competition, and fostering innovation and inclusivity. From 2019 to 2023, the Vietnam Urban Energy Security Project, funded by the US Agency for International Development with 14 million US dollars, collaborated with big cities in Vietnam to improve policies and regulations, mobilise public and private investment, and promote the adoption of innovative solutions.

In the health sector, during the fight against COVID-19, the United States donated over 24 million vaccine doses, and the US Agency for International Development provided 23.06 million US dollars in aid to Vietnam. Additionally, the US Agency for International Development implemented several projects to enhance Vietnam's capacity to prevent, detect, assess and respond to public health emergencies. These projects include Risk Mitigation and Management of Human Health Threats, One Health Workforce, and Infectious Diseases Detection and Surveillance. Notably, the Southeast Asia Regional Office of the US Centers for Disease Control and Prevention was established in Hanoi, elevating Vietnam's role as a regional health hub.

Regarding cooperation on education, the United States has aimed to strengthen relations with countries in the Indo-Pacific region. Through the Young Southeast Asian Leaders Initiative, the United States has provided scholarships, workshops, and grants to young leaders, fostering leadership development and networking opportunities in the region. The US Agency for International Development is supporting Vietnam in modernising its higher education system by improving academic quality and enhancing institutional governance. Additionally, the Partnership for Higher Education Reform is a five-year initiative running from 2021 to 2026, supporting Vietnam's three largest universities in policy advocacy, higher education reform, technology and digitalization, as well as gender empowerment for success and long-term sustainable development.

5. Conclusion

An examination of President Joe Biden's Indo-Pacific Strategy reveals its success in consolidating alliances in the region, restoring United States credibility and influence abroad, and rebuilding alliances that were strained during the Trump administration. President Joe Biden has not only built upon the strengths of the Trump administration's Indo-Pacific strategy but also addressed its evident shortcomings. Although the two administrations have adopted different strategic approaches, President Biden has sought to strengthen cooperation with countries across the Indo-Pacific region.

Although Donald Trump and President Joe Biden disagree on most issues, they share a common strategic interest in the Indo-Pacific region. The Indo-Pacific is of critical importance to the United States, and although Donald Trump has returned to office as the 47th President, he is unlikely to significantly alter the existing framework that supports US relations with the region. During his first term, in 2019, Trump and his administration introduced the Indo-Pacific Strategy, which aimed to maintain a free and open region primarily through strengthening alliances and partnerships. When the Biden administration took office in 2021, it reinforced its predecessor's approach by addressing setbacks from the Trump administration and substantially upgrading alliances and partnerships across all dimensions to support strategic competition with Beijing. While Donald Trump is known for his unpredictable leadership style, including alternating between praise and threats toward traditional US allies, his administration not only maintained but also strengthened these alliances.

Overall, both the Trump and Biden administrations strengthened or at least prevented the deterioration of alliances between Indo-Pacific nations and the United States. Indeed, US alliance engagement has been particularly robust in recent years, and it will be difficult to undermine, regardless of future administrations' decisions in the Indo-Pacific. If threats from China and North Korea continue to escalate, allies will likely continue to seek US support, regardless of the specific policy choices of a future Trump administration.

6. References

Al Jazzeera (2025): What tariffs are China imposing on the US. https://www.aljazeera.com/economy/2025/2/4/what-tariffs-is-china-imposing-on-the-us-and-why-are-they-significant.

Bond, David E. (et al.) (2025): President Trump Imposes 25%Tariff on Canada and Mexico, and 10% Tariffs on China. https://www.whitecase.com/insight-alert/president-trump-imposes-25-tariffs-canada-and-mexico-and-10-tariffs-china.

Cheng Enfu/Li Jing (2024): Changes in U.S. Grand Strategy in the Indo-Pacific and China's Countermeasures. https://monthlyreview.org/2024/07/01/changes-in-u-s-grand-strategy-in-the-indo-pacific-and-chinas-countermeasures/.

China Briefing (2025): US-China Relations in the Trump 2.0 Era: A Timeline. https://www.china-briefing.com/news/us-china-relations-in-the-trump-2-0-implications/.

Đại sứ quán và Tổng lãnh sự quán Hoa Kỳ tại Việt Nam (2023): Chiến lược Ấn Độ Dương – Thái Bình Dương của Hoa Kỳ (The United States' Indo-Pacific strategy). https://vn.usembassy.gov/vi/trang-thong-tin-chien-luoc-an-do-duong-thai-binh-duong-cua-hoa-ky/.

Doan Hung/ Le Anh (2023): Mỹ cam kết đẩy mạnh hợp tác với các quốc đảo Thái Bình Dương (The United States' Commitment to Strengthening Cooperation with Pacific Island Countries). https://www.vietnamplus.vn/my-cam-ket-day-manh-hop-tac-voi-cac-quoc-dao-thai-binh-duong-post89659 5.vnp.

Hoai Thu (2022): Mỹ công bố chiến lược Ấn Độ Dương- Thái Bình Dương mới, Việt Nam là đối tác hàng đầu khu vực (The United States Unveils New Indo-Pacific strategy, Identifies Vietnam as a Leading Regional Partner). https://vneconomy.vn/my-cong-bo-chien-luoc-an-do-duong-thai-binh-duong-moi-viet-nam-la-doi-tac-hang-dau-khu-vuc.htm.

Hương Giang (2025): Chính sách áp thuế của Tổng thống Donald Trump tác động thế nào đối với Việt Nam (The Impact of President Donald Trump's Tariff Policy on Vietnam). https://thanhtra.com.vn/tai-chinh-701717FFD/chinh-sach-ap-thue-cua-tong-thong-donald-trump-tac-dong-the-nao-voi-viet-nam-1cdf2271b.html.

Kieu Oanh (2024): Soi chi tiêu quốc phòng gần 900 USD của Mỹ (A closer look at the United States' Nearly $900 Billion Defence Budget). https://vietnamnet.vn/soi-chi-tieu-quoc-phong-gan-900-ty-usd-cua-my-2287203.html#:~:text=N%C4%83m%202024%2C%20g%C3%B3i%20chi%20ti%C3%AAu,t%E1%BB%A5c%20t%C4%83ng%20trong%20n%C4%83m%202025.

Maguire, I. (2024): Looking back Biden Administration's pacific strategy. https://www.lowyinstitute.org/the-interpreter/looking-back-biden-administration-s-pacific-strategy.

Nguyen Son (2025): Navigating US-China trade war shift, risks and gains. https://www.rmit.edu.vn/news/all-news/2025/feb/navigating-us-china-trade-war-shifts-risks-and-gains.

Nguyen Van Duong (2024): Chính sách đối ngoại của Mỹ tại khu vực Ấn Độ Dương–Thái Bình Dương dưới thời Tổng thống Joe Biden (The United States' Foreign Policy in the Indo-Pacific under President Joe Biden). https://lyluanchinhtri.vn/chinh-sach-doi-ngoai-cua-my-o-khu-vuc-an-do-duong-thai-binh-duong-duoi-thoi-tong-thong-joe-biden-5548.html.

Office of the Spokesperson (2024): The United States's enduring commitment to the Indo-Pacific: marking two years since the release of the administration's Indo-Pacific strategy. U.S. Department of State. 3.

The American Presidency Project (2023): Fact Sheet: Enhancing the U.S.-Pacific Islands Partnership. https://www.presidency.ucsb.edu/documents/fact-sheet-enhancing-the-us-pacific-islands-partnership.

The White House (2022a): Pacific Partnership Strategy of the United States. Washington D.C, 3-16.

The White House (2022b): Indo- Pacific Strategy of the United States. Washington D.C Public.

The White House (2025): Fact Sheet: President Donald Trump Imposes Tariffs on Imports from Canada, Mexico and China. https://www.whitehouse.gov/fact-sheets/2025/02/fact-sheet-president-donald-j-trump-imposes-tariffs-on-imports-from-canada-mexico-and-china/.

Tran Bich (2022): US- Vietnam Cooperation under Biden Indo Pacific strategy. https://www.csis.org/analysis/us-vietnam-cooperation-under-bidens-indo-pacific-strategy.

Tran Van Dung/Do Huy Hai (2024): Vietnam Balances between the Indo Pacific Powers. https://eastasiaforum.org/2024/02/23/vietnam-balances-between-the-indo-pacific-powers/.

U.S. Department of State (2024): The United States' Enduring Commitment to the Indo-Pacific: Making Two Years Since the Release of the Administration's Indo-Pacific Strategy. https://2021-2025.state.gov/the-united-states-enduring-commitment-to-the-indo-pacific-marking-two-years-since-the-release-of-the-administrations-indo-pacific-strategy/.

United State Studies Center (2022): What to expect from the Biden administration's Indo-Pacific strategy. https://www.ussc.edu.au/what-to-expect-from-the-biden-administrations-indo-pacific-strategy.

United States Institute of Peace (2022): A closer look at Biden's Indo-Pacific Strategy. https://www.usip.org/publications/2022/03/closer-look-bidens-indo-pacific-strategy.

York, Erica (2025): Trump Tariffs: Tracking the Economic Impact of the Trump Trade War. https://taxfoundation.org/research/all/federal/trump-tariffs-trade-war/.

Chapter 7: The European Union's Connectivity Strategy for the Indo-Pacific Region and Its Implications for Vietnam

Bui Hong Hanh

The European Union (EU) officially announced its strategy for the Indo-Pacific region in April 2021, in the context of major international actors increasingly focusing on this region. This strategy covers a wide range of issues, with the *connectivity* strategy being a particularly distinctive and characteristic aspect of the EU.

From the perspective of a country within the Indo-Pacific region, an objective study of the EU's connectivity strategy is essential. This chapter outlines three key research objectives:

- To provide an overall analysis of connectivity strategies in general and examine notable connectivity initiatives by major actors in the Indo-Pacific region.
- To summarize the core content and implementation of the EU's Connectivity Strategy in this region from 2021 to 2024.
- To draw conclusions about the EU's Connectivity Strategy in the region and its implications for Vietnam.

1. Introduction

Connectivity is a term originally used in information technology and the field of Internet connections. However, now it has been widely applied in the realms of politics and international relations, especially after efforts to establish connections between the continents of Asia and Europe in the 1990s. In July 1994, the European Commission announced *Towards a New Asia Strategy,* and shortly after, with rapid movements from both sides, the Asia-Europe Meeting (ASEM) was officially established in 1996, serving as a vivid proof for the relevance of connectivity. Building upon this foundation, in September 2018, the European Union (EU) issued a statement called *Connecting Europe and Asia – Building Blocks for an EU Strategy,* commonly known as the *EU Connectivity Strategy.* The EU commitments were to create favourable conditions for connectivity development extending from Europe to Asia. Since then, *connectivity* has become a common keyword in EU policy planning. It is also considered an essential part of the EU's strategy for the Indo-Pacific region, which was announced in April 2021.

There have been quite a few studies on the EU's Asia-Europe connectivity strategy. However, the EU's Connectivity Strategy with the Indo-Pacific region is still quite new, so there are not many studies focusing on this issue. Some examples include *EU Connectivity Strategy: Putting Words into Action* by Manuel Widman (2021), or *European Norm Trap? EU Connectivity Policy and the Case of the Global Gateway* by Tyyne Karjalainen (2023). However, these updated studies mainly focus on policy analysis and advisory proposals to the EU in implementing this Connectivity Strategy from the perspective of EU researchers.

This represents a gap when objectively assessing the EU's Connectivity Strategy for the Indo-Pacific from the perspective of a non-EU country. For a nation within the Indo-Pacific region, understanding the essence of the strategy is crucial in evaluating the feasibility and commitment of the EU to the region. By comparing it with other initiatives, it is possible to identify the advantages and limitations of the EU's approach, thereby recognizing opportunities for countries like Vietnam. Understanding the motivation behind the strategy is essential in determining whether it is a sustainable long-term initiative or merely symbolic. Additionally, it is necessary to identify the key sectors where the EU prioritizes investment and its actual capacity for cooperation. This will help develop a flexible and pragmatic collaboration strategy, avoiding excessive dependence on a single partner or passively reacting to opportunities from the EU. In other words, the research aims to provide recommendations for Vietnam to maximize the benefits of EU resources while safeguarding its national interests in the long run.

On this basis, this study employs key research methods such as policy analysis, case studies, and forecasting methods to further clarify the defined research tasks.

2. The Essence of the Connectivity Strategy

The concept of connectivity

This is a relatively new concept as a term used in international relations or political science. Although many scholars have been discussing this concept recently, there is still no official definition of connectivity. Amid various distinct geographical factors, cultural heritage, market mechanisms, political systems, and international relations practices, this concept has driven efforts towards comprehensive systematisation (Sommerer/Tallberg 2019, 399–433). In 2017, ASEM reached a consensus on the definition of connectivity. Accordingly, connectivity generally means bringing together countries, people, and societies. The concept includes hard connectivity (infrastructure projects) and soft connectivity (human-to-human or digital connections), encompassing all types of connections: land, sea, air, internet, and educational connections, as well as customs cooperation, facilitating a favourable environment for trade. ASEM also agreed that connectivity should adhere to international standards based on transparency, sustainability, and quality standards, such as implementing the Sustainable Development Goals (ASEM 2017). Building on this perspective, Ries defined "connectivity as all the methods in which countries, organisations, and societies are linked and interact globally," including material flows, information flows, hard infrastructure, soft governance measures, or socio-cultural links (Ries 2019).

On the other hand, Stec and Jakóbowski view connectivity as a way to shape "globalisation flows through strategic investments in infrastructure." (Stec/Jakóbowski 2020) Some scholars even elevate connectivity to a historical idea, like freedom or capitalism, as a concept that has evolved and transformed over time, driving contemporary changes. Therefore, connectivity is not just a tool but an impetus (Stec/Jakóbowski 2020). In the article *Connectivity and Order: An Analytical Framework*, the authors present a conceptual framework for connectivity dividing it into six areas: infrastructure, economy, institutional framework, knowledge exchange, socio-cultural exchange, and security. Their argument about connectivity also covers six issues: cooperation, replication, cushioning, disputes, prevention, and coercion (Gaens/Sinkkonen/Vogt 2023). For the EU, connectivity primarily involves networks that bring people, places, and opportunities closer together, with a particular focus on transportation, energy, digital connections, and human-to-human interactions (European Commission 2018).

In conclusion, connectivity is a multi-layered concept, combining cooperative aspects with competitive geopolitical factors and significant opportunities and challenges. Thus, *connectivity* is a multi-layered concept that encompasses aspects of cooperation, geopolitical competition, as well as significant opportunities and challenges. This study adopts a comprehensive definition of *connectivity*

> as the ability to establish linkages between actors in international relations (nations, regions, and international organisations) through various elements such as transportation infrastructure, energy, digital technology, trade, people, and institutions. Connectivity facilitates economic, cultural, and security cooperation among stakeholders.

The concept of connectivity can be roughly divided into five main areas:

1. *Infrastructure connectivity*: Includes transportation (roads, railways, seaports, aviation), energy (electric grids, gas pipelines), and telecommunications (5G networks, fibre optics).
2. *Economic connectivity*: Covers free trade agreements, global supply chains, and logistics.
3. *Digital connectivity*: Encompasses digital transformation, artificial intelligence (AI), and cross-border data flows.
4. *People-to-people connectivity*: Includes educational exchanges, labour migration, and research collaboration.
5. *Institutional connectivity*: Involves bilateral and multilateral agreements, as well as international cooperation mechanisms.

Connectivity strategy

Based on the concept and essence of connectivity, it can be affirmed that a connectivity strategy is a long-term plan aimed at enhancing infrastructure, economic, and institutional linkages between nations or regions to serve economic, political, and security development goals. Each actor in international relations may adopt a distinct approach to a connectivity strategy, depending on their interests and objectives.

Some notable examples of connectivity strategies

(a) The U.S. Connectivity Strategy

The Build Back Better World (B3W) initiative was officially announced in June 2021 at the G7 Summit, spearheaded by U.S. President Joe Biden. It was designed as a global infrastructure investment initiative, particularly targeting low- and middle-income countries. By June 2022, the B3W strategy was gradually replaced by the Partnership for Global Infrastructure and

Investment (PGII), which expanded its scope and involved more partners for the 2022–2027 period. PGII focuses on four key areas: Clean energy infrastructure; Digital technology infrastructure; Healthcare and health security; and Transportation and logistics infrastructure. The main goal of PGII is to counterbalance China's Belt and Road Initiative (BRI) by promoting sustainable development, helping partner countries upgrade their infrastructure without relying on non-transparent funding sources, and strengthening the role of the U.S. and G7 in strategic regions such as the Indo-Pacific, Africa, and Latin America. Thus, PGII can be seen as a crucial part of the geopolitical strategy of the U.S. and G7, aiming to reshape the global economic order through high-quality infrastructure investments.

(b) China's Connectivity Strategy

The Belt and Road Initiative (BRI) was announced by President Xi Jinping in 2013. It is a large-scale strategy aimed at enhancing infrastructure, trade, and investment connectivity between China and other regions worldwide. BRI consists of two main components: The Silk Road Economic Belt – linking China with Central Asia, Europe, and the Middle East through a network of roads and railways; and the 21st Century Maritime Silk Road – connecting China with Southeast Asia, South Asia, Africa, and Europe via maritime trade routes. BRI focuses on five key areas of connectivity: Infrastructure connectivity; Economic connectivity; Financial connectivity; Digital connectivity; People-to-people and Institutional connectivity. The primary goal of BRI is to expand China's economic influence by investing in global infrastructure and trade, driving economic growth, enhancing regional connectivity, and strengthening China's geopolitical position. Through the BRI, China's connectivity strategy has become one of the most ambitious and largest global connectivity programs, intensifying competition over global infrastructure and economic influence.

(c) Japan's Connectivity Strategy

Japan's Indo-Pacific Connectivity Strategy is part of its broader vision for a *Free and Open Indo-Pacific* (FOIP), first introduced by Prime Minister Shinzo Abe in 2016. This strategy focuses on three key pillars: Promoting high-quality infrastructure connectivity; Enhancing trade and economic linkages; Maintaining regional peace and stability. The strategy aims to counterbalance China's growing influence in the region while fostering economic, trade, and infrastructure cooperation in a transparent and sustainable manner.

(d) ASEAN's Connectivity Strategy

The Master Plan on ASEAN Connectivity 2025 (MPAC 2025) is ASEAN's strategy to enhance infrastructure, economic, institutional, and people-to-people connectivity across Southeast Asia. It was adopted at the 28th ASEAN Summit in September 2016 in Laos, building upon the previous Master Plan on ASEAN Connectivity 2010 (MPAC 2010). MPAC 2025 plays a crucial role in strengthening ASEAN integration, fostering economic growth, boosting trade and investment, and promoting sustainable development in the region. The strategy focuses on five key areas of connectivity: Sustainable infrastructure; Digital connectivity; Seamless logistics; Enhanced people mobility; and Institutional connectivity. MPAC 2025 is a crucial strategy for strengthening intra-ASEAN connectivity and promoting regional economic integration. While it has achieved significant progress, it still faces challenges related to financing and development disparities among member states.

In the context of globalization and intensifying geopolitical competition, major international actors such as China, the United States, the EU, Japan, and ASEAN have all introduced connectivity strategies to expand their influence and safeguard national interests. The key motivations behind these strategies include:

- *Enhancing economic influence and expanding markets*: Connectivity strategies help expand markets for goods and services, reduce transportation costs, and improve the efficiency of global supply chains. Major powers leverage these strategies to extend their economic influence, facilitate overseas investments by domestic enterprises, and gain control over supply chains.
- *Geopolitical competition and increasing global influence*: Connectivity strategies serve as tools for shaping the international order and competing for power. Major nations use infrastructure investments as soft power instruments to exert political influence, maintain and expand their strategic presence in key regions, control vital maritime routes, and counter the rise of competing powers.

- *Promoting development standards and values*: Major countries utilize connectivity strategies to export their standards and values, thereby shaping global norms in ways that benefit their domestic industries and align global development models with their national interests.
- *Strengthening security cooperation and controlling strategic spaces*: Connectivity strategies enable major powers to maintain military presence and secure key transportation routes. Maritime security cooperation, anti-piracy efforts, and cybersecurity are also integral parts of connectivity strategies. Connectivity strategies are not just about infrastructure; they represent a broader competition for influence and power in the 21st century.

Thus, the concept of connectivity is not exclusive to the EU. In recent years, many actors both within and outside the Indo-Pacific region have also introduced their own connectivity strategies. While these strategies may differ in approach, implementation models, or scale, they share a common understanding: the goal of positioning influence on the international geopolitical map.

3. *Content and Implementation of the EU Connectivity Strategy in the Indo-Pacific Region*

Content

In 2018, the Europe-Asia Connectivity Strategy was developed amidst President Donald Trump's declaration of the *America First* policy and China's implementation of the *Belt and Road Initiative* (BRI). This strategy adopts an approach based on three fundamental principles: sustainable connectivity, comprehensive connectivity, and connectivity based on international law. The objectives of the strategy include:

> (i) establishing transport links by air, road, or sea; (ii) establishing energy connections to ensure energy security with new, clean, and renewable energy sources; (iii) leveraging the economic role and influence of the EU in Asia; (iv) contributing to the creation of a sustainable development environment in the Eurasian continent through promoting mutual cooperation and understanding; and (v) facilitating the economic development of Asian countries, contributing to poverty eradication, poverty reduction, and sustainable growth; (vi) enabling better management

of goods, people, capital, and service flows; (vii) improving resource mobilization, enhancing the utilization of EU financial resources, and strengthening international partnership relations (European Commission 2018).

Based on that, the EU will cooperate with neighbouring countries and Asian partners in three directions:

- First, contributing to effective connectivity and networks between Europe and Asia through prioritized transportation corridors, digital links, and energy cooperation to serve the people and respective economies.
- Second, by establishing partnership relations, create connectivity based on common agreed rules and standards to enable better management of goods, people, capital, and service flows.
- Third, contributing to addressing significant investment gaps by improving resource mobilization, enhancing the utilization of EU financial resources, and strengthening international partnership relations (European Commission 2018).

In the 2021 Indo-Pacific Strategy, connectivity is one of the EU's seven priority areas for this region, even though the essence of connectivity can be found in the other six priorities. Essentially, the comprehension of *connectivity* in 2021 inherits the principles, objectives, and comprehension of the EU's 2018 Connectivity Strategy. In the context of the COVID-19 pandemic, the EU emphasized investment in digitalization to better connect with partners in the Indo-Pacific region. Additionally, the EU has mentioned a range of specific projects, tools, and methods to promote connectivity with this region, such as the *EU Data Gateway*, the *Neighbourhood, Development, and International Cooperation Instrument* (NDICI), also known as *Global Europe*, *European Connectivity Fund*, *Horizon Europe*, *Invest EU* etc. In this strategy declaration, the EU also highlights its ongoing efforts to engage and connect with partners and organisations in East Africa and the Indian Ocean region, seeking combined strength over north-south links and continuing its involvement in sustainable ASEM connectivity (European Commission 2018).

Therefore, it is evident that the EU's 2018 Connectivity Strategy forms the foundation for the connectivity strategy outlined in the 2021 Indo-Pacific Strategy declaration. This demonstrates a clear determination to implement connectivity efforts in this region. Successfully implementing this connectivity strategy can potentially boost the EU's political and normative power on the international stage.

Thus, the EU's Connectivity Strategy aims to promote a sustainable, inclusive, and rules-based connectivity system between Europe and other regions worldwide. The main objectives can be summarized as follows:

- *Strengthening global partnerships*: The EU seeks to expand cooperation with partner countries, particularly in the Indo-Pacific, Africa, Latin America, and multilateral organisations such as ASEAN.
- *Developing sustainable infrastructure*: Promoting high-quality, environmentally friendly, and transparent infrastructure projects while preventing debt traps for recipient countries.
- *Enhancing trade and investment*: Facilitating European businesses in expanding their markets while ensuring fair trade principles and compliance with international standards.
- *Supporting green transition and digitalization*: Assisting partner nations in transitioning to a green economy, reducing carbon emissions, and advancing digital technology.
- *Safeguarding the rules-based international order*: Ensuring stability in the global trade and economic system, maintaining freedom of navigation, cybersecurity, and protecting human rights.

This strategy also serves as the EU's response to other connectivity initiatives, particularly China's Belt and Road Initiative (BRI), reinforcing the EU's role in global geopolitical and economic structures.

Implementation

The EU's approach to implementing the Connectivity Strategy is based on three core principles, also known as the *European way*, which include sustainable connectivity, comprehensive connectivity, and connectivity based on international law. Accordingly, investments in connectivity need to align with environmental, social, economic, and financial sustainability. On this basis, the EU first develops a *soft connectivity* approach to promote consistent rules and standards and ultimately aims to ensure that *hard connectivity* projects meet desired expectations. Therefore, the EU primarily focuses on policy support, legal advice, and technical assistance for partner countries. To promote the adoption of the established standards, the EU actively engages at various levels, from overall policy aspects to specific projects. This is also the framework through which the article examines implementing the EU's strategy.

At the overall *policy level*, the EU seeks to promote and implement its soft connectivity standards primarily through relations with regional bilateral partners. The implementation of the EU's Connectivity Strategy began immediately after its declaration in 2018. First, the EU focused on promoting connections with key partners in the region, with a particular emphasis on signing agreements with key partners within the region.

In September 2019, the first partnership in connectivity between the EU and Japan was established, known as the *Sustainable Connectivity and Quality Infrastructure Partnership* (European Commission 2018). This was followed by the *Comprehensive EU-India Connectivity Partnership Agreement* in May 2021, aimed at supporting "adaptive and sustainable connectivity projects" in India and other regions such as Africa, Central Asia, and the Indo-Pacific (European Commission 2018). Additionally, in a joint ministerial statement issued in December 2020, the EU and ASEAN outlined the goal of promoting connectivity between the two regions. The EU and other regional actors also leverage its normative power by emphasising the importance of quality standards and sustainability through regional multilateral platforms, such as the ASEM forum (D'Ambrogio 2021).

The EU's connectivity strategy revolves around four pillars: energy, transportation, digital, and people-to-people connections, focusing on sustainability, security, and smart connectivity (D'Ambrogio 2021). This strategy also aims to enhance trade and investment within established rules and standards (D'Ambrogio 2021). The EU also introduces specific initiatives and directions to achieve these goals at *the level of specific projects.* The EU seeks to connect its Trans-European Transport Network (TEN-T) with corresponding networks in Asia. For energy connectivity, it promotes the efficient transition from a market-oriented approach to clean energy, contributing to the objectives of the Green Deal. By promoting digital connectivity, the EU aims to upgrade digital infrastructure and address cybersecurity risks, fostering socio-economic development in remote areas and safeguarding personal data and human rights in cyberspace. For people-to-people exchanges, activities include expanding academic mobility, exchange programs, and mutual recognition of qualifications (European Commission 2018).

To fund projects and activities related to the strategy's implementation, the EU introduced the new Multiannual Financial Framework (MFF) for 2021–2027 (European Commission 2018). Most of the funding will be allocated through NDICI, with a total budget of 79.5 billion euros (European Commission, 2018). NDICI funds all EU cooperation activities with third countries, providing additional support for geographical programs (neighbouring regions) with 60.38 billion euros, thematic programs with 6.36 billion euros, quick-reaction activities with 3.18 billion euros, and an unallocated contingency fund of 9.53 billion euros. For geographical programs, at least 19 billion euros are intended for the EU's direct neighbouring region, with approximately 8 billion euros potentially allocated for the Asian and Pacific regions (European Commission 2018).

After declaring the Indo-Pacific Strategy in 2021, the EU established the EU-Indo-Pacific Forum of Ministers. The forum, first organised in February 2022 in Paris, serves as a platform for foreign ministers from EU member countries, countries in the Indo-Pacific region, EU organisations, and other regional partners to connect, exchange ideas, and discuss practical regional cooperation issues in the region. More recently, on May 13, 2023, the second forum was held in Stockholm, co-chaired by the EU High Representative for Foreign Affairs and Security Policy, Josep Borrell, and the Swedish Minister for Foreign Affairs, Tobias Billström (as Sweden holds the EU Council Presidency). The forum focused on three aspects:

(1) Building sustainable and comprehensive prosperity together.
(2) Pursuing green opportunities and addressing global challenges in cooperation.
(3) Facing the ongoing security context in the Indo-Pacific.

This forum represents one of the regular models of operation that the EU frequently uses and exploits in the process of implementing its strategies. In summary, the EU has implemented its Connectivity Strategy in the Indo-Pacific region through the following approaches:

- *Strengthening partnerships* with countries in the region by establishing and reinforcing trade agreements and strategic partnerships with various nations and regional organisations.
- *Investing in infrastructure and technology*, including digital connectivity (such as cooperating with countries in the *India-Europe-Xpress* initiative to connect Europe with India and Southeast Asia through high-quality telecommunications infrastructure), green energy transition, and sustainable infrastructure development.
- *Promoting transparent governance*, environmental protection, and labour rights in investment projects.

- *Enhancing security and maritime cooperation*, including initiatives such as the *Coordinated Maritime Presences (CMP) in the Indo-Pacific* to support regional stability.

Regarding the implementation of *connectivity* within the Indo-Pacific Strategy during the 2021–2024 period, the strategy's rollout coincided with a challenging post-pandemic recovery phase following COVID-19, as well as the complex developments of the Ukraine conflict. These factors have made it difficult to comprehensively assess the strategy's implementation across the entire region. Therefore, in Section 4, we will focus specifically on the EU's Connectivity Strategy in Vietnam as a case study, illustrating how the EU's connectivity initiatives are being implemented in the region.

4. Implications for Vietnam

Practical implementation of the EU's Connectivity Strategy in Vietnam

For Vietnam, the EU divides its relations into nine main areas, of which at least six relationship areas (development cooperation, civil society cooperation, science, technology, and digitalisation, gender equality, fair energy transition partnership, and Erasmus+ program) are closely related to the four key focus areas of the connectivity strategy (transportation, energy, digital, and people-to-people connections).

In the field of development cooperation, the EU has adopted a new seven-year Multi-Annual Indicate Programme (MIP) from 2021 to 2027, with three priority areas:

> (i) Circular economy for climate change adaptation; (ii) Responsible business spirit and skill enhancement for decent work; (iii) Enhancing governance, rule of law, and institutional reforms, with a total planned funding of 210 million euros for the 2021–2024 period in the form of non-reimbursable aid (European Commission 2020b).

This program follows the Multi-Annual Indicate Programme 2014–2020, which contributed to Vietnam's socio-economic development, including support in various areas such as energy transition, climate action, sustainable green development, economic governance, including public financial management, digital transformation, promoting the rule of law and access to justice, etc. (European Union delegation to Vietnam 2023).

Regarding science, technology, and digitalisation, the EU's Global Gateway Strategy strongly promotes digital transformation to foster connectivity. In Vietnam, the EU Delegation cooperates through the *Team Europe* approach, together with EU member countries, to promote Digital for Development (D4D). Key areas include enhancing digital skills for circular economy platforms; enhancing circularity in the value chains of digital and electronic devices; smarter energy transitions, etc.; advanced, secure, and cyber-safe digital connections; broadband internet connections via fibre optics or satellite; digital infrastructure, etc.; and E-governance and digital literacy building.

The *Just Energy Transition Partnership (JETP) Political Statement* with Vietnam was signed on December 14, 2022, during the EU-ASEAN Summit in Brussels, between Vietnam and the International Partners Group (IPG), co-chaired by the EU and the United Kingdom. JETP aims to support Vietnam in achieving net-zero emissions, accelerating the peak of greenhouse gas emissions, and transitioning from fossil fuels to clean energy. JETP will mobilise an initial financial amount from the public and private sectors, amounting to 15.5 billion US dollars over the next three to five years (European Union delegation to Vietnam 2023).

Regarding gender equality, the EU recently funded the Green Women's Leadership Partnership between the EU and Vietnam to establish a strategic cooperative relationship with Vietnam's political and social organisations. The EU will also provide non-reimbursable aid for women-led initiatives on climate change adaptation and resilience, digital, and circular value chains. The EU expects these initiatives to promote women's leadership roles and participation in decision-making processes and empower women economically in Vietnam.

Cooperation in education is becoming an important tool for implementing the EU's connectivity strategy, promoting cross-cultural understanding and interregional connectivity, knowledge transfer, and sustainable development. The Erasmus+ 2021–2027 program supports projects, partnerships, events, and academic exchanges in education, training, youth, and sports. The program also focuses on social inclusion, green, and digital transformation while promoting youth participation in democratic life. In Vietnam, Erasmus+ funds three types of activities: Individual academic exchanges – scholarships for students and staff; Cooperation for innovation and exchange of good practices – funding for EU-Vietnam cooperation projects and some scholarships for individual students; Policy reform support primarily targeting European organisations, but Vietnamese organisations can participate as partners. The Jean Monnet program also provides funding for initiatives promoting higher-level teaching and research in the EU (European Union delegation to Vietnam 2023).

In the areas above of cooperation, the EU has implemented numerous activities and projects, including both specialised and multi-sectoral ones. Among them, there are several energy projects such as Technical Assistance for the Implementation of the EU-Vietnam Energy Facility (2018–2021) (EVEF), the Energy Sector Policy Support Programme to enhance access to sustainable energy in rural areas of Vietnam (2017–2021), Civil society meets Renewable Energy & Energy Efficiency (RE&EE) – training, seminars, and communication skills to boost RE&EE as a key tool for sustainable development and green growth strategy in Vietnam (E-Enhance) (2017–2021), etc. Furthermore, the EU Delegation in Vietnam has been actively and successfully involved in people-to-people connections, such as organising the annual Europe Days in Vietnam with various festival activities or hosting European film festivals. In May 2022, the EU Delegation in Vietnam launched the EU Alumni Network. It was introduced in a short time and has quickly gained attention by organising various activities like the Christmas Fair in 2022. *The Good Leaves Protect the Worn-out Leaves* (Cặp lá yêu thương) charity event, and recently, a series of talk shows on *Personal Data Protection in Cyberspace.*

In 2024, Vietnam continued to effectively implement free trade agreements with the EU (EVFTA). Vietnam-EU trade turnover in 2024 reached 68 billion US dollars, an increase of 16 per cent compared to 2023. The EU has become Vietnam's fourth-largest trading partner and fifth-largest investment partner, with total cumulative investment exceeding 30 billion US dollars (Lê Thị Thu Hằng 2024). It also remains Vietnam's leading ODA donor. Economic connectivity continues to be a key highlight in the implementation of the EU's connectivity strategy in Vietnam.

The implementation of the EU's connectivity strategy in Vietnam, alongside certain achievements, also faces numerous challenges from both internal and external factors. These challenges may stem from differences in standards and regulations. For instance, the EU imposes stringent requirements on labour, the environment, and corporate governance, necessitating significant reforms in Vietnam to comply. Additionally, regulations such as the Carbon Border Adjustment Mechanism (CBAM) and measures against illegal logging and fishing (IUU) exert considerable pressure on Vietnamese businesses. In economic connectivity, although the EVFTA agreement has facilitated exports, Vietnam still struggles to meet rules of origin and quality certification requirements. The EU maintains protective policies for agricultural and processed products, impacting the competitiveness of Vietnamese goods. Furthermore, foreign direct investment (FDI) inflows from the EU have yet to meet expectations due to challenges in Vietnam's business environment, legal framework, and project management transparency. Strategic priority differences between the EU and Vietnam also poses challenges. The EU emphasizes high sustainability standards, while Vietnam still seeks investment in infrastructure and basic industries. Additionally, security and defence cooperation remain limited, as the EU is not a military power in the region.

Moreover, the effectiveness of the EU's connectivity strategy in Vietnam is influenced by geopolitical and global economic factors. Competition among major powers can affect trade and investment relations between Vietnam and the EU. Global economic fluctuations, inflation, and economic downturns in Europe may reduce demand for imports from Vietnam. These challenges require Vietnam to adopt appropriate strategies to strengthen its relationship with the EU in an effective and sustainable manner.

Remarks on the EU's Connectivity Strategy

The EU's connectivity strategy stands out and differs from other countries' strategies in several key aspects:

Values and standards:

The EU's strategy is built on core values such as transparency, respect for the rule of law, human rights and environmental protection. Projects and investments must comply with high social, environmental and governance standards. In comparison, some other countries' connectivity strategies – notably BRI – tend to focus on economic and strategic interests and are sometimes criticised for their lack of transparency and regulatory standards.

Approach and cooperation:

Multilateral model: The EU adopts a multilateral approach, promoting cooperation based on the principles of mutual benefit and respect for the sovereignty of partners. This not only helps build infrastructure but also contributes to the development of digital, energy and governance sectors.

Unilateral model: Some other countries' strategies may be biased towards a unilateral approach or focus on a particular bloc, making the participation of stakeholders less diverse and equitable than the EU model.

Scope and areas of connectivity:

Multidimensional and comprehensive: The EU's connectivity strategy does not only focus on physical infrastructure such as transport, ports or railways, but also extends to areas such as digital connectivity, energy and governance cooperation. This is an effort to promote digital transformation, sustainability and long-term socio-economic development.
Focus on basic infrastructure: Some other countries' strategies may focus mainly on building physical infrastructure without paying enough attention to digital aspects, energy or sustainability standards.

Financing modalities and support conditions

Sustainable Financing: EU projects are designed with transparent financing mechanisms, to avoid public debt risks and ensure that investments are managed in a sustainable and responsible manner.
Debt and Dependency Risks: Some other connectivity models, while providing funding with initially favourable conditions, raise concerns about debt risks and long-term economic dependence for participating countries.

Strategic objectives and geopolitical impact

Diversifying Values and Stability: The EU aims to promote a connectivity model based on international standards, which not only improves infrastructure but also spreads the values of democracy, human rights and good governance, contributing to regional and international stability. Some other countries' strategies may focus primarily on expanding geopolitical influence and gaining access to strategic economic resources, sometimes raising concerns about using investments as a tool for political influence.

Thus, the main difference lies in the EU's emphasis on a model of connectivity that is inclusive, sustainable and based on transparent standards and shared values, while some other countries' strategies are more focused on economic-strategic interests and may place less emphasis on environmental, social and governance standards. The EU's Global Gateway takes a different approach from China's BRI: while the BRI heavily invests in infrastructure to expand China's influence, the Global Gateway focuses on sustainable development, ensuring transparency and avoiding debt traps. Compared to the PGII led by the U.S. and G7, the EU has been slower in implementation but benefits from long-term cooperation with partner countries, particularly in Africa and Eastern Europe. Japan's FOIP and ASEAN's MPAC 2025 primarily focus on the Indo-Pacific region, whereas the EU has a broader geographic scope but lacks a strong security dimension.

The EU's Global Gateway has a smaller financial scale compared to the BRI and PGII – 300 billion euros versus over one trillion US dollars for the BRI. Due to the EU's complex financial mechanisms and differences in priorities among member states, implementation has been slow. Additionally, the EU places less emphasis on security compared to Japan's FOIP and the U.S.'s PGII. As geopolitical concerns gain increasing attention in the region, the EU's strategy remains relatively less focused on geopolitical factors. Therefore, the EU's connectivity strategy is not a direct competitor to the BRI or PGII but rather an alternative option for countries in the Indo-Pacific region that seek to develop sustainable infrastructure without being burdened by large debts.

Suggestions for Vietnam

To develop fundamental proposals for Vietnam, it is essential to analyse and draw insights into the nature and evolving trends of the EU's connectivity strategy in the Indo-Pacific region.

The EU's connectivity strategy has not been formulated through a sole legal document. However, it has evolved through various statements, including the Global Strategy for the EU in 2016, *Connecting Europe and Asia – Building Blocks for the EU's Strategy* in 2018, the Indo-Pacific Strategy in 2021, and most recently the Global Gateway Strategy. Each statement reflects the EU's response to different contexts and times. The EU's approach to *connectivity* appears to lack a systematic and coherent framework and seems more like a patchwork (European Union delegation to Vietnam 2023). Thus, it can be observed that the EU is developing a new global connectivity concept. However, the Indo-Pacific have become focal points in the EU's connectivity strategy and may serve as a basis for expanding global connectivity.

The concept of connectivity is not exclusive to the EU. In recent years, many actors within and beyond the Indo-Pacific region have also their own connectivity. The diversity of participating actors in the region has created a context of competitive connectivity strategies. Meanwhile, a single country cannot meet the demand for investment in infrastructure and other development areas in this region. The competition arises from both sides, with major powers as the suppliers and from the demand side, with their corresponding strategies. This presents opportunities and challenges for the EU's connectivity strategy. Multiple strategies and various cooperation options may lead to conflicts arising from competition, one of the EU's major challenges.

It would be an opportunity if the EU's connectivity strategy aligned with the countries in the region and both sides found common ground. Another advantage in this situation is the EU's presence and experience as an investor in the region, making it an attractive cooperation partner. As one of the leading actors with normative power (European Union delegation to Vietnam 2023), the EU always promotes EU values, standards, and norms through policy documents, a consistent theme in its connectivity policies. Moreover, based on the foundation of normative power, the EU's connectivity projects will be built on cooperation and empowerment rather than coercion. To make cooperation advantageous, some understanding of how connectivity operates (the standards, norms, and values applied) must be shared to some extent between the EU and its connectivity partners. This is something that the EU has been working on through multilateral (with ASEAN, ASEM) as well as bilateral relations. If this strength can be harnessed, the EU will have a special advantage compared to other actors, especially when the EU's connectivity strategy includes areas where it holds a competitive advantage (e.g., security). Therefore, countries in the region recognise that the EU's role has the potential to contribute to the stability and development of the Indo-Pacific regions (European Union delegation to Vietnam 2023).

Alongside opportunities, implementing the EU's connectivity strategy will also face challenges from both sides. First, the context of regional competition mentioned earlier creates challenges in applying EU values to practical projects, especially when the recipient countries have weaker institutions, low transparency, and different standards (European Union Delegation to Vietnam 2023). Therefore, the successful implementation of these practical projects will be crucial, especially in countries facing systemic challenges in meeting the standards defined in the strategy.

Secondly, internal obstruction within the EU in maintaining and promoting consensus among member states. Is this another factor affecting the EU's connectivity strategy's clear definition and measurable goals? While this allows policy planners within the EU to maintain flexibility in decision-making and linkages with the strategy, it can also complicate the operational and monitoring processes for the effectiveness of the EU's connectivity efforts. Applying the Indo-Pacific strategy in particular and the broader connectivity strategy, in general, will be significant because it reflects the widely accepted viewpoint of the 27 member states. EU member states require a unified and coherent approach in building the action plan (European Union delegation to Vietnam 2023).

Perhaps the EU's connectivity strategy for the Indo-Pacific region is just the beginning of its global connectivity strategy. At the end of 2021, the EU announced the Global Gateway connectivity initiative, planning to invest 300 billion euros by 2027 (European Union delegation to Vietnam 2023). This initiative continues the EU's connectivity strategy since 2018. However, compared to the previous strategy, Global Gateway is more specific in its funding plan. Additionally, while the 2018 strategy focused specifically on Asia and the Indo-Pacific, the Global Gateway has much wider scope. Consequently, implementing the EU's connectivity strategy in the region will have to confront resource allocation issues. Therefore, financial commitments are considered one of the most critical challenges the EU must overcome. Completing and allocating financial and other resources for the action plan will need to be addressed through discussions with various organisations and stakeholders within and outside the EU. Thus, the success of the connectivity strategy will largely depend on the EU's management's ability to attract additional funding from international and multilateral organisations and private sector entities. Another factor hindering resource allocation and prioritising the EU's recent strategy is the situation in Ukraine. Although EU representatives assure that the war will not limit the organisation's involvement in the Indo-Pacific, it will draw the focus of political attention and EU resources, at least in the near future.

Overall, Vietnam benefits significantly from the EU's Connectivity Strategy, particularly in the areas of trade, investment, sustainable development, and digital transformation. The Global Gateway's key advantages lie in its high standards, investment in quality infrastructure, sustainability, and transparency, ensuring that partner countries are not trapped in debt. The EU is eager to strengthen ties with partners, especially in the Indo-Pacific region. Therefore, it is essential to identify the EU's strengths to prioritize cooperation in key areas, including:

Green transition and sustainable development:

- Financial support for renewable energy, with Vietnam benefiting from initiatives such as the Just Energy Transition Partnership (JETP), which helps mobilize EU funding for clean energy development.
- Climate change cooperation, with the EU supporting Vietnam in implementing emission reduction commitments, sustainable agriculture, and environmental protection.

Digital transformation and innovation:

- Developing the digital economy, with EU support in AI, big data, and cybersecurity, enhancing Vietnam's technological capabilities.
- Research collaboration, where programs like Horizon Europe provide Vietnamese businesses and universities with opportunities for research and innovation partnerships with the EU.

Additionally, Vietnam can benefit from the EU's support in maritime security, combating illegal, unreported, and unregulated (IUU) fishing, and protecting maritime sovereignty, thereby enhancing security and maritime cooperation. Strengthening connectivity cooperation with the EU will elevate Vietnam's international standing, enhance its links with ASEAN and the global economy, and position Vietnam as a bridge between the EU and ASEAN, increasing its influence in regional forums.

5. Conclusion

The EU's adoption of the Indo-Pacific strategy has been primarily symbolic so far, demonstrating political will to enhance engagement with the region in the areas of economy, security, and connectivity. The plan reveals a clear purpose of positioning the EU in global and emerging regional governance structures, focusing on strategic autonomy, comprehensiveness, and a rules-based order. However, due to both objective and subjective limitations, it would be better for the EU to concentrate on prioritized areas according to sectors and geographical regions instead of attempting to engage in all sectors and the entire region. Thus, the Indian Ocean is a reasonable choice due to its geographical proximity, trade significance, and the EU's activities in the region. Out of the seven priority areas set forth in the Indo-Pacific

Strategy, the EU can concentrate on areas where it possesses capabilities, means, and tools through trade policies or development cooperation. The EU's priority is to support partners in creating conditions for economic growth and addressing development challenges. Hence, economic issues, climate change, connectivity, etc. are fundamental concerns for both Indo-Pacific countries and the EU. The connectivity strategy can bring about new results and impacts.

In order to enhance the attractiveness and influence of the EU's normative power in the connectivity strategy, the EU's commitments in the Indo-Pacific must be based on a realistic assessment of the EU's capabilities, interests, and goals to increase the EU's visibility in the region and avoid creating disappointments that it may not meet (e.g., in the security realm). The success of the strategy and the EU's credibility as a participant in the region will need to be coordinated with important partners in the region, leading to the subsequent complementing of their initiatives. Countries in the region also expect the EU's engagement to help minimize competition between the US and China while contributing to stabilizing the regional order based on international law.

Vietnam has great potential to become a key strategic partner of the EU in the Indo-Pacific region. By leveraging trade agreements, promoting sustainable development, fostering technological innovation, enhancing security cooperation, and expanding people-to-people exchanges, Vietnam can elevate its international standing, drive economic growth, and ensure long-term sustainable development.

6. References

ASEM Pathfinder Group on Connectivity (2017): Chair Summary, European External Action Service. https://eeas.europa.eu/sites/default/files/chair_summary_apgc_21_june_2017-final.pdf.

Bui Hong Hanh/Trinh Hanh Linh (2021): Normative Power - The Case of the European Union, Communist Review, No. 971. 106–111.

D'Ambrogio, Enrico (2021): Prospects for EU-Asia Connectivity, European Parliamentary Research Service.

European Commission (2018): Connecting Europe and Asia: Building Blocks for an EU Strategy, Brussels: European Union.

European Commission (2020a): EU Budget for External Action in the next MFF. https://ec.europa.eu/commission/presscorner/detail/en/qanda_20_988.

European Commission (2020b): EU Welcomes Political Agreement on €79.5 Billion for NDICI, European Commission. https://ec.europa.eu/commission/presscorner/detail/en/ip_20_2453.

European Commission (2021): EU & India Launch Collaboration on Sustainable Connectivity. https://ec.europa.eu/commission/presscorner/detail/en/ip_21_2327.

European External Action Service (2021): Global Gate Way, https://www.eeas.europa.eu/eeas/global-gateway_en.

European Union Delegation to Vietnam (2023): https://www.eeas.europa.eu/vietnam/the-eu-and-vietnam_vi?s=184#9110.

Gaens, Bart/Sinkkonen, Ville/Ruokamo, Anu (2023): Introduction to the Special Issue: Theory and Practice of Connectivity in the Indo-Pacific-Spheres, Logics, and Regional Dynamics, East Asia. https://www.ncbi.nlm.nih.gov/pmc/articles/PMC10186308/.

Gaens, Bart/Sinkkonen, Ville/Vogt, H. (2023): Connectivity and Order: An Analytical Framework. In: East Asia, 40(2).

Karjalainen, Tyyne (2023): European Norms Trap? EU Connectivity Policies and the Case of the Global Gateway. In: East Asia, 20/3/2023. https://link.springer.com/article/10.1007/s12140-023-09403-x#Sec6.

Khanna, P. (2016): Connectography: Mapping the Future of Global Civilization. Random House.

Le Thi Thu Hang (2024): Vietnam-Europe relations: Imprints in 2024 and prospects in 2025, Government Electronic Newspaper, February 21, 2025. (21/2/2025). https://baochinhphu.vn/quan-he-viet-nam-chau-au-nhung-dau-an-trong-nam-2024-va-trien-vong-trong-nam-2025-102250221162420683.htm.

Okano-Heijmans, Maaike (2020): The EU's Value Proposition for Connectivity: Time to Choose and Focus. In: Echle, Christian (ed.): Responding to the Geopolitics of Connectivity: Asian and European Perspectives. KAS, Singapore. 11–21.

Ries, T. (2019): Security Aspects of Connectivity. EGMONT – The Royal Institute for International Relations. Security Policy Brief. https://www.egmontinstitute.be/security-aspects-of-connectivity/.

Söderberg, Marie (2020): Connectivity and Infrastructure: Can the EU-Japan Partnership Make a Difference? http://www.realinstitutoelcano.org/wps/portal/rielcano_en/contenido?WCM_GLOBAL_CONTEXT=/elcano/elcano_in/zonas_in/asia-pacific/commentarysoderberg-connectivity-and-infrastructure-can-eu-japan-partnership-make-difference.

Sommerer, T./Tallberg, J. (2019): Diffusion across International Organisations: Connectivity and Convergence. In: International Organization, 73(2), 399–433.

Stec, Grzegorz/Jakóbowski, Jakub (2020): Geopolitics of Connectivity Competition – The Curious Case of Central and Eastern Europe. https://www.grzegorzstec.com/podcasts/jakub-jakobowski-geopolitics-of-connectivity-competition-in-central-and-eastern-europe-cee.

Widmann, Manuel (2021): The EU Connectivity Strategy: Putting Words into Action. EIAS Brief Paper No.02/2021. European Institute for Asian Studies, Brussels.

Acknowledgement

The research presented in this chapter was conducted as part of the project *The EU Approach to Cooperation in the Indo-Pacific: From Strategy to Practice* during 2020–2023, with funding from Konrad-Adenauer-Stiftung (KAS) in Vietnam. I am sincerely grateful to KAS Vietnam for their generous support, which made this study possible. The views expressed in this chapter are those of the author and do not necessarily reflect the official position of KAS.

Chapter 8: Economic Cooperation of the EU with the Indo-Pacific Countries: Strengthening the Foundation of Engagement

Nguyen Van Dap

Economic cooperation is currently and must continue to be an important pillar in the relationship between the EU and the countries in the Indo-Pacific region despite the increasing geopolitical competition. For the relationship with the EU to remain important in the decisive considerations of Indo-Pacific countries, it needs to deepen economic cooperation as guided by the EU's Indo-Pacific Strategy. Based on assessing the current state of cooperation, needs and capabilities of the two sides indicate significant potential for bilateral collaboration. Additionally, broader contextual shifts – including green transition, digital transformation, changes in economic structure and growth models, and increasing geopolitical competition – are shaping the environment for bilateral relations. From this perspective, the chapter provides recommendations and proposals for the EU's economic cooperation with the Indo-Pacific region in the future. It suggests that efforts should focus on five key areas: green transition and sustainable economy, digital economy development, strengthening and ensuring global supply chains, prioritizing the services sector, and development assistance initiatives.

1. Introduction

The economic prosperity of the Indo-Pacific region is closely linked to the world's prosperity. This is a clear fact as the region has contributed to the growth engines of the world economy for more than two decades. At the same time, that prosperity increasingly ties the region to external connections: investment capital flows, technological know-how, high-quality human resources, and modern production and management methods. One of the important departures for these resources is the European Union (EU). Through a centralised production process from countries in the Indo-Pacific region, goods reach consumers worldwide through global supply chains.

However, the fluctuations in global economic growth because of wars and conflicts, geopolitical fluctuations, pandemics, potential opportunities, and threats have greatly influenced the economic relations of the EU and its member countries with countries in the Indo-Pacific region over the past two decades. The EU's economic presence and role in the region is more contested than ever before. Faced with this uncertain context, the EU has published an overall, highly directional Indo-Pacific Strategy in 2021 to guide EU actions in the region. This document identifies the objectives, methods, and priority areas in the EU's relations with countries in the region. Economic ties are considered one of the five most important pillars of the EU's Indo-Pacific Strategy, which "aims to contribute to the region's stability, security, prosperity and sustainable development." To fully assess the prospects for economic relations between the EU and countries in the region, it is necessary to first consider the parties' current backgrounds, needs and capabilities and major trends affecting this relationship before considering the promising areas in the economic relations between the two sides.

2. Main Findings

Existing foundations of economic relations

Today, the Indo-Pacific is a vibrant economic region that accounts for 60 per cent of global GDP, with three of the world's four largest economies outside the EU (China, Japan, and India) contributing two-thirds of the world's economic growth. In less than a decade, by 2030, 90 per cent of the 2.4 billion people entering the middle class will come from the Indo-Pacific (EEAS 2022). Of the 20 economies with the largest goods import and export activities, half are in the Indo-Pacific region. The situation is similar to the service import and export sector. Not only in terms of size, but Indo-Pacific also plays an important and promising role as the region is the centre of global value chains, international trade, and investment flows, as well as the forerunner of the digital economy and technological development. In the opposite direction, generating nearly 15 per cent of global GDP (purchasing power parties), the EU is one of the leading investors and providers of development aid and a major trading partner of countries in the region. Therefore, it can be said that for the EU, the Indo-Pacific region is essential for its economic growth.

The situation of bilateral trade and investment relations

For decades, trade and investment have been central to Europe's approach to the Indo-Pacific and have driven Europe's relations with the countries of the region (Grare/Reuter 2021). The total value of bilateral trade reached 1.5 trillion euro in 2019 (Europarl 2022). This figure after the pandemic, in 2022, is around 1.76 trillion euro. The Indo-Pacific is the EU's second-largest export destination and home to four of the EU's 10 largest trade partners in goods, including China, India, Japan, and South Korea. On the other hand, the EU is also among the leading trading partners of most countries in the region. This implies that the presence of the EU in the Indo-Pacific region is greater than that of Indo-Pacific countries in the EU.

From 2011 to 2021, imports of goods from the Indo-Pacific region to the EU increased more significantly than exports, which also showed steady growth. Imports increased from 515 billion Euro in 2011 to 844 billion Euro in 2021 (+64 per cent), while exports increased from 407 billion Euro to 583 billion Euro in the same period (+44 per cent). With non-EU imports growing more than exports, the EU's trade deficit with the Indo-Pacific region reached 261 billion Euro, the highest value since 2011, 109 billion Euro (Eurostat 2022) *(see Figure 1).*

Figure 1: Trade volume between EU and Indo-Pacific countries

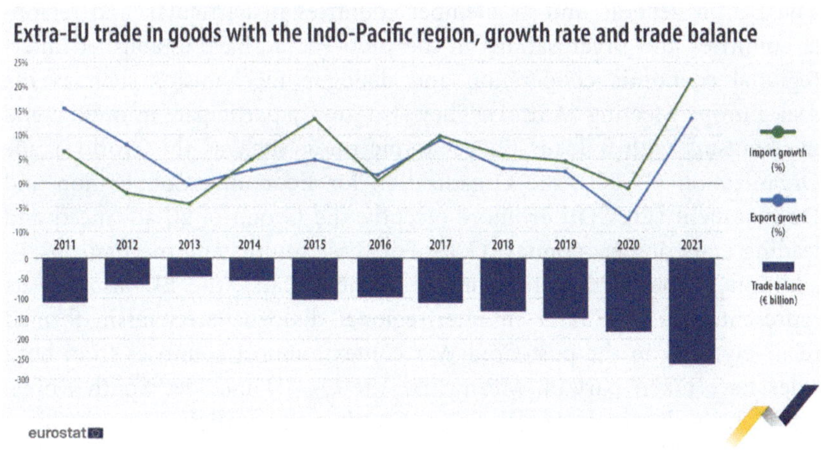

Source: https://ec.europa.eu/

The growth rate of imports and exports from the Indo-Pacific region in total imports and exports outside the EU slowed down during the peak of the COVID-19 pandemic (-1 per cent and -7 per cent in 2020 compared to 2019, respectively). However, they recovered in 2022, compared to 2020; +61 per cent for imports and +26 per cent for export. In 2022, the Indo-Pacific region accounted for a significant share of total imports (37 per cent) and exports (25 per cent) outside the EU (Eurostat 2024).

In 2023, the EU's FDI outflows accounted for 30 per cent of the globe, significantly higher than the second largest source of FDI, the US, with 21.3 per cent (Eurostat 2025), far ahead of the next FDI sources at less than 6 per cent. However, the main destinations of the EU's FDI flows are non-EU European countries and North America, with nearly two-thirds of the total amount of FDI outside the bloc. On the other hand, the EU receives an equal amount of foreign direct investment from these countries. In other words, the EU's investment relations are mainly with non-EU European countries and two North American countries, the US and Canada, the Indo-Pacific countries are not yet major investment partners of the EU. Even so, the EU remains the leading investor in some regional economies, such as ASEAN countries.

Multilateral economic cooperation platforms

The EU, in general, and its member countries in particular, and regional countries and organisations in the Indo-Pacific have established interregional economic cooperation and dialogue mechanisms such as the Asia-Europe Meeting (ASEM). They also jointly participate in multilateral mechanisms with a focus on economic ones, such as the World Trade Organization (WTO), the Organization for Economic Cooperation and Development (OECD), or, more recently, the Group of 20 advanced and leading emerging economies (G20). For these multilateral mechanisms, in addition to the participation of key member states, the EU also has its representatives. ASEM is an inter-regional dialogue mechanism formed relatively early in the post-Cold War context, almost countries from both sides have taken part in. Meanwhile, the OECD includes South Korea, Japan, Australia, and New Zealand. G20 has the participation of China, Japan, South Korea, an ASEAN country – Indonesia – Australia, and India.

The EU strongly promoted a global trade structure based on the reform of WTO rules; however, the actual failure of the Doha Round in 2008 caused the EU to shift direction towards achieving a common trade and investment framework with the Indo-Pacific as a good alternative (Grare/ Reuter 2021). However, the EU has not made any significant progress in this direction. As a result, the EU turned to an approach based on existing regional agreements in the Indo-Pacific and a bilateral approach.

> "The EU will need to strengthen its strategic trade position and level the playing field in the Indo-Pacific, given recent significant regional agreements, such as the Comprehensive and Progressive Agreement for Trans-Pacific Partnership (CPTPP) and the Regional Comprehensive Economic Partnership (RCEP)." (EU 2021)

The bilateral platforms: EU's FTAs with Indo-Pacific countries

> "It will continue to explore and negotiate ambitious trade and investment agreements in the region, such as those concluded with Japan, the Republic of Korea, Singapore and Vietnam. It will aim to conclude free trade agreements with Australia, Indonesia and New Zealand and take further steps towards the Comprehensive Agreement on Investment with China. The EU will continue to explore deepening economic relations with India." (EU 2021)

Currently, the EU has signed and is negotiating a total of 26 trade and investment agreements with partner countries/organisations of various types, such as: Free Trade Agreements (FTA), Deep and Comprehensive Free Trade Agreements (DCFTA), Investment Agreements (IA), Enhanced Partnership and Cooperation Agreement (EPCA), Partnership and Cooperation Agreement (PCA). In particular, for the Indo-Pacific region, the EU currently has 16 agreements, equivalent to 55 per cent of the bloc's trade and investment agreements, at levels from negotiation to signing pending ratification and implementation, except for the agreement with Myanmar *(see Table 2).*

Table 2: List of EU's trade, investment agreements with Indo-Pacific countries

No.	Parties	Type of agreement	Status
1	EU-Vietnam	Free Trade Agreement	In place
2	EU-South Korea	Free Trade Agreement	In place

3	EU-Papua New Guinea	Cooperation and Partnership Agreement	In place
4	EU-Sri Lanka	Cooperation and Partnership Agreement	In place
5	EU-Singapore	Free Trade Agreement	In place
6	EU-Japan	Economic Partnership Agreement	In place
7	EU-New Zealand	Cooperation and Partnership Agreement	Adoption
8	EU-China	Comprehensive Investment Agreement	Adoption
9	EU-ASEAN	Cooperation and Partnership Agreement	Being negotiated
10	EU-Indonesia	Free Trade Agreement	Being negotiated
11	EU-Philippines	Free Trade Agreement	Being negotiated
12	EU-India	Cooperation and Partnership Agreement	Being negotiated
13	EU-Australia	Cooperation and Partnership Agreement	Being negotiated
14	EU-Thailand	Cooperation and Partnership Agreement	On hold
15	EU-Malaysia	Cooperation and Partnership Agreement	On hold
16	EU-Myanmar	Free Trade Agreement	On hold

Source: European Commission (2023)

The main actors: governments, corporations, and communities

Attracting the participation of the private sector is considered a strength of European countries. In the context of China's presence and expansion of economic and financial influence in the region through state-owned or state-supported economic corporations, the public-private partnership model of EU partners offers an important experience in promoting the resources of countries in the region. In particular, the EU is using a financing model characterised by grants, low-interest loans, and guarantees aimed at promoting investment from the private sector. (Kuoman, 2023)

Large European multinational corporations soon had a solid presence in the Indo-Pacific region with financial, scientific, and technological potential and the ability to penetrate and operate in international markets, both in most civil and military fields. At the same time, small and medium enterprises are also encouraged by EU countries to internationalise their operations.

One-fifth of the expatriate communities in the EU are now from the Indo-Pacific region, including, in order of greatest number: China (including Hong Kong), India, Afghanistan, Pakistan, the Philippines, Bangladesh and Vietnam. This is one of the critical economic connection channels between the EU and countries in the Indo-Pacific region through remittances, investment, or human resources.

EU's Strategy to Indo-Pacific on economic cooperation

With the situation as analysed above, in its Indo-Pacific Strategy, the EU identifies issues of principles, methods and objectives as follows:

> "The EU will continue to promote key EU economic interests, principles and objectives including on sustainable development towards ensuring a strong, balanced, and inclusive socio-economic recovery and growth as well as sound macroeconomic policies, institutional capacity building and support for regional integration. The EU will foster dialogue with like-minded countries of the Indo-Pacific region by crafting forward-looking growth enhancement strategies for a resilient and sustainable rebound of our economies." (EU 2021)

In particular, with the experience of experiencing severe disruptions due to the COVID-19 pandemic as well as in the context of fierce strategic competition in the region, the EU emphasises supply chain issues:

> "Diversification of supply chains should contribute to the resilience of the European economy, especially for the most sensitive industrial ecosystems, and to the reduction of strategic dependencies on critical raw materials. The EU will also cooperate with Indo-Pacific countries to reform the WTO towards a sustainable and effective multilateral trading system." (EU 2021)

Mega trends impacting economic cooperation

Green transition

Greening the economy is not only a desire but has become a task of countries to achieve the climate goals set for the 21st century. Accordingly, to fulfil the commitments, countries need to change the energy structure to increase the proportion of clean and renewable energy sources while reducing the fossil energy supply as one of the most important solutions. In addition, improve resource efficiency by moving from a linear economy to a circular economy.

The ambitious goals to combat the rapid deterioration of climate change that countries committed to during the recent Conferences of the Parties to the United Nations Framework Convention on Climate Change (COP) have posed significant challenges for countries in the region, especially developing countries.

Digitalisation in economy

The trend of digitising the economy has been accelerating in recent years, especially as the world experiences the COVID-19 pandemic with the disruption of physical supply chains. At that time, e-commerce, as a leading field in the digital economy, was given more impetus to explode in many countries worldwide. For the Asia-Pacific region, 62.6 per cent of global e-commerce revenue will come from this region in 2020 and it is forecast to remain the largest market over the next decade (Reddington 2022). Other aspects of the digital economy are also experiencing rapid developments *(see Figure 2)*. Digitisation is both an important context and an urgent need for countries in the region to avoid falling behind in the context of the Fourth Industrial Revolution.

Figure 2: Electronic trade and digitisation of several Indo-Pacific economies

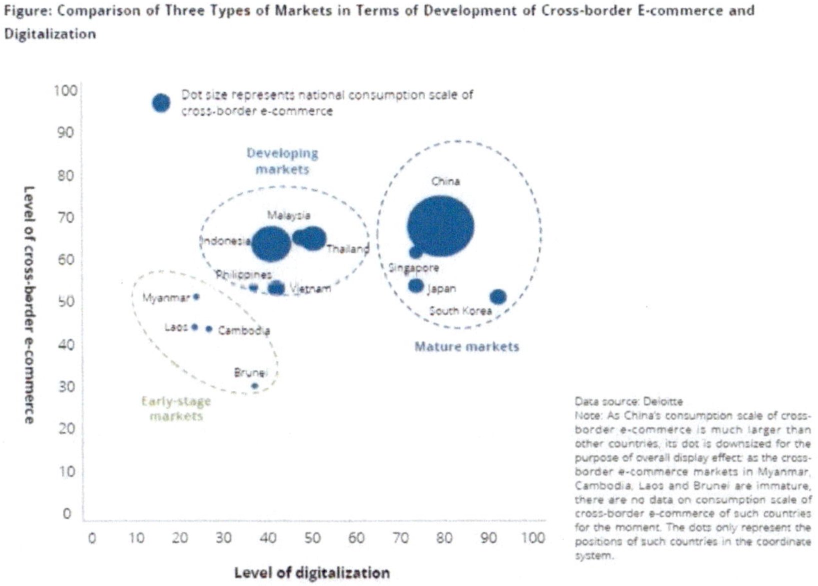

Source: https://www2.deloitte.com/

Transformation of economic structure and growth model

Most of the economies in the Indo-Pacific region are experiencing a strong structural shift in the direction of increasing the proportion of the industrial and service sectors. China and India are two emerging economies with a service sector share exceeding 50 per cent of GDP in 2015 and 2019. Except for Japan and Singapore, most of the emerging economies in the region have a service share of 40–55 per cent of GDP. Meanwhile, the industrial sector (including construction) currently accounts for 25–40 per cent of GDP in most countries in the region. Compared to 1990–2010, this sector decreased by about 10 per centage points (WB 2023).

Another notable trend is that the region's economies are shifting from a growth model based on production for export to a growth economy based on domestic consumption combined with exports. This is very important, especially in the case of *the world's factory* – China, because "every per centage point of growth in this country leads to 0.3 per centage points of growth in other Asian economies." (Georgieva 2023) Meanwhile, China's economy is slowing down and adjusting to structure after decades of a two-digit growth rate. One expected positive effect of this shift is the ability to meet climate goals, as a reduction in energy demand leads to reduced greenhouse gas emissions and relieves energy pressures (Georgieva 2023). However, this shift in China also means that other countries in the region will gradually replace China in energy consumption, especially India and Southeast Asian countries. As a driver of growth, the outcome of these shifts in the Indo-Pacific economies will have a major impact on the medium-term economic outlook in the region and globally. At the same time, they will directly affect the movement of international supply chains.

Increasing geopolitical rivalry

This is considered the biggest external challenge for the prospects of economic relations between the EU and countries in the Indo-Pacific region. The fact that Russia put troops into control of Crimea and the Donbas region in 2014 opened a war with Ukraine that continues today. The United States and Western countries have responded harshly directly to Russia through international sanctions and indirectly through support for Ukraine. Meanwhile, the hidden rivalries between China and the US have revealed themselves openly under US President Donald Trump (2017–2021), corresponding to the second term of Chinese President Xi Jinping (2012–present). The sanctions imposed on Russia and the trade war against China have put the US and Western countries in a confrontational position with two members of the BRICS bloc.

Due to the context of strategic competition, under the President Joe Biden (2021-2025) administration, the US established minilateral mechanisms on politics and security in the region without the participation of the EU or member states such as: together with Japan, Australia and India established QUAD, together with the UK and Australia AUKUS and together with Japan and Australia Blue Dot Network (BDN). In addition, the economic sector also has fierce competition between economic initiatives promoted by the US and China in the region such as the Indo-Pacific Economic Framework (IPEF), which is currently in the negotiation stage, preceded by the Trans-Pacific Partnership (TPP), and the Regional Comprehensive Economic Partnership (RCEP). While the US has called on its businesses, its allies, and partners to retract from China as the world's factory for the last three decades, China has gradually moved up the ladder in the global value chain. Therefore, economic separation and finding alternatives will require much time and resources.

Under the second Trump administration, geopolitical tensions escalated as the United States simultaneously challenged the EU with two major issues: enhancing its role in resolving the prolonged Russia-Ukraine conflict and addressing tariff pressures directly from the United States. For countries in the Indo-Pacific region, tariff pressures in trade relations with the United States forced many nations to make adjustments while facing intensified competition from the escalating United States-China rivalry. This situation diverted the focus of both the EU and Indo-Pacific countries.

In line with its interests, the EU strives to maintain a certain degree of *strategic autonomy* in the context of the growing geostrategic rivalry between the US and China. Despite their emphasis on different focuses, EU countries see the Indo-Pacific Strategy as a way to "manage the trans-Atlantic alliance" (Grare/Reuter 2021) or the EU-US relationship. At the same time, the EU also considers that "EU-China relations are multifaceted, in which China is a cooperative partner, but also an economic rival and a systemic opponent in some areas." (Europarl, 2022) This also poses significant challenges to the EU's economic presence in the Indo-Pacific region. However, the EU has many challenges in promoting economic relations in the region due to the dispersion of resources and the deepening of economic divisions.

Highly competitive cooperation fields

Transition to green and sustainable economy

The scale of *green* investment opportunities in the Indo-Pacific region is substantial. Among the major emerging markets by region, the Indo-Pacific accounts for three-quarters of investment (Fuhrmann 2021). As a result, the region offers many opportunities for activities for European governments and companies. Key areas include urban transport, municipal waste treatment, decarbonisation of heavy industry, renewable energy, climate change-responsive agriculture, low-carbon transportation, etc. Especially with its technical advantages, the EU has great potential to provide partners with technical solutions for clean energy development for Indo-Pacific countries. Nuclear technology for civilian use is one of the obvious strengths of many EU member states, especially France and Germany (only before it completely phase-outed nuclear power in April 2023). In 2019, nuclear energy share accounted for 30.5 per cent of the whole EU, higher than fossil energy sources. Meanwhile, the share of energy produced from biomass, waste, electricity and heat is 43.4 per cent (Eurostat 2022) *(see Figure 3).*

However, China's competition in this field is very strong because it soon implemented a strategy to develop renewable energy, especially wind and solar energy, and has accelerated the development of construction technology and power system management. On the other hand, electricity infrastructure development projects in particular and energy in general within the framework of the Belt and Road Initiative (BRI) not only help China have great influence in the region but also accumulates a lot of experience in implementing large projects in many countries worldwide.

The EU produces 3.9 per cent of the world, while China is the largest producer with 17.9 per cent. The United States and Russia are also the two leading energy producers in the world, with a share of 15.7 per cent and 10.5 per cent of total global energy, respectively (Eurostat 2022). However, while the US and Russia are the world's top energy exporters, the EU and China are the world's top energy importers and depend on external partners.

Figure 3: Structure of EU's energy, in comparison with the world (2019)

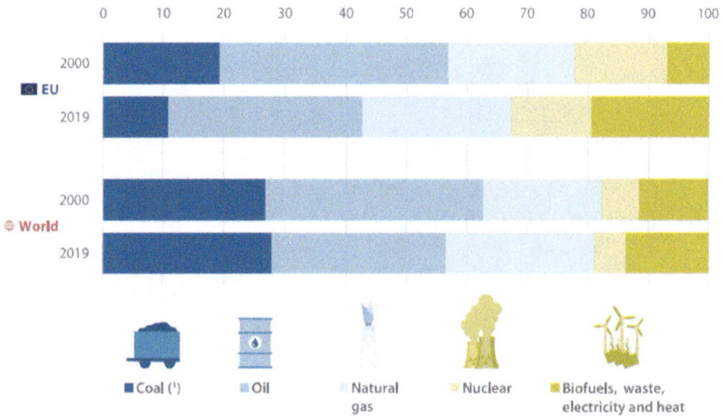

Source: Eurostat (2022)

Developing the digital economy

Information and communication technologies are ubiquitous worldwide regarding both accessibility and cost. The digital economy is entering a boom phase in many countries in the Indo-Pacific region, bringing about a major shift in the economic structure of these countries as well as in cross-border economic relations with partners inside and outside the region. The Global Gateway initiative, in effect an extension of the EU's 2018 Eurasian Connectivity Strategy, is expected to be an alternative to the Digital Silk Road (DSR) initiated by China. "The Global Gateways will support the deployment of secure and sustainable infrastructures, promote the sustainability of global supply chains, and strengthen the decision-making autonomy of EU partners." (EEAS 2022) However, in the Indo-Pacific region, it is clear that GG will have to compete fiercely with DSR.

In addition, the EU established a digital partnership with Japan, Singapore, and South Korea in late 2022 and early 2023. Digital partnerships are non-binding cooperation tools focusing on the digital transformation of the economy and society and deepening bilateral trade and investment relations. In the future, the EU can continue to expand the network of digital partner countries in the Indo-Pacific region.

Strengthening and securing the global supply chains

Through global value chains (GVCs), the degree of economic integration of the Indo-Pacific countries, including ASEAN, is the cornerstone of the Indo-Pacific economic architecture. In the context of the production shift away from China, India and Southeast Asian countries emerged as the leading alternatives and indeed, the shift is taking place in this direction. However, in the short term, China will remain a huge emerging market in the Indo-Pacific region and worldwide despite the slower and weaker post-pandemic recovery than forecasted. As a result, the world's leading EU manufacturers and suppliers will still need to go further into this market. This can be facilitated by the market coherence of countries through RCEP, where China plays a central role. An Indo-Pacific trade and economic cooperation plan must consider China and face the inevitable supply chain integration between ASEAN and China, the European Union (EU) and China, among others (Prakash 2023).

Emphasising the service sector

Currently, trade in services is increasingly accounting for a larger proportion of trade relations between the EU and countries in the Indo-Pacific region. As analysed above, these fields are becoming increasingly important along with the shift in the structure of the countries' economies. For the EU, the service sector now accounts for almost three-quarters of the bloc's total annual value added (Eurostat 2022). The EU's non-EU service exports now account for 20 per cent of the total value of global services exports, ranking first compared to other individual economies. Therefore, it can be said that the fields of financial services, banking, high-quality education, health, and tourism are the most promising sectors. Currently, investment in the financial sector accounts for 57 per cent of the total EU foreign direct investment (FDI). EU financial institutions have an efficient international network with high standards and are highly competitive in the Indo-Pacific region and worldwide.

Regarding the health sector, with the current ageing population and life expectancy at 80.1, EU countries have a high demand for workers in the healthcare sector. The cost of the EU healthcare sector currently stands at 10 per cent of GDP, or 1.7 trillion euro (Eurostat 2023). Meanwhile, most of the emerging and developing countries in the Indo-Pacific region have a young and abundant labour force, which is a potential source of human resources for this field.

Regarding education, one-third of the population over 25 years old has a university or postgraduate degree. If high school education is included, the rate is up to 80 per cent (Eurostat, 2022). As a result, universities in the EU have a strong incentive to address non-EU needs, while the Indo-Pacific region has a young population, rising living standards and a thirst for knowledge. For the health and education sectors, the EU's high quality continues to attract international students, including in the Indo-Pacific region and is a trusted choice for patients from many different countries. A significant barrier to access to these two sectors in the EU is the issue of cost. In tourism, the resources of both sides are rich and diverse.

The tourism industry in Indo-Pacific countries has also developed explosively in recent years, opening up many new opportunities for bilateral relations. From 2007 to 2019, the EU welcomed 40–42 per cent of the world's annual international tourist arrivals (Eurostar 2022). Meanwhile, the Indo-Pacific region has top destinations such as China, Hong Kong, Thailand, Macao, Malaysia, and Japan.

Development assistance

The EU is well known to date as the leading donor among industrialised countries providing development aid to the Global South countries through bilateral channels or multilateral international financial institutions such as the World Bank (WB), the International Monetary Fund (IMF) and the Asian Development Bank (ADB). Through grants, the EU continues to have effective channels to assist countries in the region in making "reasonable macro policies, building institutional capacity and supporting regional integration." (EU 2021)

3. Conclusion

The birth of the EU's Indo-Pacific Strategy in the context of great fluctuations in the region and the world is essential to be able to orient actions for the interests and position of the EU as well as to contribute to ensuring stability, security, prosperity, and sustainability in the region's development, including economic and trade aspects. The EU has relatively solid foundations for promoting economic relations with countries in the Indo-Pacific region. These are relatively clear and complete frameworks to attract the participation of the parties as well as the results achieved in the trade and investment relations between the two sides. Major trends shaping the EU's economic relations in the Indo-Pacific region include digitalisation, green transition, economic restructuring and growth patterns, and increased geopolitical competition.

In addition to the existing solid foundations, and based on general and individual advocacy trends, there are many positive prospects for the EU's economic relationship with the region in the future in five areas: transition to a green and sustainable economy, focus on the service sector, development of the digital economy, strengthening and securing global supply chains and development aid.

4. References

Borell, Josep (2021): The EU needs a strategic approach for the Indo-Pacific. https://www.eeas.europa.eu/eeas/eu-needs-strategic-approach-indo-pacific_en?s=253.

Briesen, Detlef/Minh, P. Q./Trang, N. T. T. (2021): European Indo-Pacific Strategies and Perception of Vietnam in The EU approach to Cooperation in the Indo-Pacific: From Strategy to Practice, KAS and USSH, Hà Nội.

Briesen, Detlef/Minh, P. Q./Trang, N. T. T. (2022): Perception and Involvement of Significant Actors in the EU's Indo-Pacific Strategy in The EU approach to Cooperation in the Indo-Pacific: From Strategy to Practice, KAS and USSH, Hà Nội.

Truong Dinh Chien/Nguyen Hoai Nam (2022): FDI capital flow shifting trends in the context of geopolitical fluctuations and the impact of the COVID-19 pandemic: what opportunities for Vietnam? In: Ha Van Hoi/Vu Thanh Huong (ed.): Global FDI and Vietnam's FDI attraction orientation in the new context (Vietnamese). VNU Publishing House, Hanoi.

Council of European Union (2021): Council conclusion on an EU Strategy for Cooperation in the Indo-Pacific. https://data.consilium.europa.eu/doc/document/ST-7914-2021-INIT/en/pdf.

EEAS (2022): Ministerial Forum for Cooperation in the Indo-Pacific. https://www.eeas.europa.eu/eeas/ministerial-forum-cooperation-indo-pacific_en.

European Commission (2023): Negotiations and Agreements. https://policy.trade.ec.europa.eu/eu-trade-relationships-country-and-region/negotiations-and-agreements_en.

European Parliament (2022): Resolution P9_TA (2022)0276 Indo-Pacific strategy in the area of trade and investment. https://www.europarl.europa.eu/doceo/document/TA-9-2022-0276_EN.html.

Eurostat (2022): EU trade with the Indo-Pacific region. https://ec.europa.eu/Eurotat/web/products-Eurotat-news/w/EDN-20221128-1.

Eurostat (2023): Key figures on the EU in the world – 2023 edition. https://ec.europa.eu/Eurotat/web/products-key-figures/w/ks-ex-23-001.

Eurostat (2025): Key figures on the EU in the world – 2025 edition. https://ec.europa.eu/eurostat/web/products-key-figures/w/ks-01-25-002.

Fuhrmann, Michael (2021): The European Union is set to launch a comprehensive Strategy for the Indo-Pacific. https://www.mitsui.com/mgssi/en/report/detail/__icsFiles/afieldfile/2021/09/03/2107e_fuhrmann_e.pdf.

Grare, Frederic/Reuter, Manisha (2021): Moving closer: European views of the Indo-Pacific. https://ecfr.eu/special/moving-closer-european-views-of-the-indo-pacific/.

Georgieva, Kristalina (2023): IMF says risks to financial stability have increased, calls for vigilance. Reuters. https://www.reuters.com/markets/imf-says-risks-financial-stability-have-increased-calls-vigilance-2023-03-26/.

IBEF (2023): Service Sector: Contribution to India's GDP. https://www.ibef.org/research/case-study/service-sector-contribution-to-india-s-gdp.

Kuoman, Andrea (2023): A new guideline of the EU's foreign policy: A battle for global geopolitical influence. https://www.unav.edu/web/global-affairs/a-new-guideline-of-the-eus-foreign-policy.

Malmström, Cecelia (2022): The EU should expand trade with the Indo-Pacific region. https://www.piie.com/blogs/realtime-economics/eu-should-expand-trade-indo-pacific-region.

Prakash, Anita (2023) (ed.): Regional Integration in Indo-Pacific: Connectivity, Cooperation, and New Supply-Chain Linkages, ERIA. https://www.eria.org/publications/regional-integration-in-indo-pacific-connectivity-cooperation-and-new-supply-chain-linkages/.

Reddington, Karen (2022): It's time for EU firms to capitalise on the growing Asia-Pacific market. https://www.euractiv.com/section/economy-jobs/opinion/its-time-for-eu-firms-to-capitalise-on-the-growing-asia-pacific-market/.

SIPRI (2023): Surge in arms imports to Europe, while US dominance of the global arms trade increases. https://sipri.org/media/press-release/2023/surge-arms-imports-europe-while-us-dominance-global-arms-trade-increases.

UNCTAD (2023): World Investment Report 2023. https://unctad.org/publication/world-investment-report-2023.

World Bank (2023): Services, value added (per cent of GDP). https://data.worldbank.org/indicator/NV.SRV.TOTL.ZS?locations=IN-CN-JP-TH-ID-VN-KR-MY-SG.

Acknowledgement

The research presented in this chapter was conducted as part of the project *The EU Approach to Cooperation in the Indo-Pacific: From Strategy to Practice* during 2020–2023, with funding from Konrad-Adenauer-Stiftung (KAS) in Vietnam. I am sincerely grateful to KAS Vietnam for their generous support, which made this study possible. The views expressed in this chapter are those of the author and do not necessarily reflect the official position of KAS.

Chapter 9: Navigating Norms and Interests: The European Union's Values-Based Foreign Policy in the Indo-Pacific Region

Nguyen Thi Thuy Trang

This chapter explores the European Union's (EU) values-based approach to foreign policy, particularly in its engagement with the Indo-Pacific. It examines how democracy, human rights, and the rule of law have shaped the EU's foreign policy identity and strategic actions. Tracing the historical evolution of the EU's external policy from the European Economic Community (EEC) to the Common Foreign and Security Policy (CFSP), the article highlights key treaties and institutional developments that have formalized the EU's commitment to normative diplomacy. The EU's Indo-Pacific Strategy reflects its ambition to expand influence through multilateralism, connectivity, and sustainable development. However, challenges persist, including tensions between values and economic interests, institutional constraints in decision-making, and the geopolitical complexities of great power competition. The Russia-Ukraine war has further reshaped the EU's strategic priorities, prompting a recalibration of its foreign policy. Additionally, shifting U.S. policies under the Trump administration add uncertainty to transatlantic cooperation and Indo-Pacific engagement. Despite these challenges, the EU continues to advocate a rules-based international order, though its effectiveness as a normative power depends on balancing principles with strategic imperatives. This chapter critically assesses the feasibility of the EU's values-based diplomacy in an increasingly fragmented global landscape.

1. Introduction

Values-based approaches to foreign policy have no longer been exclusive to the West, i.e., America and European countries. Many countries worldwide, on all continents, seem to gradually recognise the role of cultural, historical, normative, legal, or even religious values in building foreign policy and gaining national power. However, the link between *values* and the European Union's internal and external policies still has its ambivalences and is more commonly discussed. Part of the reason for this is perhaps because *values*, although in many cases quite abstract and undefined, are always things that Europeans think inherently belong to them, coming from Europe in a very natural way and responsible for spreading those values to the rest of the world. Many factors have shaped this perception throughout the development of Europe and the world. Among those *values*, some are universal, and it is difficult to explain why Europeans have always assumed that they are responsible for universalising those values to the whole world. The second reason is the need to unite and create a common identity in the process of European integration.

The process of integration from economic to political requires leaders to build cohesion, solidarity, and common responsibility among the people of the Union, in other words, to form *European citizenship* in the member countries. Creating a common share of values also helps European Union (EU) officials justify their public policy. The recent enlargements of the Union and the constitution-making process were also structures of opportunities for claims to define shared values. The third reason is to demonstrate the EU's role and participation in world affairs through external or foreign policy. The first President of the European Commission, Walter Hallstein, once said: "One reason for creating the European Community [was] to enable Europe to play its full part in world affairs." (Hallstein 1962, 79)

In promoting political integration and formulating a common foreign policy, values are the basic elements shaping the EU's identity and instrumental factors in approaching partners and realising specific foreign policy goals.

This article analyses the values-based approach in the EU's foreign policy in its cooperation strategy in the emerging Indo-Pacific region. The article consists of three parts: the first part is presented in chronological order, overviewing the history of the formation of the EU's common foreign policy with values as one of the constitutive factors; the next part analyses the values-based approach in the EU's common foreign policy; and the third part focuses on the values-based approach in EU's cooperation strategy in the Indo-Pacific region in the context of many ups and downs, especially the ongoing conflict in Ukraine.

2. History of the EU's Common Foreign Policy

The early European community did not have a common foreign policy. It can be said that the foundation for the EU's foreign policy is the European Economic Community (EEC) and especially the European Political Cooperation (EPC).

The European Economic Community (EEC) represents its members in foreign trade issues and plays several roles in relations with the outside world, such as promoting international trade, building free trade areas or establishing the European Development Fund. In the early 1960s, the EEC took the first steps to formulate a development policy. In 1963, the Yaoundé Convention was signed by the EEC and eighteen former colonies of six member countries. In 1969, the convention was extended for another five years. Originally, the Convention was essentially a policy for Francophone countries in Africa (Bindi 2016, 16). After the expansion of the EEC in 1973, the Convention included African members of the British Commonwealth and other former colonies in the Caribbean and Pacific. The Yaoundé Convention (1963–75) maintains the system the Treaty of Rome introduced: aid allocations over five years, channelled through the European Development Fund (EDF), and a reciprocal preference-based trade mechanism.

The European Political Cooperation (EPC) was the precursor to today's EU Common Foreign and Security Policy (CFSP). The EPC was formed in 1970 and functioned until 1993 after the CFSP was created under the Maastricht Treaty. With the EPC, the member states of the European Community then developed a system of informal cooperation on foreign policy. The main purpose of the EPC was to protect and even strengthen the influence of European countries in the international arena as global political and economic interdependence increased. At the same time, the EPC was often seen as an approach that promoted the political side of the European integration process. During the 1950s and 1960s, the EC member states twice tried to add an external dimension to the domestic market, but both failed.

In 1954, efforts to promote the European Defence Community (EDC) failed. Eight years later, the Fouchet Plan proposed a form of intergovernmental political union that suffered the same fate. The issue of political integration was stalled until the late 1960s, when the growth of political and economic activities in countries outside Europe forced members to reconsider their external policy. And the 1969 The Hague Summit gave new impetus to Europe and paved the way for implementing the EPC. The

Davignon Report (also known as the Luxembourg Report), adopted by the Foreign Ministers on October 27, 1970, in Luxembourg, has a particularly important role in shaping European foreign policy. The report stipulated regular meetings of EEC foreign ministers, meetings of heads of state, regular consultation activities on external affairs between member states and regular meetings of political leaders of member countries.

It was the Davignon/Luxembourg report that led to the formation of the European Political Cooperation (EPC) (Bindi 2016, 19). After that, the Copenhagen Report of July 23, 1973, specified the role and operating mechanism of the EPC. According to the report, the EPC establishes "a new process in international relations and Europe's first step towards achieving a coordinated action." (European Communities 1973, 6) The Copenhagen Report specifies that foreign ministers will meet four times a year and whenever they deem necessary; it emphasises the role of the Political Committee as the body tasked with the preparation of ministerial meetings and the establishment of the "Group of Correspondents" and the system of European telex (COREU).

Transatlantic relations became strained in the 1970s. Overall, the United States remained supportive of European integration until the end of the Kennedy administration (Bindi et. el. 2005). This changed in the late 1960s and early 1970s when the United States began to regard the EEC as an economic competitor and blamed the bloc for the balance of payments deficit the United States encountered. On the one hand, the US insisted that Europe contribute more to NATO expenses; on the other hand, President Richard Nixon always affirmed the American leadership over this organisation. The US also always emphasised its global responsibilities and interests, while Europe's interests were only regional in scope (Bindi 2016, 21). In response, on December 14, 1973, in Copenhagen, the Foreign Ministers of the EEC adopted the Declaration on European Identity. The goal of the Declaration is to clearly define the EEC's relations and responsibilities with the rest of the world, as well as their position in global affairs (Bindi 2016, 21). In the statement, the nine-member states asserted that:

> "European Unification is not directed against anyone, nor does a desire for power inspire it. On the contrary, the Nine are convinced that their union will benefit the whole international community ... in world affairs and to thus ... positions to contribute more that international relations have a just basis... In pursuit of these objectives the Nine should pro-

gressively define common in the sphere of foreign policy." (European Community 1973b)

On 13 October 1981, the then ten member states adopted the London Report, further outlining the functions of the EPC in internal and external issues. Subsequently, the Stuttgart Declaration of 19 June 1983 expanded the scope of action of the EPC to include "the political and economic aspects of security" (Point 3.2). The Declaration also calls for "progressive development and definition of common principles and objectives [and] the possibility of joint actions in the field of foreign policy" (Point 3.2) (European Communities 1983), and for concerted action on "international problems of law and order" – later known as Justice and Home Affairs (Bindi 2016, 24). In December 1984, the European Parliament approved a draft treaty, calling for creating a European Union with legal status and allowing closer coordination between the EPC and foreign affairs. Under the draft treaty, the European Council could also expand foreign policy coordination on defence issues and the arms trade.

In the late 1980s, dramatic changes in the international system had a major effect on Europe, bringing both hope and fear about Germany's future. European leaders wanted a solution of a united Germany in a stronger Europe. With the reunification of Germany, the EEC leaders decided to convene an intergovernmental conference to establish the European Monetary Union (EMU). In June 1990, the European Council continued to convene two intergovernmental conferences: one to debate monetary union and the second to discuss political union, including a common foreign policy. The two conferences lasted in 1991. On 7 February 1992, the Treaty of Maastricht or the Treaty of the European Union (TEU) was signed.

The Maastricht Treaty establishes a Common Foreign and Security Policy (CFSP) for the European Union, replacing the European Political Cooperation (EPC). The TEU Treaty is the second of the three pillars of the EU (European Communities 1992, Title V). The text of the Treaty guides a wide range of values to which the EU is obligated (and will uphold and promote). CFSP has the objective of protecting the common values, fundamental interests, and independence of the Union; strengthening the security of the Union and its member states by any means; maintaining peace and strengthening international security; promoting international cooperation; developing and strengthening democracy and the rule of law, respecting human rights and fundamental freedoms, as outlined in article J.1.2 of the TEU (European Communities 1992, J. 1.2).

In October 1997, the Treaty of Amsterdam (officially known as the Treaty of Amsterdam, amending the Treaty on the European Union, the Treaty establishing the European Community and several related acts) was signed and created. Under the Treaty of Amsterdam, member states have agreed to transfer certain powers from national governments to the European Parliament on various areas, including immigration policy, through civil law and criminal justice, promulgating a common foreign and security policy (CFSP), as well as implementing institutional changes to expand as new member states join the EU (European Communities 1997). The Treaty sets out new principles and responsibilities in common foreign and security policy, emphasising expressing EU values to the outside world, protecting its interests and reforming EU policies.

The Lisbon Treaty that entered into force in December 2009 removed the separate structures of the three pillars, clearly and specifically demarcating the EU's jurisdiction over policy areas. For the first time, the EU was given the legal status of "inheriting and replacing the legal status of the European Community." It also created the presidency of the European Council and the EU's high representative for diplomacy and security (vice-president of the European Council). The CFSP's role as a pillar also ends here. To ensure coordination and consistency in EU foreign policy, the Treaty of Lisbon created a High Representative of the Union for Foreign Affairs and Security Policy, de facto merging the post of High Representative for the Common Foreign and Security Policy and European Commissioner for External Relations and European Neighbourhood Policy. Since December 2011, the High Representative (HR) has been in charge of the European External Action Service (EEAS), which the Treaty of Lisbon also created. It is intended to be a common Foreign Office or Diplomatic Corps for the European Union.

The EU employs a variety of diplomatic instruments, such as political dialogue, Council conclusions, European Council statements and formal diplomatic representations of official views, known as démarches. Crisis management missions and operations and restrictive measures against third countries, namely sanctions, are among the more tangible measures available to the CFSP.

The European External Action Service (EEAS) assists the High Representative in preparing the EU's external action and ensuring its coherence and coordination. The Council of the European Union may appoint EU Special Representatives (EUSRs) with a special mandate to assist the High Representative. Several EUSRs have been mandated to represent the EU in crisis and conflict areas outside the EU. They enable the EU to have an active and comprehensive role in conflict resolution. There are nine EUSRs, of which eight have a regional mandate and one has a thematic focus.

In 2016, the EU promulgated the European Union Global Strategy (EUGS), which replaced the European Security Strategy (adopted in 2003). The EUGS highlighted the importance of strategic autonomy for the EU and stressed the need to enhance its credibility as a global player. Key aspects covered were to improve internal and external security; stabilise fragile states on the EU's perimeter; develop an integrated approach to conflict and crises; promote peace and integration; display a commitment to multilateral systems; and promote sustainable development and respect for human rights (European Union 2016).

3. *Values in EU's Foreign Policy*

From the foundation history of the European Union's foreign policy, the values in the EU's external policy play both the constitutive element of the EU's identity and a key instrument for the EU to achieve specific goals, especially those related to security.

The phrase *European values* emerged as a new political term in the 1980s, in the context of accelerated European integration and the gradual formation of the European Union. The European Values Study first popularised the phrase. This large-scale, long-term transnational research program began in 1981 and is carried out every nine years in several European countries to provide insights into the ideas, beliefs, preferences, values and attitudes of citizens across Europe (European Values Study). Since then, the *values* that are the basis of defining the common identity and formulating external policies are mentioned in different ways, *European Values*, *our values*, *common values*, or *values of Europe*" (Calligaro et. al. 2016, 10) and are interpreted differently. Article 2 of the Treaty of the European Union (the TEU) lists the values on which the EU is based:

> "The Union is founded on the values of respect for human dignity, freedom, democracy, equality, the rule of law and respect for human rights, including the rights of persons belonging to minorities. values are common to the Member States in a society in which pluralism, non-discrimination, tolerance, justice, solidarity and equality between women and men prevail." (European Union 2012)

Article 3(5) of the TEU links these values to the EU's common goals in interacting with the rest of the world:

> "In its relations with the wider world, the Union shall uphold and promote its values and interests and contribute to the protection of its citizens. It shall contribute to peace, security, the sustainable development of the Earth, solidarity and mutual respect among peoples, free and fair trade, eradication of poverty and the protection of human rights, in particular the rights of the child, as well as to the strict observance and the development of international law, including respect for the principles of the United Nations Charter." (European Union 2012)

Article 21 of the Treaty expresses the common goal of external actions:

> "The Union's action on the international scene shall be guided by the principles which have inspired its own creation, development and enlargement, and which it seeks to advance in the wider world: democracy, the rule of law, the universality and indivisibility of human rights and fundamental freedoms, respect for human dignity, the principles of equality and solidarity, and respect for the principles of the United Nations Charter and international law." (European Union 2012)

The key objectives of the European Union's Common Foreign and Security Policy (CFSP) include safeguarding the EU's common values, preserving peace, consolidating democracy and respect for human rights, fundamental freedoms, and the rule of law, as well as strengthening the EU's internal and external security (European Union 2012, Article 21). The instruments available to the Common Foreign and Security Policy (CFSP) include political and economic instruments and military and civilian crisis management instruments.

Although not always clearly defined, human rights, democracy and the rule of law are central to the EU's common values and have become an increasingly important part of the Union's internal and external policy-making process (Cremona, 2004). Commitment to promoting human rights, democracy and the rule of law as common EU values in its foreign policy approach is linked to a perception of a normative power, a great power acting according to its values and seeking to present its rules to the outside, of the European Union (Manners 2002). In addition, coherence and consistency are key concerns of policymaking in the EU, including foreign policy.

It is difficult for the EU as a "supranational actor" to react quickly to international events and thus to do strategic planning to use the means at its disposal (Muguruza et al. 2018). Thus, promoting democracy, human rights and the rule of law are long-term strategies to address the underlying causes of vulnerability, conflict and insecurity. The EU's focus on the rule of law, as a shared value and as an instrument to promote democracy, dates back to the 1990s when EU institutional actors attempted to democratise the institutional framework not only for the democracy of the EU but also for its role-playing in the world Against this background, the EU's legitimacy as a "norm power" seems to rest on its ability to translate universal norms into more concrete policies (Bickerton 2011, 35). Both one of the EU's fundamental values and an objective of EU foreign policy, the rule of law has been invoked as a "means" and "objective" to develop and legitimise a range of domestic and foreign policies (Calligaro 2016, 21).

Besides interpreting the basic values, values in EU foreign policy are sometimes divided into categories according to their own characteristics and functions. An example is the division of values into five groups: social-cultural values which are the underlying drivers of foreign policy; political values, including the trinity of human rights, democracy and the rule of law; economic values that characterise the nature of the economic system; Earth values referring to the inclusion of environmental concerns in foreign policy; and "International order values" characterising the international outlook of actors, hereby according to the EU the value of international order is "principled pragmatism" (Damen 2022, 3). In recent years, values have often been seen as part of strategic autonomy and some EU policies, such as EU enlargement, trade policy, or a combination of these policies. Several observations point to differences in the value-based approach to EU foreign policy with different countries and according to the types of values involved. For example, when cooperation on political values does not seem to work for some countries, the EU continues its efforts with economic or Earth values (Damen 2022, 3).

The EU has worked to develop a sense of its identity based on core values, which are reflected in the way the EU wants to be perceived from the outside and in its foreign policy. The process of defining the EU's common identity can also be seen as the result, as well as the cause, of foreign policy. Of course, other factors affect this process, but the demand to demonstrate and conceptualise the role of human rights, the rule of law and democracy in the EU's external policy has led the EU to see and define itself from the perspective of values concerning the world as well as to their own people.

Although integrated and affirmed in many official documents and discourses of organisations and leaders, the values-based approach in EU foreign policy faces many challenges. Many, both from inside and outside, are sceptical and even critical of the role of the EU as a driving force in foreign policy in recent times. The critical arguments focus on the following key issues:

Firstly, considering the values as the foundation of European integration in general and the EU's foreign policy agenda, in particular, is the idea of some countries, and the other reluctant members have been convinced. This can be visualised relatively easily for members joining in later expansions of the Union. However, the members of the EU have never come together to specifically discuss any foreign policy doctrine or precise criteria for developing such a policy driven by values. Although values-based foreign policy is not limited to statements of intentions or goals of the Union, the difficulty of achieving unity of strategy and action within an intergovernmental political system will undermine the role of the EU.

Secondly, the institutions and individuals empowered to represent the EU externally do not have enough authority over issues that are inherently within their jurisdiction, as provided for in the EU's Treaties. One example is the role and authority of the EU High Representative for Foreign Affairs and Security. On February 4th–6th, 2021, Josep Borrell was the first high-ranking EU official to pay a visit to Russia since 2017; however, the visit was said to be a failure. Most member states, especially Germany, were not interested in giving Borrell the authority he needed to craft a strong foreign policy. Therefore, Borrell's visit to Russia was said to lack strategy and direction. Following Borrell's visit, Russia expelled three EU diplomats. On his blog, Borrell wrote upon returning from Moscow that his visit was inherently opposed by some member states (Dempsey, 2021).

The third point is the conflict between values, principles and the core interests of the EU and its member states. On the one hand, the EU considers a model of normative power with universal values; on the other hand, it wants to maximise benefits for the Union, its member states and its people. The EU's promotion of values parallel with further engagement with third countries on key interests creates a dilemma. The EU's failure to counter (despite its critical attitude) the 17+1 Forum of China and a group of Central and Eastern European and Balkan states to advance their economic and political interests is an example, showing that the 12 EU member states participating in this forum do not take seriously the meaning of values in EU policy (Dempsy 2021). The EU's criticism of China's human rights situation or Beijing's actions in the South China Sea has been partly softened by Hungary and Greece, who are fond of achieving large Chinese investments in their infrastructure. Several other major members, including Germany and Italy, prioritise economic interests in their bilateral relations with China (Raik 2020).

Values-based approach to cooperation in the Indo-Pacific

On 16 April 2021, the Council of Europe Union issued the Conclusion of the EU's Strategy for Cooperation in the Indo-Pacific region, the geographical area from the east coast of Africa to the island nations of Asia-Pacific.

The EU's Indo-Pacific strategy must be viewed in the context of the Union's foreign and security policy developments. 2016 the EU issued the European Union Global Strategy (EUGS). The strategy emphasises the direct link between European prosperity and Asian security because European and Asian trade and investment depend on regional stability (European Union 2016). About 80 per cent of goods entering the EU transit through the Indian Ocean, and therefore the security of routes, freedom of navigation and the rule of law are crucial to the bloc (Luthra 2021).

The European Union Maritime Security Strategy (EUMSS) was adopted in June 2014 after much deliberation, with an action plan agreed in December 2014 in five key areas: External action; Maritime awareness, surveillance, and information sharing; Capability development; Risk management, protection of critical maritime infrastructure and crisis response; and Maritime security research and innovation, education and training (Council of the EU). The Action Plan was revised in June 2018 to include regional responses to global challenges in the maritime sector. The EUMSS and accompanying action plans are important in integrating maritime aspects, where maritime security is a high priority, in EU policies and its commitments to other regions, especially in the western Indian Ocean.

The EU's new Indo-Pacific strategy is an evolution of the EUGS, EUMSS and other sector-specific strategy documents. The Indo-Pacific Strategy emphasises that the EU will strengthen its strategic focus, presence, and actions in that region. It highlights the need for a long-term perspective while maintaining appropriate flexibility. It highlights seven priority areas: Sustainable and inclusive prosperity; Green transition; Ocean governance;

Digital governance and partnerships; Connectivity; Security and defence; and Human security (Council of the EU, 2021).

Such a strategy is generally expected to advance EU interests, from both bilateral and multilateral relations, in the economic, trade or security domains. However, the EU may differ from other countries' Indo-Pacific strategies, as Europe's interests are largely normative (Kliem 2022, 57). As outlined in the EU's foreign policy documents, including the Global Strategy 2016 and as analysed above, these benefits include strengthening the rules-based order, human rights, democracy, the rule of law, and sustainable development:

> "The Council considers that the EU should reinforce its strategic focus, presence and actions in the Indo-Pacific with the aim of contributing to the stability, security, prosperity and sustainable development of the region, based on the promotion of democracy, rule of law, human rights and international law." (Council of the EU 2021)

The dynamics of the Indo-Pacific concept for regional actors must be candidly re-assessed. The core driving force of this concept is neither the economic or social importance of the region nor a simple definition of geospatial. The central feature of the Indo-Pacific concept is a shift in the geopolitical order with the rise of an increasingly assertive China (Kliem 2022, 58). The first reason actors like the US, Japan, Australia or even ASEAN endorse the idea of the Indo-Pacific is not to expand trade relationships and partnerships but to redefine their strategic space and priorities as the US-led order ends. It can be said that the Indo-Pacific is the dismantling of Asia's status quo, underpinned by America's liberal hegemony (Ikenberry 2004).

The Indo-Pacific is gradually replacing previous conceptualisations of the region such as *Asia-Pacific* or *East Asia*. Supported by key players in the region, especially former Japanese Prime Minister Abe Shinzo and former US President Donald Trump, the concept of a *free and open Indo-Pacific* (FOIP) specifically symbolises a strategic reorientation to focus resources on the challenges posed by China's growing confidence and assertiveness in the region (Goldstein 2020). Research on the views of key regional actors in the second phase of this research project agrees that the Indo-Pacific has become an area of competition among major regional powers in a new era.

As a result, Indo-Pacific policies are primarily not instrumental to exploiting opportunities in the region but rather to containing Chinese power and influence (Kliem 2022, 58). And the Indo-Pacific debate is primarily a re-establishment of its denial of hegemony, which attempts to limit the extent to which China can expand its military and geo-economic reach in the region (Colby 2021). The United States and its regional partners seek to establish a new balance of power. What is most worrisome for the region's small and medium-sized players is being caught up in this geostrategic power competition or being forced to choose a side.

In this context, the fact that an engagement of an actor who identifies itself as a normative power in the Indo-Pacific debate is remarkable and perhaps is welcomed by many regional entities. Of course, the EU is interested in increasing and expanding market access in Asia, and many EU members are interested in maintaining free trade routes and stability on the important shipping routes. However, the EU had almost all that before considering and announcing its Indo-Pacific Cooperation Strategy. The key point that makes the important members of the bloc, i.e. France, Germany and the Netherlands, and the EU Commission and Parliament, realise the demand to present and participate in the region is the geopolitical shift that is taking place in this region. The EU announced its strategy for the region relatively late compared to some other important actors. But the EU Strategy represents two goals of ambivalences: first, to strengthen the Transatlantic relationship with the US through engagement and play a role in a region that the US considers a strategic priority; and second, to affirm the Union's role and participation in global affairs, counterbalancing the US's FOID strategy.

The value-based approach helps the EU better represent a normative actor's role in the region. In relations with China, the strategy text shows that the EU manages to avoid strategic competition with China by seeking dialogue and cooperation with all partners, including China. For other actors, the EU promotes an open, multilateral, and rule-based regional order through a normative approach to connectivity (based on sustainability, standards, shared values and a level global playing field) and technology (people-centred).

The EU affirms that it will promote human rights and democracy and continues to use all available disposals: dialogue and consultation on politics and human rights, trade preferences and integration of human rights considerations in all EU policies and programmes. At the same time, the EU also endorses a tough stance, such as restrictive measures (sanctions) against individuals, organisations and agencies responsible for, participate in or are involved in serious human rights violations and abuses (European Commission 2021, 1).

The EU intends to strengthen its role as a cooperative partner in the Indo-Pacific, bringing added value to the relationship with all partners in the region through comprehensive cooperation across multiple development sectors towards achieving the United Nations Sustainable Development Goals, addressing the devastating human and economic impacts of the COVID-19 crisis in many countries, and the need to ensure sustainable and inclusive socio-economic recovery while improving the resilience of health systems (Council of the EU 2021). The EU's values- and rules-based and multilateral approach supports its relationship with important regional entities, including China and ASEAN. Of course, as analysed above, when values conflict with interests, in some cases, the EU or its member states may be willing to push the former backwards if necessary.

The new context

The conflict between Russia and Ukraine that began in early 2022 resulted in tremendous changes in the international system. The large-scale war caused problems beyond the imagination of the people of Europe and the world. It also reveals many problems of actors in the current international system. A new world order with a changing role of key players may be taking shape.

The conflict started less than a year after the EU had announced its Indo-Pacific Cooperation Strategy. As hopes for a stronger role of the EU as a normative actor in global affairs grew, the war in Ukraine created anxiety and scepticism about the future of its strategic ambitions. At present, expectations for a foreign policy and an international order based on values, rules, or norms must give way to more realistic calculations and visions. The EU and its member states are primarily preoccupied with the ongoing conflict in their neighbouring region, economic recovery, energy security, and the evolving global power structure.

The war in Ukraine has also influenced the EU's strategic autonomy debate, pushing the bloc toward increased military coordination and more robust defence mechanisms. The European Peace Facility (EPF) has been significantly expanded to support Ukraine, while countries like Germany have abandoned long-standing policies of military restraint. The EU's commitment to reinforcing its defence capabilities, including discussions on a joint European army, is now central to its security agenda.

Simultaneously, the recent changes in the U.S. administration have further complicated global strategic calculations. With the return of the Trump administration, there have been significant shifts in U.S. foreign policy that have directly impacted the EU and its strategic priorities. Trump's *America First* approach has led to renewed tensions within NATO, with calls for European allies to take on a greater share of defence spending and security responsibilities. The administration's stance on Ukraine has become more ambiguous, with debates on continued military aid, potentially leaving the EU to assume a more independent role in supporting Kyiv. Additionally, Trump's renewed emphasis on trade protectionism and economic nationalism has strained transatlantic trade relations, prompting EU policymakers to reconsider economic and technological dependencies and enhance strategic autonomy.

The Trump administration has also deprioritized multilateral diplomacy in favour of bilateral deals, complicating EU efforts to coordinate collective responses to global challenges. In the Indo-Pacific, Washington has intensified competition with China but has placed less emphasis on cooperation with traditional allies, raising concerns in Europe about how to navigate the region's evolving security landscape.

In light of these developments, two scenarios can be considered regarding the EU's Indo-Pacific strategy:

> The first scenario is that the EU may continue to pursue its Indo-Pacific Cooperation Strategy as a long-term project, reaffirming its role as a global actor while adjusting its approach based on lessons from the Ukraine conflict. In this case, the EU and its member states may place greater emphasis on security cooperation in the Indo-Pacific, working more closely with partners such as Japan, India, and ASEAN to counterbalance geopolitical risks.
>
> The second scenario is the EU may be forced to shift its focus inward, prioritizing security and economic concerns closer to home. With pressing issues in Eastern Europe, the Middle East, and Africa, discussions about maintaining investments and cooperation in the Indo-Pacific may lose momentum.

Given the complexity of the Ukraine conflict and the evolving global landscape, it is too early to predict which scenario is more likely. However, one certainty is that security will remain the EU's top priority for the foreseeable future. Beyond military and economic strengthening, the EU must also reduce its dependence on Russian energy, counter China's influence in key sectors, and reassess its relationship with the U.S. to ensure greater strategic autonomy.

Despite these challenges, European public opinion remains supportive of a values-based foreign policy. A study conducted in April 2023 by the Friedrich Naumann Foundation, involving 2,752 citizens from 10 EU member states, produced rather optimistic results. Most respondents emphasized the need for the EU to focus on security, human rights, and democracy while promoting a common foreign policy on Ukraine and other global issues. This indicates that, despite geopolitical pressures, Europeans still expect the EU to uphold its core values while navigating an increasingly complex international order (Friedrich Naumann Foundation 2023).

4. Conclusion

The European Union's values-based approach to foreign policy has long been a defining feature of its global engagement. As this article has explored, the EU's foreign policy framework has evolved through various historical stages, from the European Economic Community (EEC) and European Political Cooperation (EPC) to the establishment of the Common Foreign and Security Policy (CFSP) and the adoption of key treaties such as Maastricht, Amsterdam, and Lisbon. These developments have institutionalized the EU's commitment to upholding and promoting democracy, human rights, the rule of law, and multilateralism as integral elements of its external relations.

The Indo-Pacific Strategy represents a continuation of this values-driven diplomatic agenda. By prioritizing strategic partnerships, connectivity, sustainable development, and human security, the EU seeks to reinforce its normative influence in a region marked by growing geopolitical competition. However, the implementation of this strategy is fraught with challenges. The EU must navigate tensions between its normative aspirations and pragmatic economic and security interests, institutional limitations within its foreign policy mechanisms, and the shifting dynamics of great power competition, particularly in light of China's expanding influence and evolving U.S. policies.

Furthermore, the outbreak of the Russia-Ukraine war has redefined the EU's strategic priorities, forcing the Union to recalibrate its global approach. While European public opinion still supports a values-driven foreign policy, the need for security, economic resilience, and strategic autonomy has increasingly come to the forefront. The potential return of a Trump administration in the U.S. further complicates the EU's geopolitical calculations, raising questions about transatlantic cooperation and the Union's ability to sustain its Indo-Pacific engagement amid global uncertainties.

Ultimately, while the EU remains committed to a values-based foreign policy, the extent to which these principles can drive real-world decision-making will depend on the balance between idealism and pragmatism. The Indo-Pacific Strategy reflects the EU's ambitions to position itself as a normative power in a multipolar world, but its success will be determined by the Union's capacity to adapt to geopolitical realities, enhance internal cohesion, and assert strategic influence in an increasingly contested global order.

5. References

Bickerton, Christopher (2011): European Union Foreign Policy: From Effectiveness to Functionality, New York, Palgrave-Macmillan.

Bindi, Federiga (2016): European Union Foreign Policy: A Historical Overview. Bookings: 13–40. https://www.brookings.edu/wp-content/uploads/2016/07/theforeignpolicyoftheeuropeanunion_chapter.pdf

Bindi, Federiga/D'Ambrosio, Palma (2005): Il futuro dell'Europa. Milan: Franco Angeli.

Calligaro, O. (et al.) (2016): Values in the EU policies and discourse. A first assessment. Les Cahiers du Cevipol.

Colby, Elbridge A. (2021): The Strategy of Denial: American Defense in an Age of Great Power Conflict.

Council of the European Union (2014): European Union Maritime Security Strategy. Brussels, (OR. en) 11205/14. Council of the European Union.

Council of the European Union (2021): Council conclusions on an EU Strategy for cooperation in the Indo-Pacific. Brussels.

Cremona, Marise (2004): Values in the EU Constitution: The External Dimension. In Mills and Aziz (eds.): Values in the Constitution of Europe. Ashgate, Dartmouth.

Damen, Mario (2022): Values on the Retreat? The Role of Values in the EU's External Policies. Policy Department for External Relations, Directorate General for External Policies of the Union, European Parliament. PE 639.318 - March 2022.

Dempsey, Judy (2021): Why the European Union Cannot Do Foreign Policy. Carnegie Europe. https://carnegieeurope.eu/strategiceurope/83841.

European Commission (2021): Questions and Answers: EU Strategy for Cooperation in the Indo-Pacific. Brussels, 16 September 2021.

European Communities (1973): Second report on European political cooperation in foreign policy matters. Copenhagen, 23 July 1973. http://www.cvce.eu/obj/second_report_on_european_political_cooperation_in_foreign_policy_matters_copenhagen_23_.

European Communities (1983): Solemn Declaration on European Union (Stuttgart, 19 June 1983).

European Communities (1992): Treaty on European Union. Maastricht.

European Communities (1997): Treaty of Amsterdam amending the Treaty on European Union, the Treaties establishing the European Communities and certain related acts. Amsterdam.

European Community (1973): Declaration on European Identity. Copenhagen, 14 December 1973, point II.9. http://www.cvce.eu/obj/declaration_on_european_identity_copenhagen_14_december_1973-en-02798dc9-9c69-4b7d-b2c9-f03a8db7da32.html.

European Union (2012): Consolidated Versions of the Treaty on European Union and the Treaty on the Function of the European Union (2016/C 202/01). https://eur-lex.europa.eu/legal-content/EN/TXT/HTML/?uri=CELEX:12016ME/TXT&from=EN.

European Union (2016): Global Strategy, Shared Vision, Common Action: A Stronger Europe, Brussels, June 2016.

European Values Study. https://europeanvaluesstudy.eu/about-evs/.

Friedrich Naumann Foundation (2023): European Citizen's Perspectives on EU Foreign Policy: Values, Security, and the Veto-System.

Goldstein, Avery (2020): US-China Rivalry in the twenty-first century: Déjà vu and Cold War II. China

Hallstein, Walter (1962): United Europe: Challenge and Opportunity. Harvard University Press, 1962.

Ikenberry, John (2004): American hegemony and East Asian order. In: Australian Journal of International Affairs, Vol. 58(3), 353–367.

International Strategy Review. Vol. 2, 48–62; Niall Ferguson. 2019. The New Cold War? It's with China and it has already begun. (http://www.niallferguson.com/journalism/politics/the-new-cold-war-its-with-china-andit-has-already-begun).

Kliem, Frederick (2022): The EU Strategy on Cooperation in the Indo-Pacific: A Meaningful Regional Complement? In European Strategic Approaches to the Indo-Pacific. KAS.

Luthra, Girish (2021): An Assessment of the European Union's Indo-Pacific Strategy. ORF Issue Brief No. 504, November 2021, Observer Research Foundation.

Manners, I. (2002): Normative Power Europe: A Contradiction in Terms? JCMS: Journal of Common Market Studies, 40, 235–258.

Muguzura, Cristina Churruca (2018): Human rights and democracy at the heart of the EU policy? An assessment of the EU's comprehensive approach to human rights. In EU Human Rights and Democratization Policies. Routledge. https://www.taylorfrancis.com/chapters/edit/10.4324/9781315110769-4/human-rights-democracy-heart-eu-foreign-policy-cristina-churruca-muguruza.

Raik, Kristi (2020): 17+1 Cooperation Is Turning Sour: Shared Concerns Over China Can Help Repair the Transatlantic Relationship. International Centre for Defence and Security of Estonia. https://icds.ee/en/171-cooperation-is-turning-sour-shared-concerns-over-china-can-help-repair-the-transatlantic-relationship/.

Acknowledgement

The research presented in this chapter was conducted as part of the project *The EU Approach to Cooperation in the Indo-Pacific: From Strategy to Practice* during 2020–2023, with funding from Konrad-Adenauer-Stiftung (KAS) in Vietnam. I am sincerely grateful to KAS Vietnam for their generous support, which made this study possible. The views expressed in this chapter are those of the author and do not necessarily reflect the official position of KAS.

Chapter 10: The European Union's Engagement in Southeast Asian Security

Ho Thu Thao

As part of a broader strategy for cooperation in the Indo-Pacific, the European Union (EU) has been pursuing more proactive policies and closer ties with the Southeast Asian region. Despite being recognized primarily as an economic giant, the EU has been putting much effort into developing and strengthening its role as a security actor in the region. However, questions remain about whether the EU can foster its security presence in Southeast Asia. This chapter therefore aims to examine the EU's engagement in Southeast Asia, focusing on its role as a security actor, especially with the introduction of the Indo-Pacific strategy. To achieve such aim, the chapter will firstly trace the conceptual foundations laid out by the previous researchers to conceptualize the term *security actor* in international relations. It will then examine various aspects of the EU as a security actor in Southeast Asia through qualitative analysis of EU strategies, official declarations, operational instruments, partnership, and regional perceptions. The discussions follow will attempt to bring all these elements together and lay out the current problems and prospects of the EU's engagement in Southeast Asian security.

1. Introduction

In 1991, the then-Belgian Minister of Foreign Affairs famously retorted that *Europe was an economic giant, a political dwarf, and a military worm.* For a long time, this saying has often been cited both by academia and politicians. First EU, despite being recognized first and foremost as an economic giant, has been putting much effort in developing and strengthening its role as a security actor, both regionally and internationally. The 1990s first saw the creation of Common Foreign and Security Policy (CFSP) and European Security and Defence Policy (ESDP) as EU recognized the need for independent military capabilities, then witnessed the beginning of the EU's most ambitious enlargement process which led to the transition to liberal democracies and market economies in many European post-communist countries, contributing to solidarity and security in the region. In 2004, the EU launched the European Neighbourhood Policy to further extend the ring of stability, security and prosperity to the EU's Eastern and Southern neighbouring regions. With the adoption of the European Security Strategy (ESS) in 2003, the EU identified a range of security threats and challenges, established principles and set clear objectives for advancing the EU's security interests, all of which have been reinforced even more in the following years. Entering into force in 2009, the Lisbon Treaty has officially strengthened the EU's security role by important reforms:

- Creating the post of the High Representative for Foreign Affairs and Security Policy (High Representative) and the European External Action Service (EEAS) for greater coordination in foreign policy.
- Establishing Permanent Structured Cooperation (PESCO) to deepen defence cooperation amongst EU Member States.
- Shifting ESDP to Common Security and Defence Policy (CSDP) to emphasize that security and defence since then has been core components of the EU's foreign policy.

In 2016, amid rapid global challenges, the European Union Global Strategy (EUGS) was adopted to help the EU stay the course and continue to be a reliable global power and strong security provider. The 2016 EUGS sets out the EU's core interests and principles for engaging in the wider world and gives the EU a collective sense of direction. With such policy evolution, the EU has emerged as an evolving security actor with the ability to response to both regional and international crises.

On 16 September 2021, the EU strategy for cooperation in the Indo-Pacific was adopted to increase the EU's engagement in the region, as

> "The futures of the EU and the Indo-Pacific are inextricably linked given the interdependence of the economies and the common global challenges." (European Commission 2021, 1)

As part of the wider Indo-Pacific, Southeast Asia has vital geostrategic importance and presents both significant opportunities and challenges for the EU, especially when considering that this region is home to a great concentration of political and security challenges. Therefore, forging EU's closer engagement in Southeast Asia region in general, and with the ASEAN in particular, has been a central part of Europe's strategy (Kliem 2022, 57). Even though the EU already has a long-standing partnership with the ASEAN that officially formalized in 1977, the Indo-Pacific strategy is still considered an important turning point that marks the EU's increasing presence in Southeast Asia.

However, despite EU's ambition to foster its security presence worldwide, as well as its increasingly important role in Southeast Asia, the fact that the EU has emerged and been acknowledged in the region mostly as a major trading partner and foreign direct investment (FDI) source is not likely to be changed. As revealed in a perception study carried out in many Southeast Asian countries in 2010, the EU has historically been perceived as an economic power rather than a security actor in Southeast Asia (Chaban/Holland 2010, 6). Even though the EU's relations with ASEAN have been elevated to a strategic level since 2020, and its influence in Southeast Asia has extended beyond economic domains with the introduction of 2021 Indo-Pacific strategy, questions remain about whether the EU can play any role as a global security actor in the region.

This chapter therefore aims to examine the EU's engagement in Southeast Asia, focusing on its role as a security actor, especially after the introduction of the Indo-Pacific strategy. To achieve such an aim, the chapter will firstly trace the conceptual foundations laid out by the previous researchers to conceptualize the term *security actor* in international relations. It will then examine different aspects of the EU as a security actor in Southeast Asia through qualitative analysis of EU strategies, official declarations, operational instruments, partnership and regional perceptions. The discussions follow will attempt to bring all these elements together and lay out the current problems and prospects of the EU's engagement in Southeast Asian security.

2. Literature Review

There is an extensive amount of pre-existing literature relating to the EU's engagement in Southeast Asian security. As security challenges had become more and more complex and multidimensional since the end of the Cold War, the EU has developed into a security actor and recently increased its presence in Southeast Asia, hence become a potential research object for many scholars around the world. To facilitate the research, this literature review will be organized thematically and divided into two sections.

The first section examines certain aspects of the EU as a developing security actor through the findings of several previous studies. Conducted when heated discussions towards the development of CFSP and ESDP were still going on, the paper *The Demand for Military Expenditure: Evidence from the EU15 (1961–2005)* by Eftychia Nikolaidou provides an empirical analysis of the determinants of military spending in each of the 15 core EU countries over a 44-year period. Nikolaidou explored the linkage between several variables and military expenditure and indicated that there is very little uniformity in the factors that determine each member state's demand for military expenditure (Nikolaidou 2008). Published by Annemarie Peen Rodt in 2011, the paper *Taking Stock of EU Military Conflict Management* studies EU conflict management and how the EU utilized both civilian and military means. Rodt examined five cases in which the EU had conducted military operations to manage conflicts and focused on the criteria which were used to measure to what degree the operations were successful. As concluded in the case study, the EU seemed to have a good track record regarding operational goals attainment and appropriateness of the military operations (Rodt 2011).

Like many other studies, the papers *The EU as a Security Actor: The development of political and administrative capabilities* by Pernille Rieker, *The European Union: A New Security Actor?* by Thomas Renard and *The EU, neither a Political Dwarf nor a Military Worm* by Elina Viilup recognize the emergence of the EU as a security player. Despite the reality that the EU was still far from being a coordinated and fully-fledged external actor due to limited capabilities and strategic clout, the authors positively noted the EU's political and administrative capacity as well as the growing coherence and consistency that has been slowly shown in the EU's responses to a range of security challenges. However, while Rieker believed that the most important shortcomings for the EU's security role are the lack of its organizing skills (Rieker 2007), Renard concluded that the EU primarily acts as a regional security player (Renard 2014), Viilup argued that the EU still exerts significant global influence through soft power (Viilup 2015).

Finally, through the paper *European Military Capabilities: Enablers and Constraints on EU power?* Kaija Schilde examines the material aspects of the EU power by analysing its military capabilities and the factors that both enable and constrain its role as a global security actor. The paper analyses how external threats, such as the Russia–Ukraine crisis, serve as critical junctures in the weight and means of EU military power, representing a partial but significant shift away from the overall national tendencies of reducing military spending across Europe, and the decade-long trends of strategic goals towards mobilizing EU military power outside of Europe (Schilde 2017).

The second section looks at literature regarding the security engagement of the EU in Southeast Asia. Conducted right after the release of the Indo-Pacific Strategy, as Europe was gearing up to engage Southeast Asia in the Indo-Pacific region, the paper *European Strategic Approaches in the Indo-Pacific: A View from Southeast Asia* by Nazia Hussain provides a Southeast Asian perspective of European strategic approaches in the Indo-Pacific and revealed that ASEAN still more or less harbours doubt about whether the EU can move past the asymmetrical donor-recipient nexus which has been existed between the two sides for decades, and that there is a lack of coherence in EU's approach towards ASEAN (Hussain 2021). Also published in 2021, the paper *European Maritime Security Capacity Building Assistance in Southeast Asia: Promises and Pitfalls* by Olli Pekka Suorsa focuses on Europe's efforts to enhance maritime security in Southeast Asia, highlighting both the opportunities and challenges inherent in these initiatives. It is worth noting that not only EU as a whole, but also major European powers such as Britain, France, and Germany are increasingly turning their attention to the Indo-Pacific in general and the Southeast Asia in particular. The paper provides an overview of the different maritime security capacity building tools available for the major European powers and the EU and assesses their contributions to the region's maritime security architecture and challenges therein (Suorsa 2021).

Another paper discusses practical engagement of EU in the region is *COVID-19: EU Engagement in Southeast Asia* by S. Nanthini. In this paper, Nanthini focuses on the COVID-19 outbreak as it has become clear that the pandemic poses a significant non-traditional security threat. The paper then examines the active involvement of the EU in the Southeast Asia's *COVID* -19 response, pandemic preparedness and overall disaster cooperation activities (Nanthini 2021). One of the more recent studies on this topic is the paper *The future of Europe's Southeast Asia engagement* by Prashanth Parameswaran. This paper emphasizes the evolvement on many fronts in relations between Europe and Southeast Asia and stay optimistic that the relations will likely keep developing due to several converging interests. However, Parameswaran also noted that regional and global geopolitical tensions will potentially limit or complicate the EU's engagement with some Southeast Asian countries, especially given the fact that the two sides are holding different views to several concerns (Parameswaran 2024).

While agreeing with most of Parameswaran 's comments, Eugene R.L. Tan and Joanne Lin in *Engaging Southeast Asia: The EU's role as a Resilient and Reliable Middle Power?* emphasize the preferred and trusted *third party* position that the EU has gained in Southeast Asia, as well as its reputation for "doing the right thing" in the wider interests of the global community. After breaking down certain practical limitations from both sides, the paper suggests that the EU can focus its strengths on areas of non-traditional security, rather than focusing on hard security (Tan/Lin 2024).

Scholars have acknowledged the EU's development as a security actor whose presence in Southeast Asia is increasingly acknowledged. However, the literature also shows that the EU's engagement is especially strong in non-traditional security domains such as maritime capacity building, pandemic response, disaster resilience, and development cooperation. Despite the lack of presence in traditional security domains, the EU has gained growing recognition as a trusted actor in the region through its soft power reputation and normative commitment to multilateralism. However, the EU's security role remains constrained by internal fragmentation and external expectations.

3. The EU's Security Actorness in Southeast Asia

In Southeast Asia, the EU has a long-standing partnership with the Association of Southeast Asian Nations (ASEAN). The EU-ASEAN relations have undoubtedly seen significant milestones in recent years. While ASEAN is a central international organization in Southeast Asia, the EU is widely recognized as a supranational entity with deeper institutional integration and legal authority that transcends traditional intergovernmental cooperation. Striving to become key players in shaping the regional and global political landscape, the two entities have also shared almost half a century of diplomatic ties together. Since the official establishment in 1977, despite many ups and downs, both regions have developed a comprehensive dialogue that encompasses both economic and political components.

It is worth noting that even though the early years of the partnership was mostly underpinned by development and economic cooperation, the EU seemed to recognize its security role in Asia region from very early on. The 1994 European Commission's Communication on *Towards a New Asia Strategy* revealed the fundamentally economic-oriented approach of EU towards Asia, with ASEAN being the gateway to a stronger and broader partnership between the EU and Southeast Asia. Even though there was no mention of the EU as a security actor, its objectives of contributing

> "To the development and consolidation of democracy and the rule of the law, and respect for human rights and fundamental freedoms in Asia" (European Commission 1994, 3)

can easily be associated with EU's security role in the region.

Nearly a decade after introducing the 1994-Communication, the 2003 European Commission's Communication on *A new partnership with South-East Asia* identified six strategic priorities of the EU towards ASEAN, which clearly and directly refer to EU's engagement in security matters in Southeast Asia. From this point on, EU-ASEAN relations have been driven no longer by mere economic matters as the EU began to recognize and prioritize its certain role in Southeast Asian security.

Also, some notable phrases taken out from the 2003-Communication are:

> "Supporting regional stability and the fight against terrorism," "promoting human rights," "migration and asylum, trafficking in human beings, money laundering, piracy," "organized crime and drugs." (European Commission 2003)

demonstrate how security has been understood from the EU's perspective, especially since the end of the Cold War. It is shown that the EU has been perceived security in a much broader context than the traditional, realist state-centric view of national security which mainly focuses on territorial defence. Instead, the EU tends to put much importance on a wide range of non-traditional security threats such as migration and human rights, which is no longer state-centric. The 2003 ESS adopts a *security is a precondition of development* approach, not only linking security and development but also structuring the overall strategy based on preventive engagement and effective multilateralism which seriously takes human security into account (Council 2003, 4). In 2021, the Indo-Pacific Strategy continues to assert that the EU is "a consistent defender of human rights and democracy," thereby emphasizing even more the importance of non-traditional dimension in the EU's concepts, policies and actions on security matters (European Commission 2021, 3).

To examine the engagement of the EU as a security actor in Southeast Asia, it is necessary to define the concept and connotation of the term *security actor*. While in conventional international relations, statehood has traditionally been one of the requirements for being treated as an actor in the international system, other criteria have been recently emphasized – such as autonomy and the ability to perform. Such an approach makes it possible for multilateral institutions in general and the EU in particular to be considered as actors. Thus, this chapter affirms that the EU can be considered as a security actor in the world in general and in Southeast Asia in particular. In fact, such role of the EU is increasingly recognized and supported by many scholars, based on the fact that EU institutions have been granted more powers in the security area to influence international security dynamics through a combination of capabilities, policies, and actions (Rieker 2007; Renard 2014; Viilup 2015).

However, scholars have different approaches when analysing and assessing the EU's security actorness. For example, Rieker only focuses on several key political and administrative capabilities that must be present for the EU to be considered a genuine security actor (Rieker 2007, 11) while Renard investigates the EU's security actorness through its contribution to four key security functions, namely assurance, prevention, protection and compellence (Renard 2014, 7). Focusing only on some specific aspects of the EU's security actorness leads to the absence of a comprehensive definition of security actor. This chapter thus attempts to define security actor based on the views of previous scholars on the concept of actor in international relations.

Since the late 1970s, Gunnar Sjöstedt has joined the debate on the EU's actorness and defined actor capability as a

> "Capacity to behave actively and deliberately in relation to other actors in the international system." (Sjöstedt 1977, 16)

In other words, he connects actorness with the ability to respond effectively to others' needs and to act accordingly in a given context. For the EU, this approach puts emphasizes on *internal cohesion* or its capacity to act deliberately and consistently in international politics and internal resources or its ability to identify, develop, and implement foreign and security policy (Rieker, 2007: 8).

Building and expanding on the pioneering work of Sjöstedt, Joseph and Caporaso identify four components of actorness in global politics:

(1) *recognition*, where other actors recognize, accept, and interact with the EU; (2) *authority*, where the EU's activities have a sense of legal competence; (3) *autonomy*, where the EU has a distinctive identity

and interests that are independent from other actors including its own member states; (4) *cohesion*, the degree to which the EU is able to formulate and articulate internally consistent policy preferences (Jupille/Caporaso 1998, 214).

Charlotte Bretherton and John Vogler, on the other hand, argued that actorness is constructed through the interplay of both internal and external factors (Bretherton/Vogler 2006, 2) and expanded the list of criteria for actorness by combining three interacting processes, based on the notions of opportunity, presence and capability:

(1) *Opportunity* refers to factors in the external environment which constrain or enable the EU's actorness. In other words, this signifies the structural context of the EU's actions and refers to the idea that no actor can be considered completely independent in international system; (2) *Presence* describes the EU's ability to exert influence beyond its borders. Such influence can be understood as the EU's ability to change their partners' behaviour by using different methods and resources; (3) *Capability* refers to the internal context of EU external actions, which covers the legitimate character of foreign policy priorities, the availability of foreign policy instruments and the EU's ability to utilize these instruments (Bretherton/Vogler 2006, 22).

Based on the conceptual foundations laid out by the above-mentioned researchers, it can be argued that the concept of a security actor in international relations refers to a

> recognized entity that possesses the legal authority, political autonomy and operational capability to identify and respond effectively to security threats in both traditional and non-traditional domains.

Even though it can undoubtedly be affirmed that the EU qualifies as a relevant security actor, this chapter will still rely on the above definition to assess the EU's engagement as a security actor in Southeast Asia through the examination of several key aspects:

(1) The *authority*, which means the EU must have legal and institutional foundations that authorize it to undertake external action in the field of security, typically embedded in its treaties or constitutional documents.
(2) The *autonomy*, with which the EU must possess the ability to pursue independent interests, formulate consistent policy preferences, and

maintain a distinct identity in external action, without being fully dependent on the will of its member states or other external actors.

(3) The *recognition*, or the acknowledgment by ASEAN in general and Southeast Asian countries in particular that the EU is a legitimate and relevant player in security affairs.

(4) The *capability*, which means the EU must possess the resources, instruments and means needed – either military, economic, or civilian – to effectively implement its security policy.

(5) The *responsiveness*, or the capacity of the EU to respond to security challenges in Southeast Asia. In other words, the EU's security actorness depends not only on what the EU is but also how it interacts with the region and shapes behaviours accordingly.

4. The EU's Engagement as a Security Actor in Southeast Asia

Authority

There is no doubt that the EU has the authority to undertake external actions in the field of security. The 1993 Maastricht Treaty, officially known as the Treaty on European Union (TEU), states in Article J.1(1) that the EU shall "define and implement a common foreign and security policy covering all areas of foreign and security policy." While the 1993 Maastricht Treaty introduced and created the legal foundation for the CFSP, marking the first time the EU was given an explicit mandate to act as a unified actor in foreign and security matters, the 2009 Lisbon Treaty strengthened such legal and institutional authority through the creation of the High Representative and the EEAS to centralizes the leadership and resources for the EU s external action, thus enhancing the EU's competence in external security action, both in civilian and military dimensions.

In addition to the founding treaties, other EU strategies and official declarations also emphasize the EU's authority as a security actor. While the 2003 ESS affirms the EU's role and commitment in dealing with security challenges as a global player, the 2003-Communication explicitly refers to the EU's authority to engage in external security-related action in the region. The document affirms that a variety of security concerns:

> "Constitute core objectives in external relations of the European Union and its development co-operation with third countries" and some important security issues need to be "incorporated systematically into... (the

EU's) regional and bilateral dialogues with Southeast Asia." (European Commission 2003, 14, 16)

The 2016 EUGS also confirms that the EU's external action in security issues is "grounded in the values enshrined in the Treaties," affirming its institutional legitimacy as a global security actor (European External Action Service 2016, 7). Such authority of the EU continues to be affirmed in its 2021 Indo-Pacific strategy. Thus, it has been clearly shown in the EU's founding Treaties and official documents since the early 1990s that the EU's external engagement in security matters in the world generally and Southeast Asia particularly is part of its legal competence to undertake actions in external affairs.

Autonomy

As stated in the founding Treaties, the EU operates its external actions independently through supranational bodies such as the EEAS, which serves as the EU's diplomatic corps and represents the EU as a single international actor, and European Defence Agency (EDA), which coordinates defence cooperation among member states based on EU strategic priorities and thus gives shape to an EU-level defence identity. Besides, the EU's global strategy documents such as the 2003 ESS, the 2008 Implementation Report of the ESS, the 2016 EUGS and the 2021 Indo-Pacific Strategy also articulate a unified vision that transcends national foreign policies. In these strategy documents, the EU identified a series of external security challenges, established principles and set clear objectives for advancing its security interests based on its core values, thus demonstrating an independent stance on security threats and policy priorities.

It is also emphasized in the 2003 ESS and the 2016 EUGS that the EU is a "credible and effective actor" that is "ready to share in the responsibility for global security" (Council 2003, 3), as well as to pursue the "ambition of strategic autonomy" based on its own collective interests and values (European External Action Service 2016, 4). The EU's distinct strategic goals and its autonomy in shaping its partnership with ASEAN continue to be emphasized many times through the EU-ASEAN Ministerial Meetings.

Even though interests and security threat perceptions vary widely across Europe, most European citizens agree with the security priorities identified by the EU, support the EU's CFSP and CSDP and want the EU to exert "strong leadership in world affairs" (Renard 2014, 3). These indicate that the EU's global security policy has great legitimacy among European population, which can then be translated into specific policies and concrete actions, hence emphasizing the EU's autonomy in security matters even more. In short, the EU is acting not merely as a coordination forum for member states, but as a strategically autonomous actor in security matters. Despite the lack of a common perception across Europe, the EU still be able to pursue its own independent strategies and interests in the world generally and Southeast Asia particularly, thereby maintaining a distinct identity in its foreign policy actions.

Recognition

As stated above, the EU conceptualizes security through a significantly broader and more multidimensional lens than the traditional, realist, state-centric approach that prioritizes military threats and territorial defence. Rather than focusing exclusively on defending state sovereignty, the EU has increasingly emphasized a more human-centric framework of security, where the well-being and rights of individuals are considered core to international stability. However, unlike the EU's viewpoint, for ASEAN and its member states, sovereignty remains a vital issue and is aggressively guarded by the countries, and security is still primarily viewed in the most traditional concept of national security. Even though ASEAN has recognized the serious danger of non-traditional threats, and its security policy has touched some non-traditional security issues, it still tends to categorize those threats as domestic concerns and generally showing slow progress on the development and application of such policies in reality (Jati 2016, 12). Such incompatibility of perspectives has complicated ASEAN's recognition of the EU as a security actor in the region, especially when the EU-ASEAN relationship has historically been centred around trade and investment and Southeast Asian nations seem to acknowledge the EU as a significant economic and normative partner instead of a security actor (Tan/Lin 2024). However, even though there is limited recognition of the EU as a key security actor in the region, it is still evident that Southeast Asian countries – particularly ASEAN – have increasingly acknowledged the EU's security engagement in the region, especially when the concept of security is viewed in the EU's broader perspective.

Since December 1, 2020, with the official announcement of the EU-ASEAN Strategic Partnership, the EU-ASEAN relations have gone much stronger and security dialogue has become an important component of the partnership. The EU's designation as a strategic partner by ASEAN in 2020 marked a formal recognition of its relevance in regional and global security dialogues. The 23rd ASEAN-EU Ministerial Meeting also paved the way for deeper cooperation between the two sides on counterterrorism, cyber threats, and maritime security, thereby emphasizing ASEAN's acknowledgement of the EU's securitizing role.

In the Joint Ministerial Statement of the 24th EU-ASEAN Ministerial Meeting, the two sides reaffirmed the shared values and common interests that underpin their longstanding relationship, and noted with satisfaction the continued commitment, as well as potential cooperation on a wide range of traditional and non-traditional security issues such as

> "Maritime cooperation, climate change and green growth, disaster management... combatting transnational crime and terrorism." Particularly, it is stated that "ASEAN welcomed the EU's contributions towards ASEAN Community building and regional integration efforts,"

which signals one of the most important formal recognitions from ASEAN's side on the EU's security presence in the region (Council 2024, 9).

Capacity

The founding Treaties provide a comprehensive legal framework that enables the EU to implement security policies using a wide array of military, civilian, and economic instruments. First, Article 42(1) of the Lisbon Treaty explicitly states that the EU is given "the operational capacity based on civil and military assets" which can be used in conflict prevention, peacekeeping, and crisis management operations. Further, Article 42(3) obliges EU member states to "make civilian and military capabilities available to the (EU) for the implementation of the (CSDP)," thus ensuring that military and civilian tools are accessible to the EU. Besides, while the EDA plays a vital role in strengthening the EU's military capabilities, the role of the High Representative and the EEAS is crucial for ensuring the coherent implementation of the EU's diplomatic and civilian actions under CFSP.

Other EU strategy documents mention overseas deployments of "European forces" (Council 2003, 3) with a wide range of instruments and institutional capacity to implement an external security agenda (European

Commission 2003, 26) – "thousands of men and women serving under the European flag for peace and security" (European External Action Service 2016, 4). This clearly illustrates the EU's operational capacity that enable it to act beyond its borders on security issues, especially in Southeast Asia. In addition, the 2021 Indo-Pacific Strategy also mentions several instruments to achieve non-traditional security goals in the region.

Although the EU lacks a unified military presence in Southeast Asia, there are several important instruments and mechanisms that have been employed and are still highly relevant in the region today such as:

(1) Multilateral and bilateral forums and agreements that facilitate strategic dialogue on security cooperation. Some notable examples are the EU-ASEAN Foreign Ministers Meetings; platforms such as the ASEAN Regional Forum (ARF) and the Asia-Europe Meeting (ASEM); official bilateral agreements signed between the EU and certain Southeast Asian countries; etc.
(2) The network of EU delegations in Southeast Asia which serve as on-the-ground diplomatic hubs that enable the EU to localize security priorities, respond to crises, and develop direct links with host governments and civil society in the region.
(3) Stable financial resources and financial tools that fund and improve the EU's external assistance and initiatives such as training, equipment and peace building in Southeast Asia.
(4) The mainstreaming of human rights considerations in EU policies, programmes and trade agreements that ensures a holistic security approach in the EU's external action while demonstrating its commitment to normative security role in the region.
(5) Crisis management, conflict prevention and resilience building initiatives in the region such as technical assistance in humanitarian aid, support to refugee management, and regional maritime capacity-building.

Responsiveness

Even though the EU's security policy soon obtained public legitimacy, critics have highlighted the EU's delay in updating its security strategy to reflect contemporary threats, particularly in the external dimension (Foreign Policy Association 2012; Renard 2014, 3). Since the 2003 ESS were published, long term trends had further accelerated and major events had occurred, yet there was no update in the EU's security policy upon the emerging security challenges until the adoption of the EUGS in 2016. Such a prolonged period between the 2003 ESS and its eventual update suggests a lack of strategic responsiveness and underscores challenges within the EU in promptly adapting its security policies to meet new and emerging threats.

Since the 2016 EUGS, the EU's vision and policies has been clearly established for increasing its security engagement worldwide. However, the EUGS barely mentions the security context in Southeast Asia, and the growing instability and crises to which the EU asserts that it will be *more responsive* remain mostly limited to hotspots outside the region such as the EU's neighbourhood, Middle East and Africa. Despite that, it is worth mentioning that the EU recognized one of the emerging security issues in Southeast Asia, which is the growing tension in the South China Sea, demonstrated through the EU's emphasis on its support for "freedom of navigation," maritime security and the "peaceful settlement of maritime disputes" in the region (European External Action Service 2016, 38). It is also shown from the 2021 Indo-Pacific Strategy that the EU has recognized the evolving security threats in Southeast Asia – from the "increasing tensions in regional hotspots such as in the South (China Sea)" to democracy and human rights issues under "authoritarian regimes in the region" – and adjusted its external view and posture accordingly, thus demonstrating a high degree of responsiveness to real-time regional developments (European Commission 2021, 2).

Furthermore, the external events and regional contexts have also shaped the EU's security engagement in Southeast Asia. The EU has consistently framed several non-traditional security issues in Southeast Asia such as maritime insecurity, climate change, pandemic, and cybersecurity as threats requiring collective action. On maritime security, from 2018 to 2022, the EU, Australia and Vietnam co-chaired ARF workshops focusing on issues like maritime law enforcement and cooperation (Rahman 2022). Although lacking hard power, the EU plays a growing role in regional maritime security through the launch of Critical Maritime Routes Programme II (CRIMARIO-II) in 2020 that expanded to Southeast Asia for the first time (Suorsa 2021, 124). On information and cybersecurity, ASEAN and the EU adopted the Statement on Cybersecurity Cooperation in 2019. This Statement was timely as information and cyberspace are a strategic domain where conflict, coercion, crimes, and online harms increasingly happen (Rahman 2022). On pandemic, as Southeast Asia be the first region outside

China affected by the *COVID* -19 pandemic, the EU has become actively engaged in pandemic preparedness and broader disaster cooperation efforts in the region, not just multilaterally, but also bilaterally to the individual ASEAN member states. Through the Team Europe initiative, the EU provided over 800 million euro in aid to Southeast Asia and contributed 2.2 billion euro to the COVAX Facility, allowing them to secure 1.3-billion-euro doses of vaccines for 92 low- and middle-income countries, especially developing ASEAN nations (Nanthini 2021, 147, 149).

5. Discussion

First and foremost, through examining several key aspects of a security actor in international relations, it can be affirmed that the EU has evolved into a legitimate and multidimensional security actor in Southeast Asia. Although traditionally perceived as a normative and economic power, the EU has, in recent years, strengthened its institutional and strategic foothold in regional security through a variety of mechanisms, including political dialogues, capacity-building programs, maritime cooperation, and normative engagement on non-traditional threats. The elevation of EU-ASEAN ties to a Strategic Partnership in 2020, the adoption of the EU's Indo-Pacific Strategy in 2021, and the Joint Ministerial Statement of the 24th EU-ASEAN Ministerial Meeting in 2024 all demonstrate the EU's increasing relevance in the regional security. These developments reflect a gradual but tangible shift in how the EU is recognized – not merely as a distant donor, but as a responsive actor capable of contributing to Southeast Asia's evolving security landscape. While limitations remain, particularly in terms of military projection and rapid responsiveness, the EU's political legitimacy, institutional capacity, and growing strategic partnerships provide a firm basis for affirming its role as a security actor in the region.

Besides, in Southeast Asia, the EU has primarily focused its security engagement on non-traditional areas such as maritime capacity building, health security, disaster preparedness, and climate resilience. This focus reflects the EU's comparative strengths in diplomacy, development cooperation, and soft security tools. Therefore, this chapter argues that the EU's identity as a security actor in Southeast Asia has evolved along several interconnected concepts of power.

Firstly, the concept of *normative power* positions the EU as a global actor that shapes what is considered *normal* in international relations, especially through the promotion of democracy, human rights, and the rule of law (Manners 2002). As stated throughout this chapter, the EU enjoys significant legitimacy as a normative power in Southeast Asia as it consistently commits to international law, multilateralism, human rights and a rules-based order. Such normative stance, along with the formal authority to act on foreign and security policy – which is recognized both externally and internally – gives the EU a legal and institutional mandate to engage in Southeast Asian security.

Secondly, the EU engages with security concerns as a *civilian power*, a term that captures its ability to enhance security through *non-military means* such as institutional partnerships, capacity building, and cooperative frameworks, rather than direct confrontation (Özer 2012).

Finally, the EU increasingly functions as a *middle power*, a role characterized by its capacity to engage in and address regional and global security challenges through building coalitions, mediating between great powers and promoting multilateral governance (Park 2022). Recent studies underscore that the EU has emerged as a preferred *third party* and has gained a reputation among Southeast Asian partners for *doing the right thing* and upholding multilateralism. Rather than competing directly in the sphere of hard security – an area better handled by capable member states such as France or Germany – the EU can maximize its influence by leveraging its comparative advantage in non-traditional security, regulatory diplomacy, and capacity building.

Among the aspects analysed, recognition appears to be one of the most complicated issues. Despite the EU's normative ambitions and growing engagement in the region, its role as a security actor in Southeast Asia is still met with scepticism, partly due to the incompatibility of security perspectives between the two sides: security perceptions in Southeast Asia remain state-centric and sovereignty-focused, which do not fully align with the EU's broader human-centric security concept. One might argue that since responding to non-traditional security threats and challenges on a regional level is not one of ASEAN's strengths, more space can be made for the EU to step in and engage further in the region. Yet things are more complicated than that. For instance, an ASEAN member will certainly not willing to welcome any intervention attempt when a sensitive issue like human rights is not adequately recognized and protected, especially when the situation is more or less associated with the legitimacy of the government (Nishikawa 2009). Besides, another problem that can potentially hinder the EU's security engagement in the region is the principle of non-interference, one of the core elements of the ASEAN Way, which was created to prevent unwanted foreign intervention in the domestic affairs and guarantee the independence and sovereignty of the ASEAN member states (Molthof 2012).

Such principle reinforces even further the tendency to address security matters domestically, and the high value that ASEAN countries place on state sovereignty, which can lead to the hesitation of ASEAN countries to welcome the EU's participation in both traditional and sensitive non-traditional security issues. Particularly, the EU's emphasis on human rights and democratic values, while aligned with its own principles, may not always resonate with all ASEAN member states, given the region's diverse political systems, thus limiting ASEAN acceptance of the EU as an active security actor (Djalal 2022). This partly explains why ASEAN remains cautious about external influences and only opened the door to expanded cooperation with the EU in "safe" areas such as maritime security, transnational crimes, cybersecurity, disaster relief and counterterrorism (Rahman 2022). As a result, regional recognition of the EU's security role has lagged – a weakness the EU has been striving to overcome through deeper engagement.

In terms of capabilities and instruments, the EU brings a comprehensive, if largely non-military, toolbox to Southeast Asian security. Its strengths lie in civilian and soft-power instruments such as diplomatic engagement, trade agreements, development aid, conflict prevention and capacity-building initiatives. In practice, the EU has leveraged multilateral forums and a network of EU delegations on the ground to advance security cooperation. It has also dedicated financial resources to support its policies and programs. These capabilities underscore the EU's holistic approach and multidimensional engagement in security matters. However, when it comes to hard power, the EU's limitations are evident. It lacks a standing military presence or power-projection capacity in Southeast Asia comparable to the United States or China. There is no EU army as defence remains exclusively a matter for member states, and consensus among 27 countries can be difficult to attain in time-sensitive crises. Even as European naval vessels from France, Germany and other EU countries have begun occasional forays into Indo-Pacific waters, these are national deployments rather than a unified EU force (Suorsa 2021). As part of the CSDP, by 2025, the EU launched and run over 40 operations, of which only 16 are military, yet none has been conducted in Southeast Asia (European External Action Service 2025). This constraint was apparent in the EU's historically modest security footprint in Asia and a perception of being "geographically, historically, militarily and politically distant" from the region (Chaban/Holland 2010, 9). In sum, the

EU possesses strong civilian capabilities and some enabling frameworks for security action abroad, but its military means and operational clout in Southeast Asia remain limited. This contrast between its strong soft-power tools and weak hard-power deployment is a fundamental weakness in the EU's security actorness in the region.

Another dimension to assess is the EU's responsiveness in addressing security challenges in Southeast Asia. The EU has at times demonstrated strategic adaptability, especially since the adoption of the 2016 EUGS and the 2021 Indo-Pacific Strategy, showing that the EU has become more responsive to real-time regional developments and more attuned to the security concerns of Southeast Asian partners. Moreover, the EU has gradually increased engagement in ASEAN-centric security forums and cooperation frameworks to timely address a wide range of non-traditional security challenges. Taken together, these developments reveal an increasingly responsive EU security posture in Southeast Asia, particularly in addressing non-traditional threats.

Nevertheless, weaknesses in responsiveness persist due to the EU's decision-making complexities. The EU has often been seen as slow in reacting to fast-moving crises, hampered by the need for internal consensus and by institutional procedures. For instance, the EU went over a decade between major strategy updates, from the 2003 ESS to the 2016 EUGS, despite rapidly changing threat environments. Even when policies are in place, translating them into action in Southeast Asia can be sluggish. The EU's ability to mount timely operations is constrained outside its immediate neighbourhood as it has no permanent security presence in Asia and must negotiate any involvement case by case. Moreover, as emphasized in certain studies, despite the EU's ambition to become a global security provider, for over a decade after the first police mission in Bosnia and Herzegovina in 2003, the EU had not only punched below its weight but also put a much heavier emphasis on its narrower neighbourhood than on other regions. In other words, even though the 2003 ESS recognized the EU as a global player, until before 2020 the EU seemed to only remain active at the regional level (Renard 2014, 10). Additionally, varying threat perceptions among EU member states can undercut a cohesive response. However, in practice, the EU has demonstrated more practical and concrete steps, indicating a higher degree of responsiveness to regional developments.

Yet the EU's security engagement in Southeast Asia presents a complex landscape and has not been without challenges. Firstly, unresolved economic disagreements, including those related to palm oil trade and concerns over the EU's carbon policies, have strained relations between the two sides and can overshadow collaborative efforts in security. Secondly, the EU and Southeast Asian countries often hold differing views on regional and global geopolitical issues such as the conflicts in Myanmar or the Israel-Gaza war. Such differences can complicate or hinder the EU's security engagement with some Southeast Asian countries. Thirdly, the EU's aspiration to establish a stronger security presence in Southeast Asia has been slow. For example, the EU has not yet achieved full participation in key regional defence frameworks like the ASEAN Defence Ministers' Meeting Plus, thus limiting its influence in regional security dialogues (Parameswaran 2024). Although external threats like the Russia-Ukraine conflict have increased EU military coordination, deep-rooted institutional constraints continue to limit the EU's transformation into a fully autonomous security actor (Schilde 2017).

In summary, the foregoing analysis shows that the EU has gradually transformed its role in Southeast Asia from a distant economic partner to an increasingly multidimensional security actor. The EU's profile as a security actor in Southeast Asia is characterized by significant strengths in normative legitimacy, comprehensive diplomatic and economic capabilities, and a deepening commitment to regional multilateralism. At the same time, it is hampered by weaknesses in hard security capacity, historical lack of recognition, and only gradually improving responsiveness. The EU's legitimacy as a global security actor and its resources for capacity-building are assets that can complement regional security efforts, but its influence is constrained by the absence of military presence and the need to reconcile diverse member-state interests. Balancing these strengths and weaknesses will determine how effectively the EU can contribute to Southeast Asian security in the long run. From the Southeast Asian perspective, the EU's growing security role presents both opportunities and challenges that ASEAN and its member states can navigate strategically. On the whole, ASEAN has much to gain by constructively engaging and leveraging the EU as a security partner, given the EU's resources and commitment to regional stability. At the same time, Southeast Asian nations should approach this engagement in ways that maximize mutual benefit while preserving their core interests and autonomy.

6. References

Bretherton C./Vogler J. (2006): Conceptualizing actors and actorness. In: Bretherton, C./Vogler J. (eds): The European Union as a Global Actor. London: Routledge. 12–36.

Chaban N./Holland M. (2010): Perspectives on the role of the European Union: A study of Asian stakeholders' opinion for six countries. International Institute for Democracy and Electoral Assistance. Stockholm. https://www.idea.int/sites/default/files/publications/chapters/the-role-of-the-european-union-in-democracy-building/eu-democracy-building-discussion-paper-22.pdf.

Council of the European Union (2008): Report on the Implementation of the European Security Strategy – Providing Security in a Changing World.

Council of the European Union (2003): European Security Strategy: A Secure Europe in a Better World. Brussels.

Council of the European Union (2020): Co-Chairs' press release of the 23rd ASEAN-EU ministerial meeting. https://www.consilium.europa.eu/en/press/press-releases/2020/12/01/co-chairs-press-release-of-the-23rd-asean-eu-ministerial-meeting/.

Council of the European Union (2024): Joint Ministerial Statement of the 24th EU-ASEAN Ministerial Meeting.

Djalal, D. S. (2022): A larger role from the EU in Southeast Asia: A perspective from ASEAN. Sasakawa Peace Foundation USA. https://spfusa.org/publications/a-larger-role-from-the-eu-in-southeast-asia-a-perspective-from-asean/.

European Commission (1994): Towards a New Asia Strategy (COM (94) 314 final). Brussels.

European Commission (2003): A new partnership with Southeast Asia (COM (2003) 399 final).

European Commission (2021): The EU strategy for cooperation in the Indo-Pacific (JOIN (2021) 24 final).

European External Action Service (2016): Shared vision, common action: A stronger Europe. A global strategy for the European Union's foreign and security policy.

European External Action Service (2021): European Neighbourhood Policy. https://www.eeas.europa.eu/eeas/european-neighbourhood-policy_en.

European External Action Service (2025): Missions and Operations. https://www.eeas.europa.eu/eeas/missions-and-operations_en.

European Union (1992) Treaty on European Union (Maastricht Treaty). Official Journal of the European Communities, C191.

European Union (2007): Treaty of Lisbon amending the Treaty on European Union and the Treaty establishing the European Community. Official Journal of the European Union, C306.

Foreign Policy Association (2012): Does the EU really need a new security strategy? https://fpa.org/eu-security-strategy/.

Hussain, N. (2021): European strategic approaches in the Indo-Pacific: A view from Southeast Asia. In: European strategic approaches to the Indo-Pacific. Panorama: Insights into Asian and European Affairs. Konrad-Adenauer-Stiftung. 99–114.

Jati, I. (2016): Critical perspective on ASEAN's security policy under ASEAN Political and Security Community. Dauliyah: Journal of Islamic and International Affairs, 1(1). https://ejournal.unida.gontor.ac.id/index.php/dauliyah/article/view/357.

Jupille J./ Caporaso J. (1998): States, Agency and Rules: The European Union in Global Environmental Politics. In: Rhodes, C. (ed.): The European Union in the World Community. Boulder, Colorado: Lynne Rienner. 213–230.

Kliem, F. (2022): The EU strategy on cooperation in the Indo-Pacific: A meaningful regional complement? In: European strategic approaches to the Indo-Pacific. Panorama: Insights into Asian and European Affairs. Konrad-Adenauer-Stiftung. 55–70.

Manners, I. (2002): Normative power Europe: A contradiction in terms? In: Journal of Common Market Studies, 40(2), 235–258.

Molthof, M. (2012): ASEAN and the principle of non-interference. E-International Relations. https://www.e-ir.info/2012/02/08/asean-and-the-principle-of-non-interference/.

Nanthini, S. (2021): COVID-19: EU engagement in Southeast Asia. In: European strategic approaches to the Indo-Pacific. Panorama: Insights into Asian and European Affairs. Konrad-Adenauer-Stiftung. 143–156.

Nikolaidou, E. (2008): The demand for military expenditure: Evidence from the EU15 (1961–2005). In: Defence and Peace Economics, 19(4), 273–292.

Nishikawa, Y. (2009): Human security in Southeast Asia: Viable solution or empty slogan? In: Security Dialogue, 40(2), 213–236.

Özer, Y. (2012): The European Union as a civilian power: The case of the EU's trade policy. In: Marmara Journal of European Studies, 20(2), 63–90.

Parameswaran, P. (2024): The future of Europe's Southeast Asia engagement. In: GIS Reports Online. https://www.gisreportsonline.com/r/eu-asean/.

Park, A. S. (2022). Beyond great powers: Middle power paths to resilient multilateralism. Asian Journal of Peacebuilding, 10(1), 131–157.

Rahman, M. F. A. (2022): Enhancing ASEAN-EU cooperation in non-traditional security. In: Modern Diplomacy. https://moderndiplomacy.eu/2022/12/17/enhancing-asean-eu-cooperation-in-non-traditional-security/.

Renard, T. (2014): The European Union: A new security actor? (RSCAS Working Paper No. 2014/45). Robert Schuman Centre for Advanced Studies. https://cadmus.eui.eu/bitstream/handle/1814/31267/RSCAS%202014_45.pdf.

Rieker, P. (2007): The EU as a security actor: The development of political and administrative capabilities (Working Paper No. 725). Norwegian Institute of International Affairs. https://nupi.brage.unit.no/nupi-xmlui/bitstream/handle/11250/2395770/WP_nr725_07_Rieker.pdf.

Rodt, A. P. (2011): Taking stock of EU military conflict management. Journal of Contemporary European Research, 7(1), 41–60.

Schilde, K. (2017): European military capabilities: Enablers and constraints on EU power. Journal of Common Market Studies, 55(1), 37–53.

Sjöstedt, G. (1977): The External Role of the European Community. London: Saxon House.

Suorsa, O. P. (2021): European maritime security capacity building assistance in Southeast Asia: Promises and pitfalls. In: European strategic approaches to the Indo-Pacific. Panorama: Insights into Asian and European Affairs. Konrad-Adenauer-Stiftung. 115–126.

Tan, E. R. L./Lin, J. (2024): Engaging Southeast Asia: The EU's role as a resilient and reliable middle power? Fulcrum: Analysis on Southeast Asia. https://fulcrum.sg/eng aging-southeast-asia-the-eus-role-as-a-resilient-and-reliable-middle-power/.

Viilup, E. (2015): The EU, neither a political dwarf nor a military worm. The EU: A True Peace Actor? ICIP. https://www.icip.cat/perlapau/en/article/the-eu-neither-a-p olitical-dwarf-nor-a-military-worm/.

Chapter 11: The US and EU Indo-Pacific Strategies: A Comparative Study

Nguyen Thi Thanh Thuy

The two US administrations of President Donald Trump (in the 2017–2020 term) and President Joe Biden (in the 2021–2024 term) completed the US national security strategy with a new vision for the Indo Pacific. In September 2021, the European Union (EU) also officially released its own Indo-Pacific Strategy with its own considerations for the cooperation with the Indo-Pacific partners. Since their announcement, both the US and EU Indo-Pacific Strategies have attracted great attention from scholars and observers. So far, many studies on the content and impacts of the US and EU Indo-Pacific Strategies have been carried out and published. However, the questions of what the similarities and differences of the two strategies are, or whether the two strategies complement each other or compete, as far as such similarities and differences are concerned, have not been fully answered in the published works which are related to the US and EU Indo-Pacific Strategies. In response to these research questions, my paper aims to identify similarities and differences of the two strategies and their impacts on international relations in the Indo-Pacific, of which Vietnam is a part.

1. Introduction

The United States is the world's leading economy and military superpower. The European Union is a supranational political and economic union with 27 member states in Europe. The United States and the European Union have enjoyed a close Transatlantic relationship for decades. In addition, both the United States and the European Union have great influence in global politics and international relations and have implemented their own Indo-Pacific Strategy in recent years. For the United States, the traditional strategic vision for the Asia-Pacific was expanded to the Indo-Pacific by the administration of President Trump in his 2017–2020 term. President Trump's vision for the Indo-Pacific is clearly presented in the *National*

Security Strategy of the United States of America, which was released in December 2017 (The White House 2017). Later, the administration of President J. Biden in his 2021–2024 term inherited the Indo-Pacific vision of the previous administration and officially issued an updated Indo-Pacific Strategy in February 2022. In general, the Indo-Pacific Strategy pursued by the two US administrations aims to protect US interests in the region in the context of an increasingly strategic competition between the United States and China. As a leading partner of the United States in the Transatlantic relationship, the European Union also quickly launched its own strategy for the Indo-Pacific. The fact that the United States, a leading superpower, and the European Union, a supernation, jointly launched their own Indo-Pacific Strategy has upheld the importance of the Indo-Pacific on the world geopolitical map.

In the context of the United States and the European Union together implement their Indo-Pacific strategies, both international and Vietnamese scholars have been interested in exploring how the US and EU strategies have been implemented and what impacts of the strategies have been on international and regional affairs. Regarding academic research on the US Indo-Pacific strategy, two examples could be given. The first example is an article, titled *Assessing US Indo-Pacific Strategy* for the 2017–2022 period, by Chen Jimin. The article focuses on studying the US strategic community's perception of the importance of the Indo-Pacific through the overall policy structure, consisting of theme and the operating philosophy. According to Jimin, the aim of the strategy is to maintain US dominance in the region, and it is based on the premise that China is the main competitor of the United States in the Indo-Pacific (Chen 2023). The second notable article titled *US foreign policy in the Indo-Pacific under President Joe Biden* by Nguyen Van Duong. In his article, Duong points out that the overarching goal of the United States is to restore its leadership role in the Indo-Pacific and to protect the US interests through strengthening cooperation with its allies and partners to deal with the perceived challenges, including those from China (Nguyen Van Duong 2024). Thus, the two researchers have similar assessments of the US concerns about China's challenges to the US implementation of its Indo-Pacific Strategy. Regarding the EU Indo-Pacific Strategy, two Vietnamese articles could be mentioned.

The first article is of Bui Hong Hanh, which is titled *The European Union's approach to the Indo-Pacific and some issues raised for ASEAN countries*. In her article, Dr. Hanh focuses on studying the approaches of the European Union in general and the individual EU members in particular to the Indo-Pacific. Further, Dr. Hanh initially compares the differences in the approaches of the European Union and those of the United States to the Indo-Pacific and affirms that the US approach aims to serve its global interests, especially to strengthen the US military presence in the region, while the EU approach is relatively comprehensive which covers three policy groups of economy, diplomacy and defence-security (Bui Hong Hanh 2023).

The second article of the same subject by Nguyen Thu is titled *The EU Indo-Pacific Strategy: Current Situation and Prospects*. In her article, Ms. Thu analyses objective and subjective factors which have influenced the formulation of the EU Indo-Pacific Strategy. She, then, comes to an assessment which says that the focus of the EU Indo-Pacific Strategy is to maintain a free and open Indo-Pacific for all parties in the process of building a strong and long-term partnership (Nguyen Thu 2023). Thus, the surveyed articles show that they mainly focus on studying the specific content of the Indo-Pacific strategies of either the United States or the European Union, while comparative research on the similarities and differences between the two strategies in different aspects is still limited. Therefore, comparative research needs to be done to make additions to studying the US and EU strategies for the Indo-Pacific.

In this chapter, some research questions can be raised as whether *there will be mutual cooperation between the two sides?* or whether a *kind of competition between the United States and the European Union will take place in the Indo-Pacific?* In order to find the answers for these questions, it is necessary to identify the similarities and differences in the US and EU Indo-Pacific strategies, then to explain, either possible cooperation or competition between the United States and the European Union in the Indo-Pacific, thereby possibly identifying and assessing impacts of the implementation of the US and EU Indo-Pacific strategies on the regional countries, including Vietnam. It is also noted that Vietnam is a close neighbour of China. As such, the United States, the European Union, and China are all the leading important partners of Vietnam. In this regard, the question of how this reality will impact Vietnam's policy of international cooperation is a matter of great concern. To address the above-raised research issues, the author of this article will combine two main research methods which are the policy analysis and the policy comparison, so as to clarify the contents of the US and EU strategies along with the similarities and differences between the two strategies in different aspects, including their perception of the Indo-Pacific, the goals and measures to implement their strategies in the region.

On that basis, the author will analyse and evaluate the impacts in general and those on Vietnam in particular, as results of the implementation of the US and EU strategies in the fields of security, politics, and economics in the Indo-Pacific.

2. Overview of the US Indo-Pacific Strategy

Regarding the perception of the Indo-Pacific

President Trump's administration initiated the Indo-Pacific vision, covering both the Indian Ocean and the Pacific, which is seen in the National Security Strategy (NSS) and was announced in December 2017. In the NSS-2017, China is mentioned first with many negative images such as using economic tools as enticement and punishment, imposing military threats, using infrastructure investment and trade strategies to serve its own geopolitical ambitions, threatening freedom of navigation and national sovereignty of the regional countries, etc. In the Trump administration's view,

> "Chinese dominance risks diminishing the sovereignty of many states in the Indo-Pacific. States throughout the region are calling for sustained US leadership in a collective response that upholds a regional order, respectful of sovereignty and independence." (The White House 2017)

Other notable points include responding to the perceived threats from North Korea's cyber, nuclear, and ballistic missile programs, welcoming India's emergence as a leading global power and stronger strategic and defence partner, and seeking to increase quadrilateral cooperation with Japan, Australia, and India, recognizing the Association of Southeast Asian Nations (ASEAN) and the Asia-Pacific Economic Cooperation (APEC) as centrepieces of the Indo-Pacific's regional architecture and platforms for promoting an order based on freedom (The White House 2017).

Under the Biden administration, despite adjustments to the US foreign policy, President J. Biden continues to emphasize the importance of the Indo-Pacific to the US interests. In the new Indo-Pacific Strategy, which was announced in February 2022, the Biden administration states that this region is of vital importance to the US interests in terms of military, economic, and international cooperation to ensure security and international law in the region. Therefore, the Biden administration affirms that

> "The United States is determined to strengthen our long-term position in and commitment to the Indo-Pacific... firmly anchor the United States in the Indo-Pacific and strengthen the region itself, alongside our closest allies and partners." (The White House 2022)

Like the Trump administration, the Biden administration sees China as the greatest and growing challenge to the US interests in the region, accusing China of inflicting damage on the US allies and partners and undermining human rights and international law, including freedom of navigation and the principles that have underpinned stability and prosperity in the Indo-Pacific. In addition, other challenges that are believed to threaten regional stability are also identified, which include the impact of climate change and the COVID-19 pandemic, and North Korea's nuclear weapons (The White House 2022).

Regarding the goals and measures to implement the strategy

The Trump administration puts forward three groups of goals and measures to implement its strategy, including:

- To strengthen the economy by addressing trade deficits, removing trade barriers, creating opportunities to increase US exports, and accepting new trade agreements, and modernizing the existing ones.
- To resolutely resist challenges to America from the *revisionist powers* (namely China and Russia), from the *rogue* states (namely Iran and North Korea), and from the transnational criminal organizations.
- To promote the US influence in the world through building alliances, partnerships, and coalitions based on free will and common interests, upholding international law, encouraging the promotion of economic and trade links, and dealing with non-traditional security challenges (The White House 2017).

Under the Biden administration, the Indo-Pacific Strategy sets out five main goals and implementation measures, including:

1) To promote a free and open Indo-Pacific to protect the vital interests of the United States and its close allies.
2) To build intra- and extra-regional connectivity to ensure the freedom and openness of the Indo-Pacific through the collective action of a network which includes the strong and mutually supportive alliances, and

to create a connection between the Indo-Pacific and the Euro-Atlantic region.

3) To promote prosperity in the Indo-Pacific through increasingly bilateral trade and the direct US investment in the region, which is based on the US principles and standards.
4) To strengthen security in the Indo-Pacific by maintaining the US military presence, closely coordinating with the US allies and partners to promote peace, security, stability and prosperity of the region, which is against all threats and challenges in traditional and non-traditional security issues.
5) To support the building of the regional resilience against the impacts of the 21st century transnational threats such as climate change, environmental change, etc., through close cooperation with the partners and multilateral mechanisms.

In addition, the Biden administration sets out ten key plans to implement the five groups of objectives and measures which include:

- Investment of new resources in the Indo-Pacific.
- Leadership of the Indo-Pacific Economic Framework.
- Reinforcement of the US deterrence.
- Enforcement of an empowered and unified ASEAN.
- Much support for India's rise and its regional leadership.
- Fortification and intensification of cooperation with QUAD (including US, Australia, Japan, India).
- Expansion of cooperation among the United States, Japan, and South Korea on regional security.
- Revitalization of partnerships with the Pacific Island nations and the establishment of multilateral cooperation groups in various areas.
- Support for good governance and accountability.
- Assistance to the open, resilient, secure, and trustworthy technologies (The White House 2022).

To complement the Indo-Pacific Strategy, in May 2022, the Biden administration proposed the Indo-Pacific Economic Framework for Prosperity (IPEF) with the goal of promoting prosperity in the Indo-Pacific. The IPEF includes four pillars, namely Equitable Economy, Connected Economy, Resilient Economy, and Green Economy (Trung tam WTO va Hoi nhap 2022). In fact, the IPEF is not a free trade agreement because the countries that join the IPEF are requested to follow the common agreements as set out in the IPEF.

3. *Overview of the EU Indo-Pacific Strategy*

Regarding the perception of the Indo-Pacific

In September 2021, the European Union officially released its own Indo-Pacific Strategy, stemming from the impact of different factors. In their view, EU officials acknowledge that there are close economic and trade links between the European Union and the Indo-Pacific, as stated that

> "The European Union is the top investor, the leading provider of development cooperation, and one of the biggest trading partners in the Indo-Pacific" and "current dynamics in the Indo-Pacific have given rise to intense geopolitical competition adding to increasing tensions on trade and supply chains as well as in technological, political and security areas. This is the reason why the European Union has decided to step up its strategic engagement with the Indo-Pacific." (European Commission 2021a)

However, the EU leaders' awareness of the importance of the Indo-Pacific is based on three main factors.

First, the EU organization is increasingly growing in terms of territorial scope (about 4 million square kilometres) with total population of more than 448 million people, accounting for 5.6 per cent of the world's population, and the EU trade and service exchange reach 17 trillion euros, accounting for 14 per cent of the world's trade value (European Commission 2024). Furthermore, the EU institutional framework is increasingly perfected, making the European Union a supranational entity. Thus, the strong development has placed the European Union in an increasingly high position in the international arena.

Second, the engagement of single EU member states, France, Germany, and the Netherlands in particular, is increasing in the Indo-Pacific. Being inspired with their own motives, these three countries soon become interested in the region, clearly demonstrated by the issuance of their own Indo-Pacific Strategies (France in 2018, Germany and the Netherlands in 2020). In a combined effort, France, Germany and the Netherlands jointly led the drafting of the EU Indo-Pacific Strategy (Anh Ngoc 2021).

Third, during President Trump's first term, the US-EU relations changed in a polarized direction with deep disagreements, mainly due to the impact of Trump's *America First* policy and his doubts about the basic principles of the Transatlantic relationship (Archick et al. 2020). The disagreements between the United States and the European Union have damaged the bond between them and seriously reduced the trust of the EU leaders in the United States, thereby pushing the European Union to launch a more independent foreign policy towards the United States as seen in the new Strategic Agenda for the 2019–2024 period, which was announced in June 2019. In this document, the EU leaders affirm that the European Union needs to pursue a strategic action program and increases its ability to act independently to ensure its interests, to promote its values and way of life, and to help shape the future of the world (European Council 2019).

Regarding the goals and measures to implement the strategy

The European Union advocates an increased engagement with the Indo-Pacific in building partnerships, which is aimed at strengthening the rules-based international order, addressing global challenges, and laying the foundations for a rapid, equitable and sustainable economic recovery which is believed to create the lasting prosperity. In addition, the EU engagement is aimed to promote democracy, rule of law, human rights and commitments which are widely agreed in the UN documents such as the 2030 Agenda and the Sustainable Development Goals, and the Paris Agreement on climate change (European Commission 2021b). To achieve such goals, the European Union has proposed ten groups of measures to implement its strategy, including:

1) Engaging with the Indo-Pacific partners to build more resilient and sustainable global value chains by diversifying trade and economic relations, and by developing technological standards and regulations that are in line with the EU values and principles.
2) Completing the ongoing trade negotiations and opening new trade negotiations with the regional countries, including a regional trade agreement with ASEAN.
3) Concluding negotiations on the Partnership and Cooperation Agreements with several of the regional countries.

4) Building the Green Alliances and Partnerships with the willing and ambitious Indo-Pacific partners to fight against climate change and environmental degradation.
5) Strengthening the ocean governance in the region.
6) Expanding the network of digital partnerships with the regional partners, as well as exploring the possibility of new Digital Partnership Agreements.
7) Stepping up the implementation of the Connectivity Partnerships with Japan and India, supporting other partners to improve the on-the-ground connectivity between Europe and the Indo-Pacific.
8) Strengthening cooperation on research and innovation under the Horizon Europe research program.
9) Exploring ways to enhance the naval deployments by the EU member states to help protect the sea lines of communication and freedom of navigation in the Indo-Pacific.
10) Improving the healthcare systems and pandemic preparedness for the least developed countries in the Indo-Pacific and enhancing collaborative research on communicable diseases in the context of the Horizon Europe research program (European Commission 2021b).

Immediately after the issuance of the Indo-Pacific Strategy, the European Union has carried out several activities at both multilateral and bilateral levels. For example, in February 2022, the EU-ASEAN Joint Cooperation Committee held a meeting to assess the four-year implementation of the EU-ASEAN Action Plan 2018–2022, affirming its support for maintaining and strengthening an open, fair, non-discriminatory, transparent and rules-based multilateral trading system, and working towards a follow-up Action Plan for the 2023–2037 period (European External Action Service 2022a). Another notable activity is the EU-held Ministerial Forum on Indo-Pacific Cooperation in Paris, which took place on February 22, 2022, and attracted the participation of more than 60 officials who were the representatives of the European Union itself, of the 27 EU member states, and of other 30 Indo-Pacific countries. The Forum focuses on discussing the priority areas which include sustainable and inclusive development, ecological transition, ocean governance, development of digital partnerships, enhancement of connectivity, national security, and humanitarian security (European External Action Service 2022b).

The commitments which were made at the Forum show that the European Union is gradually implementing its Indo-Pacific Strategy for economic, and trade purposes and wishes to play a larger and more independent role in the Indo-Pacific. In addition, the issues which were agreed at the Forum indicate the support of the regional countries for the EU Indo-Pacific Strategy. Regarding bilateral cooperation, that the European Union signed the Free Trade Agreement (FTA) with Singapore and Vietnam is noteworthy. The EU-Singapore FTA officially came into effect in November 2019 and the EU-Vietnam FTA was effective in August 2020. The European Union is also negotiating FTAs with other countries of the ASEAN bloc to open broader cooperation opportunities for trade and investment connectivity between the business community and people of the EU and ASEAN member countries. This is also a way for the European Union to implement the Indo-Pacific Strategy in Southeast Asia as well as across the entire Indo-Pacific.

Main points of the two US administrations' strategies in comparison

In general, the two Indo-Pacific Strategies of the two US administrations in the 2017–2024 period, as presented in the above-section of this paper, have the similarities and differences:

1) Both documents of the two US administrations are the national security strategies of the kind, covering a larger vision of the Indo-Pacific instead of the traditional one of the Asia-Pacific, and emphasizing the importance of the Indo-Pacific to US interests in different aspects.
2) Both US administrations perceive China as the biggest challenge in the US-China strategic competition in the Indo-Pacific, while clearly identifying other dangers and challenges in the non-traditional security area.
3) Both US administrations attach importance to the role of their allies and partners in the region, in which the Indian factor is a new point with greater importance, and the central role of ASEAN is promoted, which is directly related to the issue of maritime security and freedom of navigation.
4) Both US administrations focus on enhancing the US overall strength which can respond to any challenges to US interests in the region in their effort to realize the ambition of the US leadership in international issues around the world.

Essentially, the Indo-Pacific Strategy of the two US administrations have similarities in their perception of the importance of the Indo-Pacific and the common goal of protecting the US interests in the region.

However, each administration applies its own measures to achieve its goals. For example, due to the emphasis on security cooperation, the Trump administration re-launched the Quad group in November 2017 and the 2018 National Defense Strategy which is aimed at gathering forces to deal with the perceived security challenges in the Indo-Pacific. Economically, President Trump withdrew the United States from the Trans-Pacific Partnership (TPP), thus downplaying the multilateral economic cooperation. Furthermore, the Trump administration waged an unprecedented trade war between the United States and China, starting in the year of 2018, thus choosing a unilateral and direct confrontation against China. Meanwhile, the Biden administration maintained the activities of the QUAD group and built a new alliance, AUKUS (consisting of Australia, Britain, the United States), in September 2021, despite China's objections (Ke Thong 2021). Thus, the Biden administration further promoted multilateral cooperation in the security field. Economically, the Biden administration also focused on multilateral cooperation with the announcement of the IPEF, as above-mentioned in the section of this paper, which is considered a way for the United States to fill the gap of economic cooperation after the Trump administration withdrew the United States from the TPP Agreement in 2017. Thus, the Biden administration established a kind of playing style in an order which is based on international law and rules, serving the US multilateral cooperation with allies and partners to increase the US overall strength and to counter the perceived rivals, especially China, to protect the US interests in the region.

Similarities and differences in the US and EU Indo-Pacific Strategies and their impacts

Judging from the studies of the US and EU Indo-Pacific Strategies, which are presented in the three above sections, the similarities and differences along with the main impacts of the strategies can be identified, as follows.

Regarding the Indo-Pacific perception

First, both the United States and the European Union attach the importance of the Indo-Pacific to their interests, and they will therefore engage more in the region. However, the specific interests of the United States and those of the European Union are not the same, therefore the extent and the issues of their engagements in the region are also different. The two US administrations affirm that the Indo-Pacific is of vital importance to the US interests in terms of military, economic, and international cooperation to ensure the security and international law in the region. Meanwhile, the European Union is clearly aware of its close connection with the Indo-Pacific in the economic and trade fields. In this connection, the Indo-Pacific is strategically important for the European Union in terms of economics, politics, and human resources. From the EU viewpoint, the region is also valued as an important factor in shaping the international order and addressing global challenges (European Commission 2021b).

Second, despite differences between the United States and the European Union in their own resources and history of international relations with the Indo-Pacific, both want to expand their own spheres of influence and different extents of cooperation in the region. For the United States, its traditional strategic vision of the Asia-Pacific has expanded to the Indo-Pacific. Regarding the European Union, its traditional sphere of influence is no longer limited to Europe but extends to the Indo-Pacific. That the US superpower and the EU supernation have expanded their sphere of influence with different cooperation proposals has offered the Indo-Pacific countries and organizations more options for their cooperation, either with the United States or with the European Union. For example, in the investment area, both the United States and the European Union are highly developed partners with great potential for capital and development assistance. With such advanced levels, the United States and the European Union may transfer technology and provide investment capital to regional countries which are eligible to participate in either the US or the EU cooperation projects.

However, once the regional countries are accepted to participate in either the US or the EU cooperation projects, the countries must comply with either the US or the EU principles and playing rules. For example, if a country joins the IPEF trade agreement that the Biden administration has proposed, it will have to follow the US direction and leadership in accordance with the US-set principles and standards. Or, if a country joins the EU Sustainable Fisheries Partnership Agreement, it will be required to comply with the EU-set strict regulations in implementing regional, national or international fisheries conservation or management measures, to avoid being sanctioned under the IUU regulation (meaningly illegal, unreported and unregulated fishing), also branded as the IUU *yellow card* of the European Union. Thus, the cooperation opportunities of the Indo-Pacific countries with the United States and the European Union are conditional, facing certain challenges.

Regarding the goals and measures to implement the strategy.

First, both the Indo-Pacific strategies of the two US administrations identify China as the biggest challenge in the strategic competition between the United States and China in the Indo-Pacific. The US strategic documents also accuse China of causing damages to US allies and partners as well as eroding human rights and international laws which include the freedom of navigation and the principles that have brought stability and prosperity to the Indo-Pacific. To deal with the perceived Chinese challenges and threats, the two US administrations saw the need to increase the US overall strength to counter the identified challenges and threats from China, especially in the security and economic fields. As a result, the Indo-Pacific countries which choose to cooperate with the United States on the issues which are related to China must consider the sensitivity of *choosing sides* between the United States and China as far as their own national interests are not negatively affected. Unlike the US negative view on China, the European Union sees China as a partner on the global issues, as stated by Gabriele Visentin, the EU Special Envoy for the Indo-Pacific:

> "Our strategy is the one of openness to cooperation, not confrontation. We do not want to create tensions. This strategy is open to all partners, it is also open to China. The strategy does not require the partners to choose sides. It is designed to strengthen relations with the regional partners and maintain peace, free and open access to the Indo-Pacific." (Quynh Trung 2022)

Clearly, the United States and the European Union have sent different messages about their views on China's role in the Indo-Pacific, thus offering different prerequisite conditions and choices for the regional countries to consider before they decide to join either the US or the EU cooperation projects to which China is related to a certain extent.

Second, both the United States and the European Union have promoted multilateral cooperation in different areas and sizes in the Indo-Pacific. In the security field, the United States pro-actively established military alliances, typically the QUAD and the AUKUS groups, which are under the US leadership to create a kind of collective response to maintain the order, ensure freedom, security and safety of navigation in the region, and to counter China's territorial claims in the South China Sea. In addition to multilateral cooperation, the United States has stepped up bilateral security-military cooperation with its regional allies to counter the perceived threats to regional and global security such as nuclear weapons and missiles, cybercrime, and piracy (The White House 2022). Meanwhile, the European Union has proposed the multilateral security cooperation in a probable manner, as stated that it

> "Will seek to conduct more joint exercises and port calls with Indo-Pacific partners, including multilateral exercises, to fight piracy and protect freedom of navigation while reinforcing EU naval diplomacy in the region," and it "will explore ways to ensure the enhanced naval deployments by its Member States in the region." (European Commission 2021b)

Furthermore, the European Union focuses its cooperation with the prepared partners on non-traditional security issues such as the marine environmental protection, regional ocean governance, combating overfishing, support for healthcare systems and pandemic preparedness for the least developed countries in the Indo-Pacific to prevent epidemics. In the economic field, the US and EU measures to implement their own strategies are not the same. The measures of the two US administrations appear to limit opportunities for regional cooperation because the Trump administration downgraded the multilateral cooperation by withdrawing the United States from the Trans-Pacific Partnership Agreement (TPP), and the Biden administration advocated a multilateral cooperation which is under the US leadership, thus being coercive, through the Indo-Pacific Economic Framework for Prosperity (IPEF), as mentioned in the above sections of this paper. In a different manner, the EU measures of economic cooperation are a combination of both bilateral and multilateral ways. A typical example of the EU bilateral cooperation is the signing of the FTAs with Singapore and Vietnam. Regarding the EU way of multilateral cooperation, the implementation of the EU-ASEAN Action Plans is a good example, in which the European Union and ASEAN have affirmed their support for maintaining and strengthening an open, fair, non-discriminatory, transparent, rules-based multilateral trading system with the World Trade Organization at its core and the need to address barriers to international trade (European External Action Service 2022a).

Moreover, that the European Union promptly organized the ASEAN-Pacific Ministerial Forum in February 2022, soon after the announcement of its Indo-Pacific Strategy, is another example of a multilateral approach to the economic cooperation. The EU ways of implementation of its strategy appear to be more favourable and liberal, thus being more attractive, to the Indo-Pacific countries which are looking for international economic cooperation in general and the economic cooperation with the European Union in particular. In this regard, the EU ways seem to be more open-minded, but competitive, in economic cooperation in comparison with the US coercive measures.

4. Impacts on and Policy Suggestions for Vietnam

Vietnam is an important country in the Indo-Pacific for some reasons. In geographical terms, Vietnam is on the border of the South China Sea, which is the busiest maritime and trade route in Asia. It is more important that Vietnam is a neighbour of the giant China. Both Vietnam and China have been involved in territorial disputes in the South China Sea, over which China has made a claim of sovereignty with the *cow-tongue line* which covers 90 per cent of the South China Sea its aim to monopolize control over it. In other geographical aspect, Vietnam possesses Cam Ranh Bay, which is located at an inlet of the South China Sea and is considered the finest deepwater shelter, thus a perfect naval base, in Southeast Asia. In fact, Cam Ranh Bay was ever used as a military base by the French, American, and Russian armies in the 20th century. In military and political viewpoints, the bay has brought comparative advantages to Vietnam. In the context of the strategic competition in the Indo-Pacific among the superpowers, especially the United States and China, Vietnam enjoys geo-political importance. Moreover, Vietnam is rising to become a middle-income country, which can contribute to the importance of Vietnam from an economic point of view. Apart from enjoying favourable conditions in different aspects, Vietnam has pro-actively developed good cooperative relations with the world's major powers, including China, the United States, and the European Union. In relation to the United States, the Vietnam-US relationship has witnessed a great success of being upgraded to the Comprehensive Strategic Partnership in September 2023.

Regarding its relationship with the European Union, Vietnam has become one of the EU main partners in Southeast Asia with the highest number of agreements of any country in the region (Delegation of the European Union to Vietnam 2023). The most important agreements that Vietnam and the European Union signed include the EU-Vietnam Framework Agreement on Comprehensive Partnership and Cooperation, which entered into force in 2016, a Framework Participation Agreement in 2019 to strengthen bilateral security and defence cooperation, the EU-Vietnam Free Trade Agreement (EVFTA) and the Investment Protection Agreement (IPA) in 2020. So far, Vietnam has developed good relationships with the United States and the European Union, becoming an important partner for both in different fields. At present, the United States and the European Union are implementing their Indo-Pacific Strategies, Vietnam enjoys more opportunities to cooperate with these two important partners, especially in the economic area.

However, due to differences in development levels, national stature and interests, Vietnam's cooperation with the United States and the European Union cannot avoid difficulties. For example, in relation with the United States, the US policy of rallying forces in the Indo-Pacific to counter the perceived challenges from China is a sensitive issue which places Vietnam in an unfavourable and undesirable situation, given the fact that China is a giant neighbour and the leading trade partner of Vietnam. In addition, Vietnam and China have faced very fierce territorial disputes in the South China Sea. Being placed in such a dilemma, Vietnam has carefully taken the Chinese factor into account in all Vietnam's cooperation with the United States to avoid the issue of *choosing sides* at the expense of Vietnam's national interests. Further, Vietnam has been steadfast to Bamboo *Diplomacy*, which is characterized with "strong roots, firm trunk, and flexible branches", and is imbued with "the spirit, character, and the resilience of the Vietnamese people." (Nguyen Ngoc Hoi 2024)

Moreover, Vietnam has persistently pursued the so-called *Four Nos* defence policy which states that

> "Vietnam will not join any military alliance; not side with one country to counter another one; not allow foreign country to set military bases or use Vietnam's territory to counter a third country; not use force or

threaten to use force in international relations." (Quang Chuyen/Manh Ha 2022)

To this point, Vietnam's combination of the *Bamboo Diplomacy* and the *Four Nos* defence policy in its overall foreign policy is a very appropriate way to avoid getting involved in the superpowers' rivalry, while maintaining peace for Vietnam, protecting its national interests, and making active contribution to ensuring a peaceful environment in the Indo-Pacific. Regarding Vietnam's relations with the European Union, there are no sensitive political and security issues related to China as such in Vietnam's relations with the United States. However, due to differences in national development, political and legal systems, it is inevitable that there are obstacles and challenges in the economic cooperation between Vietnam and the European Union. For example, in October 2017, the European Commission (EC) issued the so-called *yellow card* IUU (meaningly illegal, unreported, and unregulated fishing) to warn against Vietnamese violations of fishing exploitation and seafood exports to the EU market, which is considered the failure to meet the EC standards and regulations.

As a result, the entire Vietnamese fishing industry has suffered significant losses which include the decreasing value of Vietnamese seafood exports to the EU market by an average of 6 to 10 per cent per year (depending on each year), and has greatly affected Vietnam's reputation, position and diplomatic relations in the international arena (Minh Phương 2024). Although such EU punishment for the Vietnamese fishing industry is serious, it is not easy for Vietnam to immediately comply with the regulations and standards of such a high-ranking partner as the European Union. Despite this, the issue of removing the EC warning *yellow card* IUU, as soon as possible, is an important task for Vietnamese authorities. Furthermore, the complete fulfilment of the task will help improve the quality and reputation of Vietnamese products which are exported to the EU market, for the sake of Vietnam's benefit in economic cooperation with the European Union and the acceleration of Vietnam's integration into the international economy, in general.

5. Conclusion

The above-presented comparative studies have shown the fundamental similarities and differences in various aspects of the US and EU Indo-Pacific Strategies for the 2017–2024 period, along with the impacts of those similarities and differences on international relations. In sum, the biggest similarity is the emphasis on the importance of the Indo-Pacific for international cooperation, thus opening many cooperative opportunities for the regional countries. The biggest difference between the US and EU strategies is the approach to the region, especially the attitude towards China – the leading power in the Indo-Pacific. While the two US administrations consider China as the biggest challenge and have imposed a fierce counterweight to China, the European Union sees China as a partner on the global issues.

The difference between the US and EU behaviour toward China has become a big challenge for many of the Indo-Pacific countries, including Vietnam, when they must deal with the problem of choosing side, either the United States or the European Union, in joining their projects which are related to the Chinese factor at any level. To this point, how to seize the opportunities and minimize the challenges in cooperation with the United States and the European Union to ensure national interests is not the easiest issues for small- and middle-sized countries in the Indo-Pacific like Vietnam. In this regard, the countries in region need to make careful and flexible calculations which depend on their own circumstances to achieve maximum benefits in cooperative relations with the United States and the European Union, while contributing to peace and common prosperity in the Indo-Pacific and the world at the same time.

Finally, it is noted that a hot political event happening in the United States has attracted the attention of the whole world. It is the result of the US presidential election, which was held on November 5, 2024, with the overwhelming victory of Trump, who becomes the 47th President of the United States for the 2025–2029 term. Donald Trump's return to the US politics, which is known as Trump 2.0, has raised great concerns globally because of the legacy of Trump's confrontative foreign policy which was pursued during his first presidential term (2017–2020). Furthermore, during the 2024 election campaign, concerns grew significantly, because of Trump's slogan of *Make America Great Again* along with his threats to re-start a trade war: imposing 60 per cent import taxes on Chinese goods and announcements for higher tariffs from other countries too. These warnings have caused great concerns in many countries around the world (VTVOnline 2024).

Following Donald Trump's official inauguration on 20 January 2025, the Trump 2.0 administration has rapidly implemented domestic and foreign policies with many unprecedented major changes. In terms of foreign affairs, the most prominent point is that the Trump administration imposed unprecedented trade tariffs on most countries in the world, including the EU, especially escalating the trade war with China. In addition, the Trump 2.0 administration also has disagreements with the EU in finding a solution to end the war between Russia and Ukraine, which broke out in late February 2022 (Hess 2025). In that context, it is highly likely that President Trump will pursue an Indo-Pacific strategy that includes new adjustments and additions and will have new, possibly unexpected implications for the Indo-Pacific region and the implementation of the EU's Indo-Pacific strategy. In this regard, the implementation of the Indo-Pacific strategies of the US and the EU from 2025 onwards will bring about new developments with far-reaching implications, which should be further examined in the coming period.

6. *References*

Acharya, Amitav (2019): Why ASEAN's Indo-Pacific Outlook Matters, East Asia Forum, 11 August 2019. https://www.eastasiaforum.org/2019/08/11/why-aseans-indo-pacific-outlook-matters.

Anh Ngoc (2021): Chau Au ap u ve An Do Duong – Thai Binh Duong da cuc (Europe cherishes a multipolar Indo-Pacific). https://vnexpress.net/chau-au-ap-u-ve-an-do-duong-thai-binh-duong-da-cuc-4232451.html.

Archick, Kristin (et al.) (2020): Transatlantic Relations: U.S. Interests and Key Issues. CRS Research. R45745. Congressional Research Service. Washington D.C. April 27, 2020.

Bui, Hong Hanh (2023): Cach tiep can khu vuc An Do Duong – Thai Binh Duong cua Lien minh chau Au va mot so van de dat ra doi voi cac nuoc ASEAN (The European Union's approach to the Indo-Pacific and some issues raised for ASEAN countries), Tap chi Cong san. https://www.tapchicongsan.org.vn/web/guest/the-gioi-van-de-su-kien/-/2018/827684/cach-tiep-can-khu-vuc-an-do-duong---thai-binh-duong-cua-lien-minh-chau-au-va-mot-so-van-de-dat-ra-doi-voi-cac-nuoc-asean.aspx.

Chen, Jimin (2023): Assessing U.S. Indo-Pacific Strategy. China-US Focus. https://www.chinausfocus.com/peace-security/assessing-us-indo-pacific-strategy.

Delegation of the European Union to Vietnam (2023): The European Union and Vietnam. https://www.eeas.europa.eu/vietnam/the-eu-and-vietnam_en?s=184.

European Commission (2021a): Questions and Answers: EU Strategy for Cooperation in the Indo-Pacific. State of the Union 2021. Brussels, 16 September 2021.

European Commission (2021b): The EU strategy for cooperation in the Indo-Pacific. Brussels, 16.9.2021. JOIN (2021) 24 final. https://www.eeas.europa.eu/eeas/joint-communication-indo-pacific_en.

European Commission (2024): Facts and figures on the European Union. https://european-union.europa.eu/principles-countries-history/facts-and-figures-european-union_en.

European Council (2019): A New Strategic Agenda 2019–2024. https://www.consilium.europa.eu/media/39914/a-new-strategic-agenda-2019-2024.pdf. Brussels, June 2019.

European External Action Service (2022a): 29th EU–ASEAN Joint Cooperation Committee Meeting Convenes Virtually. https://eeas.europa.eu/topics/external-investmentplan/110822/29th-eu-asean-joint-cooperation-committee-meeting-convenes-virtually_en.

European External Action Service (2022b): Ministerial Forum for Cooperation in the Indo-Pacific. Paris. 22 February 2022. https://www.eeas.europa.eu/eeas/ministerial-forum-cooperation-indo-pacific_en.

Hess, Amandine (2025): US-EU relations: The 31 days that shook the transatlantic partnership. https://www.euronews.com/my-europe/2025/02/20/us-eu-relations-the-31-days-that-shook-the-transatlantic-partnership. euronews 20/02/2025.

Ke Thong (2021): Ba diem khac biet cua thoa thuan My-Anh-Australia (AUKUS) (Three differences of the US-UK-Australia agreement). https://baoquocte.vn/ba-diem-khac-biet-cua-thoa-thuan-my-anh-australia-aukus-158764.html.

Minh Phuong (2024): Yeu to quyet dinh trong hanh trinh go the vang IUU (Decisive factors in the journey to remove the IUU yellow card). Bao dien tu – Đang Cong san Viet Nam. https://dangcongsan.vn/kinh-te/yeu-to-quyet-dinh-trong-hanh-trinh-go-the-vang-iuu-661372.html.

Nguyen, Ngoc Hoi (2024): Practical experience refutes distortion of Vietnamese Bamboo Diplomacy. In: National Defense Journal. http://tapchiqptd.vn/en/events-and-comments/practical-experience-refutes-distortion-of-vietnamese-bamboo-diplomacy/22317.html.

Nguyen, Thu (2023): Chien luoc An Do Duong – Thai Binh Duong cua EU: Thuc trang va trien vong (EU Indo-Pacific Strategy: Current status and prospects). Vien nghien cuu Chien luoc [Institute for Foreign Policy and Strategic Studies]. https://nghiencuuchienluoc.org/chien-luoc-an-do-duong-thai-binh-duong-cua-eu-thuc-trang-va-trien-vong.

Nguyen, Van Duong (2024): Chinh sach doi ngoai cua My o khu vuc An Do Duong – Thai Binh Duong duoi thoi Tong thong Joe Biden (US foreign policy in the Indo-Pacific region under President Joe Biden). Tap chi Ly luan Chinh tri [Political Theory Journal). https://lyluanchinhtri.vn/chinh-sach-doi-ngoai-cua-my-o-khu-vuc-an-do-duong-thai-binh-duong-duoi-thoi-tong-thong-joe-biden-5548.html.

Quang Chuyen/Manh Ha (2022): Four Nos – a policy of peace. In: National Defense Journal. http://tapchiqptd.vn/en/theory-and-practice/four-nos-a-policy-of-peace/18841.html.

Quynh Trung (2022): Hoi nghi bo truong ve An Do Duong – Thai Binh Duong: Ban nhieu ve an ninh, vang bong My – Trung (Indo-Pacific Ministerial Meeting: Much discussion on security, no US-China presence). https://tuoitre.vn/hoi-nghi-bo-truong-ve-an-do-duong-thai-binh-duong-ban-nhieu-ve-an-ninh-vang-bong-my-trung-20220223233903074.htm.

The White House (2017): National Security Strategy of the United States of America. Washington D.C., 18 December 2017. https://www.whitehouse.gov/wp-content/uploads/2017/12/NSS-Final-12-18-2017-0905.

The White House (2022): Indo-Pacific Strategy of the United States. Washington D.C., February 2022. https://www.whitehouse.gov/wp-content/uploads/2022/02/U.S.-Indo-Pacific-Strategy.pdf.

Trung tam WTO và Hoi nhap (Centre for WTO and International Trade) (2022): Khuon kho Kinh te An Do Duong – Thai Binh Duong vi thinh vuong va Y nghia doi voi Viet Nam (Indo-Pacific Economic Framework for Prosperity and its Implications for Vietnam). https://trungtamwto.vn/tin-tuc/20973-khuon-kho-kinh-te-an-do-duong--thai-binh-duong-vi-thinh-vuong-va-y-nghia-doi-voi-viet-nam.

VTVOnline (2024): Cuc dien kinh te the gioi sau ngay nuoc My chon Tong thong thu 47 (World economic situation after the day when America elected the 47th President). https://vtv.vn/the-gioi/kinh-te-the-gioi-sau-ngay-nuoc-my-chon-tong-thong-thu-47-20241107154643877.htm.

Chapter 12: Russia's Engagement with the Mekong Subregion: Theoretical Foundations, Historical Context, and Future Prospects

Tu Anh Tuan

This paper examines Russia's evolving engagement with the Mekong Subregion, analysing the theoretical foundations, historical context, and potential avenues for cooperation. It explores how geopolitical theory, neoliberal institutionalism, and soft power theory provide a conceptual framework for understanding Russia's involvement in the region. The paper traces the trajectory of Russia-Mekong relations from the Cold War era to contemporary developments, highlighting the multifaceted challenges facing the Mekong Subregion, including climate change, geopolitical competition, and fragmented cooperation mechanisms. The paper identifies key areas where Russia can make significant contributions, including climate science, integrated water resource management, sustainable agriculture, renewable energy technologies, and capacity building. It also delineates principles for effective partnership, emphasising alignment with ASEAN frameworks, open regionalism, and a focus on sustainable development. The paper argues that Russia-Mekong Subregion relations have substantial prospects for development. Russia's historical ties, combined with its technical expertise and resources, position it as a potentially valuable partner in addressing the Mekong Subregion's complex challenges. This partnership could play a role in fostering regional stability and promoting sustainable growth while also serving Russia's strategic interests in the Asia-Pacific region. The paper concludes by suggesting that Russia could leverage its historical ties and complementary resources to develop a regional strategy that aligns with the Mekong countries' development goals, benefiting both Russia and the Mekong Subregion.

1. Introduction

The Mekong Subregion is home to approximately 240 million people along the world's 12th longest river, encompassing the nations of Cambodia, Laos,

Myanmar, Thailand, and Viet Nam. This region boasts abundant natural resources, including minerals, timber, and hydropower potential, and has experienced rapid economic growth in recent years. The subregion's strategic location and burgeoning consumer market have rendered it an attractive destination for foreign investment and trade, with the development of the individual countries contributing to the overall growth and progress of the Mekong Subregion as a whole. The Mekong River Basin also plays a vital role in ensuring food security for the region and globally, with Vietnam and Thailand being two of the world's leading rice exporters, and a diverse supply of agrifood and freshwater products are also from this region. In this connection, the Mekong Subregion attracted the attention of many outside players, including Russia.

Russia's growing strategic interest in the Mekong Subregion deserves comprehensive examination, with a specific focus on identifying potential avenues for cooperation. The analysis aims to propose a set of principles that could guide the development of Russia-Mekong Subregion relations. A thorough view encompassing historical factors, the complex landscape of overlapping cooperation mechanisms, and intersecting partnership dynamics provides necessary context. Through addressing these objectives, it contributes to the broader discourse on evolving geopolitical relationships in Southeast Asia and offers insights into the potential role of Russia as a constructive partner in the Mekong Subregion's development.

In Russia's foreign policy, for a long time the topic of cooperation with Mekong Subregion has always been nested within the broader topic of Russia-Southeast Asia Cooperation. The literature review on this matter further reaffirms this fact. As Rangsimaporn (2017) points out, Russia employs a combination of hard and soft power tools across Southeast Asia, including the Mekong subregion. This approach encompasses economic initiatives, political dialogues, and cultural exchanges, demonstrating Russia's holistic view of the region. Koldunova (2018) examines Russia's engagement with ASEAN as a whole, which inherently includes the Mekong subregion. Her work highlights that Russia's approach to the Mekong countries is part of a larger strategic framework aimed at strengthening its presence in Southeast Asia. Wishnick's (2019) analysis of Russia's 'pivot to Asia' policy suggests that the country's interest in the Mekong area is part of a broader attempt to balance other major powers' influence and establish itself as a significant player in Asian affairs. Storey (2021) further underscores the interconnectedness of Russia's Mekong strategy with its wider Southeast Asian policy. Smyshlyaev (2021) is among the first Russian scholars to directly elaborate on technical areas (legal reference, water management, smart agriculture) that Russia could contribute to the Mekong Region.

2. *Theoretical Rationale for Russia's Constructive Engagement with the Mekong Subregion*

From a theoretical standpoint, multiple conceptual frameworks offer diverse perspectives and compelling rationales for the intensification of diplomatic and economic relations between Russia and the Mekong Subregion. These theoretical approaches provide nuanced lenses through which to analyse and explain Russia's enhanced engagement with the region.

From the lens of geopolitical theory (Tuathail 1996), Russia's engagement with the Mekong Subregion can be perceived as an avenue to construct and represent Russia's role and interests in the region through various discursive practices, such as political statements, economic investments, and cultural exchanges. By fortifying its ties with the region, Russia can project its image and position and safeguard its interests amidst geopolitical rivalries. Moreover, by advocating for multilateralism and nurturing cooperation among Mekong countries, Russia can contribute to regional stability and mitigate the risk of conflict. This aligns with Russia's overarching geopolitical objectives of promoting a multipolar world order. Russia's engagement with the Mekong Subregion can also be seen as part of its broader geopolitical strategy of *Pivot to the East.*

Neoliberal institutionalism (Keohane 1984) emphasises the role of constructive international institutions and cooperation in shaping international relations. Russia's involvement in regional cooperation mechanisms, such as the ASEAN-Russia Dialogue Partnership (ARDP) and its support for the Mekong River Commission (MRC), exemplifies its dedication to multilateralism and institution-building in the region. The ARDP, established in 1996, provides a platform for Russia to engage with ASEAN countries on a wide range of issues, including political, economic, and security cooperation. By participating in the ARDP, Russia can contribute to the development of norms, rules, and practices that foster cooperation and mutual understanding between Russia and ASEAN countries. Such engagement not only enhances Russia's influence in the region but also solidifies its reputation as a responsible and constructive actor dedicated to addressing shared challenges through cooperative frameworks.

Soft power theory (Nye 2004) offers a rationale for Russia's engagement with the Mekong Subregion, underscoring the use of attraction and persuasion to influence others. For Russia, the positive historical legacy of its support for the anti-colonial struggles of the Indochina countries during the Cold War era could serve as a crucial asset in expanding its soft power in the Mekong Subregion. This legacy, which is rooted in the shared values of anti-imperialism and national self-determination, provides a foundation for building trust and goodwill between Russia and the Mekong countries. By leveraging this historical connection, Russia can foster a sense of solidarity and shared purpose, which is essential for cultivating long-term relationships. This approach becomes even more important considering the rising prominence of the Global South and the resurgence of the Non-Aligned Movement (NAM), also known as *Non-Alignment 2.0*. These developments indicate that developing countries are adopting a more practical and adaptable stance when it comes to the competing influences of major powers.

3. Historical Context of Russia-Mekong Subregion Relations

The relationship between Russia and the Mekong Subregion has a rich and storied history, with its origins dating back to the Cold War era when Russia, then part of the Soviet Union, played a pivotal role in supporting the anti-colonial struggles of the Indochina countries, Viet Nam, Laos, and Cambodia. The Soviet Union provided significant military, economic, and political support to these countries, helping them in their fight for independence and nation-building efforts. For instance, the Soviet Union was the primary supplier of weapons and military equipment to Viet Nam during the Viet Nam War, and also provided substantial economic aid and technical assistance to help rebuild the country after the war. Similarly, the Soviet Union supported the anti-colonial movements in Laos and Cambodia, providing them with military and economic assistance. This steadfast support and friendship laid the groundwork for future relations between Russia and the region.

In the 1990s, following the collapse of the Soviet Union, the relationship between Russia and the Mekong region began to evolve, taking on multilateral dimensions and becoming intertwined with Russia-ASEAN relations. Russia recognised the importance of engaging with the rapidly growing economies of Southeast Asia and sought to establish closer ties with the region. A significant milestone was achieved in July 1991 when Russian representatives were invited by the Malaysian Government to attend an ASEAN Ministerial Meeting, marking the beginning of the ASEAN-Russia Dialogue (Mission of the Russia Federation to ASEAN 2024). This invitation signalled a growing recognition of Russia's potential role in the region and a desire to engage with Russia on a more formal basis.

As the relationship between Russia and ASEAN developed, Russia sought to deepen its engagement with the organisation. In July 1996, at the 29th ASEAN Ministerial Meeting in Jakarta, Indonesia, Russia was elevated to the status of a *Full Dialogue Partner of ASEAN* (Mission of the Russia Federation to ASEAN 2024). This upgrade in status was a significant development, as it provided Russia with a platform to engage with ASEAN on a wide range of issues, including political, economic, and security matters. As a Dialogue Partner, Russia participated in various ASEAN-led forums and initiatives, such as the ASEAN Regional Forum (ARF) and the East Asia Summit (EAS), which allowed Russia to contribute to discussions on regional security and cooperation.

Russia's commitment to regional peace and stability was further demonstrated on November 29, 2004, when it acceded to the Treaty of Amity and Cooperation in Southeast Asia (TAC). The TAC is a key document that sets out the principles governing relations between ASEAN member states and their partners, including non-interference in internal affairs, respect for sovereignty, and the peaceful resolution of disputes. By acceding to the TAC, Russia signalled its willingness to abide by these principles and work towards promoting peace and stability in the region. This move paved the way for the establishment of the ASEAN-Russia Dialogue Partnership (ARDP) in 2005, which aimed to strengthen political, economic, and cultural ties between the two regions. Under the ARDP framework, regular summits and ministerial meetings between Russia and ASEAN have been held to discuss various issues of mutual interest and concern. These meetings have covered a wide range of topics, including trade and economic cooperation, security challenges such as terrorism and transnational crime, and regional developments, including the Mekong region. The meetings have also provided an opportunity for Russia and ASEAN to identify areas for further cooperation and to exchange views on global and regional issues. These ongoing high-level dialogues have been instrumental in fostering a deeper understanding and collaboration between Russia and ASEAN, as well as Russia and the Mekong Subregion. In recent years, Russia has sought to further deepen its engagement with the Mekong Subregion, recognising the region's strategic importance and potential for cooperation.

Despite the significant historical foundation and potential for cooperation, recent times have seen a lack of full exploitation of the rich heritage and potential between Russia and the Mekong Subregion. While Russia has maintained strong political and diplomatic ties with the region, its economic presence in the region, particularly in terms of trade and investment, has remained relatively low compared to other major powers. Russia's trade with the Mekong countries has been modest, and its investments in the region have been limited, with only a few notable projects in sectors such as energy and infrastructure. This can be attributed to several factors, including the geographical distance between Russia and the Mekong Subregion, the lack of strong economic complementarity, and the intense competition from other major powers in the region. Additionally, Russia's own economic challenges and the need to prioritise domestic development, have limited its ability to significantly expand its economic engagement with the Mekong Subregion. As a result, Russia's economic ties with the region have not fully reflected the depth and potential of the political and historical relationship.

Since 2023, Russia's engagement with the Mekong Subregion has marked a new shift, partly as a response to Western sanctions. This pivot has manifested through various diplomatic, academic, and strategic initiatives. In 2023, through diplomatic channels in Thailand, the Russian Embassy sent some informal proposals toward forming a Mekong-Russia Cooperation framework, which is still then under consideration at the working level among Mekong members (Bunyavejchewin/Tungkeunkunt 2023). In June 2024, the Institute of Oriental Studies of the Russian Academy of Sciences hosted the International Scientific and Practical Conference *Mekong: Regional Problems and Possible Solutions* in Moscow, signifying a significant escalation in track-2 diplomatic activities. This symposium brought together scholars from Russia, Vietnam, and other countries to address critical issues in the Greater Mekong Sub-region (GMS), with a particular focus on sustainable water resource management and the need for cooperative strategies among riparian states (Vietnam News Agency 2024). Notably, a recent joint statement issued by Vietnam and Russia during President Putin's visit to Viet Nam on 20 June 2024 also highlighted Russia's commitment to enhancing "cooperation with Mekong sub-region countries across fields," reflecting a strategic partnership aimed at fostering regional stability and development (Government News 2024).

4. Key Challenges Confronting the Mekong Subregion

The Mekong Subregion finds itself grappling with a complex interplay of climate change, human activities, and geopolitical dynamics, which have far-reaching consequences for the region and its inhabitants. Some of the key issues and their implications are as follows:

First, the impacts of climate change and human activities on the Mekong River Basin are stark and measurable. According to a 2020 study by the Mekong River Commission, the basin has experienced a 0.2°C increase in average temperature per decade since 1960. This warming trend has led to more frequent and severe droughts (Mekong River Commission 2020). For instance, in 2019, the Mekong River reached its lowest levels in 100 years (Beech 2020). Human activities, particularly dam construction, have exacerbated these issues. As of 2021, there were 13 mainstream dams and over 100 tributary dams in operation or under construction in the basin. These dams have significantly altered the river's natural flow, leading to severe reduction in sediment transport to the Mekong Delta Basin (De Xin Chan/Xi Lu 2021).

Second, the geopolitical competition in the Mekong Subregion is evident in the proliferation of regional initiatives. China's *Lancang-Mekong Cooperation mechanism*, launched in 2016, has committed over 300 million US dollars in project funding. The United States led Mekong-US Partnership in 2020, pledges more than 150 million US dollars for regional projects. Japan's *Mekong-Japan Initiative for SDGs toward 2030* and India's *Mekong-Ganga Cooperation (MGC)* are other examples of major powers vying for influence in the region (Ganjanakhundee 2024). These initiatives highlight how major powers are intensifying their bids for influence, leveraging economic aid and soft power. For newer players like Russia, this crowded landscape presents a challenge to carving out a meaningful role.

Third, the proliferation of cooperation mechanisms in the Mekong Subregion has led to significant fragmentation of efforts and resources. This fragmentation is evident in the diverse focus areas of various regional initiatives. For instance, while the Mekong River Commission (MRC) primarily focuses on water resource management, other mechanisms have different priorities. The Lancang-Mekong Cooperation (LMC) emphasises connectivity, production capacity, cross-border economic cooperation, water resources, and poverty reduction. The Ayeyawady-Chao Phraya-Mekong Economic Cooperation Strategy (ACMECS) concentrates on trade and investment facilitation, agricultural cooperation, and industrial and energy cooperation. Meanwhile, the Greater Mekong Subregion (GMS) programme, supported by the Asian Development Bank, prioritises infrastructure development and economic corridors. This multiplicity of frameworks, while potentially offering diverse avenues for cooperation, also results in overlapping mandates, duplication of efforts, and inefficient allocation of resources, ultimately diminishing the overall effectiveness of regional cooperation initiatives.

Lastly, the ineffectiveness of the legal framework governing the Mekong River Basin is exemplified by the limitations of the Mekong River Commission (MRC). Despite its mandate to promote sustainable development and management of the river, the MRC has primarily functioned in an advisory capacity rather than as an executive body with arbitration powers (Hensengerth 2009). This lack of authority is further compounded by significant financial constraints. The Mekong River Commission (MRC) has experienced notable fluctuations in its operational budget over the past decade. In 2014, the MRC's funding peaked at approximately 33 million US dollars. In 2021, the amount went down to about 14.5 million US dollars for the 2021–2025 strategic plan (Viet Anh 2021). The combination of limited legal authority and diminished financial capacity has undermined the MRC's ability to address critical transboundary water management issues in the Mekong region, highlighting the need for a more robust and enforceable governance structure.

With its vast experience in managing complex water systems, its leading technologies in sustainable agriculture and renewable energy, and its deep historical legacies with individual Mekong countries, Russia has the potentials to provide valuable support to the Mekong countries as they navigate the path toward sustainable development.

5. Avenues for Russia's Constructive Engagement

Through multiple theoretical lenses, Russia's intensified engagement with the Mekong Subregion could have many layers of meaning. From the perspective of soft power theory, Russia's increased involvement has been largely well-received, thanks to the positive historical legacies of bilateral relations with the Mekong countries. This reception enhances Russia's ability to influence regional affairs through attraction and persuasion rather than coercion. Concurrently, a geopolitical analysis suggests that this proactive engagement serves to bolster Russia's strategic positioning in the region, potentially counterbalancing other major powers' influence. Furthermore, through a neoliberal institutionalist lens, Russia's approach could also contribute to and strengthen the current mechanisms such as the Mekong River Commission (MRC). Alternatively, Russia can join with China through other channels, such as China's Belt and Road Initiative (BRI) and the Lancang-Mekong Cooperation (LMC) framework. This engagement with diverse regional institutions not only aligns with neoliberal principles of international cooperation but also provides Russia with multiple avenues to leverage its expertise and resources within the Mekong Subregion. Collectively, these theoretical perspectives illuminate the multifaceted nature of Russia's strategy, highlighting its potential to simultaneously enhance soft power, improve geopolitical standing, and contribute to regional institutional frameworks.

Russia's distinctive competencies in critical domains – including integrated water resource management, climate change adaptation strategies, advanced agricultural technologies, and sustainable energy development – position it as a potentially significant contributor to the Mekong Subregion's sustainable development agenda. Given Russia's strengths, there are several avenues to consider as follows:

First, Russia's extensive expertise in climate science, environmental monitoring, and sustainable development positions it as a valuable partner for Mekong countries in addressing climate change challenges. With its advanced capabilities in satellite technology and remote data analysis, Russia can offer significant contributions to the region's climate adaptation and mitigation efforts. This collaboration could encompass joint climate research initiatives focusing on regional climate variability and vulnerability assessments, as well as the transfer of advanced monitoring and forecasting technologies. Moreover, Russia can play a crucial role in capacity building by providing training programmes on climate modelling, remote sensing, and data analysis, while also supporting the establishment of regional climate centres and early warning systems in the region.

Second, Russia can offer valuable insights and technical assistance in sustainable water resource management (Smyshlyaev 2021). As a country with vast experience in managing large river systems, such as the Volga, the Ob, and the Yenisei, Russian experts have developed advanced tools and techniques for water monitoring, modelling, and forecasting, as well as for assessing the impacts of human activities and climate change on water resources. Russia has also implemented innovative approaches to water governance, such as basin-wide management, stakeholder participation, and transboundary cooperation, which can provide useful lessons for the Mekong region. Russia can support the Mekong River Commission (MRC) and other regional bodies in developing and implementing integrated water resource management plans, which take into account the complex interactions between water, land, and ecosystems, as well as the diverse needs and interests of different water users. Russian experts can provide technical assistance in areas such as water allocation, flood control, drought management, and water quality monitoring, as well as in developing decision support systems and scenario analysis tools. Russia can also contribute to capacity building for MRC staff and national water agencies through training programmes, study tours, and joint research projects.

Third, Russia has a strong agricultural sector and has made significant strides in promoting sustainable farming practices. For example, a case study of drip irrigation technology from Russia helped a locality in Cambodia triple its rice yield while reducing water consumption by three to four times (Smyshlyaev 2021). By sharing its expertise and technologies, Russia can help Mekong countries enhance their agricultural resilience, improve food security, and reduce farming's environmental impact. This could involve collaboration on agricultural research, extension services, and the promotion of climate-smart agriculture.

Fourth, as a major player in the global energy market, Russia possesses extensive expertise in renewable energy technologies, including nuclear energy, which are very relevant to the Mekong Subregion. Russia can also share its experience in implementing innovative financing mechanisms for renewable energy projects, such as public-private partnerships, green bonds, and carbon markets. Russian financial institutions, such as the Russian Direct Investment Fund and the Eurasian Development Bank, can provide financing and investment support for renewable energy projects in the Mekong Subregion, in collaboration with local governments, development banks, and private investors. By sharing its expertise and investing in alternative clean energy projects in the Mekong Subregion, Russia could potentially help these countries reduce their reliance on hydroelectric dams.

Fifth, Russia can play a constructive role in providing best practices for reference to Mekong countries. Russia has experts on the interstate use of water, such as the organisation *Rivers Without Borders*, headed by Evgeny Simonov, which has made significant progress in settling cross-border water disputes between Russia, China, and Mongolia in the Amur River basin by using a scientific approach (Smyshlyaev 2021). By sharing scientific insights, technical expertise, and empirically derived best practices, Russia can significantly enhance regional stability and cohesion among Mekong countries. This knowledge transfer could serve as a reference model for the Mekong River Commission (MRC), thereby strengthening its institutional role. Consequently, Russia's engagement in this capacity could position it as a positive catalyst for cooperative dynamics in the region.

Lastly, Russia has a wealth of expertise in various fields, including education, science, technology, and public administration. By providing targeted capacity-building programmes and facilitating knowledge sharing, Russia can help strengthen the institutional and human resource capabilities of the Mekong countries. This could include scholarships, training programmes, and technical assistance in areas such as water resource management, climate change adaptation, and sustainable development.

6. Key Expectations for Mekong Partners

The Mekong Subregion nations share a collective vision for their region as a zone of peace, stability, and sustainable development, rather than a geopolitical arena for great power competition. Consequently, these nations have a set of implicit and explicit expectations for their development partners and external stakeholders. These expectations are designed to ensure that external engagement aligns with the region's development goals and respects the sovereignty and interests of Mekong Subregion countries. Understanding and addressing these expectations is crucial for external actors seeking to engage productively with the region and for the development of effective, mutually beneficial cooperation frameworks.

First, Mekong sub-region cooperation is one of the subregional mechanisms under ASEAN. This positioning suggests that ASEAN is the overarching framework and that the rules in the Mekong typically follow those of ASEAN. Consequently, adherence to the fundamental principles outlined in the ASEAN Treaty of Amity and Cooperation (TAC) is expected to serve as a guiding framework for such endeavours. In addition, the enrolment of new partners will need to go through the consensus of all Mekong members, following the typical *ASEAN Way* approach.

Second, the principles of open regionalism are proposed as a foundation for partnership relations. This approach advocates for diversified and multilateral relations that promote transparency and multilateralism. It discourages the formation of exclusive alliances or engagement in activities that undermine the interests of third parties. Instead, the focus is on fostering an environment of trust, inclusivity, and mutual understanding.

Third, partnership relations should transcend political considerations and remain focused on supporting peace, stability, prosperity, and sustainable development in the Mekong Subregion. Partnership endeavours should help consolidate the 1995 Mekong Agreement and support the central role of the Mekong River Commission (MRC) in coordinating technical cooperation for sustainable water management.

Fourth, the non-alignment principles have been an underlying in the mindset of Mekong Subregion countries. These ten principles established in the 1955 Bandung Conference formed the basis of the Non-Aligned Movement (NAM) and provide a robust framework for fostering enduring, trust-based relationships (UN 1955). By adhering to these principles – emphasising mutual respect, non-interference, and peaceful coexistence – Russia can enhance its soft power projection and establish itself as a reliable and principled partner in the region. This approach not only respects the historical context of the Mekong Subregion's international relations but also aligns with contemporary expectations for equitable and respectful engagement among nations.

7. Conclusion

Russia's historical ties with the Mekong Subregion provide a foundation for its potential role as a significant partner in the region's complex geopolitical and developmental landscape. Russia's extensive expertise and resources could be strategically deployed to address the multifaceted challenges confronting the area. This partnership could be operationalized through various modalities, including bilateral and multilateral agreements, collaborative research and innovation projects in sectors such as agriculture, energy, and technology, as well as capacity-building and knowledge-transfer programmes designed to empower local communities and stakeholders.

Effective engagement necessitates a nuanced understanding of both the explicit and implicit expectations of the Mekong countries. By strategically leveraging its existing political and diplomatic ties with the region and identifying niche areas for cooperation, Russia has the opportunity to cultivate a more robust and comprehensive partnership with the Mekong countries.

For Russia, such a partnership could potentially enhance its soft power projection, improve its geopolitical positioning, and establish its role as a constructive player in the region. For the Mekong Subregion, this partnership could not only strengthen political and security ties but also promote economic growth and sustainable development, aligning with the Mekong countries' developmental aspirations.

8. References

Beech, H. (2020, April 13): China limited the Mekong's flow. Other countries suffered a drought. The New York Times. https://www.nytimes.com/2020/04/13/world/asia/china-mekong-drought.html.

Bunyavejchewin, P./Tungkeunkunt, K. (2023): Mekong–Russia cooperation: Russia's unprecedented move in the Mekong Sub-Region. In: Strategic Analysis, 47(4), 404–410.

Chua, S. D. X./Lu, X. X. (2022): Sediment load crisis in the Mekong River Basin: Severe reductions over the decades. In: Geomorphology, 419, Article 108484. https://doi.org/10.1016/j.geomorph.2022.108484.

Ganjanakhundee, S. (2022, April): Interests, initiatives, and influence: Geopolitics in the Mekong Subregion. In: Asia Policy, 17(2). https://www.nbr.org/publication/interests-initiatives-and-influence-geopolitics-in-the-mekong-subregion/.

Government News (2024): Viet Nam-Russia issue joint statement. https://en.baochinhphu.vn/viet-nam-russia-issue-joint-statement-111240625132431373.htm.

Hensengerth, O. (2009): Transboundary river cooperation and the regional public good: The case of the Mekong River. In: Contemporary Southeast Asia, 31(2), 326–349.

Keohane, R. O. (1984): After hegemony: Cooperation and discord in the world political economy. Princeton University Press.

Koldunova, E. (2018): Russia and ASEAN: In search of economic synergy and political rapport. In: Contemporary Southeast Asia, 40(2), 258–283.

Mekong River Commission (2020): Mekong low flow and drought conditions in 2019–2021 [Technical Report]. MRC Secretariat. https://reliefweb.int/attachments/184b2d39-9331-3515-bd48-5c649847a7b3/Mekong-low-flow-and-drought-conditions-2019-2021df.pdf.

Mission of the Russia Federation to ASEAN (2024): ASEAN-Russia Dialogue Partnership Overview. https://asean.mid.ru/en/asean_russia/dialogue_partnership/.

Nye, J. S. (2004): Soft power: The means to success in world politics. Public Affairs.

Rangsimaporn, P. (2017): Russia's search for influence in Southeast Asia. Asian Survey, 57(6), 1079–1105.

Smyshlyaev, V. (2021, July 27): Russian key to the Mekong River. In: Russian International Affairs Council. https://russiancouncil.ru/en/analytics-and-comments/analytics/russian-key-to-the-mekong-river/.

Storey, I. (2021): Russia's defence and security cooperation in Southeast Asia. In: ISEAS Perspective, 33, 1–10.

Tuathail, G. Ó. (1996): Critical geopolitics: The politics of writing global space. Routledge.

Viet Anh (2021): Mekong River Commission secures $13 mln pledges for strategic plan. Vietnam Express. https://e.vnexpress.net/news/news/mekong-river-commission-secures-13-mln-pledges-for-strategic-plan-4299387.html.

Vietnam News Agency (2024): Moscow symposium highlights Mekong River issues. https://en.qdnd.vn/social-affairs/news/moscow-symposium-highlights-mekong-river-issues-567319.

III.
The Indo-Pacific from the Inside: The Risks and Benefits of a Geopolitical Imaginary for the Countries Concerned

Chapter 13: Strengthening Vietnam's International Position through Foreign Policy Strategy amidst Competition in the Indo-Pacific Region

Nguyen Anh Cuong

This study examines Vietnam's foreign policy strategy in the context of increasing geopolitical competition in the Indo-Pacific region, particularly amidst the growing influence of China. Focused on the principles of *multilateralization* and *diversification*, Vietnam's approach to international relations has been characterized by active participation in multilateral forums like ASEAN, ARF, and EAS, alongside the cultivation of strong bilateral ties with major powers such as the United States, Japan, and India. This strategy aims to balance Vietnam's national interests of maintaining sovereignty, economic growth, and regional security in a rapidly changing global environment. The paper explores the effectiveness of this approach in safeguarding Vietnam's sovereignty, ensuring national security, and fostering sustainable economic development. Additionally, the study evaluates the challenges faced by Vietnam in balancing these external relationships, particularly in relation to China's assertiveness in the South China Sea, and the policy implications for future strategic decisions. Through this analysis, the study offers insights into how Vietnam can refine its foreign policy to effectively respond to regional power dynamics and secure long-term stability and prosperity.

1. Introduction

Vietnam's foreign policy has undergone significant transformation in the face of increasing geopolitical competition in the Indo-Pacific region. The strategic location of Vietnam, situated at the crossroads of critical international maritime routes and surrounded by contentious areas like the South China Sea, presents both opportunities and challenges in shaping its international relations. As major powers like China, the United States, Japan, and India intensify their influence in the region, Vietnam has developed a dynamic foreign policy strategy centred on multilateralization and diversification of its international engagements. This approach aims to safeguard Vietnam's sovereignty, economic development, and national security while navigating the complex web of competing interests in the region.

One of the defining features of Vietnam's foreign policy is its emphasis on multilateralism – actively participating in organizations such as ASEAN, ARF (ASEAN Regional Forum), EAS (East Asia Summit), and APEC to ensure that its national interests are protected through diplomatic dialogue, cooperative frameworks, and regional stability. Diversification is equally critical, reflecting Vietnam's strategic decision to expand its relationships beyond any single power. This balancing act enables the country to maintain flexibility and avoid over-dependence on one particular country or bloc, particularly when managing its complex relationship with China, a key economic partner yet a source of strategic contention due to ongoing territorial disputes in the South China Sea (Thayer 2017).

Vietnam's policy of diversification is also underscored by its growing defence and economic cooperation with countries such as the United States, Japan, and India. These relationships help Vietnam strengthen its defence capabilities while also promoting sustainable economic growth through investments in technology, infrastructure, and trade. However, this strategy of balancing relations with great powers presents significant challenges, particularly given the competition between the United States and China and the implications of Vietnam's growing security cooperation with the United States on its relationship with China Trinh/Huyen Ho 2024). Furthermore, while multilateral and diversified relations have played an important role in enhancing Vietnam's international standing, the effectiveness of these strategies is not without limitations. The consensus-based decision-making structure of ASEAN, for instance, often limits the organization's ability to address urgent regional security issues decisively. This becomes particularly problematic when major powers, like China, hold substantial influence within ASEAN, which complicates efforts to resolve disputes such as those in the South China Sea Mosyakov 2020).

In this context, Vietnam's foreign policy strategy faces a delicate balancing act. It must navigate between maintaining stable and growing economic ties with China, ensuring robust defence and security cooperation with other powers, and engaging in multilateral forums to protect its national interests. This research seeks to critically assess the effectiveness of Vietnam's multilateral and diversified foreign policy strategy, evaluating its strengths, weaknesses, and potential areas for further development.

The study will also delve into the internal political dynamics of Vietnam, examining how domestic factors – such as the role of the Communist Party, public opinion, and economic constraints – affect its foreign policy decisions. Understanding the intersection of domestic politics and international diplomacy will provide a more nuanced view of Vietnam's positioning in a rapidly shifting geopolitical environment. Ultimately, this research aims to offer insights into how Vietnam can refine its foreign policy to better safeguard its sovereignty, enhance economic opportunities, and navigate the growing competition in the Indo-Pacific region. By examining Vietnam's foreign policy in this context, the study contributes to a broader understanding of the complexities small nations face when managing relations with powerful neighbours and global superpowers. This paper will offer policy recommendations for Vietnam to continue leveraging multilateralism and diversification in a manner that optimizes its long-term national security and economic growth while minimizing the risks associated with its delicate balancing act.

2. Multilateralization and Diversification of Foreign Relations Strategy

Vietnam's foreign policy strategy in the 21st century is fundamentally shaped by two key principles: multilateralization and diversification. These principles have been essential in helping Vietnam navigate the shifting geopolitical landscape in the Indo-Pacific region, where the competition for influence among major powers such as China, the United States, Japan, and India is intensifying. In a region marked by both opportunities and risks, particularly in relation to territorial disputes and economic interdependence, Vietnam has employed these strategies to maintain its sovereignty, secure its national interests, and enhance its international standing (Thuong/Oanh 2021).

Multilateralization, in the context of Vietnam's foreign policy, refers to the active and strategic participation in various regional and global multilateral frameworks aimed at fostering cooperation, managing conflicts, and building partnerships across a wide range of areas, including security, economic development, and environmental protection. Vietnam has consistently prioritized multilateral institutions like ASEAN (Association of Southeast Asian Nations), the ASEAN Regional Forum (ARF), the East Asia Summit (EAS), and APEC (Asia-Pacific Economic Cooperation) as platforms for diplomacy. These multilateral engagements provide Vietnam with the ability to safeguard its sovereignty while avoiding being caught in the sphere of influence of any single power. For instance, Vietnam's involvement in ASEAN has been pivotal in enabling the country to engage in collective regional security and economic cooperation. Through ASEAN, Vietnam has worked to address both traditional and non-traditional security challenges, such as the maritime disputes in the South China Sea, as well as regional issues like climate change, terrorism, and cybersecurity. ASEAN's central role in promoting dialogue and cooperation allows Vietnam to pursue its national interests within a framework that prioritizes regional stability, peace, and mutual respect among member states (Cuong 2024).

However, Vietnam's participation in multilateral institutions is not without its limitations. A key challenge lies in ASEAN's consensus-based decision-making process, which can be slow and sometimes ineffective in responding decisively to pressing regional security issues (De Castro 2021). The South China Sea dispute is a prime example, where ASEAN has struggled to reach a unified stance on China's territorial claims, despite Vietnam's efforts to assert its position through diplomatic channels (Thayer 2017). This limitation underscores the need for Vietnam to complement its multilateral strategy with other policy approaches, such as diversification, to balance its interests in the face of rising regional tensions.

Diversification, on the other hand, represents Vietnam's effort to expand and strengthen its bilateral relationships with key global powers, thereby reducing its dependency on any single nation or bloc. This approach has been particularly significant in Vietnam's dealings with major powers like the United States, Japan, and India, all of which play critical roles in both the security and economic dimensions of Vietnam's foreign policy. By diversifying its partnerships, Vietnam enhances its ability to mitigate risks arising from its economic reliance on China and its security concerns, particularly regarding the South China Sea (Fedorov/Garin 2023).

The relationship with the United States has evolved significantly in recent years, transitioning from one of historical suspicion to a comprehensive partnership characterized by cooperation in trade, defence, technology, and education. The US *Pivot to Asia* strategy has provided Vietnam with numerous opportunities to bolster its defence capabilities, notably through joint military exercises, maritime security cooperation, and defence technology transfers. Vietnam's alignment with the United States also complements its multilateral engagements by offering an alternative to China's growing influence in the region (Willis 2017). Nevertheless, this partnership presents its own set of challenges, especially in balancing the US-Vietnam relationship with Vietnam's need to maintain a stable economic partnership with China (Cuong 2023; Van Quyet/Nguyet 2023).

In parallel, Vietnam has forged strong ties with Japan, one of its most important economic partners. Japan has been a significant investor in Vietnam's infrastructure and technology sectors, providing not only capital but also critical know-how in areas like electronics, automotive manufacturing, and renewable energy. Japan's role in enhancing Vietnam's maritime security, particularly through the provision of patrol vessels and technical assistance, is another key aspect of their growing bilateral relations. Additionally, Japan's emphasis on a *Free and Open Indo-Pacific* aligns with Vietnam's efforts to ensure a stable and balanced regional order, free from coercive actions by any single power (Yazuru 2022).

Vietnam's strategic partnership with India, rooted in shared security concerns, particularly maritime security and the protection of freedom of navigation in the South China Sea, is another essential aspect of its diversification strategy. India has been an important partner in enhancing Vietnam's defence capabilities through the provision of military equipment, training programs, and joint exercises. This partnership is also supported by India's *Look East* policy, which emphasizes strengthening ties with Southeast Asia, and serves as a counterbalance to China's dominance in the region (Toan/Yen 2023).

Through diversification, Vietnam has managed to reduce its vulnerability to external pressures, particularly from China. However, the pursuit of this strategy requires a careful balancing act. The simultaneous cultivation of strong bilateral relations with the United States, Japan, and India must be carefully managed to avoid tensions, especially considering the strategic rivalry between the United States and China. Vietnam's ability to maintain this balance while preserving its sovereignty and security interests is a testament to the effectiveness of its diversification strategy, but it is not without its complexities. Multilateralization and diversification are not only key components of Vietnam's foreign policy, but they also form an integrated approach to navigating the complexities of regional and global politics. While multilateralism allows Vietnam to promote cooperation and stability within established regional frameworks, diversification strengthens its autonomy by broadening its international partnerships. This dual approach has proven effective in safeguarding Vietnam's national interests, but its long-term success will depend on the country's ability to adapt to emerging geopolitical challenges and continue leveraging both multilateral institutions and diversified bilateral relations to its advantage.

3. Strengthening Security and Defence Cooperation

Vietnam's foreign policy strategy in the context of increasing power competition in the Indo-Pacific region has not only focused on diplomatic engagement through multilateralism and diversification but also emphasized the critical importance of strengthening security and defence cooperation. The growing military influence of China, particularly its assertive actions in the South China Sea, as well as the broader strategic competition between the United States, Japan, and other regional powers, has necessitated Vietnam's proactive approach to enhancing its defence capabilities. This approach includes expanding military alliances, increasing defence cooperation, and engaging in joint military exercises to ensure national security and protect its sovereignty.

Vietnam's defence strategy is grounded in the concept of comprehensive security, which involves not just military strength but also economic resilience, political stability, and societal cohesion. The country's military modernization efforts, in line with this strategy, have been aimed at enhancing its self-defence capabilities while avoiding entanglements in power rivalries. To achieve this, Vietnam has expanded defence cooperation with both regional and global powers, with a particular focus on bilateral defence partnerships and multilateral security arrangements.

One of the most significant developments in Vietnam's defence strategy has been its growing military relationship with the United States. This cooperation, which began with more limited forms of engagement in the post-Vietnam War era, has expanded significantly since the normalization of diplomatic relations between the two countries in the 1990s. In recent years, Vietnam and the United States have strengthened their defence ties through joint military exercises, defence technology transfers, and shared maritime security initiatives, particularly in the South China Sea (Cuong 2024). The USA has provided Vietnam with advanced maritime patrol vessels, technical assistance for strengthening Vietnam's defence infrastructure, and training programs for the Vietnamese military. These efforts aim to enhance Vietnam's deterrence capabilities and ensure its ability to respond effectively to security threats in the region (Cuong 2024).

Vietnam's defence cooperation with the United States is also framed within the broader strategic context of the US *Pivot to Asia* policy, which emphasizes the importance of the Indo-Pacific region for global security and stability. Through this partnership, Vietnam has sought to balance its strategic relations with China while ensuring its military readiness in the face of potential territorial challenges in the South China Sea. The cooperation is not solely limited to military exercises but also encompasses intelligence sharing, counterterrorism collaboration, and joint efforts to ensure freedom of navigation in international waters – a key concern for Vietnam given the contested claims in the South China Sea (Van Quyet/ Nguyet 2023).

Parallel to its engagement with the United States, Vietnam has significantly strengthened its defence cooperation with Japan, a key strategic partner in the region. Japan has provided substantial military assistance to Vietnam, particularly in the realm of maritime security. This collaboration includes the supply of modern patrol vessels to the Vietnamese coast guard, as well as the transfer of advanced surveillance technologies. Japan's assistance aims to bolster Vietnam's ability to monitor and protect its exclusive economic zones (EEZ) in the South China Sea, which are increasingly under threat due to China's expansive territorial claims. The Japan-Vietnam defence relationship is further deepened through military exchanges, intelligence sharing, and participation in joint regional security initiatives. This cooperation is framed within the context of Japan's Free and Open Indo-Pacific Strategy, which emphasizes promoting peace, stability, and the rule of law in the region (Yazuru 2022).

The relationship between Vietnam and India has also become increasingly important in the context of regional security. India, with its *Look East Policy* and emphasis on strengthening ties with Southeast Asia, has emerged as a vital partner for Vietnam, especially in maritime security. India has provided Vietnam with modern military equipment, including naval vessels and radar systems, to help safeguard its territorial waters. Moreover, India has contributed to training Vietnam's military personnel, particularly in the areas of submarine operation and naval warfare (Toan/Yen 2023). India's support is particularly significant for Vietnam as it provides an alternative source of defence assistance, reducing reliance on China and further diversifying Vietnam's security partnerships.

Defence cooperation between Vietnam and these key partners is not limited to bilateral efforts but also extends to multilateral security frameworks. Vietnam actively participates in regional security mechanisms such as ASEAN Defence Ministers' Meeting Plus (ADMM+), ASEAN Regional Forum (ARF), and East Asia Summit (EAS). These platforms have provided Vietnam with opportunities to engage in multilateral discussions on regional security issues, including counterterrorism, disaster relief, and non-traditional security threats like cybersecurity. Vietnam's active participation in these forums strengthens its diplomatic and defence credentials, positioning it as a responsible player in regional security (Tran/Ionov 2023).

However, while these defence partnerships offer significant benefits, they also pose challenges for Vietnam. The strengthening of military ties with countries such as the United States and Japan, which have strategic interests that may not always align with Vietnam's, requires careful diplomacy. Vietnam must balance its relationships with these countries while avoiding actions that might provoke China, especially as Vietnam continues to prioritize maintaining stable economic ties with its northern neighbour. The challenge for Vietnam lies in ensuring that its defence cooperation with external partners does not upset its delicate position in the broader regional power dynamics.

Strengthening security and defence cooperation has become a cornerstone of Vietnam's foreign policy strategy in the face of rising regional tensions. Through defence partnerships with the United States, Japan, India, and active participation in multilateral security arrangements, Vietnam has significantly enhanced its defence capabilities and its ability to deter potential threats to its sovereignty. These efforts have not only strengthened Vietnam's security but also reinforced its international standing, positioning the country as an active participant in regional security affairs. However, the continued success of these strategies will depend on Vietnam's ability to navigate the complexities of regional power rivalries, particularly in managing its relationships with China while deepening its defence cooperation with other global powers.

4. Responding to the Increasing Influence of China

The growing influence of China in the Indo-Pacific region, particularly in the South China Sea, has posed a significant challenge to Vietnam's foreign policy. As China continues to assert its dominance through the construction and militarization of artificial islands, along with its expansive territorial claims over the South China Sea, Vietnam faces a delicate balancing act. On one hand, China remains Vietnam's largest trading partner, with deep economic ties that are crucial for Vietnam's continued growth. On the other hand, China's increasingly aggressive actions in the region threaten Vietnam's sovereignty, especially over its claimed territories in the South China Sea. In this context, Vietnam's foreign policy has evolved to address the growing influence of China through a combination of diplomatic, military, and legal strategies aimed at safeguarding its national interests (Dar 2023).

Vietnam's response to China's rise is rooted in its commitment to maintaining sovereignty and territorial integrity. A cornerstone of this strategy is Vietnam's active participation in multilateral platforms, where it has advocated for peaceful resolutions to territorial disputes in accordance with international law, particularly the United Nations Convention on the Law of the Sea (UNCLOS). By emphasizing the importance of rule-based international order, Vietnam seeks to gain international support for its position while pushing back against China's unilateral claims. The 2016 ruling by the Permanent Court of Arbitration in the Philippines v. China case, which declared China's claims to the South China Sea as invalid under international law, provided a legal foundation that Vietnam has repeatedly invoked in its diplomatic efforts (Gunawan et al. 2022). This ruling not only strengthened Vietnam's position in regional forums but also garnered support from the broader international community, particularly the United States, Japan, and the European Union, who have expressed their concerns over China's actions in the region.

Diplomatically, Vietnam has skilfully leveraged its multilateral relationships to counterbalance China's influence. ASEAN, as the leading regional organization, has been central to Vietnam's strategy in addressing the South China Sea disputes. Through ASEAN, Vietnam has worked to promote dialogue among claimant states and non-claimants, seeking to build consensus on the need for a peaceful resolution based on international law. However, ASEAN's consensus-based decision-making has its limitations, particularly when dealing with the influence of powerful member states like China (Chalid et al. 2016). Vietnam has thus had to engage with external powers – most notably the United States, Japan, and India – who share its concerns about the militarization of the South China Sea and China's broader regional ambitions.

The partnership with the United States has been instrumental in strengthening Vietnam's position against China. The United States has been a critical ally in enhancing Vietnam's maritime security, providing technical assistance, training, and modern defence equipment, including patrol vessels to safeguard Vietnam's Exclusive Economic Zone (EEZ) in the South China Sea. Joint military exercises and cooperation in areas like maritime surveillance, counterterrorism, and cybersecurity have further reinforced Vietnam's ability to respond to potential security threats posed by China. Moreover, the United States has supported Vietnam's stance on freedom of navigation in the South China Sea, ensuring that international maritime trade remains uninterrupted. This defence partnership serves as a critical counterweight to China's military expansion in the region (Heiduk 2022).

In addition to its relationship with the United States, Vietnam has deepened its ties with Japan and India as part of its strategy to diversify its international relations and reduce dependency on China. Japan's support has been especially significant in bolstering Vietnam's maritime security capabilities. Japan has supplied patrol vessels, radar systems, and surveillance technology, strengthening Vietnam's ability to monitor and respond to China's activities in the disputed waters. Furthermore, Japan's focus on a Free and Open Indo-Pacific aligns closely with Vietnam's objectives of preserving a stable, rules-based regional order, free from coercion and unilateral actions (Brown/Kingston 2018).

India also plays a crucial role in Vietnam's efforts to counterbalance China. With its own strategic interests in the South China Sea, particularly regarding freedom of navigation and maritime security, India has emerged as a key partner for Vietnam. India has provided military assistance, including naval vessels, and has trained Vietnam's naval personnel, thus enhancing Vietnam's ability to safeguard its maritime borders. Moreover, both countries have conducted joint military exercises to strengthen defence cooperation. India's involvement in the region, through its Act East Policy, is seen as a vital component of Vietnam's broader strategy to engage with like-minded countries to resist China's growing influence (Toan/Yen 2023).

On the military front, Vietnam has pursued modernization of its defence capabilities, particularly its navy and air force, to enhance its ability to respond to potential provocations from China. Vietnam has invested in advanced radar systems, submarines, and combat aircraft, increasing its deterrence capacity and its ability to operate in contested maritime zones (Ghosal 2024). This military buildup, however, is not intended to confront China directly but to ensure that Vietnam can defend its sovereignty if necessary. Vietnam's military modernization also serves as a means of signalling to China and the international community that it is prepared to take all necessary measures to protect its territorial claims.

The legal strategy employed by Vietnam has been equally important in responding to China's actions. Vietnam has consistently called for a resolution of the South China Sea disputes through peaceful dialogue and legal means. By invoking international law, particularly UNCLOS, Vietnam seeks to reaffirm its sovereignty over the Paracel and Spratly Islands, areas that are also claimed by China. Vietnam has also participated in international forums such as the United Nations and the International Court of Justice (ICJ) to advocate for its position. Despite the challenges of facing a much stronger China, Vietnam has remained steadfast in its commitment to using international legal frameworks to address disputes, believing that this approach not only serves its national interests but also contributes to regional peace and stability (Dar 2023; Rusmuliadi 2023).

Vietnam's response to China's increasing influence in the South China Sea has been multifaceted, involving a combination of diplomatic engagement, military strengthening, and legal advocacy. Through its strategic use of multilateral forums, defence partnerships with the United States, Japan, and India, and active participation in international legal proceedings, Vietnam has sought to safeguard its sovereignty and ensure the stability of the Indo-Pacific region. While the challenges of countering China's growing power are substantial, Vietnam's efforts to build a network of supportive partners and enhance its defence capabilities demonstrate its resilience and commitment to maintaining its national interests in an increasingly competitive and uncertain global environment.

5. Economic Development and Foreign Investment

Economic development and the attraction of foreign investment have become pivotal components of Vietnam's foreign policy strategy, especially in the context of the country's position in a rapidly transforming global economy and a strategically contested Indo-Pacific region. As Vietnam seeks to strengthen its international standing, the country has pursued an open-door policy to foreign investors and worked diligently to improve its domestic business environment. At the heart of this strategy is the commitment to fostering sustainable economic growth, ensuring economic resilience, and reducing its vulnerability to external shocks, particularly in the face of increasing economic rivalry in the region, most notably from

China. Vietnam's economic policy, shaped by its engagement with global markets and international partners, underscores its drive for industrial modernization, technological innovation, and increased trade diversification (Jia et al. 2022).

Central to Vietnam's approach to economic development is its participation in international trade agreements. Membership in organizations such as the Comprehensive and Progressive Agreement for Trans-Pacific Partnership (CPTPP), the EU-Vietnam Free Trade Agreement (EVFTA), and the Regional Comprehensive Economic Partnership (RCEP) has provided Vietnam with access to new markets and opportunities for investment, particularly in high-tech industries and sustainable sectors. These free trade agreements (FTAs) have significantly enhanced Vietnam's trade relations with major global economies, including Japan, the United States, and the European Union, creating a favourable environment for foreign companies to invest in the country (Goh, 2016). As a result, Vietnam has become an attractive destination for foreign direct investment (FDI), particularly in industries such as electronics, textiles, and automotive manufacturing (Bobowski 2019; Le 2023).

Foreign investment has been instrumental in driving Vietnam's economic transformation over the past few decades. The country has become one of the leading destinations for FDI in Southeast Asia, with significant investments from multinational companies such as Samsung, Intel, and LG. These companies have not only contributed to Vietnam's manufacturing capacity but also facilitated the transfer of critical technologies, enhanced the skill set of the Vietnamese workforce, and improved the quality of domestic products. This shift towards higher value-added industries is key to Vietnam's ambition to move up the global value chain and reduce its reliance on low-cost manufacturing (Asada 2020). For example, Vietnam has become one of the largest exporters of electronics in the region, with Samsung alone accounting for a substantial portion of its exports. In addition to manufacturing, foreign investments have been instrumental in developing Vietnam's infrastructure and financial sectors, areas critical for ensuring long-term economic growth.

While FDI has been a key driver of economic growth, Vietnam's approach to attracting investment has also involved improving its investment climate. The government has implemented a series of economic reforms aimed at reducing bureaucratic hurdles, enhancing transparency, and providing tax incentives for foreign investors. These reforms have been critical in boosting investor confidence and increasing the inflow of capital into the country. Additionally, Vietnam has been expanding its special economic zones and industrial parks, which have become magnets for foreign companies seeking to benefit from competitive wages, skilled labour, and access to international supply chains. These zones are designed to foster a more conducive environment for high-tech industries, as well as to attract capital-intensive projects that contribute to the country's long-term development goals.

Furthermore, economic diversification has been a priority for Vietnam as it seeks to reduce its dependence on any single sector or market. While the manufacturing sector has traditionally been the backbone of the Vietnamese economy, the country has increasingly focused on expanding its services sector, including finance, information technology, and tourism. Vietnam has made significant strides in developing a digital economy, with the rise of e-commerce, fintech, and digital platforms being seen as essential to the country's economic future. Investments in startups and technology ventures are expected to further catalyse economic diversification, ensuring that Vietnam remains competitive in the rapidly evolving global economy.

Vietnam's economic development strategy is also closely tied to its efforts to foster regional integration. By promoting economic cooperation with neighbouring countries and regional powers such as Japan, India, and South Korea, Vietnam has positioned itself as a vital link in the growing network of global supply chains. This regional integration not only offers Vietnam access to broader markets but also allows the country to capitalize on strategic partnerships in areas such as energy, technology, and defence cooperation. In particular, Vietnam's collaboration with Japan has proven crucial in advancing infrastructure development, including the construction of transport networks, the establishment of smart cities, and the transfer of clean energy technologies. Similarly, economic cooperation with India has focused on sectors like agriculture, information technology, and maritime security, all of which are critical to Vietnam's economic resilience and sustainability in the long run.

At the same time, Vietnam has worked to reduce its economic dependence on China by diversifying trade relationships and seeking alternative supply chains. The ongoing trade tensions between China and the United States have opened new opportunities for Vietnam to serve as a regional manufacturing hub, with many companies shifting their production from China to Vietnam to avoid tariffs and take advantage of Vietnam's more favourable trade agreements with the US and the EU. This shifting landscape has made Vietnam an increasingly attractive alternative to China, not only for manufacturing but also for sectors such as electronics, automotive, and renewable energy. This trend reflects Vietnam's growing importance as a regional economic player and its ability to adapt to the evolving dynamics of global trade (Hayakawa 2024).

Despite these successes, challenges remain. One of the most pressing issues for Vietnam is the need to continue improving its institutional capacity and governance framework. The country's rapid economic growth has placed significant pressure on its infrastructure, labour markets, and environmental resources. In particular, Vietnam must balance the demands of industrialization with the need for sustainable development. Issues such as environmental degradation, urbanization, and the cost of living in major cities pose significant challenges to ensuring that the benefits of economic growth are distributed equitably across society. Furthermore, maintaining political stability and social cohesion while opening the economy to foreign investment will be critical for Vietnam as it continues to integrate further into the global economy.

Economic development and foreign investment have been central to Vietnam's strategy for strengthening its position in the global economy. Through active participation in international trade agreements, targeted economic reforms, and the diversification of its industrial base, Vietnam has positioned itself as one of the most dynamic economies in Southeast Asia. However, continued success will require addressing structural challenges, promoting sustainable development, and ensuring that the benefits of growth are widely shared among the population. As the country continues to attract foreign investment and expand its economic partnerships, Vietnam's strategic positioning as an open, competitive, and resilient economy will be key to its long-term prosperity.

6. Regional Dialogue and Cooperation

Regional dialogue and cooperation have been foundational elements of Vietnam's foreign policy, particularly in the context of the Indo-Pacific region, where strategic competition between major powers has intensified. For Vietnam, a country with deep historical ties to its neighbours and an interest in regional stability, engagement in regional multilateral frameworks has been key to promoting peace, managing security concerns, and advancing economic development. The centrality of ASEAN in Vietnam's regional strategy reflects the country's commitment to multilateralism and its belief in the importance of a unified, collaborative approach to regional challenges.

ASEAN, as the primary regional organization, has allowed Vietnam to not only contribute to regional security but also to influence the regional agenda on issues such as trade, maritime security, and non-traditional security threats like terrorism and climate change. Vietnam has leveraged ASEAN to advocate for the peaceful resolution of disputes in the South China Sea, where it faces overlapping territorial claims with China. Through ASEAN, Vietnam has sought to establish a rules-based order that promotes freedom of navigation and the protection of international law, particularly in the context of maritime rights and sovereignty disputes (Thayer 2017).

ASEAN's consensus-based decision-making process, however, has its limitations. Despite Vietnam's active efforts to rally support within ASEAN, the organization's ability to act decisively in addressing regional conflicts – especially in relation to China's assertiveness in the South China Sea – has been constrained. ASEAN's ability to adopt collective positions has often been undermined by the differing interests of its member states, some of whom are more economically dependent on China than others. In this context, Vietnam has been increasingly proactive in seeking support from external partners, particularly the United States, Japan, and India, to counterbalance China's growing influence in the region (Lee/Hiep 2021).

Beyond ASEAN, Vietnam has deepened its engagement with bilateral and multilateral dialogues with key regional powers. The United States, with its strategic *Pivot to Asia* policy, has become an important partner for Vietnam, particularly in the areas of security and trade. Vietnam's growing defence and security cooperation with the United States have included joint military exercises, the transfer of defence technology, and increased intelligence-sharing to counter regional threats such as terrorism and cyber-attacks. These collaborative efforts contribute to maintaining peace and stability in the South China Sea, an area of critical importance to both Vietnam and the broader international community. Vietnam has supported the US's stance on the freedom of navigation in international waters, advocating for the protection of international shipping lanes that are essential to global trade (Van Quyet/Nguyet 2023).

Similarly, Vietnam's strategic relationship with Japan has been marked by significant cooperation in maritime security and economic development. Japan, which has its own interests in maintaining a stable Indo-Pacific region, has supported Vietnam with both military and non-military assistance, including the provision of patrol vessels, maritime surveillance systems, and training for Vietnamese coast guard personnel. This support strengthens Vietnam's ability to protect its exclusive economic zone (EEZ) in the South China Sea while also enhancing the overall security environment in Southeast Asia. Japan's Free and Open Indo-Pacific Strategy, which promotes regional stability and inclusive growth, aligns closely with Vietnam's interests in fostering an environment free from coercion and military escalation (Yazuru 2022).

The relationship between Vietnam and India is another critical element in its strategy of regional engagement. India's *Look East* policy, which emphasizes strengthening ties with Southeast Asia, has facilitated deepening defence and security cooperation between the two countries. Vietnam and India have conducted joint naval exercises, collaborated on maritime security, and worked together to enhance regional stability through initiatives such as the ASEAN Defence Ministers' Meeting Plus (ADMM+). These cooperative activities help to counterbalance China's growing dominance in the region. India's involvement in Vietnam's regional security framework not only bolsters its maritime capabilities but also ensures that Vietnam has strong, diversified partnerships in the face of China's assertive behaviour (Sitaraman 2016).

Vietnam's regional diplomacy is also marked by its active participation in multilateral security and economic forums such as the East Asia Summit (EAS), the ASEAN Regional Forum (ARF), and the Asia-Pacific Economic Cooperation (APEC). These platforms have allowed Vietnam to play an active role in addressing pressing issues such as climate change, natural disasters, and terrorism while promoting economic integration and trade liberalization across the Indo-Pacific region. Through these engagements, Vietnam has contributed to shaping the regional agenda, particularly in terms of promoting peace, stability, and prosperity, in line with its national interests and its broader commitment to multilateralism.

Vietnam's participation in these forums not only enhances its diplomatic standing but also provides the country with a platform to engage in confidence-building measures and build strong regional partnerships that help it address both traditional and non-traditional security challenges. For instance, through the ASEAN Regional Forum (ARF), Vietnam has been able to engage with countries such as the United States, China, Russia, and Australia in dialogues on regional security issues, thereby positioning itself as an influential voice in shaping the regional security architecture.

While Vietnam's active participation in regional dialogue and cooperation has contributed to its success in maintaining a relatively stable security environment, it faces several challenges. The primary challenge lies in the continuing influence of China, particularly within ASEAN, where some members are reluctant to confront Beijing's territorial claims and actions in the South China Sea. Additionally, while Vietnam has forged strong partnerships with countries like the United States, Japan, and India, these partnerships are not without complexities. Vietnam must carefully navigate its relationships with these external powers to avoid alienating China while ensuring its sovereignty is upheld.

Regional dialogue and cooperation are critical to Vietnam's foreign policy strategy, allowing the country to enhance its security, strengthen economic ties, and contribute to regional stability. By leveraging ASEAN as a primary platform for engagement, while also fostering strong bilateral and multilateral partnerships with countries such as the United States, Japan, and India, Vietnam has successfully positioned itself as a key player in the Indo-Pacific region. Despite the challenges posed by China's growing influence, Vietnam's active participation in regional security and economic dialogues ensures that it continues to play a central role in shaping the future of the Indo-Pacific, promoting peace, stability, and prosperity for all. As regional dynamics evolve, Vietnam's diplomatic agility will remain crucial in navigating the complexities of an increasingly multipolar world order.

7. Some Evaluations and Policy Implications

Vietnam's foreign policy strategy, shaped by the principles of multilateralization and diversification, has proven to be both adaptable and resilient in the face of growing regional competition, particularly with the rising influence of China. By focusing on multilateral cooperation through platforms like ASEAN and diversifying its strategic relationships with key global powers, including the United States, Japan, and India, Vietnam has successfully maintained its sovereignty, enhanced its security, and fostered economic development. However, despite the apparent successes, there are several areas where the strategy could be refined, and its long-term sustainability evaluated.

One of the key strengths of Vietnam's foreign policy has been its ability to balance relationships with major powers while avoiding alignment with any single state. Through its active participation in multilateral frameworks, Vietnam has skilfully ensured that no country has undue influence over its domestic and foreign policy decisions. The country's commitment to a multilateral, rules-based international order has been crucial in asserting its sovereignty over disputed territories, particularly in the South China Sea. Its engagement with ASEAN has also enhanced its diplomatic standing, allowing it to address both regional and global challenges in a cooperative manner (Thayer 2017). This diplomatic agility, combined with its growing defence partnerships, has significantly elevated Vietnam's international profile, making it an increasingly influential voice in regional and global affairs.

However, Vietnam's reliance on multilateralism also brings limitations. The ASEAN consensus-based decision-making process, for instance, can sometimes stymie decisive action, particularly when the interests of member states diverge significantly, as seen in the ongoing tensions over the South China Sea. Despite Vietnam's diplomatic efforts within ASEAN, it has been difficult to achieve a unified stance on issues related to China, whose growing economic influence over many ASEAN members has undermined collective action (Thayer 2017). ASEAN's inability to present a unified response to China's assertiveness in the South China Sea exemplifies the constraints of multilateralism when confronted with the interests of powerful neighbours. Thus, while Vietnam's approach of leveraging ASEAN is crucial, it is also necessary for Vietnam to cultivate more effective bilateral relationships with external powers who share its concerns about China's regional ambitions.

The strategy of diversification of Vietnam's foreign relations has been another significant success. By building strong defence and economic ties with countries like the United States, Japan, and India, Vietnam has mitigated the risks of over-reliance on any single partner, particularly China. These bilateral relationships have been key in providing Vietnam with both the military support to safeguard its sovereignty and the economic partnerships to promote sustainable development. Vietnam's collaboration with Japan, for example, has resulted in the provision of critical maritime security assets and investment in infrastructure, while its relationship with the United States has advanced cooperation on defence, trade, and regional stability (Yazuru 2022).

However, managing these partnerships requires careful balancing. As Vietnam strengthens ties with the United States, it risks straining its relationship with China, with whom it shares deep economic interdependence. This delicate balance has been a constant challenge for Vietnam's foreign policy, as its strategic partnerships with external powers – while beneficial – could be perceived by China as counterproductive to the status quo. The risk of provoking China, particularly through military cooperation with the United States and Japan, requires Vietnam to continuously adapt its diplomatic strategies to avoid escalating tensions in the region.

In terms of economic development, Vietnam's active engagement in international trade agreements like the CPTPP, EVFTA, and RCEP has facilitated access to new markets and attracted foreign investment, contributing to its rapid economic growth. The inflow of foreign direct investment (FDI) has supported the country's industrialization and technological advancement, while partnerships with key investors such as Samsung, LG, and Intel have enhanced Vietnam's position in global supply chains (Eckardt 2018). Despite these successes, challenges remain in terms of economic sustainability. The need for further economic diversification remains a priority, as Vietnam is still heavily dependent on low-cost manufacturing and foreign investments in certain sectors. As the global economy moves towards digitalization and green technologies, Vietnam must continue to innovate and enhance its workforce's skill set to stay competitive.

Policy implications for Vietnam's foreign strategy are clear: continued engagement with multilateral frameworks will be essential, but it must be complemented by a stronger emphasis on bilateral diplomacy with key global powers and a more flexible approach to defence and economic cooperation. Vietnam's current strategy of balancing ties between the United States and China has allowed it to maximize its economic benefits while maintaining sovereignty. However, the shifting global order – marked by the growing competition between the US and China – requires Vietnam to re-assess its policy framework regularly. It may need to consider expanding its partnerships with other regional powers, such as South Korea and Australia, to strengthen its position and reduce dependency on any single power.

Security and defence cooperation should continue to be a central aspect of Vietnam's strategy, but it must be carefully managed to avoid confrontation with China. Vietnam's military modernization efforts and defence partnerships with countries like the United States and Japan are critical for safeguarding its sovereignty, but Vietnam should also prioritize confidence-building measures and cooperative security mechanisms that allow for de-escalation of tensions in the South China Sea and other contested areas.

Finally, the economic dimension of Vietnam's foreign policy should continue to focus on fostering technological innovation and infrastructure development, while also addressing the challenges of sustainability and inclusive growth. By diversifying its economic base and reducing dependence on traditional industries, Vietnam can strengthen its economic resilience and enhance its long-term stability. It is essential that Vietnam continues to align its foreign policy with global trends, such as digitalization and green energy, to ensure that it remains competitive and adaptive to the evolving global economy.

Vietnam's foreign policy strategy of multilateralism and diversification has proven effective in navigating the complexities of regional geopolitics, but it is not without challenges. By refining its diplomatic approach, deepening defence cooperation, and fostering sustainable economic development, Vietnam can continue to safeguard its national interests and enhance its position on the global stage. The future of Vietnam's foreign policy will depend on its ability to balance the competing pressures of regional power dynamics while securing its sovereignty, stability, and prosperity in an increasingly interconnected world.

8. Conclusion

Vietnam's foreign policy strategy, characterized by the principles of multilateralization and diversification, has played a critical role in navigating the increasingly complex geopolitical landscape of the Indo-Pacific region. Amidst the rising influence of China, the growing competition between global powers, and evolving regional security dynamics, Vietnam has managed to safeguard its sovereignty, foster economic development, and enhance its international standing. By focusing on regional dialogue through ASEAN and expanding its strategic partnerships with key players such as the United States, Japan, and India, Vietnam has effectively built a flexible, resilient foreign policy framework that aligns with its national interests.

The success of Vietnam's strategy lies in its ability to balance diplomatic engagements with diverse global powers while mitigating the risks of overreliance on any single nation. The multilateral approach through ASEAN and other international frameworks has not only ensured that Vietnam remains a key player in regional security but also provided it with a platform to assert its sovereignty over the contested South China Sea. However, the limitations of ASEAN's consensus-driven approach, particularly in addressing the assertiveness of China, highlight the need for Vietnam to continuously adapt its diplomatic and defence strategies to reflect the evolving regional power dynamics.

Vietnam's efforts to diversify its foreign relations have been particularly crucial in reducing its dependency on any single partner, particularly China, which remains both a key economically and a source of strategic tension. Through stronger defence ties with the United States, Japan, and India, and increasing engagement in defence and economic cooperation, Vietnam has created a multi-faceted approach to enhance its national security and economic resilience. Despite the successes of these partnerships, the need for careful diplomacy remains paramount, as Vietnam must navigate the delicate balance between strengthening ties with global powers and maintaining its strategic relationship with China.

The country's economic development strategy, driven by its active participation in international trade agreements and its focus on attracting foreign investment, has fuelled rapid industrialization and technological progress. However, economic sustainability remains a challenge, particularly as Vietnam continues to transition from low-cost manufacturing to more advanced sectors like technology, green energy, and high-tech industries. The country's growing presence in global supply chains and increasing exports reflect the benefits of its open economic policies, but it must continue diversifying its economy to remain competitive in an increasingly digitalized and environmentally conscious global market.

Looking ahead, Vietnam's foreign policy strategy must continue to evolve in response to the shifting dynamics of the Indo-Pacific and the broader international system. The rising influence of China, coupled with the ongoing competition between global powers, presents both opportunities and challenges for Vietnam. In particular, Vietnam's ability to balance its partnerships, enhance its defence and economic capabilities, and address regional security concerns will be crucial in determining its long-term stability and prosperity.

Ultimately, Vietnam's approach to foreign policy has proven successful in safeguarding its interests and enhancing its role in regional and global affairs. However, continued engagement in multilateral diplomacy, deepening defence cooperation, and fostering sustainable economic development will be essential for Vietnam to navigate the complexities of an increasingly interconnected and competitive world. By refining its strategy to address both emerging challenges and opportunities, Vietnam can continue to strengthen its position as a responsible, resilient, and influential actor in the Indo-Pacific and beyond.

9. References

Asada, H. (2020): Effects of Foreign Direct Investment and Trade on Labor Productivity Growth in Vietnam. In: Journal of Risk and Financial Management. https://doi.org/10.3390/jrfm13090204.

Bobowski, S. (2019): An insight into trade patterns in HDD industry between CPTPP countries. In: International Days of Statistics and Economics 2019. https://doi.org/10.18267/pr.2019.los.186.17

Brown, J. D. J./Kingston, J. (2018): Japan's Foreign Relations in Asia. Routledge.

Chalid, A. M. (et al.) (2016): ASEAN's Role in Responding the United States and the Philippines Military Cooperation on the South China Sea Conflict. In: The Journal of international studies, 1, 5–22. https://doi.org/10.24198/intermestic.v1n1.2.

Cường, N. A. (2023): Vietnamese online media leaders' and citizens' perspectives on Vietnam-US relations. In: Humanities and Social Sciences Communications, 10(1), 864.

Cường, N. A. (2024): Cooperation and Struggle Between Vietnam and the United States: Impediments to Improved U.S.-Vietnam Relations. In: Journal of American-East Asian Relations, 31(1), 75–110. https://doi.org/https://doi.org/10.1163/18765610-31010004.

Cuong, N. X. (2024): Vietnam's Marine Environmental Security: Cross-Border Challenges and Vietnam concept. Journal of People, Plants, and Environment. https://doi.org/10.11628/ksppe.2024.27.3.237.

Dar, K. B. (2023): THE SOUTH CHINA SEA DISPUTE AND SINO-VIETNAMESE RECONCILIATION. In: Journal of International Studies. https://doi.org/10.32890/jis2023.19.1.2.

De Castro, R. (2021): Under the shadow of the giants: The ASEAN in search of a common strategy in a fluid and perilous Indo-Pacific region. In: Asian Journal of Comparative Politics, 7, 282–301. https://doi.org/10.1177/20578911211014598.

Eckardt, S./Mishra, D./Dinh, V. T. (2018, April 17, 2018): Vietnam's manufacturing miracle: Lessons for developing countries. The Brookings Institution. https://www.brookings.edu/articles/vietnams-manufacturing-miracle-lessons-for-developing-countries/.

Fedorov, N./Garin, A. (2023): Defense and economic cooperation of India and Vietnam in link with problems of the South China Sea. In: The Russian Journal of Vietnamese Studies. https://doi.org/10.54631/vs.2023.71-111035.

GHOSAL, A. (2024): US ambassador to Vietnam says US arms manufacturers could help boost Vietnam's military capabilities. AP. https://apnews.com/article/vietnam-arms-weapons-exposition-manufacturing-0257d237db09c22a8694a1964ea96941.

Gunawan, Y. (et al.) (2022): Dispute Resolution between the Philippines and China: Fishing Activities in the South China Sea. In: UNISCI Journal. https://doi.org/10.31439/unisci-141.

Hayakawa, K. (2024): Exports to the US and Imports from China during the US-China Tariff War: Evidence from Regional Trade Data in Vietnam. In: SSRN Electronic Journal. https://doi.org/10.2139/ssrn.4954162.

Heiduk, F. (2022): Security in the Indo-Pacific https://doi.org/10.18449/2022RP11.

Jia, G./Wang, R./Wong, C. H. (2022): Literature Review on Foreign Direct Investment of Vietnam. In: Advances in Social Science, Education and Humanities Research. https://doi.org/10.2991/assehr.k.211220.214.

Le, T. A. T. (2023): Macroeconomic factors and trade balance: An analysis of Vietnam's relations with RCEP countries. In: International Journal of ADVANCED AND APPLIED SCIENCES. https://doi.org/10.21833/ijaas.2023.08.011.

Lee, J./Hiệp, L. H. (2021, 15/03/2021): Việt Nam, ASEAN và Đối đầu Mỹ-Trung ở Ấn Độ Dương-Thái Bình Dương [Vietnam, ASEAN and US-China Confrontation in the Indo-Pacific]. Nghiên Cứu Quốc Tế. https://nghiencuuquocte.org/2021/03/15/viet-nam-asean-va-doi-dau-my-trung-o-an-do-duong-thai-binh-duong/.

Mosyakov, D. (2020): Vietnam's Politics as a Factor of Peace and Stability in the South China Sea Dispute. 5–11. https://doi.org/10.31696/2072-8271-2020-3-3-48-005-011.

Rusmuliadi, R. (2023): Non-Claimant States Perspectives on the South China Sea Dispute. In: Lampung Journal of International Law. https://doi.org/10.25041/lajil.v5i1.2717.

Sitaraman, S. (2016): Rising Chinese Power and Territorial Assertiveness in the South China Sea: India-Vietnam Strategic Partnership as a Counterbalancing Endeavor. 403–423. https://doi.org/10.1007/978-3-319-26152-2_19.

Thayer, C. A. (2017): Vietnam's Foreign Policy in an Era of Rising Sino-US Competition and Increasing Domestic Political Influence. In: Asian Security, 13(3), 183–199. https://doi.org/10.1080/14799855.2017.1354570.

Thuong, N. L. T./Oanh, N. (2021): Vietnam in the Indo-Pacific Region: Perception, Position and Perspectives. In: India Quarterly, 77, 129–142. https://doi.org/10.1177/09749284211005036.

Toan, L. B. K./Yen, V. H. (2023): MARITIME STRATEGIC COOPERATION BETWEEN INDIA AND VIETNAM: PROMOTING REGIONAL SECURITY AND ECONOMIC GROWTH IN THE INDO-PACIFIC. In: Russian Law Journal. https://doi.org/10.52783/rlj.v11i3.1384.

Tran, Z. T./Ionov, E. M. (2023): The Role of ASEAN and Vietnam in Counterterrorism. In: Международные отношения. https://doi.org/10.7256/2454-0641.2023.1.39746.

Trinh, V. D./Huyen Ho, D. (2024): Vietnam's Response to the US Indo-Pacific Strategy in the Context of a Rising China. In: Journal of Current Southeast Asian Affairs, 43, 120–147.

Van Quyet, L./Nguyet, N. T. A. (2023): U.S.-Vietnam maritime security cooperation in the South China Sea: From the Obama administration to the current Biden administration. In: Cogent Arts & Humanities, 10. https://doi.org/10.1080/23311983.2023.2231697.

Willis, C. (2017): The Obama Pivot to Asia: An Analysis of the Fundamentals University of North Florida. https://digitalcommons.unf.edu/cgi/viewcontent.cgi?article=1825&context=etd.

Yazuru, W. (2022): NEW STRATEGY JAPANESE MILITARY IN THE ASIA PACIFIC REGION AND THE IMPACT ON INTERNATIONAL SECURITY STABILITY. In: Jurnal Pembaharuan Hukum. https://doi.org/10.26532/jph.v9i2.23803.

Chapter 14: Sharing Common Interests between India's Indo-Pacific Oceans Initiative and ASEAN Outlook on the Indo-Pacific

Tran My Hai Loc, Vu Thi Anh Thu, Nguyen Van Duong and Tran Thi Thuy

This chapter examines the similarities and differences between India's Indo-Pacific Oceans Initiative (IPOI) and the ASEAN Outlook on the Indo-Pacific (AOIP), two significant frameworks shaping the strategic and economic landscape of the Indo-Pacific region. It begins by outlining the core principles of both initiatives, emphasizing their shared commitment to a free, open, and inclusive Indo-Pacific. Both frameworks prioritize regional stability, sustainable development, and cooperation on key challenges, including maritime security, connectivity, and environmental sustainability. The analysis highlights areas of alignment, where shared objectives present opportunities for collaboration, while also addressing critical differences in strategic focus, member-state priorities, and responses to the region's shifting geopolitical dynamics. Particular attention is given to the influence of major powers, especially China, and the diverse stances within ASEAN member states regarding engagement with India and China. These factors reveal the complexity of achieving cohesion between the two frameworks. The chapter concludes by assessing whether IPOI and AOIP truly align in their strategic interests and how such alignment, if present, can be strengthened through focused cooperation. Conversely, it examines the most significant barriers to alignment, including differing strategic outlooks, regional sensitivities, and competing interests, which complicate deeper integration. Through this comprehensive analysis, the chapter contributes to understanding the potential and limitations of IPOI-AOIP collaboration in fostering a resilient, stable, and inclusive Indo-Pacific order.

1. Introduction

In recent years, the Indo-Pacific region has emerged as a focal point of global geopolitics, with major powers actively shaping its dynamics. Notable strategies include Japan's Free and Open Indo-Pacific, the U.S. Indo-Pacific Strategy, Canada's Indo-Pacific Strategy, India's Act East Policy and IPOI, Korea's Indo-Pacific Strategy, and ASEAN's Indo-Pacific Outlook. Other influential parties, such as the European Union, the United Kingdom, France and Germany, have also shown a growing interest in the region's dynamics. While the exact strategic definition of the Indo-Pacific remains fluid and varies among stakeholders, it is undeniable that the region serves as a central point for aligning national and regional strategies that affect global security and stability.

For ASEAN and India, the Indo-Pacific holds particular importance (Lin 2022, 3). Both entities recognize the region's growing influence on their own security and economic development. ASEAN, a central player in Southeast Asia, has long been committed to fostering peace, stability, and cooperation in the region, while India, as a rising regional power, has increasingly looked to assert its strategic influence over the Indo-Pacific, particularly through its maritime capabilities and partnerships (Ladwig 2024). These shared interests in the region's peace and prosperity are reflected in the strategic documents adopted by both ASEAN and India to guide their engagement in the Indo-Pacific.

Over the past few years, ASEAN and India have increasingly worked together to align their strategic interests in the Indo-Pacific. This collaboration reached a significant milestone in November 2021 when ASEAN and India adopted the Joint Statement on Cooperation on the ASEAN Outlook on the Indo-Pacific for Peace, Stability, and Prosperity in the Region, during the 18th ASEAN-India Summit (The ASEAN Secretariat 2021). The Joint Statement seeks to deepen the ASEAN-India strategic partnership and explores convergences between the AOIP and IPOI. It emphasizes shared values and common principles, such as the commitment to a rules-based international order, sustainable development, and the importance of maritime security. The statement also identifies potential areas for cooperation, aligning with the four priority areas of the AOIP: maritime and economic cooperation, connectivity, sustainable development, and other mutual interests (ASEAN 2023, 2). This agreement serves as a clear indication that ASEAN and India are committed to working together to address the evolving challenges and opportunities in the Indo-Pacific region.

Despite this growing cooperation, the alignment between the AOIP and IPOI is not without its challenges. While both frameworks share a common commitment to peace, stability, and prosperity in the region, they also reflect differences in their strategic priorities, regional roles, and approaches to leadership. ASEAN's approach, centred around multilateralism and consensus, contrasts with India's more assertive regional engagement, particularly through initiatives like the Quad. These differences raise important questions about the extent to which ASEAN and India share common interests and whether their approaches to the Indo-Pacific are truly aligned, or if they represent competing visions for the region's future.

This chapter aims to explore the strategic benefits and differences between the IPOI and AOIP, specifically focusing on whether ASEAN and India truly share common interests and to what extent these interests align. By examining these two frameworks, the paper seeks to shed light on the broader dynamics of ASEAN-India relations and the potential for future cooperation in the Indo Pacific. It will analyse the shared priorities of both parties, assess the potential areas of divergence, and consider how ASEAN and India might navigate these challenges to strengthen their strategic partnership in the Indo-Pacific.

2. Similarities between IPOI and AOIP

In 2019, at the East Asia Summit in Bangkok, Prime Minister Narendra Modi announced India's Indo-Pacific Oceans Initiative (IPOI). According to the Ministry of External Affairs of India, this is an open, global initiative based on existing regional cooperation structures and mechanisms, focusing on seven pillars (see Image 1):

> maritime security, marine ecology, maritime resources, capacity building and resource sharing, disaster risk reduction and management, scientific, technological, and academic cooperation, and trade connectivity and maritime transport (Ministry of External Affairs 2020c).

In addition to these pillars, the concepts of *strategic autonomy* and inclusiveness are central to India's IPOI initiative. Currently, India largely maintains friendly relations with most countries and stakeholders in the region, especially ASEAN. The result of this approach is the Security and Growth for All in the Region (SAGAR) initiative, promoted through India's maritime diplomacy in the Indo-Pacific. This also reflects India's desire to manage maritime security and governance in the Indian Ocean region.

Image 1: Seven pillars of IPOI

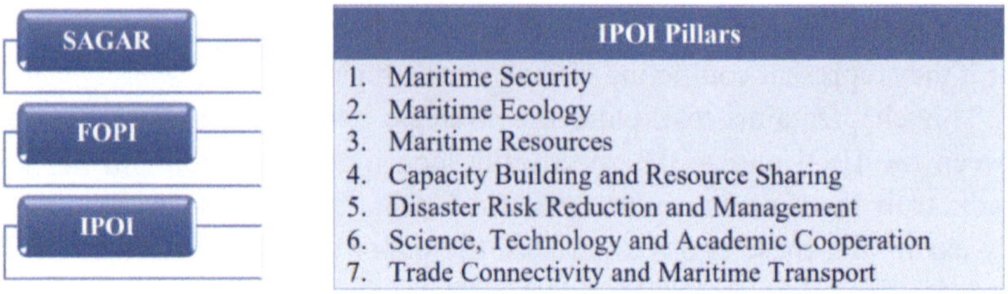

Source: Chauhan et al. 2020, 9

In the context of major powers increasingly focusing their strategies on the region, ASEAN launched AOIP in 2019 as a strategic response to address the escalating geopolitical tensions and the growing influence of major countries. AOIP reflects ASEAN's desire to maintain regional stability, ensure the future of ASEAN, and avoid dependence on the will of any major powers. This affirms ASEAN's position of remaining neutral in the competition for influence within the ASEAN region. This outlook aims to promote practical and tangible cooperation with ASEAN's external partners in four key areas: maritime cooperation, economics, connectivity, and sustainable development (Wau/Tay 2020).

Both initiatives aim for a peaceful, stable, and sustainably developed region; however, they do not exist independently but rather complement and support each other in many areas. Both IPOI and AOIP stem from the need to build an open, free, inclusive Indo-Pacific region based on international law, ensuring the central role of countries in the region. While IPOI focuses on promoting maritime cooperation, trade, sustainable development, and maritime resource management (Ministry of External Affairs 2020b), AOIP emphasizes the central role of ASEAN within the regional structure (Yoshimatsu 2023, 36), laying the foundation for cooperation in areas such as economic connectivity, maritime cooperation, sustainable development, and people-to-people exchanges. These commonalities are also very well captured in the ASEAN-India Joint Statement on cooperation on AOIP, which now acts as a beacon to guide our engagement in the region (Singh 2022).

IPOI's success depends on the involvement of key regional countries, with ASEAN playing a crucial role. To make IPOI effective, India requires ASEAN's support in diplomacy, security, and economics. ASEAN is a leading regional organization in the Indo-Pacific, with key mechanisms like the East Asia Summit, ASEAN Regional Forum, and ASEAN Defence Ministers' Meeting-Plus. ASEAN's active participation not only boosts IPOI's legitimacy and effectiveness but also helps India enhance its influence through soft power, minimizing negative reactions from other major powers.

In maritime security, India places great importance on freedom of navigation and the rule-based order, especially in the South China Sea and the Indian Ocean. Key ASEAN coastal countries such as Indonesia, Vietnam, Malaysia, and the Philippines could cooperate with India in ensuring maritime security, combating piracy, protecting trade routes, and enforcing international law. At the same time, ASEAN also plays a vital role in promoting economic connectivity and regional infrastructure. With its rapid development and being India's fourth-largest trading partner, ASEAN can collaborate with India on projects such as the India-Myanmar-Thailand Economic Corridor and the expansion of maritime trade routes, contributing to economic integration and the realization of IPOI's goals. Conversely, ASEAN also has strategic benefits from cooperating with India under the IPOI framework, particularly in the context of increasing regional geopolitical competition. Cooperation with India helps ASEAN maintain a strategic balance and avoid over-dependence on a single great power like China or the United States. Furthermore, ASEAN can leverage India's strengths in information technology, artificial intelligence, and digital technologies to drive digital transformation and develop the digital economy. Additionally, ASEAN and India can engage in deep cooperation in security and defence, including military training and cybersecurity. ASEAN countries such as Vietnam, Indonesia, and the Philippines could benefit from India's support in strengthening defence capabilities and safeguarding maritime sovereignty. Thus, IPOI and AOIP not only provide strategic benefits for both India and ASEAN but also contribute to shaping a peaceful, stable, and sustainably developed Indo-Pacific region.

Based on the concepts and frameworks of both sides, the shared and harmonized interests of both parties can be seen the seven core pillars of IPOI align with four key priorities of AOIP. This convergence suggests that IPOI and AOIP are not mutually exclusive; rather, they are complementary frameworks that can collaboratively contribute to the shared objective of fostering a peaceful, stable, and sustainably developed Indo-Pacific region. The common vision for cooperation between IPOI and AOIP centres on fostering regional stability, sustainable development, and prosperity through aligned efforts across various pillars. Both frameworks prioritize maritime security, with shared goals of ensuring safe seas and enhancing cooperation to address piracy and other maritime challenges. Connectivity, a core focus of both, can be strengthened through joint efforts in trade routes, digital infrastructure, and port connectivity. Sustainability is another key area of overlap, as both aim to protect marine biodiversity, combat pollution, and promote sustainable fisheries. Economic cooperation and resource management can be harmonized by combining efforts in sustainable exploitation of maritime resources, ensuring equitable development. Capacity building and resource sharing, integral to both frameworks, would empower local institutions and enhance resilience against maritime challenges. Additionally, disaster risk reduction and management can be strengthened through collaborative disaster response systems, particularly in light of climate change. Finally, both frameworks recognize the importance of science, technology, and academic cooperation, fostering innovation in marine research, climate science, and blue economy technologies. Through these synergies, IPOI and AOIP can work together to create a more secure, sustainable, and prosperous Indo-Pacific region (see Table 1).

India has been actively implementing IPOI and supporting AOIP by enhancing maritime security cooperation and strengthening defence ties with ASEAN member states. Through joint exercises, training programs, and coordinated patrols, India has expanded its naval presence in Southeast Asia. In addition to maritime engagement, India is implementing three key activities to deepen its defence cooperation with ASEAN. First, it is increasing joint training and exercises for ASEAN states' land, sea, and air forces, regularly hosting Southeast Asian military personnel within its sovereign spaces. Second, India is advancing bilateral and multilateral security dialogues with ASEAN nations to foster stronger defence partnerships. Third, India is emerging as a significant arms exporter to ASEAN, making steady progress despite competition from established suppliers. These efforts underscore India's broader commitment to regional stability and security.

Table 1: Identified broad-areas of cooperation

Sectors	AOIP	IPOI
Maritime Cooperation	Freedom of Navigation and Overflight	Maritime Security
	Peaceful Dispute-settlement	**Capacity Building and Resource Sharing**
	Promote Maritime Connectivity	

Sectors	AOIP	IPOI
	Maritime Safety & Security	
	Promote Maritime Commerce	
	Address Transnational Crime (e.g., trafficking in persons or illicit drugs, sea-piracy, robbery and armed robbery against ships at sea, etc.)	
	Develop a Blue Economy	Maritime Resources
	Sustainable Management of Marine Resources	
	Address Marine Pollution	**Capacity Building and Resource Sharing**
	Mitigate impacts of Sea-level Rise	
	Tackle Marine Debris	
	Preserve and Protect the Marine Environment and Biodiversity	Maritime Ecology
	Promote 'Green' Shipping	**Capacity Building and Resource Sharing**
	Protect the Livelihood of Coastal Communities	
	Support Small-scale Fishing Communities	
	Technical Cooperation in Marine Science Collaboration (R & D; sharing of experience and best practices, capacity-building, managing marine hazards, raising awareness on marine and ocean-related issues, etc.)	Science, Technology and Academic Cooperation
Connectivity (Connecting the Connectivities)	Reinforce existing MPAC 2025	Trade Connectivity and Maritime Transport
	Mobilize resources for connectivity projects via regional public-private partnerships (PPP)	**Capacity Building and Resource Sharing**
	Promote regional public-private partnerships (PPP) for infrastructure projects	
	Explore potential synergies with sub-regional frameworks (e.g., IORA, BIMSTEC, BIMP-EAGA, MGC, ACMECS, etc.)	
	People-to-people connectivity (including academia and business communities)	

Sectors	AOIP	IPOI
UN Sustainable Development Goals 2030	Utilization of the digital economy	IPOI's underpinning as a whole
	Align regional development with the SDGs	
Economic and Other Areas of Cooperation	Trade Facilitation and Logistics Infrastructure and Services	Trade Connectivity and Maritime Transport **Capacity Building and Resource Sharing**
	Climate Change and Disaster Risk Reduction and Management	Disaster Risk Reduction and Management
	Maritime Implications of Industrial Revolution 4.0	

Source: Chauhan 2020

A notable example is the ASEAN-India Maritime Exercise in 2023, co-hosted with Singapore, which included all ten ASEAN nations and featured eight naval vessels (Laos, being a landlocked country, and Cambodia do not have naval vessels) (Suri 2023). Additionally, India has elevated its security partnerships by engaging in bilateral and trilateral military exercises with Singapore, Thailand, and Indonesia. The upgrading of ASEAN-India relations to a Comprehensive Strategic Partnership in 2022 has further deepened cooperation, as seen in the first ASEAN–India Defence Ministers' Informal Meeting in Cambodia, which signalled India's intent to strengthen regional defence collaboration (Solanki 2024). The meeting was a clear indication to China that India wanted to step up its defence cooperation with ASEAN and ASEAN member states.

Beyond maritime engagement, in 2021, India extended a 100 million US dollar credit line to Manila to support defence purchases, further strengthening bilateral ties (Menon 2022). This growing partnership reflects the Philippines' strategic shift away from its previous alignment with China under President Duterte. India has expanded its arms exports to ASEAN, notably with the Philippine Army's acquisition of the BrahMos coastal-defence missile system. To advance its defence diplomacy, India is expanding its network of defence attachés across ASEAN, underscoring its commitment to regional stability and security (Solanki 2024).

Economically, India is expediting the ASEAN-India Trade in Goods Agreement (AITIGA) review, promoting secure and resilient supply chains, and enhancing connectivity through projects like the India-Myanmar-Thailand Trilateral Highway, with plans for expansion into Laos, Cambodia, and Vietnam. In the field of emerging technologies, India is deepening cooperation with ASEAN on AI, blockchain, 6G, fintech, and digital connectivity, reinforced by the ASEAN-India Fund for Digital Future. India is also prioritizing climate action, renewable energy, and environmental protection, aligning with ASEAN's bio-circular-green economy model (MEA 2024). In public health, India is working with ASEAN on vaccine security, medical research, and traditional medicine to enhance healthcare resilience. Additionally, India is strengthening people-to-people ties through initiatives like the ASEAN-India Year of Tourism 2025, fostering educational exchanges and sustainable tourism development.

At the multilateral level, India supports reforms in global governance, advocating for a more equitable international financial system that reflects the interests of the Global South. Furthermore, India is expanding cooperation with sub-regional frameworks such as IORA, BIMSTEC, Indonesia-Malaysia-Thailand Growth Triangle, Singapore-Johor-Riau Growth Triangle, Brunei Darussalam-Indonesia-Malaysia-Philippines East ASEAN Growth Area, and Mekong-Ganga Cooperation, ensuring inclusive regional growth (MEA 2024). Through its commitment to ASEAN centrality, India remains engaged in ASEAN-led mechanisms, including the ASEAN-India Summit, East Asia Summit, ADMM-Plus, and the Expanded ASEAN Maritime Forum, reinforcing its role as a key partner in promoting regional stability and sustainable development.

3. Differences between IPOI and AOIP

Although there are many shared interests between the AOIP and IPOI, mutual strategic differences, the ever-growing role of China in the region, strategic competition among major powers, and differences in the approaches of ASEAN member countries have led to the lack of a fully comprehensive and robust cooperation between the two frameworks as initially anticipated. These factors have created challenges in aligning the priorities and strategies of the two initiatives, hindering more effective collaboration.

Firstly, the mutual strategic differences between IPOI and AOIP primarily stem from their divergent priorities, security approaches, engagement mechanisms, and responses to major power competition.

One of the most prominent strategic differences between IPOI and AOIP is their approach to security and regional stability. India envisions IPOI as a platform for strengthening maritime domain awareness (MDA), naval cooperation, capacity building, and sustainable use of ocean resources. AOIP, by contrast, does not frame security in adversarial terms. ASEAN's approach to regional security under AOIP is non-militarized, diplomatic, and consensus-driven, emphasizing confidence-building measures and dialogue rather than deterrence. Unlike IPOI, which fosters strategic coordination with select partners, AOIP promotes inclusive engagement with all Indo-Pacific actors, including China and the United States. ASEAN's historical commitment to regional neutrality and strategic autonomy means AOIP avoids framing the Indo-Pacific as a contested geopolitical area. This distinction reflects ASEAN's caution in avoiding entanglement in major power rivalries, ensuring that AOIP remains a platform for dialogue rather than competition.

Another key difference is their engagement mechanisms and strategic partnerships. IPOI follows a flexible, aligns with India's preference for bilateral and multilateral cooperation, particularly with like-minded partners. Furthermore, IPOI is designed to complement existing regional mechanisms such as the Indian Ocean Rim Association and the Indian Ocean Naval Symposium, reinforcing India's leadership in the maritime domain. AOIP, in contrast, operates within ASEAN's institutional multilateralism, ensuring that ASEAN-led mechanisms remain central to regional governance. Unlike IPOI's selective engagement with like-minded partners, AOIP follows a consensus-based approach, where decisions reflect the collective stance of all ASEAN members. This ensures equal representation of small and large ASEAN nations, maintaining ASEAN's unity and credibility.

Second, the expansion of China's influence is one of the most significant factors leading to strategic differences between IPOI and AOIP. China has significantly increased its presence in the Indo-Pacific region through island reclamation, naval expansion, military base construction, and infrastructure investments via the BRI (Aditya et al. 2024, 64, 72). This has raised maritime security concerns, especially for India, as China expands its influence over the Indian Ocean and strategic sea routes. As a result, IPOI focuses on enhancing maritime security cooperation, strengthening MDA, and ensuring freedom of navigation, indirectly countering China's activities (Saha/Mishra 2020). In contrast, AOIP does not emphasize security but rather focuses on multilateral cooperation. Many ASEAN countries have deep economic ties with China, particularly Cambodia, Laos, and Myanmar, making ASEAN more inclined to maintain a neutral and non-confrontational stance. Even ASEAN nations with territorial disputes with

China, such as Vietnam and the Philippines, prefer diplomatic negotiations and multilateral mechanisms rather than joining initiatives that might escalate tensions with Beijing. Thus, China's rising is a dominant factor contributing to the differences between IPOI and AOIP. These differing priorities illustrate the contrasting approaches: IPOI tends to be more assertive in its positioning against China's influence, while AOIP emphasizes diplomacy and inclusivity to maintain regional balance and cooperation

Thirdly, the competition between major powers, particularly between the United States and China, is another critical factor leading to the differences between IPOI and AOIP. As the region becomes a key point for geopolitical rivalry, IPOI is considered to be closely aligned with the U.S.-led vision of a Free and Open Indo-Pacific, positioning itself as a counterbalance to China's growing influence, particularly through its Belt and Road Initiative and assertive maritime activities (Basu 2020, 170). The IPOI's emphasis on security cooperation, infrastructure development, and maritime capacity building reflects its underlying objective of offering alternative frameworks to China's regional dominance, thereby reinforcing the U.S.-backed notion of a rules-based order. In contrast, AOIP adheres to ASEAN's long-standing principle of neutrality, consciously avoiding framing China as a strategic competitor. ASEAN's economic and strategic interests necessitate balancing relations with both Washington and Beijing, fostering a more inclusive approach that integrates Chinese investments without directly confronting its BRI (Brandon 2024, 7). This neutral stance allows ASEAN to maintain strategic autonomy, ensuring that the region does not become a battleground for great power competition. Consequently, while IPOI's alignment with U.S. objectives implicitly positions it against China, AOIP's commitment to non-alignment seeks to preserve regional stability by avoiding overt involvement in the U.S.-China rivalry. Thus, the broader geopolitical context of U.S.-China competition remains a significant factor in the distinct pathways taken by IPOI and AOIP.

Fourthly, ASEAN's ten member states have diverse interests, leading to differences in their approaches to Indo-Pacific issues, which contributes to the variations between AOIP and IPOI. Some ASEAN countries, such as Vietnam, Indonesia, and the Philippines, take a firmer stance on maritime security, particularly concerning disputes in the South China Sea. These countries advocate for ASEAN to adopt stronger measures to ensure freedom of navigation and uphold international law. However, there are notable differences in how various ASEAN countries perceive the role of India in the region and its potential to enhance cooperation (Louis,2024). While certain countries in ASEAN may view India as a crucial partner for regional stability, the level of commitment to strengthening bilateral ties with India varies significantly due to cultural, economic, and social factors.

Some ASEAN nations, such as Vietnam, Indonesia, and the Philippines, take a firmer stance on maritime security, particularly concerning disputes in the South China Sea. These countries advocate for ASEAN to adopt stronger measures to ensure freedom of navigation and uphold international law, are more inclined to deepen their cooperation with India, recognizing its strategic significance in balancing China's influence in the region. Cambodia, Laos, and Myanmar, which have closer economic and political ties with China, tend to adopt a more cautious approach when it comes to engaging with India (Chingchit 2021, 14). This is influenced by their stronger alignment with China, both economically and politically, as well as by historical ties that favour China's influence in the region. These countries are less likely to prioritize or actively seek to expand their relationships with India in comparison to other ASEAN nations. The differences in engagement also reflect the varying levels of India's cultural presence in these countries, such as the size of the Indian diaspora, the prominence of Little India neighbourhoods, the number of Indian students, and the general cultural exchange between India and ASEAN countries.

For example, Singapore, with its large Indian community and significant economic ties to India, may be more inclined to engage with India on various fronts, including trade, technology, and defence cooperation (High Commission of India in Singapore 2024). Vietnam, with its comprehensive strategic partnership with India, has a long history of diplomatic relations and shared interests. The relationship is further strengthened by cultural and historical ties, including the influence of Indian religions, particularly Hinduism and Buddhism, in Vietnamese culture. These historical and cultural connections have fostered a deeper mutual understanding between the two countries, paving the way for strong collaboration in various fields such as defence, trade, and energy. Vietnam is also keen on expanding its cooperation with India, especially in maritime security, due to both nations' shared interest in countering China's assertive policies in the South China Sea. The Indian diaspora in Vietnam is relatively small, but the people-to-people exchanges, and cultural diplomacy play a significant role in strengthening bilateral ties. India's growing presence in Vietnam's defence and trade sectors reflects the importance of the strategic partnership, further enhancing the cooperation between the two nations in addressing regional security issues and fostering economic development. Countries such as Cambodia and Laos may not perceive the same urgency in strengthening relations with India, given their deeper cultural and economic ties with China. Consequently, the bilateral relationships between India and individual ASEAN member states vary significantly, shaped by these factors.

This divergence in perceptions and priorities among ASEAN nations complicates efforts to build a cohesive regional strategy that fully integrates India's role in the Indo-Pacific. While some countries see India as a vital partner for regional security and economic growth, others remain more cautious, primarily due to their own national interests, historical alliances, and geopolitical considerations. This disparity in engagement contributes to the challenges faced by initiatives like the AOIP, as it attempts to balance these varying interests and perspectives in its approach to regional cooperation. Consequently, the differing levels of engagement with India result in a fragmented approach to bilateral cooperation within ASEAN, which limits the effectiveness of collective strategies involving India.

In contrast, IPOI does not face internal divisions like ASEAN. As an initiative led by India, IPOI can freely choose its strategic partners without having to accommodate the diverse interests of multiple states. By collaborating with countries that share its security concerns, IPOI can more effectively advance initiatives related to maritime security, infrastructure development, and blue economy cooperation. This difference results in distinct operational methods for AOIP and IPOI. AOIP must ensure consensus among all ASEAN members before advancing any initiative, making its decision-making process slower and more diplomatic in nature.

4. Some Comments about Common Interests between IPOI and AOIP

IPOI and AOIP are two significant frameworks that play a central role in addressing the Indo-Pacific region's complex geopolitical, environmental, and security challenges. They are being implemented effectively and have developed since 2019. On a multilateral level, the synergy between IPOI and AOIP can create a framework for cooperation to address security challenges in the region based on respect for international law, with the common goal of peace, stability, cooperation, and development. Moreover, IPOI helps ASEAN member countries enhance their capabilities through maritime security and defence cooperation, strengthening ASEAN's central role in leading negotiations with major powers. For example, ASEAN has led negotiations involving competing partners, including the Regional

Comprehensive Economic Partnership Agreement, which is set to take effect in 2022. Without neutrality, ASEAN would not have been able to connect China with Australia, Japan, and twelve other Asia-Pacific countries to form this largest trade bloc in the world.

One of the primary common interests between the IPOI and the AOIP is the commitment to maintaining peace and stability in the Indo-Pacific region. Both frameworks prioritize regional stability by advocating a rules-based order, adherence to UNCLOS, and cooperative security to safeguard the Indo-Pacific's vital maritime routes to prevent conflict and promote dialogue on shared challenges.

Another key challenge faced by both the IPOI and AOIP is the differing approaches to their primary objectives, which leads to barriers in cooperation despite sharing many common visions on fundamental interests. The IPOI, in particular, focuses on enhancing maritime cooperation to ensure security in the Indo-Pacific region. Its objectives, which are designed to foster stability, peace, and development, subtly aim to balance China's growing influence through a set of seven key goals. Similarly, AOIP does not aim to create new mechanisms or replace existing ones. Instead, its primary objective is to restore ASEAN's leadership and establish its agenda for multilateral cooperation in the region through ASEAN-led institutions. This is particularly significant in the context of rising unilateralism and the growing prominence of alternative forms of engagement, including bilateral, trilateral, quadrilateral, and limited multilateral frameworks, within the Indo-Pacific region. Furthermore, India's increasing ambition to play a prominent role in the Indo-Pacific poses a challenge to ASEAN's central position in the region. The lack of a unified regional outlook among ASEAN member states further complicates the organization's ability to effectively lead in addressing the region's complex challenges. As a result, India may find it more difficult to rely solely on ASEAN-led mechanisms to advance its interests in the Indo-Pacific.

Looking ahead, there is potential for both initiatives to find common ground, particularly in areas of sustainable development, infrastructure cooperation, and non-traditional security issues such as climate change and humanitarian assistance. However, for meaningful collaboration to occur, both India and ASEAN will need to manage their differences by focusing on areas of mutual interest while respecting the divergent strategic priorities of their member states. This will require ASEAN to find ways to accommodate India's desire for a more security-focused role in the region while ensuring that its core principle of neutrality is maintained. Similarly, India may need to recognize ASEAN's preference for a non-confrontational and inclusive approach to avoid exacerbating tensions with China. The future of IPOI and AOIP cooperation will depend on their ability to bridge these differences and engage in constructive dialogue that strengthens regional governance and promotes a stable, secure, and prosperous Indo-Pacific.

Under the framework of the IPOI, India has invited Vietnam to participate in this initiative. The initiative was launched in the context of both India and Vietnam facing an increasingly aggressive China, with both countries also dealing with border disputes with China. The Indian Ministry of External Affairs stated,

> "India and Vietnam have agreed to strengthen bilateral cooperation in line with India's Indo-Pacific Oceans Initiative and ASEAN's Outlook on the Indo-Pacific to achieve security, prosperity, and shared growth for all in the region." (Ministry of External Affairs 2020a)

On this basis, Vietnam and India can collaborate to create a shared vision and a working plan to strengthen bilateral relations and jointly promote the region's prosperous development.

With ASEAN's strategic position and its vision of independence and neutrality in relations with great powers, Vietnam can pursue an independent and autonomous foreign policy, maintaining a balanced approach in its economic relations with both China and the United States. However, the dynamics of U.S.-China relations depend on many unpredictable variables and uncertainties. Vietnam can only adjust its policy and prepare to respond to various scenarios to best serve its national interests and minimize potential adverse impacts. Participation in the IPOI allows Vietnam to advance common security and prosperity goals for the region while ensuring sustainable development through cooperation with key partners such as India on issues like maritime security, environmental protection, and economic connectivity. Furthermore, the strengthening of cooperation between India and Vietnam under the IPOI framework further affirms Vietnam's independence and proactive stance in protecting its national interests amid regional disputes with China, aligning with ASEAN's vision of maintaining strategic balance and ensuring a stable and peaceful region.

5. Summary

With the announcement of the AOIP and the IPOI in 2019, the Indo-Pacific region has increasingly become the focal point of India and ASEAN's strategic initiatives. IPOI and AOIP reflect a shared commitment to maintaining regional peace, security, and stability. While the IPOI and AOIP exhibit common priorities, such as promoting maritime security, ensuring the sustainability of marine resources, and fostering multilateral cooperation, they diverge in their institutional approaches and specific priorities, driven by their distinct geopolitical perspectives.

The IPOI is focused primarily on ocean governance, with a particular emphasis on maritime security and environmental sustainability (Luthra 2022). India's approach within the IPOI is rooted in its desire to enhance its regional influence by emphasizing responsible ocean management and fostering deeper partnerships with neighbouring and extra-regional states. In contrast, the AOIP is more comprehensive and diplomatic in its approach. The AOIP encompasses a broader range of regional issues, including political and economic cooperation, infrastructure development, and the promotion of a rules-based international order. ASEAN's approach is rooted in inclusivity and balancing the diverse interests of Indo-Pacific stakeholders. It seeks to promote stability through dialogue and multilateral cooperation, with ASEAN acting as the central coordinating body for regional initiatives (Qiao-Franco/Karmazin/Kolmaš 2024, 7).

Despite their different emphases, both the IPOI and AOIP share common interests in the sustainable development and security of the Indo-Pacific. A key commonality between these frameworks is their shared commitment to ensuring peace and stability in the region through a cooperative, rules-based approach to regional governance. The Indo-Pacific is critical to global trade, with key maritime routes passing through it, making the preservation of maritime security a priority for both initiatives.

However, as much as there is alignment in priorities, there are also challenges, both within the IPOI and the AOIP, as well as between India and ASEAN in their broader regional engagement. One of the key challenges for ASEAN in the context of the AOIP is its difficulty in asserting effective leadership in the Indo-Pacific. ASEAN's position as a central actor in shaping the regional order is increasingly being questioned (Mueller 2019, 178). The organization's internal fragmentation and the absence of a unified collective outlook on the Indo-Pacific construct have hampered its ability to present a coherent vision and exert leadership. ASEAN's declining unity and the limitations of its mechanisms for addressing emerging challenges, particularly in light of the growing influence of external powers such as China, have led some analysts to argue that ASEAN centrality is becoming obsolete (Yaacob 2024). This lack of cohesion has profound implications for ASEAN's ability to lead regional initiatives, including its role in the AOIP. The diverse priorities of ASEAN member states – ranging from economic integration to security concerns – make it difficult for the organization to adopt a unified approach to Indo-Pacific issues (Hoang Thi Ha 2021).

In contrast, India's approach to the Indo-Pacific, particularly through the IPOI, has been more assertive, reflecting its ambitions to become a leading regional power. India's growing engagement in the region, coupled with its strategic partnerships with countries like the United States, Japan, and Australia in the framework of the Quad reflects a desire to play a more prominent role in shaping the regional order. However, India faces the challenge of balancing its strategic interests with those of ASEAN, particularly as ASEAN continues to struggle with internal divisions and the shifting balance of power in the region (Vinodan/Kurian 2024). India's growing geopolitical clout makes it clear that it cannot rely solely on ASEAN to meet its strategic goals in the Indo-Pacific.

This divergence in leadership aspirations has created a situation where ASEAN and India may need to reassess and recalibrate their approach to regional cooperation. As ASEAN and India work towards enhancing their comprehensive strategic partnership, both sides must find ways to sustain their alignment in addressing the dynamic challenges of the Indo-Pacific. The evolving geopolitical landscape, marked by the increasing competition between major powers, requires a fresh approach to regional cooperation that goes beyond traditional institutional frameworks. ASEAN has a strict principle of non-interference in the internal affairs of its member states, and as such, has played a crucial role in regional economic integration. ASEAN has always been cautious about any clear constraints on China, partly because China has closer relations with some ASEAN members than with others (Miller 2023). Active dialogue between ASEAN and India, identifying common ground, and supporting each other will serve as a bridge to narrow the strategic gap between the two.

In short, IPOI and AOIP reflect their shared commitment to Indo-Pacific stability, but differences in institutional approaches complicate cooperation. To maximize their Comprehensive Strategic Partnership, both must find common ground and explore new collaborations. Additionally, the role of individual ASEAN members, particularly Vietnam, will be vital in advancing this partnership. As one of the key maritime nations in the region, Vietnam has significant potential to contribute to both the AOIP and IPOI. With ongoing projects and opportunities for enhanced bilateral naval cooperation between India and Vietnam, both countries can serve as pillars of support for the broader ASEAN-India partnership. Strengthening Vietnam's involvement in these initiatives will foster stronger bilateral ties and enhance the overall strategic alignment of ASEAN and India in the Indo-Pacific region.

7. References

Aditya, M. F./Amin, K./Paramitha, D. I. (2024): China's Military Engagement in The Pacific Region: Implications for Australia's Defence and National Security Policy. In: Papua Journal of Diplomacy and International Relations, 4(2), 63–84.

ASEAN (2023): ASEAN Outlook on the Indo-Pacific. https://asean.org/wp-content/uploads/2021/01/ASEAN-Outlook-on-the-Indo-Pacific_FINAL_22062019.pdf.

Basu, Titli (2020): Sino-US Disorder: Power and Policy in Post-COVID Indo-Pacific. In: Journal of Asian Economic Integration, 2(2), 159–179.

Brandon, John J. (2024): Introduction. In: U.S.–China–Southeast Asia Relations: Challenges and Opportunities for Regional Cooperation. The Asis Foundation.

Chauhan, P. (2020): ASEAN Outlook on Indo-Pacific (AOIP) and Indo-Pacific Oceans Initiative (IPOI): Complementarities and Cooperation. Paper Presented at the 6th AINTT Roundtable.

Chauhan, P. (et al.) (2020): Indo-Pacific Cooperation: AOIP and IPOI. AIC Working Paper, 3.

Chingchit, Sasiwan (2021): Myanmar's Relations with China and India: The ASEAN Perspectives. In: South Asia Scan (13). https://www.isas.nus.edu.sg/wp-content/uploads/2021/07/FINAL-South-Asia-Scan-13.pdf.

High Commission of India in Singapore (2024): India-Singapore Relations. Singapore.

Hoang Thi Ha (2021): ASEAN Navigates between Indo-Pacific Polemics and Potentials. In: ISEAS Perspective, 49. https://www.iseas.edu.sg/wp-content/uploads/2021/03/ISEAS_Perspective_2021_49.pdf.

Indian Council of World Affairs (2022): IPOI Indo-Pacific Oceans Initiative: Towards a Sustainable and Prosperous Indo-Pacific Region. Indian Council of World Affairs.

Ladwig, Walter (2024): The Indo-Pacific in Indian Foreign Policy. The Royal United Services Institute for Defence and Security Studies. https://rusi.org/explore-our-research/publications/policy-briefs/indo-pacific-indian-foreign-policy.

Lin, Joanne Lin (2022): Can ASEAN and India Share a Common Outlook and Approach in the Indo-Pacific? In: ISEAS Perspective I, 86, 1–11.

Louis, Yanitha Meena (2024): The Importance of Being Earnest: Strengthening ASEAN-India Relations in an Evolving World. Fulcrum. https://fulcrum.sg/asean focus/the-importance-of-being-earnest-strengthening-asean-india-relations-in-an-evolving-world/.

Luthra, Girish (2022): The Indo-Pacific region, maritime focus, and ocean governance. Observer Research Foundation. https://www.orfonline.org/expert-speak/the-indo-pacific-region-maritime-focus-and-ocean-governance.

MEA (2024): Joint Statement on Strengthening ASEAN-India Comprehensive Strategic Partnership for Peace, Stability and Prosperity in the Region in the context of the ASEAN Outlook on the Indo-Pacific (AOIP) with the support of India's Act East Policy (AEP). Ministry of External Affairs, Government of India.

Menon, Jay (2022): Philippines to buy India's BrahMos missiles. The Times Aerospace. https://www.timesaerospace.aero/news/defence/philippines-to-buy-indias-brahmos-missiles.

Miller, Manjari Chatterjee (2023): Cooperation Between ASEAN and the Quad is Critical for Indo-Pacific Stability. Council on Foreign Relations. https://www.cfr.org/blog/cooperation-between-asean-and-quad-critical-indo-pacific-stability.

Ministry of External Affairs (2020a): 17th India-Vietnam Joint Commission Meeting. Government of India. https://www.mea.gov.in/press-releases.htm?dtl/32912/17th_IndiaVietnam_Joint_Commission_Meeting.

Ministry of External Affairs (2020b): EAM's remarks at CII Partnership Summit 2020. Government of India. https://www.mea.gov.in/Speeches-Statements.htm?dtl/33309.

Ministry of External Affairs (2020c): Indo-Pacific Division Briefs. Government of India. https://www.mea.gov.in/Portal/ForeignRelation/Indo_Feb_07_2020.pdf.

Mueller, Lukas Maximilian (2019): ASEAN centrality under threat – the cases of RCEP and connectivity. In: Journal of Contemporary East Asia Studies, 8(2), 177–198.

New Delhi Times (2020): India invites Vietnam for its Indo-Pacific Oceans Initiative. https://www.newdelhitimes.com/india-invites-vietnam-for-its-indo-pacific-oceans-initiative-ipoi/.

Qiao-Franco, Guangyu/Karmazin, Aleš/Kolmaš, Michal (2024): The Indo-Pacific and the Next Phase of ASEAN Centrality. In: Journal of Current Southeast Asian Affairs, 0(0), 1–23.

Saha, Premesha/Mishra, Abhishek (2020): The Indo-Pacific Oceans Initiative: Towards a Coherent Indo-Pacific Policy for India. Observer Research Foundation. https://www.orfonline.org/research/the-indo-pacific-oceans-initiative-towards-a-coherent-indo-pacific-policy-for-india.

Singh, Gurjit (2022): The India ASEAN AOIP-IPOI cooperation. Observer Research Foundation.: https://www.orfonline.org/expert-speak/the-india-asean-aoip-ipoi-cooperation.

Solanki, Viraj (2024): India's increased defence and security engagement with Southeast Asia. International Institute for Strategic Studies: https://www.iiss.org/online-analysis/online-analysis/2024/04/indias-increased-defence-and-security-engagement-with-southeast-asia/.

Suri, Moksh (2023): Acting East on the seas: India's naval cooperation with ASEAN. The Interpreter. https://www.lowyinstitute.org/the-interpreter/acting-east-seas-india-s-naval-cooperation-asean.

The ASEAN Secretariat (2021): ASEAN-India Joint Statement on Cooperation on the ASEAN Outlook on the Indo-Pacific for Peace, Stability, and Prosperity in the Region. https://asean.org/wp-content/uploads/2021/10/71.-ASEAN-India-Joint-Statement-on-Cooperation-on-the-ASEAN-Outlook-on-the-Indo-Pacific-for-Peace-Stability-and-Prosperity-in-the-Region-Final.pdf.

The ASEAN Secretariat (2023): ASEAN Outlook on the Indo-Pacific. https://asean.org/wp-content/uploads/2021/01/ASEAN-Outlook-on-the-Indo-Pacific_FINAL_22062019.pdf.

Vinodan, C./ Kurian, Anju Lis (2024): Strategic Autonomy and India's Hedging Policies in the Indo-Pacific. In: Journal of Asian Security and International Affairs, 11(4), 475–495.

Wau, Jessia/Tay, Simon (2020): The Indo-Pacific Outlook: a new lens for ASEAN. East Asia Forum. https://eastasiaforum.org/2020/04/20/the-indo-pacific-outlook-a-new-lens-for-asean/.

Yaacob, Rahman (2024): The Translator: ASEAN Centrality. The Interpreter. https://www.lowyinstitute.org/the-interpreter/translator-asean-centrality.

Yoshimatsu, Hidetaka (2023): ASEAN and Great Power Rivalry in Regionalism: From East Asia to the Indo-Pacific. In: Journal of Current Southeast Asian Affairs, 42(1), 25–44.

Chapter 15: The Implementation Process of the US Indo-Pacific Strategy in Relation with Vietnam (2021–2024)

Nguyen Thi My Hanh

The transformations in global politics have led to the emergence of the Indo-Pacific Strategy (IPS) under the Biden administration, aimed at maintaining US influence and presence in the region. Within this strategic framework, Vietnam has been recognized by the United States as a country of strategic importance, sharing multiple common interests, and as a promising and potential *partner*. During President Biden's tenure (2021–2024), the United States has continuously strengthened relations and expanded cooperation with Vietnam across various sectors, particularly in security and economic domains. In September 2023, bilateral relations were officially elevated to a new level. This study seeks to examine whether the development of US-Vietnam relations aligns with the IPS agenda and whether these advancements contribute to achieving IPS objectives. The article explores US-Vietnam relations from 2021 to 2024, arguing that this relationship follows a traditional foundation while undergoing significant adjustments in line with IPS directives. In other words, IPS has played a crucial role in shaping and guiding the evolution of US-Vietnam relations. The developments and outcomes of bilateral relations essentially reflect the process of implementing the United States IPS in Vietnam.

1. Introduction

The Indo-Pacific Strategy (IPS) was officially announced by the Biden administration on February 11th, 2022, highlighting that

> "The United States is committed to an Indo-Pacific that is free and open, connected, prosperous, secure, and resilient." (The White House 2022a)

Alongside several other key policy documents released in 2022 – such as The Administration's Approach to the People's Republic of China (Secretary Blinken Speech) issued by the US Department of State on May 26, 2022, the National Security Strategy (NSS) released on October 12, 2022

(The White House 2022b), and the National Defense Strategy (NDS) published on October 27, 2022 (U.S. Department of Defense 2022) – the United States' policy in the Indo-Pacific has been clearly articulated, featuring notable shifts in its regional approach and policy implementation. The Biden administration's IPS builds upon and refines the Free and Open Indo-Pacific (FOIP) Strategy established during the Trump administration while incorporating adjustments to align with broader foreign policy objectives. These modifications primarily aim to contain China, maintain US influence, and ensure continued US presence in the region.

These strategic adjustments reflect a heightened prioritization of the Indo-Pacific region in US foreign policy, stemming from a recognition of the region's immense strategic and economic significance to the United States. US interests can only be effectively advanced if Washington remains deeply engaged in the Indo-Pacific and actively strengthens the region itself (The White House 2022a).

Regarding the content of the Indo-Pacific Strategy (IPS), in pursuit of the goal of "a free and open Indo-Pacific that is more connected, prosperous, secure, and resilient," the National Security Strategy (NSS) outlines five key pillars (The White House 2022a):

1. To advance a free and open Indo-Pacific.
2. To build connections within and beyond the region.
3. To drive regional prosperity.
4. To bolster Indo-Pacific security.
5. To build regional resilience to transnational threats (The White House 2022a).

The Biden administration introduced an Indo-Pacific Action Plan, which integrates multiple diplomatic, economic, and security initiatives to reinforce its strategic objectives. Vietnam in particular and Southeast Asia in general are recognized by the US as having an important role in the IPS framework. This is reflected in the official statement within the IPS:

> "We will focus on every corner of the region, from Northeast Asia and Southeast Asia, etc." and "Like ASEAN, we see Southeast Asia as central to the regional architecture." (The White House 2022a)

These statements underscore the strategic importance of Vietnam and Southeast Asia within the broader US vision for the Indo-Pacific. The development of US-Vietnam relations serves as a key foundation for ensuring a long-term and stable US presence in the region.

Examining the IPS in general and its practical implementation through US-Vietnam relations holds both theoretical and practical significance. From a theoretical perspective, it enables an empirical assessment of IPS execution in a Southeast Asian nation, allowing for a clearer positioning of Vietnam within the US strategic vision. From a practical standpoint, it provides Vietnam with insights for potential foreign policy adjustments, enabling adaptation to the evolving geopolitical landscape and deeper integration into global and regional frameworks. To achieve the research objectives, the study employs key research methodologies, including policy analysis, historical analysis, comparative analysis, and synthesis. These approaches aim to highlight the strategic context of IPS inception, its core principles, implementation mechanisms, and its application in Vietnam.

This study is based on primary sources, primarily official documents issued by the Biden administration, which serve as key *puzzle pieces* in constructing a comprehensive picture of the United States' new foreign policy in the Indo-Pacific region. Additionally, updates on security cooperation, economic relations, and cultural exchanges between the United States and Vietnam, as provided by the United States Mission to Vietnam, have been utilized to ensure a well-rounded analysis. Regarding secondary sources, the study draws on several scholarly works, including "Vietnam and ASEAN in the U.S. Indo-Pacific Strategy" (Hương 2022) and *An Overview of Policy Documents on the Indo-Pacific Issued by the Biden Administration in 2022* (Nghiên cứu Biển Đông 2023). These writings provide a broad perspective on the Biden administration's Indo-Pacific Strategy (IPS), as well as the opportunities and challenges facing Vietnam within this geopolitical framework. These sources form the foundational knowledge upon which this study examines the implementation of the IPS in US-Vietnam relations from 2021 to 2024.

2. The Process of Implementing the US Indo-Pacific Strategy in Relations with Vietnam (2021–2024)

Since its inception, the Indo-Pacific Strategy (IPS) has been actualized through extensive and comprehensive implementation across various domains, including diplomacy, security, economy, and culture, throughout the region, particularly in ASEAN, Southeast Asia, and Vietnam. Vietnam's role aligns with all five strategic pillars, encompassing rule-based order, maritime order, as well as cooperation in economy, trade, supply chains, and responses to non-traditional security challenges (The White House 2022a).

Advancing freedom and openness in ASEAN, Southeast Asia, and Vietnam

The concept of *Freedom and Openness* in the Indo-Pacific Strategy (IPS) under the Biden administration places particular emphasis on sovereignty, independence, international law, and democratic values, as well as principles and regulations in emerging domains. The United States has pledged to

> "Build support for rules-based approaches to the maritime domain, including in the South China Sea and the East China Sea," while also emphasizing its "support for a stronger and more unified ASEAN." Vietnam, alongside Indonesia, Singapore, and Malaysia, has been recognized as a key partner, in addition to the two treaty allies, the Philippines and Thailand (The White House 2022a).

From a multilateral perspective, since the inception of the IPS, the United States has supported its partners, including Vietnam, in upholding international maritime law in the South China Sea and has condemned China's harassment of vessels exercising their right to freedom of navigation. The Vietnam Coast Guard has actively participated in the Southeast Asia Maritime Law Enforcement Initiative (SEAMLEI). The cooperation between the US Coast Guard and the Vietnam Coast Guard, along with other maritime agencies, stands out as a significant achievement in bilateral relations. During her visit to Vietnam from May 29 to June 1, 2023, US Coast Guard Commandant Admiral Linda L. Fagan underscored the United States' commitment to collaborating with Vietnam and other key partners in the Indo-Pacific to promote a rules-based international maritime order. She also affirmed that the US Coast Guard would provide sustained support in addressing activities that undermine national sovereignty and in enhancing capacities to combat illegal, unreported, and unregulated (IUU) fishing (Minh 2023).

Maintaining and advancing practical diplomatic and political engagement with Vietnam

In its Indo-Pacific Action Plan, the United States has committed to "expanding bilateral cooperation across Southeast Asia" (The White House 2022a).

Since assuming office, the Biden administration has paid significant attention to strengthening US-Vietnam relations, contributing to the realization of a *free and open Indo-Pacific.*

Strengthening and advancing US-Vietnam bilateral relations

The political and diplomatic relations between the United States and Vietnam have been shaped by the *Comprehensive Partnership* established in 2013, which has been reinforced through joint statements issued in 2015, 2016, and 2017 (U.S. Department of State 2021).

Under the Biden administration, the United States has actively promoted a

> "Free and open Indo-Pacific" and has expressed a strong commitment to "working with" Vietnam to enhance US engagement in the region (The White House 2021). Washington has explicitly acknowledged Vietnam as a key partner in its broader efforts to materialize a "free and open Indo-Pacific." (The White House 2022a)

The deepening of US-Vietnam relations aligns with the broader US strategy of building a robust network of partnerships in Southeast Asia, fostering regional collective capacity, and advancing coordinated action in the evolving geopolitical landscape. Regarding policy implementation, between 2020 and 2021, the United States conducted multiple high-level visits to Vietnam, including those of Secretary of State Mike Pompeo (2020) and Vice President Kamala Harris (2021). Vice President Harris's first official visit to Asia, which included stops in Vietnam and Singapore, underscored the strategic importance of these Southeast Asian nations to the United States. This visit served as a clear indication of Washington's commitment and long-term engagement in the region. The primary objective was to expand bilateral relations and deepen cooperation based on shared strategic interests.

In September 2023, President Joe Biden's visit to Vietnam marked a significant milestone as the two countries elevated their diplomatic ties to a *Comprehensive Strategic Partnership.* This development ushered in a new chapter in US-Vietnam relations and was widely regarded as a critical step toward maintaining regional stability and reinforcing the United States' global strategic balance. The United States has expressed its commitment to collaborating with Vietnam in strengthening the rule of law and governance while ensuring peace and security in the Indo-Pacific region. Since then, the United States has continued to uphold substantive diplomatic and political engagement with Vietnam. High-level exchanges between the two nations have remained active, particularly through visits by Vietnam's President and Prime Minister to the United States, as well as delegations from the United States Congress, including bipartisan congressional missions to Vietnam. Additionally, the two sides have expanded discussions through regular annual bilateral dialogues, including the *US-Vietnam Human Rights Dialogue* and the *US-Vietnam Labor Dialogue* (U.S. Mission Vietnam 2024).

Fostering US-Vietnam people-to-people exchanges

In alignment with the broader goal of the Indo-Pacific Strategy (IPS) to "build connections within and beyond the region," the United States has emphasized that "our relationship not only links our governments but also connects our people" (The White House 2022a). Through expanded educational and cultural cooperation, people-to-people exchanges have been strengthened, contributing to the deepening of US-Vietnam relations. Currently, there are over two million Vietnamese Americans and more than 30,000 Vietnamese students studying at US educational institutions, making them the fifth-largest group of international students in the United States (U.S. Department of Treasury 2023). Following the elevation of bilateral ties to a *Comprehensive Strategic Partnership* in September 2023, the US Department of State signed a *Memorandum of Cooperation (MOC)* with Vietnam's Ministry of Education and Training (MOET) to promote collaboration with US institutions and further internationalize Vietnam's higher education sector (U.S. Mission Vietnam 2024). The governments of both countries have also supported professional exchanges among representatives of governmental organizations, political parties, and research institutions.

Beyond the expansion of educational collaboration, efforts to promote US cultural engagement in Vietnam have also been significant. Various cultural exchange events in Hanoi and Ho Chi Minh City have brought together both local and expatriate communities, fostering mutual understanding and strengthening cultural ties between the two nations. A notable example was the inaugural *Vietnam-US Cultural Festival* in June 2023. Additionally, in March 2024, the two countries signed a *Memorandum of Understanding (MOU) on Culture and Public Affairs* to enhance cooperation in museum partnerships and cultural heritage preservation activities (U.S. Mission Vietnam 2024).

In practice, people-to-people exchanges have deepened US-Vietnam relations at the individual and grassroots levels, which, in the long term, will support the expansion of US educational service exports and tourism. US support for English language training, higher education, and human resource development will enable Vietnam to maximize its potential as a knowledge-based economy. These joint efforts between the United States and Vietnam lay a crucial foundation for mutual understanding, playing a pivotal role in advancing the US-Vietnam strategic partnership in substantive ways and contributing to the realization of the US Indo-Pacific Strategy.

US-Vietnam economic development cooperation

Economic cooperation is considered a key pillar of the Indo-Pacific Strategy (IPS), aimed at fostering and promoting a prosperous region. This marks a significant shift, reflecting the comprehensive nature of IPS, which goes beyond security concerns emphasized in the *Free and Open Indo-Pacific (FOIP)* strategy of the previous administration. Economic cooperation – centred on promoting free and fair trade, upholding high labour and environmental standards, and fostering sustainable development – is a core component of the economic pillar.

The United States prioritizes investment to drive innovation, enhance economic competitiveness, and expand opportunities for all people in the region. Aligned with this approach, US-Vietnam economic development cooperation has been continuously strengthened and expanded across multiple sectors.

Enhancing US-Vietnam trade and investment

The United States and Vietnam have maintained effective cooperation in trade and investment since 1995. Under the Biden administration, bilateral trade relations have witnessed significant growth, yielding tangible results. In 2022, bilateral trade reached 139 billion US dollars, marking a more than 300-fold increase compared to 1995 (U.S. Embassy and Consulate in Vietnam 2023).

According to the Bilateral Relations Factsheet released by the Biden administration in April 2021, bilateral trade and US investment in Vietnam have expanded substantially (U.S. Department of State 2021). The United States remains Vietnam's largest export market, with exports valued at nearly 97 billion US dollars in 2021. In the first two months of 2024 alone, total US-Vietnam trade in goods reached 17.4 billion US dollars, reflecting a nearly 34 per cent increase compared to the same period in 2023. Data from Vietnam's Import-Export Department (Ministry of Industry and Trade) indicate that Vietnam's trade surplus with the United States is estimated at 12.5 billion US dollars, an increase of 36.6 per cent year-over-year (Dung/Xuân 2024). As of March 2023, Vietnam had become the eighth-largest trading partner of the United States, while the United States became Vietnam's first export market to surpass 100 billion US dollars in trade volume. In terms of foreign direct investment (FDI), US investments in Vietnam totalled 11.4 billion US dollars, making the United States the 11th-largest foreign investor in the country (People's Army Newspaper 2023). Vietnam's top exports to the United States include textiles, footwear, and electronics, while its main imports from the United States consist of soybeans and cotton. Additionally, Vietnam has attracted investment from major US corporations such as Apple, Coca-Cola, PepsiCo, SpaceX, Pfizer, and Amazon Web Services, highlighting the increasing economic integration between the two nations.

From its part, the Vietnamese Government has established a relatively favourable environment to attract further investment from US companies. In particular, Vietnam's corporate regulatory authorities have prioritized fostering innovation and sustainable development in trade and investment. Vietnam and the United States have also strongly supported each other in multilateral economic organizations, including the Asia-Pacific Economic Cooperation (APEC), the International Monetary Fund (IMF), the World Bank (WB), and the World Trade Organization (WTO). Through close cooperation in these multilateral platforms, both nations have gained a deeper understanding of each other's trade policies, thereby facilitating enhanced trade and investment relations.

In May 2022, the United States launched the Indo-Pacific Economic Framework for Prosperity (IPEF) with 14 countries across the Indo-Pacific region. IPEF serves as the United States' response to fill the gap left by its withdrawal from the Trans-Pacific Partnership (TPP) under President Donald Trump. As an initial partner, Vietnam has actively worked with the Biden administration to finalize agreements across all four IPEF pillars:

(i) Trade; (ii) Supply Chains; (iii) Clean Energy, Decarbonization, and Infrastructure; (iv) Tax and Anti-Corruption (U.S. Trade Representative 2022).

Although bilateral trade disputes have occasionally arisen between the two countries, most have been resolved through diplomatic negotiations. A notable example is the bilateral agreement addressing the timber trade dispute (Office of the U.S. Trade Representative 2021). Furthermore, the Biden administration removed Vietnam from the list of "currency manipulators" and "unfair trade practices" (Federal Register 2021), reflecting improved economic cooperation and regulatory transparency between the two nations.

Trade and investment relations between the United States and Vietnam have experienced significant growth, bringing mutual benefits to both nations. While challenges remain, including trade imbalances, protectionist measures, and other trade-related issues, both countries recognize that maintaining a strong and stable relationship serves their best interests. Given the vast potential for further expansion, the United States and Vietnam continue to explore opportunities to enhance bilateral trade and investment cooperation in the years to come.

Investing in an innovation-driven economy and advancing scientific and technological cooperation

The United States has implemented the workforce development initiative to enhance skills training, technical expertise, and workforce development at all levels through public-private partnerships and expanded institutional collaboration between the United States and Vietnam. This initiative includes a 4 million US dollars investment package, which also funds the International Technology Security and Innovation (ITSI) Grant – administered by Arizona State University – to support capacity-building activities (U.S. Mission Vietnam 2024).

Strengthening US-Vietnam business community relations

Since the elevation of bilateral diplomatic ties to their highest level, numerous US business delegations have visited Vietnam to engage in direct collaboration with Vietnamese enterprises. Notable examples include visits by the US-ASEAN Business Council delegation and the Semiconductor

Industry Association in 2024. Additionally, the Export-Import Bank of the United States (EXIM) and the Vietnam Development Bank signed a 500 million US dollars Memorandum of Understanding (MOU) to facilitate US export financing. This agreement aims to support Vietnam's green economic transition, infrastructure development, and climate-related projects (U.S. Mission Vietnam 2024). Vietnam has increasingly been recognized by US businesses as a strategic market in the region, with many view it as "reliable partners and resources in fostering mutual priorities and economic purposes." (Tuoitrenews 2023)

Between 2021 and 2024, US-Vietnam economic cooperation across multiple sectors has significantly contributed to Vietnam's economic prosperity, which in turn has supported regional economic growth. These efforts align fully with the objectives of the US Indo-Pacific Strategy (IPS).

Enhancing US-Vietnam security cooperation

Strengthening security in the Indo-Pacific region is the fourth strategic objective outlined in the US' Indo-Pacific Strategy (IPS) (The White House 2022a). Recognizing Vietnam's strategic importance in the Indo-Pacific, the Biden administration has repeatedly emphasized its commitment to expanding and deepening security cooperation with Vietnam. The United States affirms that US-Vietnam security cooperation is built upon a shared commitment to strengthening defence collaboration and a mutual determination to address regional security challenges (U.S. Mission Vietnam 2021). High-level defence exchanges have taken place between the two countries, underscoring their growing security partnership. Vice President Kamala Harris's visit to Vietnam in August 2021 further reinforced bilateral ties through a commitment to

> "Supporting Vietnam in enhancing its maritime security capabilities and law enforcement capacity." (Embassy of the Socialist Republic of Vietnam in the United States of America 2021)

These efforts contribute to advancing a free and open Indo-Pacific, aligning with broader US regional security goals. The United States and Vietnam have also focused on United Nations peacekeeping operations, disaster relief, humanitarian assistance, military medicine, and capacity building for the Vietnam Coast Guard. The inaugural International Defence Exhibition hosted by Vietnam in December 2022, which featured participation from the Aerospace, Defence, and Security (ADS) delegation, serves as tangible evidence of bilateral defence cooperation. As part of Vietnam's efforts to modernize and diversify its defence supply chain, the United States has affirmed its commitment to "becoming a part of this process," with the US defence industry expressing readiness to serve as a resource and partner for the Vietnamese Government in its military modernization and technological innovation (U.S.-ASEAN Business Council 2022). The presence of the aircraft carrier USS Ronald Reagan, alongside the guided-missile cruisers USS Antietam and USS Robert Smalls in Da Nang in June 2023, underscores the two nations' shared interest in enhancing security and defence collaboration.

Security and law enforcement cooperation between the two countries has also been significantly strengthened, particularly following the upgrade of bilateral relations in September 2023. Vietnam has joined the Global Coalition to Address Synthetic Drug Threats, aiming to curb the flow of synthetic drugs within the region and globally. Additionally, the United States has provided technical assistance to Vietnam's Ministry of Industry and Trade in amending chemical regulations, integrating precursor substances into the legal framework, and aligning national legislation with international best practices on chemical weapons control. The United States Department of Homeland Security and the Department of State, in collaboration with the US Coast Guard, are working with the Vietnamese Government on port security to safeguard the US supply chain from trade fraud and other non-proliferation risks (U.S. Mission Vietnam 2024).

Under the Biden administration, US-Vietnam security relations have largely been a continuation and enhancement of policies pursued by previous US administrations. The impetus behind the United States' efforts to deepen security cooperation with Vietnam is primarily driven by its Indo-Pacific security strategy, particularly aimed at countering China and maintaining influence in the region.

US efforts to strengthen cooperation in climate, energy, environment, and public health

Global challenges such as climate change, pandemics, and natural disasters are directly affecting security and development in the Indo-Pacific region, including Vietnam. The Biden administration has sought to mobilize resources and enhance international cooperation to address these pressing issues, laying the groundwork for "building regional resilience to 21st-century transnational threats," which constitutes the fifth objective of the Indo-Pacific Strategy (IPS) (The White House 2022a). In Vietnam, the United States has engaged in various initiatives aimed at improving climate resilience, energy transition, environmental conservation, and public health. To contribute to addressing the climate crisis, the United States has strengthened its partnership with Vietnam through the implementation of projects such as the Mekong Delta Coastal Habitat Conservation Project; the signing of the Just Energy Transition Partnership (JETP) Declaration; and the establishment of the Climate Change Entrepreneurship Hub (CCE Hub) on September 27, 2023 – the first of its kind in Asia and the second in the world (U.S. Mission Vietnam 2024).

In terms of strengthening public health, the United States has closely collaborated with Vietnam to reinforce its healthcare system, contributing to the country's efforts in combating the COVID-19 pandemic and enhancing resilience against potential future pandemics. The United States Centers for Disease Control and Prevention (CDC) have been working with Vietnam's healthcare system to provide technical support for disease surveillance and response to infectious disease threats.

The United States' strengthened cooperation with Vietnam in climate, energy, environmental, and public health initiatives reflects its commitment to a key nation in the Indo-Pacific. This collaboration contributes to building a region that is resilient to the impacts of non-traditional security challenges.

3. The Role and Impact of the Indo-Pacific Strategy (IPS) on Vietnam

The role of IPS in shaping and developing US-Vietnam relations

Under the Biden administration (2021–2024), US-Vietnam relations have largely continued and expanded upon the policies of previous administrations, particularly those of President Obama and President Trump. The United States continues to place significant importance on its relationship with Vietnam, with bilateral cooperation becoming increasingly substantive, effective, and in-depth. A key question arises: to what extent has IPS played a role in this development?

The Biden administration has aligned US-Vietnam relations with the five core objectives of IPS. Continuing many concepts introduced under the

Free and Open Indo-Pacific (FOIP) strategy during the Trump administration, IPS has positioned Vietnam as a critical component of the US strategic framework for the region. This is due in large part to Vietnam's strategic value, stemming from its geographic location and central position in regional security dynamics. Vietnam serves as a gateway along key maritime routes connecting the Indian and Pacific Oceans, and its position on the eastern flank of the Indochinese Peninsula – bordering China, Laos, and Cambodia – enhances its role as a bridge between mainland and maritime Southeast Asia. Moreover, Vietnam's location along the north-south shipping lanes linking East Asia and Northeast Asia with the Indian Ocean, the Middle East, Africa, and Europe further underscores its maritime significance. The country's extensive coastline also provides logistical advantages, allowing naval vessels, including warships, to access commercial ports such as Da Nang and Cam Ranh Bay for refuelling, maintenance, and logistical support.

The United States has recognized Vietnam as a key *partner* in both security and economic domains, as well as a critical contributor to the emerging regional security architecture. The United States considers its national interests closely intertwined with the Indo-Pacific, where China's growing economic and military influence is perceived as a challenge to the regional order and a direct threat to US strategic interests. IPS under the Biden administration, much like FOIP under the previous administration, has been designed to counterbalance China, ensuring continued US presence and influence in the region. Within this strategic framework, Vietnam is viewed as an important regional player that shares key strategic interests with the United States. It has been directly referenced in IPS, indicating its significance as a more pivotal strategic partner than even some of the United States' traditional allies, such as the Philippines and Thailand, or the most populous Southeast Asian nation, Indonesia. Similarly, Vietnam was identified as a leading nation in the Indo-Pacific Economic Framework for Prosperity (IPEF) launch statement. Additionally, Vietnam – alongside Singapore – is one of the few Southeast Asian nations explicitly mentioned in the Interim National Security Strategic Guidance (INSSG), reflecting its growing strategic role. US Deputy Secretary of State Daniel Kritenbrink has reaffirmed Vietnam's position as a core partner in all five pillars of IPS (Nghiên cứu Biển Đông 2023).

Based on the assessment of Vietnam's *value* in the Indo-Pacific Strategy (IPS), the Interim National Security Strategic Guidance (INSSG), and the Indo-Pacific Economic Framework for Prosperity (IPEF), US-Vietnam relations (2021–2024) have evolved in alignment with the strategic directions outlined in these key policy documents. While the bilateral relationship has been shaped by the efforts of both nations since the normalization of ties in 1995, its current trajectory strongly reflects the objectives of US foreign policy in response to emerging global and regional dynamics. Vice President Kamala Harris's visit to Vietnam underscored the strategic significance that the United States attributes to a former adversary with a distinct political system. It also demonstrated Washington's commitment to moving beyond historical legacies and focusing on future-oriented cooperation – an approach designed to strengthen the US position amid China's rapid rise. The Biden administration's decision to remove Vietnam from the list of *currency manipulators* further illustrated its intent to eliminate trade-related obstacles imposed under the Trump administration, fostering greater economic engagement between the two countries. The Biden administration recognized that a rigid approach to trade issues with Vietnam could have negative repercussions for the broader bilateral relationship, particularly at a time when Washington sought to integrate Vietnam into its network of regional partners to counter China's growing assertiveness and influence in the Indo-Pacific.

Thus, US-Vietnam relations *are not partnerships based on shared values, but rather cooperation rooted in political calculations and mutual interests.* Vietnam's strategic importance in advancing US foreign policy priorities in the Indo-Pacific has become increasingly evident.

The impact of the Indo-Pacific Strategy (IPS) on Vietnam

Shortly after the United States officially announced the Indo-Pacific Strategy (IPS) in February 2022, the spokesperson of Vietnam's Ministry of Foreign Affairs stated that Vietnam welcomes cooperative initiatives in the Indo-Pacific that contribute to regional peace, stability, cooperation, and development, while respecting international law, the legitimate rights and interests of all nations, and upholding ASEAN centrality (Huong 2022). In practice, IPS (2022) and the Free and Open Indo-Pacific (FOIP) framework (2017) share notable similarities with Vietnam's foreign policy objectives and national interests. The Biden administration has consistently expressed support for a strong, independent, and prosperous Vietnam (U.S. Department of State 2021). The United States commitment to multilateralism, ASEAN centrality, and engagement on key transnational issues such as climate change, cybersecurity, and development inequalities aligns with Vietnam's diplomatic priorities (The White House 2022a).

> Strategic implications: Given Vietnam's strategic location and its potential to influence U.S. policy in the Indo-Pacific, IPS provides Vietnam with an opportunity to enhance its international standing. As the United States deepens its focus on Vietnam, this increased visibility is likely to be echoed by United States allies and partners, further facilitating Vietnam's independent, diversified, and multilateral foreign policy. This engagement supports Vietnam's national interests, enabling it to strengthen international integration while maintaining its strategic autonomy. However, Vietnam's strategic importance may diminish if United States attention is diverted to other regional partners as Washington expands its competition with China into new geographical domains (Nghiên cứu Biển Đông 2023).

> Security implications: The United States promotion of a rules-based order, including in maritime security and the South China Sea, its support for multilateralism, and its opposition to coercive and unilateral actions, align with Vietnam's security interests. The adherence of all regional actors to international law benefits Vietnam – a smaller nation – by preserving peace, stability, and national sovereignty. Moreover, US-Vietnam security cooperation offers Vietnam opportunities to strengthen its defence capabilities. The US implementation of *integrated deterrence* in the South China Sea, which involves building the maritime capacities of regional partners alongside US military advancements, allows Vietnam to receive additional assistance in maritime law enforcement. Initiatives such as the Pacific Deterrence Initiative (PDI) and the Indo-Pacific Maritime Domain Awareness (IPMDA) program – championed by the QUAD – enhance Vietnam's situational awareness of maritime activities. IPMDA also provides a new platform for maritime security cooperation, enabling Vietnam to broaden its network of partners in addressing maritime disputes (Nghiên cứu Biển Đông 2023).

Nonetheless, challenges coexist with opportunities. Great power competition – especially between the United States and China – raises concerns about Vietnam's strategic autonomy and the risk of entrapment in major-power rivalry. The National Security Strategy (NSS) emphasizes ideological competition between democratic and non-democratic systems, an area where Vietnam and the United States have fundamental differences.

Economic implications: Through US-led initiatives such as the Indo-Pacific Economic Framework for Prosperity (IPEF), Vietnam has opportunities to advance economic development, including post-pandemic recovery, sustainable growth, market and supply chain diversification, and digital transformation. As the United States strengthens new supply chains, Vietnam could position itself as a key manufacturing hub in the region.

However, each pillar of IPEF presents potential risks for Vietnam. For example, in the supply chain pillar, the United States may seek to restrict the transfer of dual-use technologies to China, requiring participating countries to tighten export controls and technology transfer regulations – potentially limiting Vietnam's control over its supply chains. This is particularly significant given that Vietnam imports core technologies and exports a large volume of electronics to China – one of its largest export markets (Nghiên cứu Biển Đông 2023).

Diplomatic implications: The United States has reinforced its commitment to ASEAN centrality by appointing an Ambassador to ASEAN, expanding diplomatic engagement, and aligning with ASEAN's Indo-Pacific Outlook (AOIP). These efforts align with Vietnam's regional strategy and provide new opportunities for engagement with US-led multilateral mechanisms, including the QUAD (Nghiên cứu Biển Đông 2023). However, IPS also presents diplomatic challenges, particularly in terms of regional cohesion. The United States tendency to prioritize certain bilateral partners and allies – including Vietnam – has created divisions within ASEAN. Notably, IPEF does not include Laos or Cambodia, and the Summit for Democracy excluded Singapore, signalling potential fractures within ASEAN unity as the United States focuses on select regional actors.

4. Conclusion

The Indo-Pacific region has emerged as the centre of geopolitical and geoeconomic competition, attracting significant engagement from major powers. The United States has identified the Indo-Pacific as its primary strategic battleground, actively working to expand its influence in the region. As the Biden administration deepens US engagement in Southeast Asia, Vietnam – owing to its strategic geographic position and rapidly growing economy – has gained greater importance in US foreign policy. Over the past four years, the Biden administration has built upon the achievements of previous administrations to further advance the US-Vietnam strategic partnership across multiple domains, including security – an area traditionally sensitive for both nations. The growing assertiveness of China in the South China Sea and the increasing prominence of non-traditional security threats – such as cybersecurity, transnational crime, climate change, pandemics, and human trafficking – have further deepened bilateral cooperation. Both the United States and Vietnam recognize that their partnership serves mutual interests, leading to stronger commitments in bilateral and multilateral initiatives. For the Biden administration, strengthening ties with Vietnam aligns with Washington's broader Indo-Pacific strategy, reinforcing US presence in the region while maintaining a free and open Indo-Pacific. For Vietnam, upgrading relations with the United States is seen as an opportunity to preserve regional peace and stability, promote economic cooperation and development, and maintain independence and autonomy in foreign policy. The growing convergence of strategic interests has propelled US-Vietnam relations to new heights.

The US-Vietnam relationship (2021–2024) can be regarded as a model partnership shaped by the US Indo-Pacific Strategy. While the historical foundations of bilateral relations remain significant, it is evident that the relationship has been profoundly influenced by new dynamics, emerging motivations, a shifting strategic vision, evolving objectives, and newly devised implementation strategies within the US Indo-Pacific framework. From Vietnam's perspective, the partnership with the United States exemplifies how a smaller nation can leverage great power competition to its advantage. However, opportunities and challenges will always coexist, requiring Vietnam to remain vigilant and adaptive in navigating the evolving geopolitical landscape.

5. References

Dung, K./Xuân, T. (2024): Cơ hội thúc đẩy quan hệ hợp tác kinh tế – thương mại Việt Nam – Hoa Kỳ (Opportunities to promote economic and trade cooperation between Vietnam and the United States). In: Communist Party of Vietnam Electronic Newspaper. https://dangcongsan.vn/kinh-te/co-hoi-thuc-day-quan-he-hop-tac-kinh-te-thuong-mai-viet-nam-hoa-ky-666031.html.

Embassy of the Socialist Republic of Vietnam in the United States of America (2021): White House highlights enhancement of US-Vietnam comprehensive partnership. https://vietnamembassy-usa.org/vi/node/6743.

Federal Register (2021): Determination on action and ongoing monitoring: Vietnam's acts, policies, and practices related to currency valuation. https://www.federalregister.gov/documents/2021/07/28/2021-16095/determination-on-action-and-ongoing-monitoring-vietnams-acts-policies-and-practices-related-to.

Hương, L. (2022): Việt Nam và ASEAN trong chiến lược Ấn Độ Dương – Thái Bình Dương của Mỹ (Vietnam and ASEAN in the US Indo-Pacific strategy). In: Tuổi Trẻ Online. https://tuoitre.vn/viet-nam-va-asean-trong-chien-luoc-an-do-duong-thai-binh-duong-cua-my-20220218083303189.htm.

Minh, S. (2023): Mỹ đề cao hợp tác với Việt Nam thúc đẩy trật tự hàng hải quốc tế (US enhances cooperation with Vietnam to promote international maritime order). Lao Động Newspaper. https://laodong.vn/the-gioi/my-de-cao-hop-tac-voi-viet-nam-thuc-day-trat-tu-hang-hai-quoc-te-1199273.ldo.

Nghiên cứu Biển Đông (2023): Tổng quan các văn bản chính sách về Ấn Độ Dương – Thái Bình Dương của chính quyền Biden năm 2022 (Overview of the Biden administration's Indo-Pacific policy documents in 2022). https://nghiencuubiendong.vn/tong-quan-cac-van-ban-chinh-sach-ve-an-do-duong-thai-binh-duong-cua-chinh-quyen-biden-nam-2022.56481.anews.

Office of the U.S. Trade Representative (2021): USTR announces agreement between the United States and Vietnam to resolve timber Section 301 investigation. https://ustr.gov/about-us/policy-offices/press-office/press-releases/2021/october/ustr-announces-agreement-between-united-states-and-vietnam-resolve-timber-section-301-investigation.

People's Army Newspaper (2023): Deputy spokeswoman: Vietnam ready to cooperate with U.S. https://en.qdnd.vn/foreign-affairs/bilateral-relations/deputy-spokeswoman-vietnam-ready-to-cooperate-with-u-s-550569.

Tuoitrenews (2023): Biggest ever U.S. business delegation comes to Vietnam to seek investment opportunities. In: Tuổi Trẻ News. https://tuoitrenews.vn/news/business/20230322/biggestever-us-business-delegation-comes-to-vietnam-to-seek-investment-opportunities/72207.html.

The White House (2021): Interim national security strategic guidance. https://www.whitehouse.gov/wp-content/uploads/2021/03/NSC-1v2.pdf.

The White House (2022a): Strategy of the United States. https://uploads.mwp.mprod.getusinfo.com/uploads/sites/124/2023/06/U.S.-Indo-Pacific-Strategy.pdf.

The White House (2022b): Biden-Harris administration's national security strategy. https://www.whitehouse.gov/wp-content/uploads/2022/10/Biden-Harris-Administrations-National-Security-Strategy-10.2022.pdf.

U.S.-ASEAN Business Council (2022): U.S.-ASEAN Business Council brings American defense industry delegation to Vietnam. http://www.aseanmatters.org/press-release/2022/12/07/us-asean-business-council-brings-american-defense-industry-delegation.

U.S. Department of State (2021): U.S. relations with Vietnam. https://www.state.gov/u-s-relations-with-vietnam/.

U.S. Department of State (2022): The administration's approach to the People's Republic of China. https://www.state.gov/the-administrations-approach-to-the-peoples-republic-of-china/.

U.S. Department of Defense (2022): 2022 National Defense Strategy of the United States. https://media.defense.gov/2022/Oct/27/2003103845/-1/-1/1/2022-NATIONAL-DEFENSE-STRATEGY-NPR-MDR.PDF.

Chapter 16: Vietnam-South Korea Relations (2009–2024): A Retrospective and Prospective Analysis

Ngo Tuan Thang

Situated within the same Asian region, Vietnam and South Korea share several notable similarities, including comparable national scale, historical experiences, and cultural affinities. Their economies and human resources exhibit mutually beneficial complementarities, and both nations are aligned in their aspirations for regional and global development and peace. Diplomatic relations between Vietnam and South Korea were formally established on December 22, 1992, followed by the establishment of a *Comprehensive Partnership for the 21st Century* in August 2001. These foundational milestones inaugurated a new era in the relationship between the two countries and peoples, leading to successive upgrades in their bilateral ties to a *Strategic Cooperative Partnership* (October 2009) and subsequently a *Comprehensive Strategic Partnership* (December 2022). Transcending historical differences and past obstacles, the relationship between Vietnam and South Korea has demonstrably matured into a substantive and exemplary model for bilateral relations within East Asia. As the South Korean Ambassador to Vietnam, Oh Young Ju, has aptly described, this bilateral relationship represents a *miracle* in the diplomatic history of both nations. To elucidate this dynamic, this chapter provides an overview of key developments in Vietnam-South Korea relations, with a particular focus on the outcomes achieved over the past 15 years (2009–2024) across various domains, including political and diplomatic engagement, economic cooperation, defence and security collaboration, as well as cultural, educational, and tourism exchanges. Additionally, the study offers several recommendations to further advance the bilateral partnership between the two countries in the future.

1. Introduction

Vietnam-South Korea relations have become a subject of significant research interest for both domestic and international scholars. However, studies on this topic vary in scope and depth, reflecting diverse research approaches and perspectives.

Directly related to the topic of Vietnam-South Korea relations, several studies have been published. Notable works include the book *Vietnam-South Korea: A quarter-century of shared development* by Lee Han Woo and Bui The Cuong (2015); the book *Vietnam-South Korea: 25 Years of cooperation and development (1992–2017) and prospects toward 2022* by Nguyen Van Lan (2019; the article *Friendly and Partnership-Based Relationship Between Vietnam and South Korea: The Nature, Current Development, and Future Prospects* by Nguyen Hoang Tien and Dinh Ba Hung Anh (2019); and the book *30 Years of economic and social cooperation between Vietnam and South Korea: Exploring sustainable cooperation strategies for the future* by Kwak Sung-il, Beak Yong-Hun, Lee Han Woo, and colleagues (2021). Tunchinmang Langel (2022) published the study *Outlook on South Korea and Vietnam's Progression Towards a Comprehensive Strategic Partnership.* Additionally, author Pham Thuy Trang (2024) published the article *Vietnam-South Korea political and diplomatic Relations (2009–2022).* These studies provide a comprehensive and in-depth analysis of the historical evolution and dynamics of Vietnam-South Korea relations since the establishment of diplomatic ties in 1992. Through their research, the authors examine the current state of bilateral cooperation across key sectors, highlight the strengths and limitations of the relationship, and propose strategic directions to further elevate Vietnam-South Korea relations to new heights.

Regarding South Korea's New Southern Policy (NSP), which highlights Vietnam's role and position in Vietnam-South Korea relations, several studies have been disseminated. These include the book *Vietnam in South Korean President Moon Jae-in's New Southern Policy*, edited by Pham Hong Thai (2020); Huynh Tam Sang (2020) authored the article *South Korea-Vietnam Relations in the Context of South Korea's New Southern Policy*; Phan Van Ran and Nguyen Thu Ha (2022) co-authored the article *Vietnam in South Korea's New Southern Policy* and so on. It can be said that the implementation of the NSP has had a significant impact on the Vietnam-South Korea Strategic Cooperative Partnership. The aforementioned studies have provided readers with a clearer understanding of South Korea's policy toward the region, particularly its emphasis on Vietnam. Moreover, these works contribute to the theoretical foundation for policymaking, helping to maximize the positive effects of the NSP on Vietnam's development while ensuring the sustainable interests of both nations.

It is evident that studies on Vietnam-South Korea relations exhibit a systematic and diverse approach. However, a comprehensive academic study that focuses on Vietnam-South Korea relations from 2009 to 2024 across multiple dimensions, while identifying existing challenges and providing policy recommendations for future bilateral development, remains a significant omission in the current literature. In this chapter, the author will conduct an in-depth analysis of Vietnam-South Korea relations during the 2009–2024 period across various sectors. By doing so, this study aims to further enrich and deepen the understanding of Vietnam-South Korea relations. While this chapter primarily concentrates on the bilateral dimension of Vietnam-South Korea relations, it also underscores the growing influence of Indo-Pacific geopolitical discourse on inter-state engagements. South Korea's Indo-Pacific Strategy (2022) and its prior NSP have redefined the strategic rationale behind its engagement with Southeast Asia, positioning Vietnam as a core partner. As such, understanding Vietnam-South Korea ties provides critical insight into how broader regional strategies are embedded in and influence bilateral frameworks.

2. Overview of Vietnam-South Korea Relations before 2009

The relationship between Vietnam and South Korea has a long-standing historical foundation. One of the earliest and most significant links was established when Prince Lý Long Tường of Vietnam's Lý Dynasty migrated to Korea, where he founded the Lý Hoa Sơn clan, leaving a profound and enduring influence on Korean society (Hwang Gwi Yeon 2003, 41).

During the modern era, interactions between Vietnam and South Korea remained limited due to their distinct historical trajectories. The 1975–1982 period saw Vietnam-South Korea relations confined to private trade via intermediaries, with no formal diplomatic interaction (Lee Han Woo 2020, 165). From 1983 onward, Vietnam-South Korea trade relations gradually expanded, shifting from indirect exchanges to direct transactions and limited non-governmental interactions. A significant milestone in fostering bilateral engagement was Vietnam's participation in the 1988 Seoul Olympics, which facilitated informal contacts between representatives of both countries. Following this event, diplomatic ties continued to improve through unofficial visits by Vietnamese leaders to South Korea (Lee Han Woo 2020, 165; MOFA 2025).

In 1990, Vietnam and South Korea initiated diplomatic negotiations through their embassies in Thailand, aiming to accelerate the normalization of bilateral relations. This effort culminated in the signing of an agreement to establish liaison offices in April 1992, a critical step towards full normalization. Accordingly, South Korea inaugurated its Liaison Office in Hanoi on August 17, 1992, followed by Vietnam establishing its Liaison Office in Seoul on November 24, 1992 (MOFA 2025). On December 22, 1992, Vietnam and South Korea officially established diplomatic relations. On the same day, South Korea inaugurated its embassy in Hanoi. On Vietnam's side, the Vietnamese Embassy in Seoul was established in March 1993. To further enhance economic cooperation and cultural exchange in southern Vietnam, South Korea opened a Consulate General in Ho Chi Minh City in November 1993 (MOFA 2025).

Following normalization, bilateral cooperation quickly expanded across multiple sectors. The period 1992–2009 witnessed a series of high-level visits between Vietnam and South Korea. Key visits included Vietnamese leaders such as Prime Minister (PM) Võ Văn Kiệt (1993), President Trần Đức Lương (2001), PM Phan Văn Khải (2003), and National Assembly (NA) Chairman Nguyễn Văn An (2004). On the South Korean side, prominent visitors included PM Lee Young Dug (1994), NA Chairman Kim Soo Han (1996), President Kim Young Sam (1996), and President Kim Dae-jung (1998). Other visits included PM Lee Han Dong (2002), NA Chairman Park Kwan-yong (2003), President Roh Moo-hyun (2004), PM Lee Hae-chan (2005), and NA Chairman Kim Won-ki (2006) (MOFA 2025).

Nearly two decades after the establishment of diplomatic relations, the partnership witnessed significant elevation. During President Trần Đức Lương's visit to South Korea in 2001, the two countries agreed to a Comprehensive Partnership, followed by an upgrade to a Strategic Cooperative Partnership during President Lee Myung-bak's visit to Vietnam in 2009. Notably, among Vietnam's diplomatic partners from the early 1990s, South Korea became the first to attain strategic partner status (Lee Han Woo 2020, 161). Conversely, Vietnam became the fourth country to establish a strategic cooperative relationship with South Korea, following the US, China, and Russia.

The expansion of bilateral relations was supported by a series of important agreements across diverse areas, including economic, trade, investment, transportation, culture, and legal cooperation (Vu Tuyet Loan 2007; Nguyen Duy Loi 2022, 47; MOFA 2025).

Economically, bilateral trade surged from 500 million US dollars in 1992 to 9.8 billion in 2008 (Langel 2022). South Korea emerged as a major investor in Vietnam, contributing to numerous large-scale projects. Vietnam's participation in the ASEAN-Korea Free Trade Agreement (AKFTA) in 2007 further facilitated economic expansion, despite some challenges regarding tariff reductions and implementation schedules (Nguyen Duy Loi 2022). Furthermore, South Korea's ODA to Vietnam, amounting to 1.255 billion US dollars from 1995 to 2010 (Nguyen Minh Trang 2021, 74).

Between 1992 and 2008, cultural, educational, and scientific-technical exchanges between Vietnam and South Korea flourished. These dynamic interactions laid a solid foundation for the comprehensive development of Vietnam-South Korea relations from 2009 to 2024 across all sectors.

3. The Evolution of Vietnam-South Korea Relations (2009–2024)

In the field of political and diplomatic relations

Political and diplomatic relations have constituted a cornerstone of Vietnam-South Korea cooperation, demonstrating the critical role of high-level engagement in shaping broader bilateral ties. Between 2009 and 2024, the relationship was continuously strengthened, expanded, and deepened, underpinned by growing mutual trust cultivated through sustained bilateral and multilateral exchanges.

At the bilateral level, Vietnam-South Korea relations have been demonstrated through frequent high-level visits and dialogues between the leadership of the ruling parties, states, governments, and national assemblies.

Firstly, Party-to-Party diplomacy progressed markedly. The Communist Party of Vietnam (CPV) initiated high-level political exchanges with South Korea through General Secretary Đỗ Mười's visit (1995), followed by those of General Secretary Nông Đức Mạnh (2007) and General Secretary Nguyễn Phú Trọng (2014). These engagements were further reinforced through phone communications, notably between General Secretary Nguyễn Phú Trọng and Presidents Moon Jae-in (2021) and Yoon Suk Yeol (2022), and between General Secretary Tô Lâm and President Yoon Suk Yeol (2024).

High-level engagements between political party leaders from South Korea and Vietnam have also been actively pursued. In August 2011, Kim Chung Kwon, Secretary-General of the Grand National Party (GNP) of

South Korea, visited Vietnam. The two parties signed the *Memorandum of Understanding (MOU) on Strengthening Cooperation between the CPV and the GNP*. In October 2014, the CPV and the ruling Saenuri Party signed a *Cooperation Agreement for the 2015–2016 period*, building upon the MOU signed in 2011 (Youn Dae-Yeong/Nguyen Van Kim/Nguyen Manh Dung 2014, 318). In December 2018, Deputy PM Trịnh Đình Dũng visited South Korea and held a meeting with Lee Hae-chan, Chairman of the Democratic Party of Korea (DPK). In March 2019, Chairman Lee Hae-chan led a delegation from the DPK to Vietnam and a *MOU on Cooperation* was signed between the two parties.

Secondly, high-level visits between state, government, and parliamentary leaders of both countries continued to be maintained.

On the South Korean side, presidential visits to Vietnam included President Lee Myung-bak (October 2009), President Park Geun-hye (September 2013), President Moon Jae-in (March 2018), and President Yoon Suk-yeol (June 2023). Notably, since President Kim Young-sam's visit in 1996, all six successive South Korean presidents have undertaken state visits to Vietnam early in their terms. This is an exceptionally rare phenomenon, clearly demonstrating a strong bipartisan consensus among South Korean leaders in recognizing Vietnam as a key strategic partner. On the Vietnamese side, there were two state visits by the President and five visits by the Prime Minister to South Korea. The two Presidents who made official visits were President Trương Tấn Sang (2011) and President Nguyễn Xuân Phúc (2022). The Prime Ministers of Vietnam who visited South Korea included PM Nguyễn Tấn Dũng, who visited three times (2009, 2012 and 2014); PM Nguyễn Xuân Phúc (2019); and PM Phạm Minh Chính (2024). During President Trương Tấn Sang's visit in 2011, President Lee Myung-bak emphasized South Korea's role as

> "Vietnam's most sincere and close friend" and "its best and most practical partner." (Báo Điện tử Chính phủ 2011)

In 2022, President Nguyễn Xuân Phúc's state visit was particularly significant, representing his first as president, the first Vietnamese presidential visit to South Korea in over a decade, and the inaugural foreign state visit since President Yoon Suk-yeol's inauguration.

A key outcome of these high-level visits was the elevation of bilateral relations to new strategic levels. In 2009, the *Strategic Cooperation Partnership* was established during President Lee Myung-bak's visit to Vietnam. This was succeeded by the elevation to a *Comprehensive Strategic Partner-*

ship formalized in a landmark Joint Statement during the Nguyễn Xuân Phúc's 2022 visit to South Korea. To further enhance and substantiate the "Comprehensive Strategic Partnership", during President Yoon Suk-yeol's state visit to Vietnam in 2023, both countries agreed to sign and implement the *Action Programme for the Implementation of the Vietnam-South Korea Comprehensive Strategic Partnership* (hereinafter referred to as the *Action Program*).

Thirdly, regarding cooperation between the National Assemblies, Vietnam and South Korea have maintained a close relationship through high-level visits and long-term collaboration. Chairmans of the South Korean National Assembly who have paid official visits to Vietnam include Chung Ui-hwa (2015), Chung Sye-kyun (2017), Park Byeong-seug (2020), and Kim Jin-pyo (2023). Meanwhile, Vietnamese parliamentary leaders have also visited South Korea, including Chairman Nguyễn Phú Trọng (2008), Chairman Nguyễn Sinh Hùng (2013), Chairwoman Nguyễn Thị Kim Ngân (2018), and Chairman Vương Đình Huệ (2021).

The National Assemblies of Vietnam and South Korea have agreed to enhance exchanges in legislative experience, encourage inter-parliamentarian collaboration, and promote the activities of thematic groups such as women and young parliamentarians.

Fourth, with a proactive approach, intergovernmental dialogue mechanisms expanded considerably. Bilateral engagement was strengthened through mechanisms such as: the economic dialogue at the Deputy Prime Minister level; the Joint Committee on industrial, trade, and energy cooperation at the Ministerial level; the Joint Committee for the implementation of the VKFTA at the Ministerial level; the Joint Committee on science and technology cooperation at the Ministerial level; the Inter-governmental committee on economic, scientific, and technical cooperation at the Vice-Ministerial level; the Defence policy dialogue at the Vice-Ministerial level; the Security dialogue at the Vice-Ministerial level; and the Strategic dialogue on Diplomacy, Security, and national defence at the Vice-Ministerial level.

In South Korea's regional foreign policy, Vietnam is regarded as a key partner in Southeast Asia. During the initial phase of the New Southern Policy (2017–2019), South Korea prioritized integrating its diplomatic efforts to enhance relations with Vietnam within the broader ASEAN cooperation framework. However, in the second phase (2020–2022), this approach was adjusted as high-level meetings between the two countries' leaders increasingly focused on aligning the Vietnam-South Korea strategic partnership with the South Korea-Mekong cooperation framework. This shift enabled South Korea to fully capitalize on Vietnam's unique "dual role" in 2020, when Vietnam concurrently held the ASEAN Chairmanship and served as the coordinating country for ASEAN-South Korea relations (Phan Thi Anh Thu 2023, 7). In South Korea's Indo-Pacific Strategy, announced in December 2022, President Yoon Suk-yeol reaffirmed Vietnam's pivotal role in the regional strategy and "the ASEAN-Korea Solidarity Initiative." Furthermore, Vietnam was the first country with which South Korea signed the *Framework Agreement on climate change Cooperation* (2021). Vietnam has welcomed and supported South Korea's expanded role in maintaining peace, stability, and development in the region, while reaffirming South Korea as a long-term strategic partner.

Beyond bilateral engagements, Vietnam and South Korea demonstrate strategic partnership through their active participation in multilateral forums. This shared commitment underscores a convergent foreign policy approach characterized by the principles of peace, friendship, diversification, and multilateralization, with a common objective of fostering regional and global peace, stability, security, cooperation, and development.

Vietnam and South Korea have maintained strong collaboration by mutually supporting each other's nominations for international organisations. Specifically, Vietnam and South Korea alternated support in elections to the United Nations Human Rights Council, with South Korea securing membership for the 2013–2015 term and Vietnam for the 2014–2016 and 2023–2025 terms. Similarly, both countries backed one another's bids for seats on the United Nations Economic and Social Council, with South Korea elected for the 2014–2016 term and Vietnam for the 2016–2018 term. Further, Vietnam endorsed South Korea's successful elections to the International Law Commission (2017–2021), the Committee on Economic, Social, and Cultural Rights (2019–2022), the Human Rights Council (2020–2022), and the United Nations Board of Auditors (2020–2026). In return, South Korea has actively supported Vietnam's candidacy for a non-permanent seat on the United Nations Security Council (UNSC) for the 2008–2009 term. South Korea played a key role in assisting Vietnam in successfully serving as a non-permanent UNSC member for the 2020–2021 term and as ASEAN Chair in 2020. South Korea has also strongly backed Vietnam in its role as the coordinator for ASEAN-South Korea relations from 2021 to 2024. South Korea has supported Vietnam in hosting the Partnering for Green Growth and the Global Goals 2030 Summit in 2025.

Alongside bilateral parliamentary cooperation, both Vietnam and South Korea place significant emphasis on parliamentary collaboration within multilateral frameworks. At the regional level, the two countries actively collaborate through organisations such as the ASEAN Inter-Parliamentary Assembly (AIPA), the Asia-Pacific Parliamentary Forum (APPF), the Asia-Europe Parliamentary Partnership Meeting (ASEP), and the Standing Committee on Social and Cultural Affairs of the Asian Parliamentary Assembly (APA). Globally, both nations coordinate within the ASEAN+3 Parliamentary Group and the Asia-Pacific Geopolitical Group (APG). In the Inter-Parliamentary Union (IPU), Vietnam and South Korea have consistently supported each other's initiatives and nominations. Notably, both served as APG representatives on the IPU Executive Committee during the 2008–2011 term. Additionally, during the 128th IPU Assembly held in Ecuador (March 2013), South Korea actively supported Vietnam's successful bid to host the 132nd IPU Assembly in 2015, further cementing their robust multilateral parliamentary cooperation.

In the field of economics

Economic, trade, and investment cooperation forms the core of Vietnam-South Korea relations. South Korea is a leading partner, ranking as Vietnam's largest foreign investor, second-largest ODA provider, and third-largest trade partner (Thanh Tu 2018; Mai Thi Dinh 2023).

Bilateral trade

Vietnam and South Korea have established a comprehensive economic cooperation framework, combining both broad and sector-specific initiatives. A key foundation is the Vietnam-Korea Free Trade Agreement (VKFTA), which entered into force on December 20, 2015. To further institutionalize economic dialogue, President Moon Jae-in proposed a high-level economic dialogue in 2018, resulting in Deputy Prime Minister-level meetings held in Seoul (2019) and Hanoi (2023).

Beyond bilateral agreements, both countries actively engage in multilateral frameworks such as the Indo-Pacific Economic Framework for Prosperity (IPEF) and the Regional Comprehensive Economic Partnership (RCEP). They have also prioritized enhancing trade facilitation and expanding cooperation in areas like e-commerce and information technology workforce development, recognizing the growing importance of digital trade and innovation (Báo điện tử Chính phủ 2023).

Bilateral trade growth illustrates the deepening partnership. Between 1992 and 2009, trade volume remained below 10 billion US dollars. However, since 2010, trade volumes expanded rapidly, consistently achieving double-digit growth. A major milestone was reached in 2012 when bilateral trade exceeded 20 billion US dollars, three years ahead of the original target (Mai Thi Dinh 2023). By 2015, trade volume had surged to 37.6 billion US dollars (a 74-fold rise since 1992) (Phan Thanh Hoan/Jeong Ji Young 2016, 68), it more than doubled to 81.5 billion US dollars by 2024. Despite the COVID-19 pandemic (2020–2022), this upward trajectory remained unaffected *(see detailed data below).*

Chart 1: Vietnam-South Korea trade volume (2009–2024)

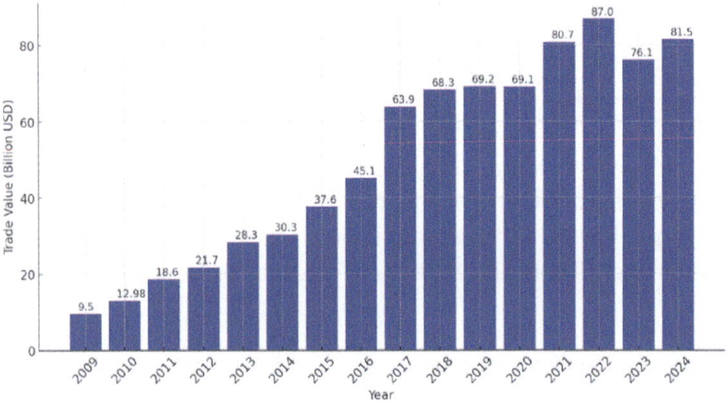

Source: Author's compilation from Phan Thanh Hoan/Jeong Ji Young 2016; Nguyen Minh Trang 2021; Hoang Manh Dung 2024

From 2009 to 2024, South Korea consistently ranked among Vietnam's top export and import markets. In 2010, South Korea officially surpassed Japan to become the world's second-largest supplier of goods to Vietnam (Nguyen Minh Trang 2021, 80). Prior to 2009, Vietnam primarily exported raw and processed goods. However, after 2009, Vietnam's exports to South Korea diversified to include 40 key product categories spanning both the agricultural and industrial sectors, with industrial goods making up the majority (Nguyen Minh Trang 2021, 82).

In 2014, Vietnam became South Korea's eighth-largest trading partner. By 2022, Vietnam surpassed Japan to become South Korea's third-largest trading partner for the first time, trailing only China and the United States (Kim 2021; Hoang Manh Dung 2024).

Investment

Since 2011, South Korea has consistently been one of the largest foreign direct investors (FDI) in Vietnam (Thanh Tu 2018). The expansion of major South Korean conglomerates such as Samsung, SK, LG, Lotte, and Hyundai has not only driven economic growth but also generated employment, advanced technology transfer, and elevated Vietnam's role in the global supply chain (Nguyen Duy Loi 2022).

Between 2009 and 2019, South Korean FDI in Vietnam surged markedly. In 2013, South Korea's FDI in Vietnam reached 3.8 billion US dollars, rising to 7.32 billion in 2014. South Korea became the largest foreign investor in Vietnam in 2014, leading in total investment capital, number of projects, and geographic coverage, with the presence of numerous multinational corporations. In 2019, South Korea's total FDI in Vietnam reached 7.92 billion US dollars, accounting for approximately 20.8 per cent of total FDI inflows (Nguyen Minh Trang 2021, 106; Doan Thi Tra Thu 2022; Truong Thu Ha 2023, 44).

During the 2020–2024 period, despite the impact of the COVID-19 pandemic and the global economic downturn, South Korea maintained a significant level of investment in Vietnam. In 2023, over 500 South Korean projects were recorded, exceeding 5 billion US dollars in capital (Vaibhav/Nguyen Quang Anh 2024). Notably, in 2024, FDI from South Korea reached 7 billion US dollars, bringing its cumulative investment in Vietnam to over 92 billion (Truong Thu Ha 2023, 44) *(see detailed data below).*

Chart 2: South Korean FDI in Vietnam (2009–2024)

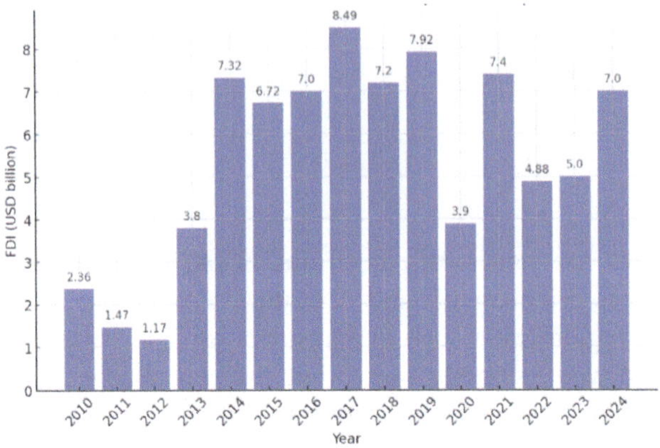

Source: Author's compilation from Truong Thu Ha 2023, 44; Vaibhav/Nguyen Quang Anh 2024

One of the key drivers behind South Korea's investment in Vietnam is the combination of competitive labour costs, favourable investment policies, and stable economic growth potential. Major corporations like Samsung have transformed Vietnam into a strategic manufacturing hub, contributing approximately 20 per cent of the country's total export value (Nguyen Duy Loi 2022). Investment patterns show a shift beyond manufacturing and mining into banking, finance, securities, and high technology. While direct investment-often with 100 per cent foreign ownership-dominates, indirect investment has gradually increased. South Korean enterprises have expanded their presence from 53 provinces in 2017 to 59 provinces by 2022 (Doan Thi Tra Thu 2022), highlighting the deepening and diversification of investment ties.

Official Development Assistance (ODA) from South Korea to Vietnam

South Korea stands as one of Vietnam's most significant providers of ODA, ranking second only to Japan. Conversely, Vietnam is the largest recipient of South Korean ODA. Between 1990 and 2009, South Korea's ODA to Vietnam grew at an average annual rate of 71 per cent (Tran Toan Thang et al. 2016). From 2009 to 2024, South Korean ODA to Vietnam focused on key areas such as green growth, infrastructure development, and human resource training. During the 2012–2015 period, South Korea provided 1.2

billion US dollars in concessional loans through the *Economic Development Cooperation Fund* (EDCF) (Truong Thu Ha 2023). This figure rose to 1.5 billion US dollars in the 2016–2020 period (Nguyen Duy Loi 2022).

In addition to concessional loans, South Korea has also prioritized grant aid. In 2011, Vietnam was officially designated as a key partner in South Korea's ODA cooperation strategy, with three priority areas: green growth, infrastructure development, and human resource training (Huynh Tam Sang 2023). In 2024, South Korea committed 200 million US dollars in grant aid for the 2024–2027 period (Báo điện tử Chính phủ 2023).

South Korea's ODA has played a significant role in improving infrastructure, enhancing education quality, and strengthening Vietnam's resilience to climate change. Key infrastructure projects, including expressway networks, overpasses, and high-tech zones, have been partially funded by South Korean ODA (Lee Han Woo 2020).

In the field of defence and security

Scholars assert that Vietnam-South Korea defence and security cooperation has evolved from symbolic engagements to substantive and institutionalized collaboration, reflecting a more comprehensive bilateral relationship.

Defence cooperation

The defence partnership between Vietnam and South Korea serves as a key pillar of bilateral relations. A significant aspect of defence cooperation is the establishment and sustained operation of high-level dialogue mechanisms. Since 2011, the two nations have institutionalized the Vice-Ministerial strategic dialogue on diplomacy, security, and defence, which has convened on five occasions by 2023. Furthermore, the Vietnam-South Korea Vice-ministerial defence dialogue has been consistently maintained, with the inaugural session of the strategic defence dialogue held in 2012. As of April 2024, eleven such dialogues have been convened. In addition to these dialogue mechanisms, the two nations have formalized their defence cooperation through the signing of several key agreements, including a MOU on information security (2012), a MOU on Military information security (2014), a Record of Discussion on Addressing the Consequences of Post-War Mines and Unexploded Ordnance (2016), and a Joint Vision Statement on defence cooperation towards 2030 (2018). Cooperation has expanded into defence industry development, arms trade, joint production, and technology transfer, with South Korea supplying 6.6 per cent of Vietnam's arms imports during 2017–2021 (Huynh Tam Sang 2023). By 2024, South Korea had delivered four second-hand vessels to Vietnam (Thu Phuong 2024).

South Korea has made substantial contributions to assisting Vietnam in addressing the legacies of war, particularly in dealing with unexploded ordnance (UXO). Through the Korea International Cooperation Agency, the South Korean government has provided a total of 34 million US dollars in funding for two UXO clearance projects in Vietnam. During the period of 2018–2021, South Korea extended non-refundable aid amounting to 20 million US dollars for the implementation of the *Vietnam-Korea Cooperation Project for Overcoming the Consequences of Post-War Mines and UXO* in the provinces of Binh Dinh and Quang Binh. For the 2024–2026 period, South Korea is providing 14 million US dollars in funding for the *Vietnam-Korea Mine Action for Peace Village* project (Cổng thông tin điện tử Bộ quốc phòng 2024).

Cooperation between the two countries in the field of air defence and air force has yielded significant results. Vietnam has regularly sent representatives to events organized by the Korean Air Force Academy and participated in the Seoul International Aerospace & Defense Exhibition (Seoul ADEX 2023). Both nations have implemented pilot and air defence officer training programmes, contributing to the enhancement of Vietnam's defence capabilities. Additionally, Vietnam and South Korea have actively cooperated in UN peacekeeping operations. The two countries have exchanged expertise, provided training support for officers participating in peacekeeping missions, and coordinated humanitarian activities and regional security assistance efforts.

Security cooperation

Bilateral security relations extend beyond law enforcement cooperation to encompass maritime security, transnational crime prevention, humanitarian assistance, and disaster relief.

In 2021, Vietnam and South Korea agreed to boost maritime security cooperation, focusing on strengthening the Vietnam People's Navy. In 2022, President Yoon Suk-yeol emphasized that South Korea would continue to support Vietnam in enhancing its maritime law enforcement capabilities

(Nguyen Duy Loi 2022). A salient instance of defence cooperation is South Korea's transfer of two decommissioned Pohang-class corvettes to Vietnam, thereby augmenting the latter's maritime defence capabilities. Between 2017 and 2019, South Korean Navy destroyers made three port calls in Da Nang, engaging in communication exercises with the Vietnam People's Navy (Huynh Tam Sang 2023).

Cooperation between Vietnam's Ministry of Public Security and South Korea's National Police Agency has also deepened substantially. The 2005 Cooperation Agreement and the 2015 MOU on the Korean Desk and Vietnam Desk operations have provided a solid legal framework for collaboration in crime prevention, fugitive apprehension, and citizen protection. By 2023, the two sides had established seven pairs of cooperative mechanisms between police forces in various localities (Khong Ha 2023). The deputy-ministerial security dialogue has been regularly maintained, with the seventh session held in Hanoi in 2019, alongside six editions of the deputy-ministerial police cooperation conference by 2024 (Thu Phuong 2024).

Of particular significance is South Korea's provision of two patrol vessels to the Ministry of Public Security of Vietnam, coupled with the implementation of training programmes for two operational crews. This collaborative effort aims to enhance Vietnam's capacity in combating transnational crime. Furthermore, the Vietnam People's Public Security Forces and the Korean National Police Agency have engaged in cultural and sporting exchange activities. In 2023, a delegation from the Vietnam Public Security Forces undertook its inaugural exchange visit to South Korea. Subsequently, in September 2024, Commissioner General of the Korean National Police Agency Cho Ji Ho led a high-level delegation to Vietnam and participated in the second iteration of the Vietnam-Korea police cultural and sports exchange programme.

In other fields

From 2009 to 2024, the cooperation between Vietnam and South Korea has experienced significant and comprehensive development across various sectors, including culture, education, people-to-people exchanges, tourism, healthcare, and science and technology.

In the field of culture and people-to-people exchanges, since 2009, exchanges have been continuously strengthened. A major contributor to the enhanced ties is the widespread popularity of the Korean Wave (Hallyu) in Vietnam. K-pop music, Korean dramas, fashion, and Korean entertainment products have garnered immense popularity among Vietnamese youth. Conversely, Vietnamese cuisine, particularly dishes like *Pho* and *Bun Cha*, has become increasingly popular in South Korea, helping bring Vietnam's image closer to the Korean people (Nguyen Duy Loi 2022). The Korean Cultural Center in Hanoi, operational since 2006, has played a pivotal role in cultural promotion through exhibitions, cultural exchanges, and Korean language education (Youn Dae-Yeong/Nguyen Van Kim/Nguyen Manh Dung 2014, 311). Numerous cultural and artistic festivals have been organized to enhance mutual understanding and exchange between the people of the two countries. A notable example is the *We Are Together* Festival, first held in 2017, which by 2024 had been hosted six times.

The strong ties between the people of the two countries are also reflected in impressive figures: on average, there are thousands of flights connecting Vietnam and South Korea every month, nearly 5 million people travel back and forth each year, more than 70 localities have established friendly cooperative relations. The presence of approximately 300,000 Vietnamese citizens in South Korea and 200,000 South Koreans in Vietnam, alongside 90,000 multicultural families, reflects the deepening inter-societal bonds (Voice of Vietnam 2024).

In the field of education, bilateral cooperation has expanded significantly, supported by agreements such as the 2017 MOU on Education Promotion. Educational collaboration between Vietnam and South Korea has significantly increased, driven by expanded government scholarships and university partnerships, leading to more Vietnamese students studying in South Korea. In 2019, Vietnam was the second-largest country of origin for international students in South Korea, with 37,426 students. Of the more than 160,165 international students enrolled in higher education programmes in South Korea, Vietnamese students accounted for 23.4 per cent, a 14-fold increase compared to 2009 (Nguyen Minh Trang 2021, 131). In 2023, out of 1.43 million foreign nationals in South Korea, approximately 201,000 were Vietnamese students, showcasing the rapid growth of the Vietnamese student community there (Langel 2022).

In the field of tourism, after the signing of the government-level Tourism Cooperation Agreement in 2002, the number of tourists between the two countries has continuously increased. The signing of the MOU on Tourism promotion for the 2023–2024 period has laid a solid foundation for both countries to continue developing sustainable tourism, promoting economic and cultural exchanges (Báo Nhân dân 2023). South Korea has also become a key source market for Vietnamese tourism. From 2015 to 2019, the number of South Korean tourists visiting Vietnam experienced a remarkable surge, rising from 1.1 million to 4.3 million (Thanh Tu 2024). Since 2016, South Korea has been the second-largest country of origin for tourists to Vietnam. However, by 2023, South Korea became the country with the largest number of visitors to Vietnam, with approximately 3.6 million South Korean tourists visiting Vietnam out of a total of 12.6 million international tourists (Thanh Tu 2024). Conversely, Vietnam emerged as South Korea's leading source of Southeast Asian tourists, with 420,000 Vietnamese visiting South Korea in 2023, ranking fifth globally (Khanh Van 2024).

In the field of healthcare. During the COVID-19 pandemic, South Korea was one of the first countries to support Vietnam by providing 1.1 million doses of AstraZeneca vaccines in 2021, helping control the spread of the virus (Tạp chí Cộng sản 2023). Additionally, the two countries have worked closely in exchanging doctors, transferring medical technology, and training healthcare professionals. This cooperation has not only enhanced the quality of healthcare services in Vietnam but also created opportunities for hospitals and healthcare organisations in both countries to grow together.

In the field of science and technology, since 2009, the South Korean government has actively increased support for Vietnam in the areas of science, technology, and education. Building on the 1995 government-level agreement, Vietnam and South Korea established a Joint Committee on Science and Technology, which by October 2023 had convened nine sessions. In 2019, the Ministry of Science and Technology of Vietnam signed an agreement with Ministry of Science and Information and Communications Technology of South Korea to co-fund joint research projects for the period 2019–2022.

High-technology collaboration is exemplified through landmark initiatives. The 2010 agreement between Hoa Lac High-Tech Park and Chungnam Science Park set the stage for deeper engagement. The Vietnam-South Korea Technology Incubator in Cần Thơ, launched in 2015, has supported numerous startups and SMEs. Most notably, the Vietnam-South Korea Institute of Science and Technology (V-KIST), inaugurated in Hanoi in January 2023, stands as a symbol of the robust science and technology partnership. As South Korea's largest non-refundable aid project globally, V-KIST has been pivotal in modelling Vietnam's first public research unit after the Korean system, promoting innovation and sustainable development.

4. Certain Issues Pertaining to Vietnam-South Korea Relations

Although positive results have been achieved in Vietnam-South Korea bilateral relations from 2009 to 2024, there are still some issues in the areas of economy, defence, and socio-cultural relations.

Firstly, in the field of economic, the persistent trade imbalance constitutes a salient issue. The disparity in economic development levels between the two nations is a structural characteristic: while South Korea has achieved the status of a developed capitalist economy, Vietnam continues its path toward industrialization and modernization, aiming to become a developed industrialized nation by 2045. This asymmetry significantly influences trade patterns. A noteworthy point is that in the joint statement on the Vietnam-South Korea Strategic Cooperative Partnership, the leaders of both countries set a goal to

> "Make efforts to cooperate for a balanced bilateral trade balance." (Báo Quân đội nhân dân 2009) Similarly, in the 2022 Joint Statement on the Comprehensive Strategic Partnership, they agreed "to promote stable growth in bilateral trade towards balance." (Báo điện tử Chính phủ 2022)

This is a very meaningful commitment for Vietnam, as the country has continuously experienced a trade deficit with South Korea for many years (Thanh Thanh 2023). The main reason is that Vietnam imports heavily from South Korea, mainly high-tech products, machinery, and electronic components. Meanwhile, Vietnam mainly exports raw materials, low value-added products, and lacks diversification in product types to South Korea. *(See the data table below).*

Table 1. Vietnam-South Korea trade balance (exports-imports) (2009–2022) (value: billion US dollars)

Year	2009	2010	2011	2012	2013	2014	2015	2016	2017
Value	*-4,9*	*-6,67*	*-8,46*	*-9,95*	*-14,06*	*-14,56*	*-18,67*	*-20,75*	*-31,91*
Year	2018	2019	2020	2021	2022				
Value	*-29,44*	*-27,21*	*-27,8*	*-34,36*	*-37,8*				

Source: Author's compilation from Thanh Thanh 2023; Hoang Manh Dung 2024

In 2022, although the two countries set the goal of "striving to achieve a bilateral trade turnover of 100 billion USD by 2023, aiming for 150 billion USD by 2030," (Báo điện tử Chính phủ 2022) this target has not been met (*as shown in Chart 1*). The reasons for this include the impact of the COVID-19 pandemic, global inflation, and disruptions in supply chains. Therefore, in the coming period, both countries will need to make significant efforts, as outlined in the *Action Program* of 2023, which states:

> "Both sides will strengthen close cooperation through effective measures, such as enhancing the role of the bilateral economic cooperation channels to ensure stable and balanced growth in bilateral trade. The goal is to strive to reach a trade volume of 100 billion USD as soon as possible and aim for 150 billion USD by 2030." (Báo điện tử Chính phủ 2023)

Secondly, in the field of defence and security, defence cooperation has not yet matched the potential of both sides. The exchange of weapons and military equipment between the two countries remains at a relatively low level, with cooperation activities primarily focused on technical aspects and individual projects. There is a lack of long-term strategic cooperation. South Korea has become the third-largest arms supplier to Vietnam, mainly through the transfer of used equipment, such as the Pohang-class frigates, which contrasts with the technology transfer agreements or joint development cooperation that South Korea typically has with its other strategic partners. Vietnam-South Korea security cooperation still has many areas for improvement. Although the two countries have established dialogue channels, actual cooperation has not seen significant progress beyond information sharing and the exchange of experiences. Furthermore, South Korea's support for enhancing Vietnam's maritime law enforcement capabilities remains limited, primarily through the provision of ships and personnel training.

Thirdly, in the field of cultural and educational cooperation, Vietnamese culture has not had many opportunities to penetrate daily life in South Korea. Although the South Korean government has prioritized strengthening cultural exchange between the two countries, opportunities for South Koreans to directly engage with Vietnamese culture in South Korea remain limited. The state of training cooperation between the two countries remains one-sided and unbalanced. The clearest evidence of this imbalance is the large number of Vietnamese students studying in South Korea. As of 2023, Vietnam had 43,361 students in South Korea, making it the second-largest source of international students in the country. In contrast, the number of

South Korean students studying in Vietnam remains relatively low (Nguyen Thi Huyen Trang 2022).

Another aspect of this imbalance is evident in the uneven development of Korean Studies in Vietnam compared to Vietnamese Studies in South Korea. In Vietnam, more than 40 universities have rapidly expanded their Korean Studies programmes. Conversely, research on Vietnamese Studies in South Korea is still limited to only a few universities. One of the key reasons for this disparity is the difference in the level of development between the higher education systems of the two countries (Nguyen Thi Huyen Trang 2022; Do Thi Thu Trang 2023, 65).

The issue of community integration for Vietnamese workers and brides in South Korea is also a noteworthy concern. Language barriers, cultural differences, and even social prejudices sometimes create challenges for them. These difficulties can reduce the effectiveness and sustainability of people-to-people exchanges and cultural cooperation between Vietnam and South Korea.

5. Recommendations for Enhancing Cooperation

Looking back on the fifteen-year journey since the establishment of the Strategic Cooperative Partnership (2009–2024), the challenges that have emerged are merely minor deviations within an overwhelmingly positive trajectory, marked by significant accomplishments fostered through the joint efforts of Vietnam and South Korea. To further substantialize the relationship between Vietnam and South Korea, the author proposes the following recommendations:

First and foremost, to deepen political relations and mutual trust, Vietnam and South Korea should continue to enhance exchanges, dialogues, and high-level engagements through party, government, and parliamentary channels, as well as among leaders at ministerial, sectoral, and local levels, both bilaterally and multilaterally. At the same time, bilateral cooperation mechanisms should convene regularly and alternately in both countries to promptly address any challenges that arise.

Second, in the economic sphere, addressing the persistent trade imbalance must be a top priority. South Korean investments should be increasingly directed toward Vietnam's processing, manufacturing, and high-technology sectors to enhance the sophistication and value of Vietnamese exports. In parallel, South Korea's support for technology transfer initiatives would bolster Vietnam's production capacity and global competitiveness. Expanding market access for Vietnamese goods, particularly agricultural products and processed foods, is another strategic avenue that should be actively pursued.

Third, regarding defence and security cooperation, it is critical for South Korea to expand its support for strengthening Vietnam's maritime law enforcement capabilities. Joint efforts should also prioritize cybersecurity cooperation, given the growing complexity and severity of cyber threats. Regular strategic and defence dialogues at all levels must be maintained to build mutual confidence and identify new areas for collaboration. Furthermore, close coordination within regional frameworks such as ASEAN, alongside enhanced consultations on security challenges in the Asia-Pacific, including the South China Sea and the Korean Peninsula, will contribute significantly to maintaining regional peace and stability.

Finally, to further deepen bilateral relations, Vietnam and South Korea should focus on strengthening cultural and social exchanges in a more balanced manner. South Korea should consider supporting the establishment of Vietnamese cultural centres in South Korea, expanding Vietnamese language education and specialized Vietnam studies programmes, and regularly organizing high-profile Vietnamese cultural events in South Korea. Additionally, enhancing integration support programmes for Vietnamese workers and brides in South Korea is essential to mitigate unnecessary risks. On Vietnam's side, encouraging and facilitating the active participation of non-governmental organisations, universities, businesses, and individual South Koreans in cooperative activities is crucial, alongside maintaining and strengthening good relations with the South Korean government. Moreover, academic cooperation between universities in both countries should become more substantive and in-depth, fostering meaningful exchanges and collaboration.

6. Conclusion

Since the normalization of ties in 1992, and particularly between 2009 and 2024, Vietnam-South Korea relations have demonstrated robust connectivity despite their distinct political systems. A shared history, cultural ties, and aligned development objectives have contributed to significant advancements. Key features include significantly enhanced political trust, broader and deeper cooperation across sectors, and a strengthened foundation of mutual understanding and friendship between the two Peoples.

With a strong historical foundation built on continuous efforts by the Peoples and leaders of both nations and reinforced by the Comprehensive Strategic Partnership framework and the Action Program, Vietnam and South Korea can be optimistic about a future of even deeper and more diverse cooperation. Guided by the motto *cooperate, win together, and grow together*, this partnership will undoubtedly contribute significantly to promoting peace, stability, and shared prosperity in the region and across the world. Furthermore, the special relationship between Vietnam and South Korea, symbolized by the spirit of *good friends, good partners, and good in-laws*, will continue to be maintained and further developed.

Importantly, as the Indo-Pacific emerges as a central geopolitical construct, South Korea's foreign policy frameworks-particularly the NSP and the Indo-Pacific Strategy-have reaffirmed Vietnam's strategic relevance as a pivotal partner in Southeast Asia. In this context, Vietnam-South Korea ties serve not only as a bilateral success story but also as a model of strategic partnership aligned with broader Indo-Pacific dynamics. Reinforcing this alignment will elevate both nations' regional standing and promote a rules-based order.

7. References

Báo điện tử Chính phủ (2011): President Truong Tan Sang's state visit to South Korea was a complete success. https://baochinhphu.vn/chuyen-tham-cap-nha-nuoc-cua-chu-tich-nuoc-truong-tan-sang-toi-han-quoc-da-thanh-cong-tot-dep-102109236.htm.

Báo điện tử Chính phủ (2022): Joint Statement between Vietnam and South Korea on the Comprehensive Strategic Partnership. baochinhphu.vn. https://xaydungchinhsach.chinhphu.vn/toan-van-tuyen-bo-chung-viet-nam-han-quoc-ve-quan-he-doi-tac-chien-luoc-toan-dien-119221206095430676.htm.

Báo điện tử Chính phủ (2023): Action Program for the Implementation of the Comprehensive Strategic Partnership between Vietnam and South Korea. baochinhphu.vn. https://baochinhphu.vn/chuong-trinh-hanh-dong-trien-khai-quan-he-doi-tac-chien-luoc-toan-dien-viet-nam-han-quoc-102230624154446942.htm.

Báo điện tử Chính phủ (2024): Prime Minister Phạm Minh Chính successfully concludes official visit to South Korea. baochinhphu.vn. https://baochinhphu.vn/thu-tuong-pham-minh-chinh-ket-thuc-tot-dep-chuyen-tham-chinh-thuc-han-quoc-102240704085741576.htm.

Báo Quân đội nhân dân (2009): Joint Statement between Vietnam and South Korea on Strategic Cooperative Partnership. In: People's Army Newspaper (October 22, 2009). https://www.qdnd.vn/chinh-tri/tin-tuc/tuyen-bo-chung-viet-nam-han-quoc-ve-viec-thiet-lap-quan-he-doi-tac-hop-tac-chien-luoc-283485.

Chiang, Min-Hua (2020): South Korea's New Southern Policy: Motivations, implementations and implications. EAI Background Brief No. 1525, National University of Singapore. https://research.nus.edu.sg/eai/wp-content/uploads/sites/2/2020/12/EAI BB-No.-1525-South-Koreas-new-southern-policy-2.pdf.

Cổng thông tin điện tử Bộ quốc phòng (2024): The 11th Vietnam-Republic of Korea defence policy dialogue took place in Hanoi. Bqp.vn (April 24, 2024). https://www.mod.gov.vn/en/detail?current=true&urile=wcm:path:/mod/sa-mod-en/sa-en-news/sa-en-news-rela/the-11th-vietnam-republic-of-korea-defence-policy-dialogue-took-place-in-hanoi.

Do, Thi Thu Trang (2023): Vietnam-Korea Education Cooperation (2000–2020). Master's thesis in International Studies, VNU-University of Social Sciences and Humanities).

Doan, Thi Tra Thu (2022): South Korean investment in Vietnam since the two countries established a Comprehensive Strategic Partnership (2009). In: Political Theory Journal. http://lyluanchinhtri.vn/home/index.php/quoc te/item/4486-dau-tu-cua-han-quoc-vao-viet-nam-tu-khi-hai-nuoc-thiet-lap-quan-he-doi-tac-chien-luoc toan-dien-2009.html.

Hoang, Manh Dung (2024): 30 Years of Vietnam-South Korea Trade Relations and the Feasibility of the Target to Increase Bilateral Trade Turnover to USD 100 Billion. In: Journal of Economics and Forecasting (October 30, 2024). https://kinhtevadubao.vn/30-nam-quan-he-thuong-mai-viet-nam-han-quoc-va-tinh-kha-thi-cua-muc-tieu-nang-kim-ngach-thuong-mai-song-phuong-len-100-ty-usd-30226.html.

Huynh, Tam Sang (2023): What to expect from the Vietnam-South Korea comprehensive strategic partnership. Yusof Ishak Institute. https://www.iseas.edu.sg/articles-commentaries/iseas-perspective/2023-4-what-to-expect-from-the-vietnam-south-korea-comprehensive-strategic-partnership-by-huynh-tam-sang/.

Khanh Van, Truong Giang (2024): Promoting Vietnamese tourism in South Korea through The Magnificent Vietnam event. VietnamPlus (April 18, 2024). https://www.vietnamplus.vn/quang-ba-du-lich-viet-nam-tai-han-quoc-qua-su-kien-the-magnificent-vietnam-post940909.vnp.

Khong Hà (2023): Strengthening Vietnam-South Korea relations to a new stage. In: Public Security News (April 7, 2023). https://cand.com.vn/su-kien-binh-luan-thoi-su/dua-quan-he-viet-nam-han-quoc-len-tam-cao-moi-i689288/.

Kim, Hyun-jae (2018): Milestone for South Korea-Vietnam relations. The Korea Times. https://www.koreatimes.co.kr/www/opinion/2025/02/137_256017.html.

Kim, Sea Young (Sarah) (2021): How South Korea Can Upgrade its Strategic Partnership with Vietnam. https://keia.org/the-peninsula/how-south-korea-can-upgrade-its-strategic-partnership-with-vietnam/.

Korea Joongang Daily (2022): Vietnam, Korea shelve the past for a closer future. https://koreajoongangdaily.joins.com/2022/10/24/national/diplomacy/korea-vietnam-trade/20221024170720933.html.

Langel, Tunchinmang (2022): Outlook on South Korea and Vietnam's progression towards a Comprehensive Strategic Partnership. In: Indian Council of World Affairs, 1–10. https://www.researchgate.net/publication/366987679_Outlook_on_South_Korea_and_Vietnam's_progression_towards_a_Comprehensive_Strategic_Partnership.

Le Mau Lam (2022): Vietnam-South Korea Relations: 30 Years in Review and Development Orientation in the New Context. Nhan Dan Online (November 21, 2022). https://nhandan.vn/quan-he-viet-nam-han-quoc-30-nam-nhin-lai-va-dinh-huong-phat-trien-trong-boi-canh-moi-post726067.html.

Lee, Han Woo (2020): Road to normalization between South Korea and Vietnam: Factors and policy-making process. In: VNU Journal of Social Sciences and Humanities, 6(2), 160–180.

Mai, Thi Dinh (2023): Vietnam-South Korea Comprehensive Strategic Partnership and Future Orientations. In: Communist Review Online (June 15, 2023). https://tapchicongsan.org.vn/tin-binh-luan/-/asset_publisher/DLIYi5AJyFzY/content/quan-he-doi-tac-hop-tac-chien-luoc-toan-dien-viet-nam-han-quoc-va-nhung-dinh-huong-trong-tuong-lai.

Ministry of Foreign Affairs (MOFA) (2023): Action Program for Implementing the Vietnam-South Korea Comprehensive Strategic Partnership. https://baochinhphu.vn/chuong-trinh-hanh-dong-trien-khai-quan-he-doi-tac-chien-luoc-toan-dien-viet-nam-han-quoc-102230624154446942.htm.

MOFA (2025): Basic Information on the Republic of Korea and Vietnam-South Korea Relations. https://mofa.gov.vn/vi/cn_vakv/ca_tbd/nr040818112237/ns070621160315.

Nguyen, Duy Loi (2022): Vietnam-South Korea trade and investment cooperation: 30-year milestone and orientation. Vietnam Social Sciences, 5(211), 45–64. http://admin.tapchikhxh.vass.gov.vn/upload/pdf/2022/11/23/6.-nguyen-duy-loi_1.11_23112022222311.pdf.

Nguyen, Hoang Tien/Dinh, Ba Hung Anh (2019): Friendly and partnership-based relationship between Vietnam and South Korea: The nature, current development, and future prospect. In: International Journal of Research in Finance and Management, 2(1), 30–36.

Nguyen, Minh Trang (2021): Vietnam-South Korea strategic partnership in economic (2009–2020). Doctoral thesis, majoring in International Relations, VNU-University of Social Sciences and Humanities.

Nguyen, Thi Huyen Trang (2022): Vietnam-South Korea education and training cooperation: looking back 30 years. In: TNU Journal of Science and Technology, 227(09), 210–218. https://jst.tnu.edu.vn/jst/article/view/5778/pdf.

Nguyen, Thuy Giang (2020): The formation of the Korean community in Hanoi. In: Journal of Social Sciences and Humanities, 6(1), 109–125.

Pham, Thuy Trang (2024): Vietnam-South Korea political and diplomatic relations (2009 - 2022). In: TNU Journal of Science and Technology, 229 (11), 333–340.

Phan, Thanh Hoan/Jeong, Ji Young (2012): An analysis of Korea-Vietnam bilateral trade relations. MPRA Paper No. 48312. https://mpra.ub.uni-muenchen.de/48312/1/MPRA_paper_48312.pdf.

Phan, Thanh Hoan/Jeong, Ji Young (2016): Potential Economic Impacts of the Vietnam-Korea Free Trade Agreement on Vietnam. In: Journal of East Asian Economic Integration Vol. 20, No. 1 (March 2016), 67–90. https://koreascience.kr/article/JAKO201614138121983.pdf.

Phan, Thi Anh Thu (2023): Vietnam-South Korea diplomatic relations under President Moon Jae-in. In: Northeast Asian Studies] 4(266), 3–12.

Thanh Giang (2024): Initiatives to promote, stimulate, and draw Korean tourists to Vietnam. VietnamPlus (June 23, 2024). https://www.vietnamplus.vn/quang-ba-xuc-tien-thu-hut-khach-du-lich-han-quoc-toi-viet-nam-post960620.vnp.

Thanh Thanh (2023): Vietnam cautious over trade deficit rise with South Korea. In: Vietnam Investment Review (June 7, 2023). https://vir.com.vn/vietnam-cautious-over-trade-deficit-rise-with-south-korea-102406.html.

Thanh Tu (2018): Vietnam-South Korea Strategic Cooperative Partnership – 25 Years of Development. In: Communist Review Online (December 2, 2018). https://tapchicongsan.org.vn/quoc-phong-an-ninh-oi-ngoail/-/2018/53343/quan-he-doi-tac-hop-tac-chien-luoc-viet-nam---han-quoc---25-nam-phat-trien.aspx.

The Saigon Times (2023): Vietnam has huge trade deficit with South Korea (January 5, 2023). https://english.thesaigontimes.vn/vietnam-has-huge-trade-deficit-with-south-korea/.

The Strait Times (2024): South Korea's international student population jumps tenfold in 2 decades. straitstimes.com (October 30, 2024). https://www.straitstimes.com/asia/east-asia/south-korea-s-international-student-population-jumps-10-fold-in-2-decades.

Thu Phuong (2024): Opens a new chapter in relations between Vietnam and South Korea. Vietnamplus.vn (March 12, 2022). https://www.vietnamplus.vn/mo-ra-giai-doan-moi-trong-quan-he-giua-viet-nam-va-han-quoc-post833779.vnp.

Tran Toan Thang (et al.) (2016): Regional Inter-Dependence and Vietnam-Korea Economic Relationship (December 30, 2016). In: KIEP Research Paper, Studies in Comprehensive Regional Strategies 16–10. https://ssrn.com/abstract=2953860.

Truong, Thu Ha (2023): Strengthening economic ties: The impact and potential of South Korean FDI in Vietnam. In: The EUrASEANs: Journal on Global Socio-Economic Dynamics, 4(41), 41–49.

Vaibhav, Saxena/Nguyen, Quang Anh (2024): Vietnam-South Korea: Expanding relations and opportunities with key partners. https://chambers.com/articles/vietnam-south-korea-expanding-relations-and-opportunities-with-key-partners.

Voice of Vietnam (VOV) (2024): PM Chinh's visit to RoK achieve great success: FM. Vov.vn (July 4, 2024). https://english.vov.vn/en/politics/pm-chinhs-visit-to-rok-achieve-grea-success-fm-post1105717.vov.

Vu, Khoan (2017): Vietnam-South Korea: From former foes to strategic partners. Tuoi Tre Newspaper Online (December 22, 2017). https://tuoitre.vn/viet-nam-han-quoc-tu-cuu-thu-thanh-doi-tac-chien-luoc-20171222101703533.htm.

Vu, Tuyet Loan (2007): 15 Years of the Vietnam-South Korea Comprehensive Partnership. In: Communist Review. https://tapchicongsan.org.vn/hoat-ong-cua-lanh-ao-ang-nha-nuoc/-/2018/10731/15-nam-quan-he-doi-tac-toan-dien-viet-nam---han-quoc.aspx.

Youn, Dae-Yeong/Nguyen, Van Kim/Nguyen, Manh Dung (2014): History of Vietnam-South Korea relations (1862–1945). Labor Publishing House, Hanoi.

Chapter 17: China's Strategy in the Indo-Pacific Region

Hoang Hue Anh and Pham Thao Nguyen

The global geopolitical centre of gravity is shifting from Europe to the Indo-Pacific region, where an intense strategic rivalry is unfolding between the United States and China. This article examines China's approach to the Indo-Pacific within the context of geopolitical competition, identifying the country's regional ambitions, strategic challenges, and opportunities. China's strategy is focused on establishing a China-centric regional order, expanding its influence through the Belt and Road Initiative, and forging economic and security links. The country is pursuing energy security via economic corridors such as the China-Myanmar Economic Corridor and the China-Pakistan Economic Corridor, while asserting maritime control in the South and East China Seas. Furthermore, China utilises discursive power to shape regional norms, reinforce its international status, and counter the United States' Indo-Pacific strategy by undermining Washington's alliance or exploiting its strategic vulnerabilities. However, China is facing significant challenges from the strategic responses of the United States and its allies, as well as serious domestic issues that may constrain its regional ambitions.

1. Introduction

> "The Indo-Pacific will be... the epicenter of 21st century geopolitics." The U.S. National Security Strategy 2022 (The White House 2022)

The global geostrategic centre of gravity is shifting from Europe to the Indo-Pacific region. Indeed, for a region to become the geopolitical centre of the world, it must meet two conditions:

- *First*, it must comprise one or more of the world's most influential powers.
- *Second*, it must be the region of the most intense competition for influence among major powers.

China is rising rapidly, whereas the European powers are in decline to such an extent that their global influence has been surpassed by several Asian nations. The combined GDP of Russia and the European Union is now less than that of ASEAN and China combined. Military expenditure among major powers in Europe and Asia paints a similar picture. Moreover, no European country currently possesses the potential to emerge as a superpower capable of challenging the future global order in the manner that China does. With the rise of the United States' strategic rival, China, and an increasingly prosperous Indo-Pacific region, the Indo-Pacific is poised to become the primary theatre of fierce competition for influence between the United States and China. The two superpowers will engage in intense rivalry across economic, technological, and military domains in the region. Furthermore, the global geopolitical centre was historically a focal point of ideological competition. The ongoing competition is further accelerating the shift of the global geopolitical centre from the West to the East. This chapter will explore issues relating to China's strategy towards the Indo-Pacific region.

2. Strategic Vision

Firstly, regarding the use of terminology, China adopts the concept of the *Asia-Pacific*, deliberately avoiding the term *Indo-Pacific* to boost legitimacy, promote the country's value system, and safeguard their central role in the region. Geographically, the term *Asia-Pacific* refers to the part of Asia located along the Pacific Ocean, comprising three main subregions: Northeast Asia, Southeast Asia, and Oceania (specifically the southwestern Pacific). The term *Indo-Pacific* is understood in broader terms as a connected space spanning the Indian and Pacific Oceans, stretching from the eastern coast of Africa to the western coast of the United States (Das 2019).

To date, no official Chinese document has employed the term *Indo-Pacific* (Kai/Li 2020). For instance, in China's Defence White Paper released in July 2019, the term "Asia-Pacific" was repeated ten times, while *Indo-Pacific* was entirely absent (Lu 2019). This is similarly reflected in the official speeches of the Chinese Government both domestically and internationally, as well as in the country's academic research. China's deliberate avoidance of the *Indo-Pacific* concept reflects its cautious and critical stance towards the United States' Indo-Pacific Strategy (IPS). From the Chinese perspective, this term is associated with a US-led strategy intended to contain China's rise (Feng 2020). The concept of the Indo-Pacific, openly supported by the United States, Japan, Australia, and India, poses a threat to China's interests in the region. The Indo-Pacific notion highlights a significant geopolitical vacuum that is increasingly being filled by the Quad countries, particularly India, Japan, and Australia (Sarkar 2020).

The term used by China also carries deeper discursive implications. Chinese scholars argue that following humanity's entry into the maritime age, the expanding Mediterranean-Atlantic order fostered a global colonial system, drawing the Asia-Pacific region into this storm and relegating it to a peripheral region in the global political economy. It was only after two devastating world wars and the collapse of colonial systems that the region embarked on a process of reconstructing order, exploring and utilising indigenous resources, and reaching a common understanding. As a result, the Asia-Pacific has emerged as a centre of wealth and power in the contemporary world, with openness and freedom becoming the new trends in regionalism (Sun 2022).

However, closely associated with the *Indo-Pacific* concept is the Indo-Pacific Strategy, which marks the return of the Mediterranean–Atlantic order in the Asia-Pacific region, the revival of Cold War mindset, and a zero-sum game mentality, thereby drawing the region once again into the trap of geopolitical conflict. In short, China asserts that the Asia-Pacific order represents a natural developmental process, arising from the region's intrinsic needs. By contrast, the Indo-Pacific order seeks not only to *erase* the region's established identity and dismantle the existing and effective structures of regional cooperation, but also to undermine the achievements in peace and development that regional countries have built over several decades, with the ultimate aim of reimposing an Atlantic order upon the Asia-Pacific (Sun 2022). Sarkar (2020) argues that the Asia-Pacific is a long-standing regional concept promoted by China, which reflects the country's leading position in the region. It embodies the strengths of Asian economic multilateralism, aligns with China's strategic vision and priorities, and supports the country's economic rise. In response to the United States' launch of the *Indo-Pacific Economic Framework* in Japan in 2022, China declared that it would unwaveringly promote open regionalism and cooperation with trade partners in the Asia-Pacific to pursue a shared future (China Daily 2022). Thus, the term *Asia-Pacific* has become an effective discursive instrument for China, serving to bolster its legitimacy, secure its long-term strategic interests and central role in the region.

3. Strategic Objectives

Promoting the regional vision based on Chinese national identity

Beijing's approach to the Indo-Pacific is closely intertwined with its identity and historical experience in the region. According to Ogden and Jones (2023), China's perspective is highly distinctive and shapes its regional strategy. China seeks to develop an approach highlighting shared values among Asian civilisations, while reflecting traditional elements of Chinese culture such as *harmony* and *tolerance*. This viewpoint was articulated by President Xi Jinping in 2014, when he emphasised the concept of "Asian collective security" (He 2018, 121). In elaborating this concept, Xi stressed that security must be inclusive – contrasting sharply with the exclusive security frameworks of the West – and should be based on *Asian values*, which serve as a counterargument to the values underpinning Western democracy. This line of argument resonates with traditional Chinese perspectives on global and regional order. For instance, the Belt and Road Initiative (BRI) represents a comprehensive and inclusive approach to membership, welcoming all states, international organisations, and regional bodies wishing to join this grand project (Xinhua 2017a). As of February 2025, 149 countries signed up to the BRI (Green Finance & Development Centre 2025). Demir (2022) describes the BRI as a typical example of *inclusive regionalism*. China's regional vision also asserts that Asian countries should act collectively in pursuit of common interests, with China having a central role as a benevolent leader (Ogden/Jones 2023).

Establishing a China-centric regional order

China's aspiration to assume a leading role in the region stems from its historical status and strategic interests. Historically, China was the dominant regional power for millennia, and the Chinese view this status as a natural order, akin to the *Mandate of Heaven*, linking it to a moral mission. The country's remarkable economic rise following more than four decades of reform and opening up has strengthened its international status and fuelled a renewed nationalism, thereby reviving a vision closely associated with China's historic identity as the *Middle Kingdom*. This has reignited China's ambition to reclaim its rightful place on the global stage, with the first step being the establishment of its position as a regional great power.

To enhance its influence within the region, China seeks cooperative relationships and formal recognition from other states. China's status and the recognition of that status lie at the heart of a China-centric regional order and shape Beijing's worldview regarding the contemporary Indo-Pacific. From Beijing's perspective, if other states acknowledge and respect China's power and centrality, the region will reap economic rewards through win-win bilateral relationships or through formal multilateral platforms such as the Asian Infrastructure Investment Bank (AIIB) or the Belt and Road Initiative (BRI) (Ogden/Jones 2023).

China's engagement in regional infrastructure projects may be seen as a critical connectivity strategy aimed at building key relationships and networks to bolster its influence. While it is undeniable that China's strategy has enhanced regional connectivity, it has also reinforced China's central role in infrastructure development in ways that create asymmetric dependencies (Loke/Gou 2025).

Striving to transform from a continental power into a two-ocean and continental superpower

After centuries of primarily seeing itself as a continental power, recent Chinese policy statements have clearly articulated Beijing's ambition to become a maritime power. The 2013 Defence White Paper set out a "strategy to exploit, utilise and protect the seas and oceans, and build China into a maritime power" (Ministry of Defence of China 2013). The Military Strategy White Paper 2015 further asserted that "the traditional mentality that land outweighs sea must be abandoned" and greater emphasis should be placed on "managing the seas and oceans," with the objective of building China "into a maritime power" (The State Council Information Office of China 2015). This maritime ambition has been directed from the highest level (Scott 2019). In 2013, President Xi Jinping emphasised the need to "strategically manage the seas" and to intensify efforts towards transforming China into a maritime great power (Martison 2015). In 2017, Xi further stressed that

> "a strong navy... is a pivot for building the nation into a great maritime power." (Xinhua 2017b)

Medcalf (2019) argues that the Maritime Silk Road (MSR) essentially represents a two-ocean strategy – or an Indo-Pacific strategy with Chinese characteristics – connecting economic, security, and diplomatic efforts from China's western Pacific coastline across the sea lanes of Southeast Asia to the Indian Ocean, Africa, and the Persian Gulf. China seeks to increase control over the South China Sea and the East China Sea to expand its presence across the western Pacific and the Indian Ocean (Scott 2019), striving to become a two-ocean superpower.

The maritime domain is increasingly playing a central role in China's grand strategy, partly due to the painful lessons from its *century of humiliation* and Zheng He's lingering regrets. Zheng He's maritime expeditions during the fourteenth century traversed the Indian Ocean as far as the southern coast of Africa. His flagship, measuring over 90 metres in length and 45 metres in width, remains the largest wooden ship known to have been built. Zheng He's largest expedition mobilised 317 ships - an astonishing number even by today's standards - whereas Columbus's second expedition (1493-1496) consisted of 17 ships, and the largest of which was less than half the size of Admiral Zheng He's flagship. However, under the conservative policies of the Ming dynasty, China abandoned its maritime ambitions, failing to evolve into a maritime power. And that was one of the main reasons why the country gradually fell behind Western powers in the following decades, ultimately suffering the *century of humiliation*. Thus, China's contemporary grand strategy of becoming a maritime power can be seen as an effort to rectify this profound historical regret.

Pursuing the rejuvenation of the Chinese nation

China's current grand strategy is built upon the premise of a strategic environment in which the country faces a *once-in-a-century strategic opportunity* to achieve national development goals. At the 19th National Congress of the Chinese Communist Party, President Xi Jinping expressed the ambition of transforming China into a "great modern socialist country" that is "prosperous, strong, democratic, culturally advanced, harmonious and beautiful" (Xinhua 2017c). Diplomatically, China's aim is to position itself at the centre of the global stage, ultimately establishing itself as a global superpower. This ambition is encapsulated in the *Chinese Dream of national rejuvenation*. The country's Indo-Pacific strategy is fundamentally designed to serve its ultimate objective of realising the Chinese Dream.

4. Strategic Content

Economic connectivity

China's connectivity strategy has become a fundamental pillar of Xi Jinping's foreign policy, reflecting a strategic effort to enhance the country's influence, reshape global interactions, and redefine interdependencies worldwide. China views its wealth and influence as being intrinsically linked to its role as a regional connector. Leveraging its comparative advantage in infrastructure, China uses this connectivity strategy to rally diverse nations around shared development goals. Since the birth of the BRI, Chinese leaders have emphasized the critical role of infrastructure connectivity in regional development. Xi Jinping described the BRI as the "wings" of regional growth, with "connectivity" serving as a vital lifeline and infrastructure as its essential "skeleton" (Loke/Gou 2025). China's growing ambitions into the Indo-Pacific has evolved from merely securing maritime oil transportation routes to undertaking large-scale infrastructure projects along the Maritime Silk Road. According to Pu (2019), the geo-economic agenda of BRI has the potential to establish a new economic, diplomatic, and security framework under China's leadership.

China's relentless efforts in economic diplomacy have become increasingly pronounced through the BRI since 2013, demonstrating its quick engagement with regional actors across the Indo-Pacific in trade and investment. All countries, both large and small, have welcomed and facilitated Chinese investment. Since the East Asian financial crisis in the late 1990s, China has emerged as the largest trading partner and an increasingly important investor in numerous coastal nations in the Indo-Pacific. Overall, China's expanding trade and investment activities across the Pacific and Indian Ocean coastal regions have transformed the Strait of Malacca from a choke point into a bridge, fostering the prospect of the confluence of the two maritime regions into an Indo-Pacific system (Borah 2022, 131).

Enhancing security

Energy security: addressing the Malacca dilemma through CMEC and CPEC

China is increasingly facing with an urgent issue of *energy security* to sustain the rapid economic development of a country with a population exceeding one billion. Before 1995, China was an oil-exporting country. However, since 1995, an increasingly industrialized and modernized China has become a nation with a growing demand for imported oil and gas. China's largest external energy supply comes from the Middle East, with imported energy flows passing through the Indian Ocean, the Strait of Malacca, and the South China Sea before reaching China. The risk of supply disruption by the Indian and the US Navy is commonly referred to as the *Malacca Dilemma*. This has spurred China's urgent need to ensure the security of its energy transportation routes (Scott 2019). To mitigate the risks associated with a potential maritime blockade at the Strait of Malacca, China has sought to develop two critical alternative routes. The first is the China-Myanmar Energy Corridor (CMEC), centred on oil and gas pipelines running from the deep-water port of Kyaukpyu to Kunming in southwest China. The second is the China-Pakistan Economic Corridor (CPEC), which extends from Gwadar along Pakistani coast, through the Indus Valley and into Xinjiang, connecting the Maritime Silk Road with the Eurasian Land Bridge under the framework of the BRI.

Maritime security: territorial claims in the South China Sea and East China Sea

The 21st century has been heralded as *the century of oceans*, marked by fierce competition among global powers over strategic maritime interests. Consequently, maritime security in the Indo-Pacific has become a *hot* focus of major powers' maritime foreign policies (Nguyen Tuan Binh et al. 2024), with China playing a particularly prominent role. The Indo-Pacific region is now facing a number of maritime security challenges. Numerous disputes – including those in the East China Sea, South China Sea, Indian Ocean, and around the Senkaku/Diaoyu Islands – are considered potential flash-points with the risk of escalating into a Sino-American conflict (Echle et al. 2020, 126). Additionally, piracy and armed robbery at sea have made the Strait of Malacca, the South China Sea, and the Indian Ocean among the most dangerous waters in the world (Nguyen Tuan Binh et al. 2024). China wants to become a *maritime power* to safeguard its energy supply routes across the Indian Ocean, strengthen its Maritime Silk Road initiative, and assert control over disputed territories in the East China Sea and South China Seas. Hence, China's strategy of becoming a maritime power is deeply intertwined with maritime security, especially concerning disputed islands and its maritime trade and energy transport routes (Liu 2016).

Security agreements: security pact with the Solomon Islands

In 2022, the Pacific Islands region came under the spotlight when China proposed security agreements with several Pacific Island nations. China's growing interest in the Pacific was clearly demonstrated through the signing of a security pact with the Solomon Islands in April 2022. This agreement enabled China to expand its maritime strategic presence in the Pacific, potentially establishing its second overseas military base after Djibouti. The pact significantly enhanced China's hard power, encompassing both economic and military dimensions in the region, while also yielding soft power benefits by facilitating similar agreements with other Pacific Island countries. According to Hammond (2023), a key objective for China is to break through the maritime containment posed by the "first and second island chains" to expand its presence in the Indo-Pacific.

Shaping regional rules

Under Xi Jinping's leadership, Beijing has intensified its efforts to develop normative and discursive power aiming at *telling China's story well*, further promoting its central role, and shaping the regional rules. China's remarkable economic rise has propelled it to the forefront of international narratives, including those concerning geopolitical discourse on the Indo-Pacific. China's growing capability to influence the international system has driven a measured yet assertive engagement with regional developments across the Indo-Pacific and with other regional actors. Under the Xi administration, China introduced a vision of a *Community of Shared Future*, encompassing bilateral, regional, and global dimensions. To realise this vision, China has recently promoted several global initiatives – the Global Development Initiative, the Global Security Initiative, the Global Civilisation Initiative, and the BRI. These initiatives encompass every aspect of international cooperation at both regional and global levels. Cooperation activities under these initiatives are largely led by China, reflecting Chinese values and supporting its national interests. At the same time, the Regional Comprehensive Economic Partnership (RCEP) represents the region's largest multilateral economic arrangement, connecting the economies of 15 Indo-Pacific countries and accounting for over 30 per cent of global GDP

(Singh/Marwah 2023). Notably, the United States is not a party to RCEP, and that underscores China's leading role in setting the regional rules.

China is also intensifying the use of discursive tools to distinguish between the objectives and prospects of the FOIP and the BRI. Beijing argues that FOIP is fully security-oriented, framing it as a strategy that could revive Cold War dynamics. Commenting on the US strategy, Chinese Foreign Ministry Spokesperson Wang Wenbin stated:

> "This strategy that resurrects the Cold War mentality and bloc politics has nothing new and no future but will only bring division and turbulence to the Asia-Pacific." (Ministry of Foreign Affairs of China 2022)

Meanwhile, China declared its wholehearted commitment to advancing the Belt and Road Initiative (BRI), with progress and development as its foundational principles (Debnath 2024). Although China is an external power to the Indian Ocean Region, it is increasingly seeking deeper engagement with the Indian Ocean Rim Association (IORA), currently holding the status of an observer. Since 2022, China has initiated the China–Indian Ocean Region Forum, thereby establishing a new platform for regional dialogue. The forum is also part of China's broader ambition to become a maritime power, serving as a mechanism through which Beijing can advance its global initiatives.

Building a maritime power: a multi-layered strategy

The maritime domain has increasingly played a central role in China's grand strategy. After centuries of primarily viewing itself as a continental power, China today aspires to become a two-ocean and continental power. To achieve this, China is pursuing a *multi-layered approach*. The first layer focuses on defending its *near seas* – the Yellow Sea, East China Sea, and South China Sea. More recently, China has extended its strategic perimeter by incorporating the defence of the *far seas*, intended to enhance its capability to actively secure the near seas. According to China's Military Strategy White Paper 2015, the People's Liberation Army Navy (PLAN)

> "Will gradually shift its focus from offshore waters defence to the combination of offshore waters defence with open seas protection." (The State Council Information Office of China 2015)

To implement this strategy, China is enhancing its capability to deploy military forces in support of long-range operations, including military infrastructure and dual-use facilities around the Indian Ocean rim. Beijing's goal is to establish an

> "Arc-shaped strategic zone that covers the Western Pacific Ocean and Northern Indian Ocean." (Erickson 2017, 110)

To fulfil these strategic ambitions, China is building both the capabilities and infrastructure necessary for deploying naval forces in the *far seas* – the waters of the Western Pacific and Indian Ocean. China's expanding overseas interests are fuelling ambitions beyond its territorial waters and disputed maritime zones, particularly in these *far seas* beyond the Yellow Sea, East China Sea, and South China Seas. Chinese maritime operations in distant waters now include regular anti-piracy missions off the Horn of Africa, surface and submarine patrols in the Indian Ocean, and deployments to the Mediterranean, North Sea, and Arctic (Cooper/Shearer 2017).

China also plans to develop a *blue-water navy*, which constitutes a key component of the PLA modernisation programme. A blue-water navy refers to forces capable of operating across oceans (Scott 2019). China envisions

> "That the Chinese navy must grow into a blue-water navy" because "China is growing into a global power and should have a navy that fits its status." (Li 2013)

Therefore, China's maritime policy is based on the goal of developing a blue-water navy capable of maintaining its presence in the *island chains* of the Pacific and expanding into a *two-ocean* naval force with operational reach not only in the Pacific but also in the Indian Ocean (You 2016). This objective has been included in the PLA's Science of Military Strategy 2013, which articulated the vision of China's strategic area encompassing the Western Pacific and Northern Indian Ocean (Erickson 2016).

Fully aware that it currently lacks military capabilities to win a major conventional war at an acceptable cost, China is employing a sub-threshold approach avoiding triggering a conventional warfare: In its near seas, China is employing strategies to alter the status quo while avoiding large-scale conventional conflict, almost always keeping its actions below the threshold of outright warfare (Cooper/Shearer 2017). China is placing greater emphasis on ambiguity, asymmetric capabilities, and incremental tactics to change the status quo without resorting to a direct war. Specifically, China is employing grey zone conflict tactics to alter regional realities without provoking large-scale conventional conflict (Cooper/Shearer 2017).

China's countermeasures to the United States' Indo-Pacific Strategy

In the Indo-Pacific, China's primary concerns centre on the US-led alliance network and its associated activities, such as joint military exercises, forward deployments, joint patrols, key security partnerships, and initiatives like the Quad. Beijing believes that the United States has been increasingly committed to containing China's rise by reinforcing alliances, value-based minilateral arrangements, and the so-called "NATOisation of the Indo-Pacific" (Loke/Gou 2025). Within the Chinese academic circles and policy-making communities, three main approaches to the US-Indo-Pacific Strategy (IPS) have emerged.

The first approach views the IPS as a robust security alliance, asserting that it poses a serious security threat to China (Han 2022). The Biden administration's emphasis on multilateralism and institutionalisation is seen in its efforts to encourage allies to play a more proactive role, enhance economic cooperation and non-traditional security engagement, counter China's regional economic strategy, and promote a shared *democratic identity* to strengthen Washington's alliance system in the Indo-Pacific. Chinese analysts argue that while China cannot fully engage in hard balancing against the United States, limited hard balancing strategies may help secure its core national interests. The proposed measure includes implementing a limited hard balancing strategy, reinforcing internal balancing efforts, and pursuing external balancing, particularly through strategic partnerships with Russia (Han 2022).

The second approach does not interpret the IPS as a "NATO in Asia" but rather as an "alliance network", centred around a US-led hub-and-spoke system in Asia (Han 2022). This network is less institutionalised than a formal alliance like NATO, and the strength of the ties within this type of alliance is generally weaker. Middle and smaller powers of the network retain considerable policy autonomy and are incentivised to pursue their own national interests. Such characteristics allow China to adopt soft strategies, such as soft balancing and division (separating weak links), to counter threats from this alliance network. Under this approach, Beijing has gradually shifted from an assertive posture to a more conciliatory and adaptive stance towards the Indo-Pacific concept (Debnath 2024). While consistently advocating the discourse of *Asia-Pacific* regionalism, China has become more open to Indo-Pacific visions, particularly inclusive ones that are not overtly designed to counter China. Moreover, China employs various measures to reassure neighbouring countries concerned about its rising power by promoting narratives of a peaceful, benevolent China, in contrast to a United States that favours military force and arms race.

The third approach argues that the IPS has inherent weaknesses and is destined to fail (Han 2022). According to this approach, the IPS represents an instance of US *imperial overstretch*, as it seeks to coordinate the foreign policies of nations within a vast geographic region that exhibits significant differences in domestic institutions, culture, religion, and levels of development. Such a complex project is deemed unfeasible given the perceived relative decline of US power and influence in the region. Therefore, China's strategy only needs focus on what the country is already doing – namely, adhering to strategic focus and pursuing long-term national objectives. Key measures include maintaining the sustainability of its political system, enhancing Party leadership, deepening reforms, and realising the vision of Chinese-style modernisation.

4. Opportunities and Challenges

China's Indo-Pacific strategy clearly presents opportunities for both China itself and other regional countries.

Liu (2019) argues that the MSR is increasing China's geostrategic influence in the Indo-Pacific and has the potential to reshape the global economic model. As part of the Belt and Road Initiative (BRI), the MSR is defined as a grand plan for trade and infrastructure development along maritime routes, connecting China through Southeast Asia, South Asia, the Middle East, Africa, and Europe. Through new efforts to facilitate trade and infrastructure cooperation, the MSR can further tighten bilateral ties between China and relevant countries while also establishing additional regional cooperation networks. This initiative will enable China to expand its influence and cooperation with its partners. From an economic perspective, all infrastructure projects not only generate future business activities but also contribute to China's broader strategic ambitions. Currently, China is emerging as a new driving force behind globalisation, regionalisation, and free trade through the MSR, bringing shared prosperity to the Indo-Pacific.

To successfully implement its soft balancing strategy in the Indo-Pacific, China needs to continue providing public goods, such as investment, trade, and regional stability, particularly for countries reluctant to align with the United States to contain China. Therefore, state-led economic initiatives, including the BRI, play a critical role in Beijing's response to the Indo-Pacific Strategy. Public goods such as vaccines, cybersecurity, critical and emerging technologies (CET), and guidelines for the long-term sustainability of outer space activities – delivered through the BRI – are becoming increasingly vital to the economic needs of regional countries. China's provision of such public goods can, in turn, enhance its influence as a responsible power in the region, promote economic interests, and realise its regional and global initiatives. Nonetheless, China also faces significant challenges in implementing its Indo-Pacific strategy.

China's expanding presence across the Indo-Pacific to safeguard its interests has raised concerns among regional powers. This move has triggered balancing act against Beijing. At the end of 2016 and 2017, Japan and the United States respectively called for a *Free and Open Indo-Pacific* (FOIP), followed by France's 2018 proposal for an *Indo-Pacific axis* (l'axe Indo-Pacifique), comprised of regional "democracies" concerned about China's growing influence (Scott 2019). These developments reflect the dynamics of a security dilemma, wherein China's growing presence in the Indo-Pacific prompts other regional actors to cooperate in counterbalancing Beijing. Major powers have proposed a series of alternative infrastructure initiatives: the Indo-Pacific Strategy has strengthened cooperation on economic and non-traditional security issues to counter China's strategy in the region; the US-backed Blue Dot Network; Quad Infrastructure Coordination Group and initiatives such as the Quad Semiconductor Supply Chain Initiative aimed to undermine China's regional leadership.

China's MSR has also lost some of its initial appeal, with clear signs of disillusionment emerging in various parts of the Indo-Pacific, where debt burdens have worsened. Countries including Cambodia, Sri Lanka, Pakistan, the Maldives, and Djibouti have been facing debt levels ranging from significant to high risk (Chen 2018; Hurley et al. 2018). Many BRI projects have been implemented rapidly in recent years, often lacking strategic focus, which has placed China in financial difficulties. After a decade, the Chinese Government has acknowledged these issues and adjusted the nature of BRI projects to make them *small and beautiful*, but the effectiveness of their implementation remains to be seen. In particular, China's overseas economic projects are now being carried out in an increasingly challenging geopolitical environment, facing security risks from both external and domestic conditions, slowing growth rate, demographic crisis, local government debt issues, and real estate crisis – all of which create structural challenges that China cannot easily resolve in the short term.

5. Conclusion

China's Indo-Pacific strategy represents a significant shift in the country's geostrategic thinking and conduct, underpinned by an ambition to establish a China-centric regional order. Through the implementation of initiatives such as the BRI, China has not only expanded its economic influence but also gradually developed networks of partnerships, institutions, and norms to promote its leadership role in the region. Nevertheless, this strategy has encountered substantial challenges, most notably the strategic responses of the United States and its allies, which have triggered concerns and balancing act of regional actors. The contradiction of China's approach is evident in its simultaneous pursuit of open cooperation and assertive defence of core interests, particularly in the domain of maritime security. China is currently capitalising on institutional and connectivity gaps in the Indo-Pacific, yet faces risks related to ambiguities in its regional strategic messaging. In the current turbulent geopolitical landscape, China's Indo-Pacific strategy is both a manifestation of a rising power and a major test of its ability to shape a stable, harmonious, and sustainable regional order.

6. References

Binh, N. T. (et al.) (2024): The strategic adjustments of China, India, and the US in the Indo-Pacific geopolitical context. In: Journal of Liberty and International Affairs, 10(1), 173–191.

Borah, R. (2022): The strategic relations between India, the United States and Japan in the Indo-Pacific. World Scientific.

CCTV News (2023, October 19): High-quality joint construction of the Belt and Road, Xi Jinping promotes the construction of this three-dimensional network. CCTV News. https://news.cctv.com/2023/10/19/ARTIvtlMk6CypcYRizqWS8oc231019.shtml.

Chen, W. (2018, April 19): BRI Fruitful but debt risk an issue. China Daily. https://www.chinadaily.com.cn/a/201804/19/WS5ad8293da3105cdcf6519467.html.

China Daily (2022, May 31): China all for 'open' regional pacts to spur prosperity. https://en.ndrc.gov.cn/netcoo/goingout/202205/t20220531_1326689.html.

Cooper, Z./Shearer, A. (2017): Thinking clearly about China's layered Indo-Pacific strategy. In: Bulletin of the Atomic Scientists. https://doi.org/10.1080/00963402.2017.1364005.

Das, U. (2019, July 13): What is the Indo-Pacific? The Diplomat. https://thediplomat.com/2019/07/what-is-the-indo-pacific/.

Debnath, B. (2024): From assertion to accommodation? Explaining China's evolving response to the Indo-Pacific strategy. In: Journal of Polity and Society, 16(1). https://journalspoliticalscience.com/index.php/i/article/view/269.

Demir, E. (2020): Competing regional visions: China's Belt and Road Initiative versus the Indo-Pacific Partnership. In: Rossiter, A./Cannon, B. J. (eds.): Conflict and cooperation in the Indo-Pacific. Routledge. 94–114.

Echle, C. (et al.) (2020): Responding to the geopolitics of connectivity: Asian and European perspectives. Konrad-Adenauer-Stiftung.

Erickson, A. S. (2016): China's blueprint for sea power. In: China Brief, 16(11), 5.

Erickson, A. S. (2017): Doctrinal sea change, making real waves: Examining the maritime dimension of strategy. In McReynolds, J. (ed.): China's evolving military strategy. Jamestown Foundation. 101–139.

Feng, L. (2020): The recalibration of Chinese assertiveness: China's responses to the Indo-Pacific challenge. In: International Affairs, 96(1), 9–27. https://doi.org/10.1093/ia/iiz226.

Green Finance & Development Center (2025): Countries of the Belt and Road Initiative (BRI). https://greenfdc.org/countries-of-the-belt-and-road-initiative-bri/.

Han, Z. (2022): China's view and counter-strategies toward the Indo-Pacific strategy. In: AEI Insights, 8(1), 60–74.

Hammond, J. (2023): China's security agreement with the Solomon Islands: Wider implications for geopolitics in the South Pacific. In: Journal of Indo-Pacific Affairs. https://media.defense.gov/2023/Nov/14/2003340194/-1/-1/1/VIEW%20HAMMOND%20-%20JIPA.PDF.

He, B. (2018): Chinese expanded perceptions of the region and its changing attitudes towards the Indo-Pacific: A hybrid vision of the institutionalization of the Indo-Pacific. In: East Asia, 35(2), 117–132. https://doi.org/10.1007/s12140-018-9297-7.

Hurley, J./Morris, S./Portelance, G. (2018): Examining the debt implications of the Belt and Road Initiative (Policy Paper No. 121). Center for Global Development. https://www.cgdev.org/sites/default/files/examining-debt-implications-belt-and-road-initiative-policy-perspective.pdf.

Kai, H./Li, M. J. (2020): Understanding the dynamics of the Indo-Pacific: US–China strategic competition, regional actors, and beyond. In: International Affairs, 96(1), 1–7. https://doi.org/10.1093/ia/iiz242.

Li, X. (2013, August 2): China sails through First Island Chain. China Daily. https://www.chinadaily.com.cn/china/2013-08/02/content_16863833.htm.

Liu, F. K. (2019): Maritime Silk Road Initiative changing geopolitical configuration in the Indo-Pacific. In: Zou, K./Wu, S./Ye, Q. (eds.): The 21st Century Maritime Silk Road: Challenges and opportunities for Asia and Europe. Routledge. 65–77.

Liu, Z. (2016, July 3): India's political goals hinder cooperation with China on Belt, Road. In: Global Times. https://www.globaltimes.cn/content/992047.shtml.

Loke, B./Guo, X. (2025): China's coalition-building in the Indo-Pacific: Strategies of connectivity and association. In: Australian Journal of International Affairs. https://doi.org/10.1080/10357718.2025.2471351.

Lu, H. (2019, July 24): China issues white paper on national defence in new era. Xinhua. http://www.xinhuanet.com/english/2019-07/24/c_138253180.htm.

Martinson, R. (2015): Jinglue Haiyang: The naval implications of Xi Jinping's new strategic concept. In: China Brief, 15(1), 6.

Medcalf, R. (2019): The Indo-Pacific with Chinese characteristics. Politique étrangère (3). https://shs.cairn.info/journal-politique-etrangere-2019-3-page-49?lang=en&tab=texte-integral.

Ministry of Defense of China (2013, April): The diversified employment of China's armed forces (White Paper). http://www.china.org.cn/government/whitepaper/2013-04/16/content_28556911.htm.

Ministry of Foreign Affairs of China (2022, February 14): Foreign Ministry Spokesperson Wang Wenbin's Regular Press Conference on February 14, 2022. https://www.mfa.gov.cn/eng/xw/fyrbt/lxjzh/202405/t20240530_11347223.html.

Ogden, C./Jones, C. (2023): Chinese conceptions of the Indo-Pacific: The impact of identity and history. In: Kratiuk, B. (eds.): Handbook of Indo-Pacific studies. Routledge India. 343–365.

Pu, X. (2019): One mountain, two tigers: China, the United States, and the status dilemma in the Indo-Pacific. In: Asia Policy, 14(3), 25–40.

Sarkar, M. G. (2020): China and Quad 2.0: Between response and regional construct. In: Maritime Affairs, 16(1), 110–130.

Scott, D. (2019): China's Indo-Pacific strategy: The problems of success. In: The Journal of Territorial and Maritime Studies, 6(2), 94–113. https://www.jstor.org/stable/26912752.

Singh, S./Marwah, R. (2023): China's engagement and the Indo-Pacific. In: Singh, S./Marwah, R. (eds.): China and the Indo-Pacific. Palgrave Macmillan. xx–xx.

Sun, X. (2022): Yíntài háishì Yàtài? – Kōngjiān yǎnhuà, dìyuán chóngxǔ yǔ qūyù zhìxù wèilái (Indo-Pacific or Asia-Pacific? – Spatial evolution, geopolitical restructuring and the future of regional order). Yàtài ānquán yǔ hǎiyáng yánjiū [Asia-Pacific Security and Maritime Studies], (2).

The State Council Information Office of China (2015, May): China's military strategy. http://english.gov.cn/archive/white_paper/2015/05/27/content_281475115610833.htm.

The White House (2022): National security strategy. https://bidenwhitehouse.archives.gov/wp-content/uploads/2022/10/Biden-Harris-Administrations-National-Security-Strategy-10.2022.pdf.

Xinhua (2013, July 31): Xi advocates efforts to boost China's maritime power. Xinhua News Agency. http://en.people.cn/90785/8348224.html.

Xinhua (2017a, June 20): Full text of the vision for maritime cooperation under the Belt and Road Initiative. https://english.www.gov.cn/archive/publications/2017/06/20/content_281475691873460.htm.

Xinhua (2017b, May 24): Xi calls for strong, modern navy. http://www.xinhuanet.com//english/2017-05/24/c_136312062.htm.

Xinhua (2017c, October 18): China Focus: Xi unveils plan to make China great modern socialist country by mid-21st century. http://www.xinhuanet.com/english/2017-10/18/c_136688933.htm.

You, J. (2016, July): China's emerging Indo-Pacific naval strategy. In: Asia Policy, 22(July), 11–19.

Chapter 18: Japan's New Plan for a Free and Open Indo-Pacific: Opportunities and Challenges

Nguyen Thu Hang and Nguyen Vo Huyen Dung

In May 2023, Prime Minister Fumio Kishida unveiled Japan's new plan for a Free and Open Indo-Pacific (FOIP), aiming to promote peace, stability, and prosperity in the region. Through launching the four pillars of cooperation for FOIP, this new plan not only signifies Japan's commitment to upholding a rules-based international order but also presents a roadmap for fostering economic integration and security cooperation across the expansive Indo-Pacific region. Drawing on secondary research and analysis of official documents, this article first provides an in-depth analysis of Japan's new plan for a FOIP then examining its opportunities and challenges under Prime Minister Kishida's leadership. In term of opportunities, Japan has the potential to strengthen its strategic partnerships with like-minded countries, such as the United States, Australia, and India, while also enhancing its economic ties with Southeast Asia and other key regions. Moreover, its presence may help to reduce tensions and conflicts in the region, promoting a more stable and predictable environment which indirectly enhances Japan's position in the region. However, the plan also faces significant challenge such as China's influence in the region. Also, the FOIP initiative will require Japan to adapt its traditional approach to diplomacy and international relations, which may be difficult given its often cautious and incremental approach to foreign policy. Moreover, Japan's own economic and military capabilities may be stretched thin by the increasing demands of FOIP implementation. Furthermore, the plan's success will depend on the ability of Japan to build consensus among regional stakeholders, which may be challenging given the diverse interests and priorities of countries in the region. Basing on these findings, some implications of Japan's new plan for regional security and economic dynamics, as well as its potential impact on Japan's relations with key partners and stakeholders will also be explored.

1. Introduction

The Indo-Pacific region has emerged as a crucial geopolitical and economic centre, shaping the global order in the 21st century. Japan's vision for a Free and Open Indo-Pacific (FOIP), was first introduced in 2016 by Prime Minister Abe and further refined in 2023 by Prime Minister Kishida, represents a strategic framework aimed at ensuring stability, prosperity, and the rule of law in this dynamic region. Given the increasing competition among major global powers and the shifting security landscape, analysing Japan's New FOIP plan is essential for understanding the future trajectory of regional cooperation and security. Regarding academic research on Japan's FOIP, some studies have been done which can be summarized as following.

Chhay Lim in the article *Japan's New Plan for a Free and Open Indo-Pacific: What Does It Mean for Southeast Asia?* argues that this New Plan under Kishida's administration is not a newly foreign policy of Japan, it's rather an enhancement of Japan's existing FOIP from the former Prime Minister Abe Shinzo. However, with its four pillars, Japan is expected to lead the Indo-Pacific region basing on a rule-based order. Chhay Lim also discusses that ASEAN still has a vital role for Japan and with its ASEAN Outlook on the Indo-Pacific (AOIP), ASEAN is believed to share some common values with Japan's New FOIP plan, contributing to maintaining the region's prosperity and security. Lim concludes that basing on the current situation and under the impact of Japan's New FOIP plan, Japan and ASEAN will further promote their cooperation in many fields which may bring up more opportunities and challenges for both in the coming time (Lim 2023).

Another comprehensive analysis of Japan's FOIP strategy, particularly in the context of China's growing regional dominance has been provided by Smith in *Japan's FOIP and the Challenge of Chinese Influence*. According to the author, Japan's FOIP serves as a counterbalance to China's Belt and Road Initiative (BRI). Smith argues that while Japan's FOIP promotes inclusivity and multilateral cooperation, it also reflects a broader strategic effort to curb China's influence in key geopolitical areas such as the South China Sea and the Indian Ocean. Smith also emphasizes some challenges that Japan may face in fully realizing its FOIP vision due to financial constraints, regional scepticism, and the need for closer coordination with like-minded partners (Smith 2021).

In *Japan's Strategic Interests in the Global South: Indo-Pacific Strategy*, Hisahiro Kondoh also discusses the Japan's New Plan for A Free and Open

Indo-Pacific but from a different perspective when analysing the influence of Japan through its Official Development Assistance (ODA) for countries in the region. After evaluating the effectiveness and limitations of Japanese Aid, Kondoh suggests some implications for Japan regarding its leadership role in setting norms and rules which all countries can benefit from. With more focus on the needs of developing countries, Japan's New FOIP plan, especially in terms of development aid, Japan is expected to proactively contribute to forming a stable and prosperous community while still pursuing its national interests (Kondoh 2024).

M. Green, in the article *Japan's FOIP Strategy: Diplomacy and Regional Influence* explores Japan's FOIP strategy from a diplomatic perspective, analysing how Japan has actively engaged regional and global partners to promote its vision. The article discusses Japan's reliance on multilateral forums, including ASEAN, QUAD, and G7, to reinforce FOIP principles. Green highlights Japan's diplomatic outreach in Southeast Asia, emphasizing how Japan positions itself as a reliable alternative to China's economic influence. The study also examines the role of ODA as a tool for advancing FOIP-related infrastructure and economic connectivity. Green concludes that while Japan has successfully promoted FOIP as a normative framework, its ability to enforce these principles remains limited without stronger military and economic commitments (Green 2020).

Current studies mainly focus on analysing Japan's New FOIP plan which consider Japan's role in the region as well as economic implications, security and strategic alliances. However, there is still limited study on Japan's opportunities and challenges after announcing its New FOIP plan, especially in the context of complex changes in Indo Pacific region. Therefore, in-depth research is necessary for providing a more comprehensive approach towards this issue. By exploring Japan's New FOIP plan, this study aims to provide a comprehensive understanding of how Japan is positioning itself in the Indo-Pacific region amidst evolving geopolitical dynamics. The findings will contribute to the broader discourse on international security, economic cooperation, and diplomatic relations in one of the world's most strategically significant regions.

2. Overview of Japan's New Plan for Free and Open Indo-Pacific

In 2007, Japan's FOIP concept was first introduced in Prime Minister Abe's speech *Confluence of the Two Seas* in the Indian Parliament with the idea of a *broader Asia*. At that time, although this first FOIP vision was announced to promote "democracy, rule of law, freedom and human rights," (Ministry of Foreign Affairs of Japan 2007) it was believed that this vision was mainly driven by the increasing Chinese threat. Therefore, this first FOIP strategy was implicitly designed to counter China's BRI and its assertive policies. Until 2016, during Prime Minister Abe's second administration, Japan's FOIP strategy was officially launched. In this strategy, Abe once again emphasized the confluence of the two oceans (Indian and the Pacific Oceans) and the two continents (Asia and Africa). Three pillars were identified to realize free and open Indo-Pacific including:

- Promotion and establishment of the rule of law, freedom of navigation, and free trade.
- Pursuit of economic prosperity.
- Commitment for peace and stability (Ministry of Foreign Affairs of Japan 2016).

Sixteen years later, on March 20, 2023, Japan's FOIP again dated back to India when during Prime Minister Kishida's visit to this country, in his speech titled *The Future of the Indo-Pacific*, Japan's New Plan for FOIP was announced with important message *Together with India, as an Indispensable Partner*. Four new pillars are set forth which are described *to be suited for the history's turning point*:

- Principles for Peace and Rules for Prosperity.
- Addressing Challenges in an Indo-Pacific Way.
- Multi-layered Connectivity.
- Extending Efforts for Security and Safe Use of the Sea to the Air (Ministry of Foreign Affairs of Japan 2023).

So, what can be seen here is Prime Minister Abe's FOIP strategy and Prime Minister Kishida's New FOIP plan share a common vision but have distinct differences in approach, focus, and execution. In other words, Kishida's New FOIP plan is a policy enhancement of the existing Abe's FOIP strategy. Comparing these two strategies, some key points can be withdrawn as following:

Table 1: Comparison of Abe's FOIP and Kishida's FOIP since 2016

Aspect	**Prime Minister Abe's FOIP (2016–2020)**	**Prime Minister Kishida New FOIP (2023–present)**
Main Objective	Promote a free, open, and rules-based Indo-Pacific	Evolve FOIP into a more inclusive and practical strategy
Key Pillars	Rule of law, freedom of navigation, economic connectivity, security cooperation	Rule of law, connectivity, security, and addressing global challenges (e.g., climate, health)
Geopolitical Emphasis	Countering China's BRI, strengthening ties with QUAD (United States, Japan, India, Australia)	More engagement with Global South, ASEAN centrality, and regional inclusivity

Source: The authors

In short, Prime Minister Abe's FOIP is more strategic and security-driven, focusing on countering China through a strong alliance network while Prime Minister Kishida's New FOIP is more inclusive and development-oriented, aiming to expand Japan's influence beyond security by promoting economic growth, sustainability, and diplomatic engagement with the Global South. Therefore, Abe's FOIP is about setting the foundation and reinforcing Japan's geopolitical positioning while Kishida's New FOIP is about adapting to a more complex global order, emphasizing cooperation, inclusivity, and regional stability rather than direct strategic competition.

3. Opportunities of Japan's New FOIP Plan

Japan's New FOIP plan has been built upon its longstanding commitment to a free, open and rules- based Indo Pacific which emphasizes inclusivity, economic cooperation, and multilateral diplomacy. This shift creates significant opportunities for Japan to strengthen its global position while ensuring long-term regional stability.

First is the opportunity to strengthen strategic partnerships with like-minded countries. One of the core advantages of Japan's New FOIP is its potential to deepen cooperation with nations that share similar values of democracy, free trade, and the rule of law. These partnerships can strengthen Japan's strategic influence and contribute to a more stable Indo-Pacific. In term of US-Japan alliance, Japan's New FOIP obviously quite aligns with the U.S. Indo-Pacific Strategy, thus providing an opportunity to further enhance military coordination through joint exercises, intelligence sharing, and deterrence measures against regional threats like China's maritime assertiveness or North Korea's missile program. Japan's investment in defence technology collaboration such as AUKUS-related projects and advanced military systems also strengthens its role as a key United States ally (U.S. Department of Defense 2024). Moreover, Japan's increase in economic and technological cooperation, particularly in semiconductors, AI, and supply chain resilience can bolster the alliance beyond security matters.

Not only with the United States, but Japan can also expand cooperation with countries within the QUAD framework through deepening maritime security, cyber defence, and infrastructure development in the Indo-Pacific. Japan can enhance defence technology collaboration with India, expanding their joint military exercises, defence exports, and maritime security initiatives in the Indian Ocean (Singh 2023). It also can strengthen ties with Australia through energy cooperation such as LNG supply and hydrogen projects which ensuring energy security and promoting sustainable growth (Australian Department of Foreign Affairs and Trade 2022). Besides, Japan's New FOIP offers an opportunity to work with European partners like France, Germany, UK, and the EU on Indo-Pacific security and economic initiatives, particularly in infrastructure development and clean energy projects. With this New FOIP plan, Japan has a chance to coordinate with G7 allies on critical technology, economic security, and climate change which reinforces Japan's global leadership role.

Secondly, a key priority of Japan's New FOIP is to strengthen economic ties with Southeast Asia, South Asia, and the Pacific Islands. These regions are crucial for Japan's long-term economic and strategic goals. ASEAN nations are major trading partners for Japan, and FOIP provides an opportunity to deepen engagement in infrastructure, digital transformation, and supply chain resilience. The Regional Comprehensive Economic Partnership (RCEP) allows Japan to further expand trade and investment, particularly in automobile manufacturing, electronics, and digital trade. Japan's digital and cybersecurity collaboration with ASEAN nations helps strengthen regional resilience against cyber threats and misinformation (Asian Development Bank 2022).

Strengthening economic integration with the Southeast Asia is not Japan's only option. The New FOIP also allows Japan to enhance engagement with South Asia and the Pacific Islands. India is a major economic and strategic partner, with opportunities to increase joint investments in industrial corridors, high-speed rail projects, and energy cooperation (Thanh Van 2024). Meanwhile, Pacific Island nations are crucial for maritime security and regional stability, and Japan's FOIP promotes climate change adaptation, fisheries management, and sustainable development projects to enhance engagement. The Indo-Pacific Economic Framework (IPEF) provides Japan with an opportunity to shape trade rules, digital trade, and climate-friendly supply chains, reinforcing its economic leadership (Nagy 2023).

Thirdly, this plan helps Japan contribute to regional stability and conflict prevention. It emphasizes diplomacy and confidence-building measures to reduce tensions and prevent regional conflicts, strengthening Japan's position as a stabilizing force in the Indo-Pacific. In terms of maritime security and rule of law enforcement, Japan can enhance coast guard cooperation and maritime surveillance with ASEAN and Pacific nations, helping counter illegal fishing, smuggling, and maritime coercion. Japan can also provide capacity-building assistance to nations with weaker naval capabilities which reinforces Japan's influence and supports regional security. Moreover, Japan's active engagement in United Nations Convention on the Law of the Sea (UNCLOS) strengthens international legal mechanisms to prevent unilateral maritime claims (Harada 2023).

By supporting ASEAN centrality, Japan helps promote peaceful dispute resolution mechanisms, particularly in the South China Sea. This strengthens Japan-ASEAN defence dialogues and expands security cooperation in areas such as counterterrorism, cybersecurity, and non-traditional security threats like pandemics, climate disasters, contributing to building trust and long-term stability. Unlike Abe's FOIP, Kishida's version takes a more diplomatic approach by engaging China in economic and regional discussions while still countering its excessive influence. Japan's infrastructure and economic investments in Southeast Asia, Africa, and the Pacific help prevent overreliance on China's BRI while fostering regional development. The engagement with China through multilateral mechanisms such as ASEAN-led forums and the Comprehensive and Progressive Agreement for Trans-Pacific Partnership (CPTPP) allows Japan to shape economic rules without direct confrontation (WTO Center 2022).

Finally, Prime Minister Kishida's New FOIP helps Japan strengthen its global leadership role. Through this new plan, Japan has an opportunity to establish itself as a global leader in sustainable development by promoting green technology, climate adaptation initiatives, and digital transformation. Moreover, Japan can become a bridge between the Global South and developed nations, ensuring that developing countries receive transparent, high-quality investments rather than debt-driven projects. Being a trusted diplomatic mediator that fosters multilateral cooperation and regional stability, Japan can further position itself as a key player in shaping the 21st-century Indo-Pacific order.

To conclude, Japan's New FOIP plan presents significant opportunities to foster strategic partnerships, economic ties, and regional stability. By focusing on inclusivity and long-term cooperation, Japan can strengthen security ties with the United States, India, and Australia; enhance economic leadership in Southeast Asia and South Asia; act as a stabilizing force in the Indo-Pacific and expand its global leadership role. It can be said that, by leveraging these opportunities, Japan can *solidify its influence in the Indo-Pacific, support regional stability, and ensure long-term economic and security benefits* for itself and its partners.

4. Challenges of Japan's New FOIP Plan

Japan's New FOIP plan seeks to promote a rules-based order, enhance economic and security ties, and counter unilateral coercion in the region. However, its implementation faces significant geopolitical, diplomatic, economic, and strategic challenges. These challenges stem from China's influence, Japan's cautious approach to foreign policy, its limited economic and military resources, and the difficulty of building regional consensus among diverse stakeholders.

For the *first* challenge, China is the dominant economic and military power in the region, and its influence presents a major obstacle to Japan's New FOIP objectives. China's BRI has already deeply integrated many Indo-Pacific nations into Chinese-funded infrastructure, trade, and financial networks. According to the Green Finance & Development Center's latest statistic in Feb 2025, 149 countries have signed BRI agreements which means many nations in Southeast Asia, South Asia, and the Pacific Islands are heavily relying on Chinese investment (Green Finance & Development Center 2025).

Unlike Japan's rules-based transparent financing model, China often provides faster, flexible, and less bureaucratic funding, making it an attractive partner for developing nations. This results in the fact that some Indo-Pacific states fear losing access to Chinese markets and investments if they engage too closely with Japan's New FOIP plan. So, the matter is if Japan wants to compete with China's economic influence, Japan needs to provide an alternative to dept-heavy BRI projects which requires Japan to offer an infrastructure financing that is both attractive and sustainable for developing nations. Furthermore, overcoming China's economic leverage over ASEAN and South Asian countries means Japan must deepen bilateral economic partnerships, trade agreements, and digital connectivity projects.

Besides economic aspects, security tensions in the East and South China Sea also reflect Chinese influence in this region. China's maritime assertiveness and territorial claims in the South China Sea and East China Sea directly threaten Japan's FOIP vision of a rules-based order. China's militarization of artificial islands and rejection of international legal rulings challenge Japan's efforts to uphold UNCLOS. Especially in the context while some ASEAN nations like the Philippines and Vietnam welcome Japan's security role, others such as Thailand, Indonesia, and Malaysia are reluctant to confront China due to their economic ties (Bibhudatta 2021).

Secondly, Japan's historical preference for non-confrontational diplomacy presents a challenge in implementing the New FOIP plan, which requires a more proactive approach. Japan has historically been cautious in taking leadership roles in geopolitical affairs, preferring multilateral engagement. Unlike the United States or China, Japan lacks a strong tradition of strategic assertiveness in its foreign policy. The New FOIP plan demands quicker decision-making, stronger diplomatic engagements, and a willingness to challenge rival powers, which is not Japan's usual approach. So, it is the Japan's political and bureaucratic culture that makes Japan difficult to shift from a reactive to a proactive diplomatic stance. Meanwhile balancing economic engagement with assertive geopolitical strategy is a new challenge that Japan has yet to fully navigate (Alonso-Trabanco 2022).

Another actor that contributes to Japan's cautious and incremental foreign policy approach is Article 9 of Japan's 1947 Constitution. Article 9 of Japan's pacifist constitution limits its ability to take military action beyond self-defence (Prime Minister of Japan 1947). Unlike the United States, China, or India, Japan cannot deploy forces or establish military bases abroad in the same way. Any military expansion or new security commitments under FOIP could face domestic political resistance. In other words, increasing Japan's security commitments in the Indo-Pacific without violating its pacifist constitution is a key limitation and expanding defence cooperation under FOIP may face political and public opposition.

Thirdly, Japan's ability to lead New FOIP plan is constrained by its own economic and defence capabilities. Japan's slow economic growth, high national debt, and aging population make it difficult to sustain large-scale New FOIP. Competing with China's massive infrastructure investments requires long-term financial commitments that may be difficult for Japan to maintain. Japan's private sector investment in the Indo-Pacific is still developing, making it harder to match China's state-backed projects. Therefore, Japan finds it difficult to sustain long-term FOIP investments despite domestic economic challenges and to encourage private sector participation in FOIP-related projects to reduce reliance on government funding. Besides, Japan's military limitations also cause challenges for Japan when Japan's Self-Defence Forces (JSDF) are smaller compared to regional military powers like China and India. Moreover, Japan lacks large overseas military bases, making power projection in the Indo-Pacific more difficult (Porter 2023). So, Japan's problem here is how to enhance its military capabilities without triggering an arms race and to build regional security partnerships to compensate for its limited military reach.

The *last* significant challenge is the difficulty in building regional consensus which means Japan must be able to align diverse regional interests. This depends on Japan's ability to convince ASEAN that FOIP is not an anti-China initiative due to ASEAN's mixed reactions to New FOIP plan. Some ASEAN nations support FOIP's security aspects, while others fear being caught in United States-China rivalry. ASEAN states prioritize economic development over strategic competition, making them cautious about fully aligning with New FOIP plan. So, Japan needs to balance economic and security cooperation to maintain ASEAN's trust. Not only with the ASEAN nations, but Japan also faces difficulty in managing relations with other Indo-Pacific players. While India prioritizes strategic autonomy and is cautious about deep military commitments, Pacific Island nations prioritize climate change issues over military security ones, requiring Japan to offer tailored engagement strategies. In other words, to successfully build regional consensus, Japan must be able to *create flexible cooperation models* that accommodate diverse regional priorities and *avoid overdependence on QUAD partners* while strengthening ties with non-QUAD states.

Overall, while Japan's New FOIP plan has strategic importance, but it faces major obstacles in countering China, overcoming its diplomatic restraint, managing resource constraints, and building regional consensus. Addressing these challenges will require adaptive diplomacy, strategic partnerships, and sustained economic and security engagement which are obviously big challenges for Japan in the contemporary context.

5. Policy Implications for Vietnam

Japan's New FOIP plan presents a strategic roadmap focused on enhancing regional security, economic resilience, and multilateral cooperation. Vietnam, as a key regional player with strong ties to both Japan and ASEAN, must navigate the opportunities and challenges presented by Japan's FOIP strategy. Some policy implications for Vietnam can be outlined as following.

In term of strengthening strategic and security cooperation, Vietnam needs to enhance maritime security and defence collaboration with Japan as well as managing the China factor in security policy. As Japan's New FOIP strongly advocates for freedom of navigation in the Indo-Pacific, particularly in contested waters like the South China Sea, Vietnam can deepen cooperation with Japan through joint maritime patrols and exercises to enhance operational coordination; expanding defence aid from Japan, including coast guard vessels and surveillance technology; strengthening intelligence-sharing mechanisms regarding regional threats. Vietnam can work with Japan to push for stronger ASEAN-led security mechanisms that reinforce the rule of law in maritime disputes. To enhance strategic coordination in regional forum, Vietnam should engage with Japan's FOIP-aligned partners like the United States, Australia, and India in multilateral defence dialogues. Towards Chinese influence in the region, on the one hand, Vietnam needs to balance relations with China through carefully navigating Japan's New FOIP plan to avoid provoking China to maintain diplomatic stability with Beijing. On the other hand, Vietnam can make use of the supply chain diversification of Japan's New FOIP to reduce dependence on China for critical goods and components.

As Japan remains one of Vietnam's largest investors, particularly in investment in infrastructure, industrial zones, and high-tech manufacturing, Vietnam should leverage FOIP's emphasis on sustainable and resilient infrastructure, securing Japanese ODA for key projects (Bich Thuy 2025). Vietnam can position itself as a key hub in Japan's efforts to restructure supply chains away from China. Moreover, strengthening high-tech manufacturing, particularly in electronics, semiconductors, and automotive industries, will ensure Vietnam's greater integration into Japan's value chains. This will also encourage technology transfer agreements to boost Vietnam's industrial capacity. Beside enhancing Vietnam's role in Japan-led supply chains, Vietnam also should promote digital and green economy cooperation with Japan to strengthen economic ties with this world-top-five-economy. Therefore, specific policies for advancing the digital economy as well as sustainable development and green energy should be prioritized for Vietnam's further growth.

As an influential ASEAN member, Vietnam should contribute to strengthening ASEAN Centrality through advocating for ASEAN-led mechanisms to ensure regional security and economic stability; leading initiatives in maritime dispute resolution and supply chain resilience through ASEAN-Japan cooperation and promoting a more proactive ASEAN stance on FOIP while ensuring inclusivity to prevent alienating China. Although Vietnam is not a formal member of QUAD, it still can benefit from FOIP-linked initiatives, such as infrastructure development financing from QUAD partnerships or technology and innovation collaborations with QUAD economies. Furthermore, being a member of both CPTPP and RCEP, Vietnam can leverage CPTPP and RCEP for economic diplomacy. The focus of Japan's New FOIP plan on trade connectivity which aligns with Vietnam's economic strategy of maximizing benefits from regional trade pacts will, to some extent, support Vietnam's role in broader FOIP alliances.

Last but not the least, to fully capitalize on Japanese FOIP-related investments, Vietnam needs improving project approval processes for foreign investments; strengthening anti-corruption measures to ensure transparent and efficient use of FOIP funding; and enhancing intellectual property protection to attract Japanese tech companies. Vietnam should modernize its regulatory environment to accommodate FOIP-aligned developments through strengthening maritime laws to align with international standards, e.g. UNCLOS 1982, as well as updating investment laws to attract more high-tech and green investments from Japan. It can be said that only with effective institutional and legal reforms which focus on improving governance and investment climate along with upgrading legal frameworks for security and trade, Vietnam can maximize Japan's New FOIP plan benefits.

In summary, Vietnam stands to gain significantly from Japan's New FOIP plan, but policy adjustments are essential to maximize benefits while managing risks. By effectively integrating into Japan's New FOIP plan, Vietnam can enhance its geopolitical standing, economic resilience, and regional influence, while safeguarding national security interests in an increasingly complex Indo-Pacific environment.

6. Conclusion

Japan's New FOIP plan presents a mix of opportunities and challenges for regional stakeholders, including Vietnam. On one hand, the initiative offers economic benefits, increased infrastructure investment, and strengthened security partnerships, particularly in maritime defence. It also reinforces ASEAN's central role in shaping a stable, transparent and rules-based regional order, which aligns with Vietnam's broader diplomatic and economic objectives. On the other hand, the New FOIP plan presents challenges that require careful navigation. Balancing relations with China, a dominant economic partner and regional power, remains a critical concern. As Japan and other QUAD nations push for a more assertive Indo-Pacific strategy, Vietnam must avoid actions that could provoke tensions with Beijing while still securing the benefits of closer strategic cooperation with Japan. Additionally, ensuring effective policy implementation and overcoming bureaucratic or logistical hurdles in infrastructure and defence cooperation will be key to maximizing the plan's potential. The geopolitical complexities of the region, including competing territorial claims in the South China Sea, also necessitate a measured and calculated response from Vietnam's leadership.

To sum up, for Vietnam, a pragmatic approach is necessary to maximize FOIP's economic and strategic advantages while avoiding unnecessary tensions. By deepening economic collaboration with Japan, enhancing maritime security cooperation, and maintaining a balanced foreign policy, Vietnam can position itself as a key player in the Indo-Pacific. Ultimately, Japan's FOIP initiative serves as a catalyst for Vietnam to strengthen its regional influence, economic resilience, and security posture in a rapidly changing geopolitical landscape. By adopting a pragmatic and forward-looking approach, Vietnam can emerge as a key player in the Indo-Pacific landscape, ensuring its long-term economic prosperity and national security.

7. References

Singh, Aditi (2023): India-Japan ties: Boosting Cooperation in Indo-Pacific Defence, Invest India. https://www.investindia.gov.in/team-india-blogs/india-japan-ties-boosting-cooperation-indo-pacific-defence.

Bibhudatta, Amlan (2021): China's Relationship with ASEAN: An Explainer, Observer Research Foundation. https://www.orfonline.org/research/china-relationship-asean-explainer.

Asian Development Bank (2022): The Regional Comprehensive Economic Partnership Agreement – A New Paradigm in Asian Regional Cooperation. https://www.adb.org/sites/default/files/publication/792516/rcep-agreement-new-paradigm-asian-cooperation.pdf.

Australian Department of Foreign Affairs and Trade (2022): Clean hydrogen collaboration with Japan. https://www.dfat.gov.au/about-us/publications/trade-investment/business-envoy/business-envoy-february-2022/clean-hydrogen-collaboration-japan.

Bich Thuy (2025): Japanese firms seeking expansion in Vietnam, Vietnam Investment News. https://vir.com.vn/japanese-firms-seeking-expansion-in-vietnam-121800.html#:~:text=Japan%20remains%20in%20the%20top,flows%20from%20Japan%20to%20Vietnam.

Lim, Chhay (2023): CSEAS Analysis, Institute for International Studies and Public Policy, No. 6, June 2023.

Green Finance & Development Center (2025): Countries of the Belt and Road Initiative. https://greenfdc.org/countries-of-the-belt-and-road-initiative-bri/.

Green, M. (2020): Japan's FOIP Strategy: Diplomacy and Regional Influence. In: International Studies Review, 22(3), 89–102.

Harada, Yu (2023): Evaluating Japan's South China Sea Policy: A Qualified Success? In: Contemporary Southeast Asia, Yusof Ishak Institute, Vol.45. No.1 (April 2023), 30–54

Alonso-Trabanco, Jose Miguel (2022): Japan: An Empire Reawakened? In: Geopolitical Monitor. https://geopoliticalmonitor.com/japan-an-empire-reawakened/.

Kondoh, Hisahiro (2024): Strategic Japan, Center for Strategic and International Studies, May 2024.

Ministry of Foreign Affairs of Japan (2007): Confluence of the Two Seas. https://www.mofa.go.jp/region/asia-paci/pmv0708/speech-2.html.

Ministry of Foreign Affairs of Japan (2016): Free and Open Indo-Pacific. https://www.mofa.go.jp/files/000430632.pdf.

Ministry of Foreign Affairs of Japan (2023): The Future of Indo-Pacific. https://www.mofa.go.jp/files/100477739.pdf.

Prime Minister of Japan and His Cabinet (1947): Constitution of Japan. https://japan.kantei.go.jp/constitution_and_government_of_japan/constitution_e.html#:~:text=Article%209.,means%20of%20settling%20international%20disputes.

Porter, Samuel P. Porter (2023): A Solution for Japan's Military Mismatch. In: Foreign Policy. https://foreignpolicy.com/2023/03/15/japan-military-defense-navy-army-kishida-personnel-gsdf-msdf-jsdf/.

Smith, J. (2021): Japan's FOIP and the Challenge of Chinese Influence. In: Global Policy Journal, 10(5), 67–89.

Nagy, Stephen (2023): The IPEF: Japan's Economic Realism and Approach to Indo-Pacific Engagement, Resilience, and Rule-Setting. KAS. https://kas-japan.or.jp/wp-content/uploads/2023/11/The-Making-of-the-Indo-Pacific-Economic-Framework-for-Prosperity-IPEF.pdf.

Thanh Van (2024): Vietnam, India economic cooperation to thrive following strengthening of strategic partnership. In: Vietnam Investment Review. https://vir.com.vn/vietnam-india-economic-cooperation-to-thrive-following-strengthening-of-strategic-partnership-113260.html.

U.S. Department of Defense (2024): AUKUS Partners Consider Cooperation with Japan. https://www.defense.gov/News/News-Stories/Article/Article/3734336/aukus-partners-consider-cooperation-with-japan/.

WTO Center (2022): What is the CPTPP and why is China eager to join? https://wtocenter.vn/chuyen-de/19553--what-is-the-cptpp-and-why-is-china-eager-to-join.

Chapter 19: Strengthening Japan's Soft Power in Southeast Asia through Development Diplomacy

Vu Thi Anh Thu

Southeast Asia is a region of geopolitical and geoeconomic significance associated with Japan's strategic interests. Since the 1980s, Japan has implemented foreign development assistance policies for neighbouring countries. This chapter examines recent modifications in Japanese Official Development Assistance (ODA) policy within the Southeast Asian region to align with the *Free and Open Indo-Pacific* vision and to compete with Chinese development cooperation policy. The chapter explores how development diplomacy might augment Japan's soft power in the region via the lens of interdependent theory and analytical methodology. This chapter asserts that through substantial development diplomacy aimed at developing countries in the region and efficient utilisation of ODA in recipient countries, Japan has obtained various national benefits beyond economic interests, including trust from ASEAN populace which bolsters its soft power in the region. In contrast, ASEAN countries perceived Japanese ODA contribution as a catalyst of socio-economic progress and a strategic leverage in counterbalancing China's influence, especially as most ASEAN countries pursue a neutral foreign policy. This recognition demonstrates Japan's positive role in maintaining peace, stability, and prosperity in the region.

This research has been funded by Hanoi University of Social Sciences and Humanities – Vietnam National University under grand number CS.2025.27.

1. Introduction

After the end of World War II, Japan received financial contributions from the International Monetary Fund (IMF), the International Bank for Reconstruction and Development (IBRD), and trade support from the General Agreement on Tariffs and Trade (GATT) to rebuild and recover the country. Thanks to that, Japan's economy grew rapidly, and it is no longer a recipient of aid. The signing of the Colombo Plan for Cooperative Economic and Social Development in Asia and the Pacific (Colombo Plan) in 1954 marked the first recognition of Japan's ODA to developing countries in the Asia-Pacific region. As a member of the Development Assistance Committee of the Organization for Economic Co-operation and Development (DAC-OECD), Japan uses public financial resources to provide grants and concessional loans to developing countries through a method known as *Official Development Assistance* (ODA) to support these countries in promoting economic development and welfare. The first ODA Charter in 1992 shaped Japan's basic philosophy, including the imperative of humanitarian assistance; recognition of the interdependent relationships between nations; the necessity of environmental conservation; and support for developing countries' self-help efforts. Later, Japan revised the 1992 ODA Charter three times to attract financial support from the private sector to expand the scope of the government's international development cooperation policy for developing countries. The contents mentioned in the ODA Charters (which were later renamed Development Cooperation Charters) include trade, investment, and social issues such as gender, health, education, environment and climate change, narrowing the income gap, institutional reform, etc. With the change in the scope of support, expanding the entities involved in providing support, etc. the Japanese Government has shifted from economic to development diplomacy to align with the international context after 2000 and to assist developing countries in achieving the Millennium Development Goals (MDGs) and the Sustainable Development Goals (SDGs) initiated by the United Nations. Moreover, since Prime Minister Shinzo Abe officially announced the *Free and Open Indo-Pacific (FOIP) vision* in 2016, Japan has implemented various diplomatic policies to enhance its influence in the Indo-Pacific region, with Southeast Asia as the focal point, to compete with the rise of Chinese sponsorship through the Belt and Road Initiative. Development Diplomacy is used as one of Japan's soft approaches to complement traditional diplomacy with the aim of creating an inclusive and comprehensive strategy of influence, engagement, and reform mobilisation to developing countries.

The chapter consists of three parts:

- first, examining the factors influencing the shift from Japan's ODA policy to Development Cooperation;
- second, analysing the implementation of Japan's international support in several countries in the region;

- third, discussing the benefits Japan gains from international support through development diplomacy.

The chapter discovers that the benefits Japan gains from development diplomacy are not only about trade (which is conducted through the tool of economic diplomacy) but also include national security benefits and Japan's influence over Southeast Asian countries. The effectiveness of ODA in recipient countries has demonstrated the support of aid-receiving countries for Japan in international forums and the trust in the quality of ODA from Japanese funding. This is the driving force behind Japan's positional competition with China in Southeast Asia.

2. Factors Influencing the Transition from ODA to Development Cooperation Policy in Japan

In 1954, Japan joined the Colombo Plan, and its ODA has contributed to the development of developing countries and addressed changing global issues. Japan joined the Organisation for Economic Co-operation and Development (OECD) in 1964 and became a member of the OECD Development Assistance Committee (DAC). In 1974, Japan established the Japan International Cooperation Agency responsible for ODA. The Japanese economy developed rapidly in the following 30 years, facilitating an increase in ODA volume and helping Japan rank among the world's top donors by 1989, surpassing the United States (MOFA 2024a).

After the Cold War, with the dissolution of the Soviet Union, Japan's ODA and that of other DAC-OECD countries supported the former socialist countries in implementing institutional reforms and democratisation processes and helped fragile states to build peaceful states. With the adoption of the ODA Charter in 1992, Japan established a philosophy following which ODA is *to support for the self-help efforts of developing countries towards economic take-off*, and Japan's ODA will help ensure the efficient and fair distribution of resources and *good governance* in developing countries, meeting basic social needs while promoting healthy economic development and environmental conservation (MOFA 1999).

Although the 1997–1998 Asian financial crisis did not significantly impact Japan, the economy had to overcome its own long-term difficulties. The Japanese Government is forced to cut the budget and emphasise the quality of ODA rather than the quantity, setting requirements for the implementation of ODA in a strategic, transparent, and effective manner. Additionally, the international situation at the end of the 20th century and the beginning of the 21st century saw significant upheavals: globalisation has stimulated increasing economic dependence; the issues of global counterterrorism and national security have received particular attention. The United Nations also set the MDGs to eradicate poverty and inequality in developing countries. In line with the MDGs, Japan amended the ODA Charter in 2003 with the aim of a

> "Contribution to the peace and development of the international community, and thereby to help ensure Japan's own security and prosperity." (MOFA 2003)

The securitisation of Japan's ODA was mentioned after the terrorist attacks in the United States in September 2001. The 1992 ODA Charter, amended in 2003, clearly expresses the connection between ODA and national interests, but it always upholds the principle that the support policy is non-political and non-military. Japan's shift in vision regarding ODA policy aligns with the new development strategy initiated by DAC-OECD, *Shaping the 21st Century: The Contribution of Development* in 1996, which acknowledges the role of "strong self-interest" of both donor countries and recipient countries (OECD 1996).

The participation of South-South development cooperation in foreign aid has introduced new donors with partnership principles that differ from the traditional North-South funding model. China has emerged as a South-South donor for countries in the Southeast Asia region and more broadly in the Indo-Pacific region, and in Africa, with the principles of its flexible foreign aid policy being non-interference, non-conditionality, and economic cooperation based on mutual benefits. With an equal approach among development partners, China demonstrates competition in the *international aid market* – which is considered the playground of traditional North-South DAC-OECD donors, particularly in competing for influence with Japanese donors in the Indo-Pacific region, especially in Southeast Asia. Domestically, Japan continues to face challenges such as population decline, labour shortages, prolonged financial difficulties, and rising social welfare costs. In that context, Japan revised the 2003 ODA Charter in 2015 and renamed it the Development Cooperation Charter (Charter). According to the 2015 Charter, the term *development cooperation* refers to

> "International cooperation activities that are conducted by the government and its affiliated agencies for the main purpose of development in developing regions."
>
> In this connection, *development* "is used in a broader sense rather than in the narrow sense; it also encompasses such activities as peacebuilding and governance, promotion of basic human rights and humanitarian assistance." (MOFA 2015)

Through international development cooperation, the Japanese Government aims to attract additional financial resources beyond ODA from the private sector, individuals, funds, etc., to foster the realisation of SDGs in developing countries. The 2015 Charter reflects a change in the approach of Japan's foreign aid: first, extending cooperation based on a whole-of-nation approach, which includes not only the government but also the private sector and local governments; second, expanding the scope of cooperation not restricted to that of past ODA; and third, building mutually beneficial relations through equal partnership with developing countries. Development cooperation provides one of the most important means for Japan in its agile implementation of such diplomacy. It carries significance as an "investment for the future." (MOFA 2015) In addition, the 2015 Charter emphasises that "one of the major purposes of ODA was to contribute to Japan's vital national interests of peace and security" to serve the National Security Strategy enacted in 2013 by the second Abe administration.

To address the risk of instability in the security of the Indo-Pacific region, particularly the threats to maritime security and safety in the Bien Dong and the East China Sea, the concept of a Free and Open Indo-Pacific (FOIP) was officially disseminated by the second Abe administration in 2016 to ensure national interests and enhance Japan's diplomatic capacity to meet the expectations of the international community. The amendment of the 2015 Development Cooperation Charter in 2023 reaffirms a contribution to "building a peaceful, stable and prosperous international community under a free and open order directly leads to Japan's national interests" in light of the *New Plan for Free and Open Indo-Pacific* and the National Security Strategy issued in 2022. It also continues the use of ODA flows and private funds to support economic growth and achieve the SDGs in developing countries, while loans from emerging donors, which do not pay much attention to debt sustainability, are unlikely to contribute to the growth of recipient countries. The 2023 Charter presents new direction for development cooperation to enhance effective and strategic and sustainable use of foreign aid models as one of the most diplomacy tools to create a peaceful, stable and prosperous environment for the world and for Japan. The 2023 Charter continues to promote Japan's foreign aid philosophy of adhering to universal values, including human security, human rights, freedom, democracy, and the rule of law in developing countries (MOFA 2023). Through this, Japan aims to maintain the trust of the public abroad in the quality of its foreign aid through development diplomacy to compete with the influence of China's Belt and Road Initiative.

3. Development Diplomacy as a Contribution to Soft Power

Development diplomacy has been active since the early 21st century to help developing countries achieve the MDGs (2000–2015) and the Paris Agreement on Climate Change in 2015, and later the SDGs (2016–2030). Development diplomacy through foreign aid is seen as a

> "Soft mechanism to shape the agenda, persuade, and evoke goodwill towards the donor." (Ney 2011, 20–21)

Therefore, the area of diplomacy is also expanding, becoming more diverse and mutually influential, such as environmental, health, energy, cultural and sports diplomacy. The scope of diplomats' activities is broader, ranging from negotiations, communications, representation, consular duties to trade promotion, cultural exchange, and public relations. Therefore, the participation of various entities as either donors or recipients of aid, especially the involvement of experts and technicians and other functional ministries facilitates more in-depth and smoother diplomatic discussions and negotiations. In the context of an increasingly interdependent international system, Cárdenas (1995) argues that:

> "The achievement of economic growth in one country increasingly depends on the performance of others... The importance of ODA, depends not only on its volume or magnitude, but also on its political dimension as a symbol of the commitment of the so-called donor community which needs to recognize interdependence as a central feature."

Therefore, development diplomacy can be understood as diplomatic activities of donor countries aimed at helping or cooperating with developing countries in various ways such as providing grants or loans, transferring technology or knowledge, etc., to address the challenges faced by developing countries such as poverty, social inequality, security instability, and environmental pollution. At the same time, development diplomacy also helps donor countries secure remote security, strengthen partnerships in various political, economic, and security aspects to share common prosperity and peace. According to Morgenthau (1962):

> "The transfer of money and service from one government to another performs here the function of price paid for political service rendered or to be rendered", and he commented foreign aid is "the real innovations which the modern age has introduced into the practice of foreign policy."

Lancaster (2007) further adds that the primary purpose of donor countries is not to promote human welfare but rather a means for diplomatic purposes to ensure international security and that of the donor country itself. Thus, the ODA provided to developing countries for poverty alleviation is not the priority goal of the donor countries; their national interests gained from international assistance are the top priority. Zielinska (2016) emphasises development aid is closely related to soft power because:

> "it shapes positive attitudes, including gratitude and admiration toward the donor; it servers transmission of information about the donor and the values it stands for; it raises interest in the donor country; and it is also often based on non-material resources that a donor state has to offer, such as knowledge and know-how; achievements and discoveries in sciences, technologies, environment, health, political system, social life and so on."

It is likely that development diplomacy has a dual role: it is not only a means of nurturing national soft power but also relies on the resources of soft power to achieve the goals of public diplomacy towards donor countries. Gulrajani et al. (2020, 7–9) argue that

> "Development diplomacy refers to the repurposing of aid in such a way that its claims to service public diplomacy ambitions and aspirations while simultaneously achieving development goals."

She believes that it is the "democratisation of diplomatic activity," in which a network of diplomacy is established, including various actors such as international officials, civil society, international journalists, transnational corporations, strategists, scientists, and individuals who all have the potential to influence. Thus, development diplomacy encompasses the characteristics of network and public diplomacy: diversity in actors and two-way communication, with both short-term and long-term orientations aimed at building relationships between donor countries and recipient countries and towards the development goals of the recipient countries. More and more donors are participating in the *foreign aid market*, particularly emerging donors with South-South cooperation modality, accompanied by flexible cooperation policies, non-interference in internal affairs, and untied aid which are attracting the interest and willingness of developing countries to receive foreign aid. Development cooperation is also viewed under the economic diplomacy aspect in the foreign policy of donor countries to serve their own interests.

The driving force behind Japan providing ODA is *aid for trade and investment* which can take place through the export of machinery and equipment, sending technical experts, transferring knowledge to developing countries, and importing resources from recipient countries while supporting the private sector in foreign direct investment. The fierce competition between traditional Northern and Southern donors requires Japan to adopt new diplomatic strategies to enhance its *soft power* to serve the goals of its aid for trade and investment, and in a second step for aid for peace, national security, and prosperity. With the *non-military* and *non-political* statements in its development cooperation modality, Japan wants to emphasise the soft approach of foreign aid to seek the trust and unwavering support of recipient countries. Development diplomacy is the path that helps Japan increase its soft power regarding the public of the host country. Development diplomacy is a specific form of public diplomacy; it is a process of building a positive image abroad, improving Japan's bilateral relations, international role and position on the basis of aid transfers aimed at promoting the development and well-being of developing countries (Zielinska 2016). Besides the realist perspective in international relations theory that national interests determine the goals, methods, and measures of foreign policy, the neoliberal perspective considers the international environment and public opinion, which can have a certain influence on national interests. The Japan's Development Cooperation Charter in 2023 emphasises that

> "Such efforts will in turn benefit Japan itself in a number of ways, including by promoting friendly relations and people-to-people exchanges with other countries, and by strengthening Japan's standing in the international arena" (MOFA 2003c).

The section below attempts to examine Japan's influence in recipient countries of the Southeast Asia region through development diplomacy.

4. Implementation of Japan's Development Diplomacy

Japan's distribution of foreign aid has focused on Southeast Asia in particular and the Indo-Pacific region in general for the past five decades because it

> "Represents a unique case a combination of vital security stakes and crucial sustainability issues." (Prabhu/Basu 2024)

The former Prime Minister Shinzo Abe officially announced his vision for the Free and Open Indo-Pacific (FOIP) in his keynote address at TICAD VI held in Kenya in 2016. Abe's vision for FOIP has received support from many countries such as the US, France, India, Australia, and the EU with the hope of developing the region as *international public goods.* A FOIP vision provides three pillars to realise Japan's efforts of foreign aid in the Indo-Pacific region, including Southeast Asia:

(i) promotion and establishment of the rule of law, freedom of navigation, free trade;
(ii) pursuit economic prosperity; and
(iii) commitment for peace and stability.

Southeast Asia is a region with geopolitical and geoeconomic significance linked to Japan's strategic interests. Financial support activities in the form of war reparations payments for some countries began in 1955, but hidden behind them were commercial motives. In 1960, the Association of Southeast Asian Nations (ASEAN) was established by five countries: Singapore, Malaysia, the Philippines, Thailand, and Indonesia, with the aim of enhancing cooperation and regional economic development. Initially, Japan provided ODA to these five countries to coordinate with each other to counter the threat of communism and to expand Japan's export market. Excessive investment and the flow of goods primarily from Japan to Southeast Asia pressured local industries, leading to concerns regarding a new Japanese economic imperialism. Violent protests took place against Japan before Prime Minister Kakuei Tanaka's visit to Southeast Asia in 1974. Later, during the 67th visit of Japanese Prime Minister Takeo Fukuda to Southeast Asia in 1977, he delivered a speech titled *Japan's Southeast Asia Policy* with three principled commitments:

- First, Japan "rejects the role of a military power... and contributes to the peace and prosperity of Southeast Asia, and the world community."
- Second, Japan will do its best for consolidating the relationship of mutual confidence and trust based on "heart-to-heart" understanding with these countries, in wide-ranging fields covering not only political and economic areas but also social and cultural areas.
- Third, Japan will be an equal partner of ASEAN and its member states and actively cooperate with them in efforts to strengthen their solidarity and strength, along with other countries (known as the *Fukuda Doctrine*) (ASJA).

He proposed providing ODA to establish a *Cultural Exchange Fund* and approved the *Joint Industrialisation Cooperation Project* proposed by ASEAN and increasing the amount of ODA distributed to countries. The Fukuda Doctrine was reiterated in the foreign policies of subsequent Japanese prime ministers towards Southeast Asia. Japan wishes to establish a relationship of trust with ASEAN based on *mutual benefit* and promote comprehensive exchanges, adhering to the principle of peace with the commitment that Japan never seeks to become a military power. Following that, Prime Minister Koizumi Junichiro called for the establishment of a new partnership with ASEAN in a speech in Singapore in January 2002 based on the new concept of *acting together – advancing together* (MOFA 2002). Since Prime Minister Shinzo Abe officially announced the FOIP initiative in 2016, with a particular focus on the Southeast Asian region, ODA funding for countries in the region has concentrated on several areas where Japan has strengths as well as those that align with the development needs of the recipient countries:

Firstly, Japan provides development funds to developing countries to support the construction of infrastructure and the procurement of equipment and materials necessary for economic and social development, such as the development of public services in the fields of education, healthcare, environment, transportation, clean water supply, and wastewater treatment, which are unlikely to be profitable. During the COVID-19 outbreak, Japan provided approximately 38 billion Japanese Yen in grant aid for health and medical equipment and technical cooperation to eleven countries in East Asia. Since January 2022, Japan has also provided additional vaccines of approximately 4.46 million doses manufactured in Japan to Viet Nam and Indonesia, bringing the total number of vaccines under bilateral aid to COVAX facility to 27.08 million doses (MOFA 2023b).

Low-middle-income countries in the Mekong River region have received the most Japanese ODA over the past 20 years of implementing the UN's MDGs and SDGs. Japan focuses on three priority areas in the Mekong region:

> (i) environmental and urban issues, (ii) sustainable natural resource management and utilisation, and (iii) inclusive growth. In 2020, Japan provided at least one billion Japanese yen to five countries in the Mekong Region (Cambodia, Laos, Myanmar, Thailand, and Vietnam) through Grant Assistance for Grass-Roots Human Security Projects (MOFA 2022).

After COVID-19, Japan announced the *Five Points of Cooperation* at the 12th Mekong-Japan Summit held in November 2020, including the *Mekong SDGs Investment Partnership* to support the implementation of development projects by private sector and others. Japan is implementing grants for several projects such as Grant Assistance for Grass-Roots Human Security Projects which serve small communities. For Myanmar, Japan has stopped providing ODA when the military government engaged in violent acts and detained anti-government individuals. But Japan continues to provide humanitarian assistance through international organisations to the people of Myanmar, such as food, health, water and sanitation, shelter and protection, and to offer oxygen concentrators and personal protective equipment such as masks to respond to COVID-19 (approximately 26.8 million US dollars in 2022) (MOFA 2023b).

Secondly, Japan provides concessional loans or investments by its private companies for the development of essential infrastructure such as roads, railways, bridges, airports, electrical engineering infrastructure, Irrigation and Flood Control, Public Health and Medicine centres. Japan desires the formation of overseas loan and investment projects to develop transportation in the Mekong region, such as the Vientiane International Airport in Laos, development of the East-West Economic Corridor Highway in Myanmar, construction of the Ho Chi Minh urban railway in Vietnam, and construction of the Bangkok MRT (Red Line) in Thailand, the Sihanoukville Port in Cambodia. (MOFA 2022). Japan has also extended the Emergency Support Loan for COVID-19 Crisis Response, totalling 225 billion Japanese yen, to five countries, considering the economic impacts. (MOFA 2023b).

Thirdly, Japan provides technical assistance to developing countries through grants or concessional loans for the development of human resources, institutional development, dissemination of technology, and R&D

necessary for their economic and social development, such as through the dispatch of experts, provision of equipment, and acceptance of technical training participants in Japan.

Supporting the *Master Plan of ASEAN Connectivity 2025* (declared at the 2016 ASEAN Summit Meetings), Japan signed the Japan-ASEAN Technical Cooperation Agreement in 2019 to encourage ASEAN to consolidate its unity and centrality. Japan provides 5.5 million Japanese yen through the Japan-ASEAN Integration Fund (JAIF) to establish the ASEAN Centre for Public Health Emergencies and Emerging Disease (MOFA 2023b). In addition, Japan has supported the training of personnel and provided the logistics system for the ASEAN Coordinating Centre for Humanitarian Assistance on Disaster Management (AHA Centre).

Japan also organises training workshops on cybersecurity, infrastructure management and waste management, logistics, as well as training on public international law, etc. Furthermore, based on the *Japan-ASEAN Connectivity Initiative* announced at the Japan-ASEAN Summit in 2020, Japan has added nearly two trillion Japanese yen to infrastructure projects connecting land, air, and sea corridors and provided non-material support in the form of human resource development for 1,000 individuals, contributing to enhanced connectivity over three years from 2020 (MOFA 2023b). Japan promotes quality infrastructure investment to assist ASEAN countries. Japan trains human resources capable of carrying out advanced operations and maintenance of infrastructure funded by Japan's ODA. Japan has transferred technology and expertise to other countries so that they can independently develop infrastructure projects with funding from Japan.

A portion of Japan's ODA capital has been used to develop industrial human resources and higher education in ASEAN countries since the 1980s. The Human Resource Development Institutions supported by Japan have been established in ten ASEAN countries with the aim of *co-creating talent*. The hallmark of Japan's international cooperation is its focus on supporting education for developing countries. Kayashima (2022) showed that from the early years of its ODA programs, higher education cooperation assistance for developing universities has been one of the pillars of Japan's ODA policy. This international cooperation aims to build partner universities capacity in teaching, research and community service in developing countries. The purpose of Japan's ODA in the field of education and training is to help developing countries learn useful experiences from Japan, develop human resources to become local partners of Japanese companies (MOFA 2023c).

Japan's ODA technical assistance focuses on higher education and vocational training programs in the fields of engineering, health, agriculture, and technology, which recipient countries need to develop their human resources. At the same time, Japan also seeks to obtain a supply of foreign labour to work in Japan to compensate for the workforce shortage due to an aging population. ASEAN countries established the ASEAN University Network/ASEAN Engineering Education Development Network (AUN/SEED-Net) project starting from 2002 onwards. The network has attracted 26 top universities in the ASEAN region and 14 Japanese universities to participate. The common activities of the network are student exchange and joint programs to promote the quality improvement of engineering education and research in ASEAN countries (Kayashima 2022).

Implementing the *Innovative Asia* initiative, Japan's ODA provides a stream of scholarships to attract undergraduate and graduate students, and interns from ASEAN countries to study and work in Japan. The scholarship sources come from the annual Asian Development Bank-Japan Programs, Japan-IMF Scholarship Programs for Asia, Asia Kakehashi Scholarship Projects, and scholarships from local government and local international associations. Students in Japan come from other countries in Asia, with the top countries of origin being China (114,255 in 2021 and 103,882 in 2022), Vietnam (49,469 in 2021 and 37,405 in 2022), and Indonesia (5,792 in 2021 and 5,763 in 2022) (Erudera News 2024). Although the number of students coming to Japan for study in 2022 decreased compared to 2021, overall, Japanese universities and the country itself remain attractive to young students.

Some prestigious universities in Japan, such as the Tokyo Institute of Technology, Toyohashi University of Technology, and Kyushu University for engineering projects; Kyushu University, Okayama University, and the University of Tokyo for agricultural projects; and the University of Tokyo, Keio University, and Toyama University for medical projects, have participated in ODA's higher education programs. They send lecturers to teach, exchange, and collaborate on research with partner universities in Southeast Asia. Kayashima (2022) remarks that the participation of Japanese universities in ODA projects is considered "an international activity that is relatively easy and effective for them to engage in." Furthermore, participating in ODA projects can lead to international academic exchanges or the reception of foreign students after the completion of ODA projects. The internationalisation of higher education in Japan aims to implement the Higher Education Policy in the Globalisation Era, issued by the Japan University Council in 2000. Japan's ODA provides funding to build universities in several countries, such as Kosen schools (Colleges of Technology) in Thailand, and Vietnam-Japan University in Hanoi, Vietnam. This not only benefits ASEAN universities by allowing them to use Japan's internationalisation programs but also attracts foreign students to study in Japan.

In 2024, the Japanese parliament enacted an amended law to expand residency and social welfare policies, allowing foreign workers and students to stay in Japan longer to work in certain fields such as railway and road transportation, forestry, and agriculture after graduation (Nikkei Asia 2024). The relaxation of immigration policies aims to attract young foreign workers for companies as Japan faces a declining population. As of February 2023, Japan's working population is 74 million people and is estimated to decrease to 70 million by 2030 and around 50 million by 2050. Therefore, "attracting foreign workers is not an act of kindness, but an imperative for Japan." (Yoshikawa 2023) As of 2022, Japan has disbursed the most ODA (net disbursement) to five countries: the Philippines, Cambodia, Thailand, Myanmar, and Laos, across all three forms of grants, concessional loans, and technical cooperation. Meanwhile, countries like Malaysia, Vietnam, and Indonesia have gradually reduced the amount of capital disbursed from Japan's ODA (Statista 2024).

Fourth, Japan supports maintaining peace, stability, and prosperity in Southeast Asia. The *ASEAN Outlook on the Indo-Pacific* (AOIP) in 2019 shares some common values between the ASEAN Community and Japan's FOIP, such as maintaining peace, stability, and prosperity in the region; respecting the rule of law, openness, freedom, transparency, and inclusiveness; promoting closer economic cooperation, and thereby enhancing trust and confidence (ASEAN 2019). In addition, Japan has expanded the exploration of other priority areas for cooperation with ASEAN, including maritime cooperation, connectivity, and SDGs, and strengthening economic supply chains, as well as other potential areas of cooperation.

The commitments in the Strategic Partnership Agreement or the Comprehensive Strategic Partnership Agreement that Japan signed with ASEAN countries serve as the basis for Japan's aid contributions to several non-traditional security areas, such as Japan enhancing cooperation with Malaysia, the Philippines, Vietnam, Thailand, and Indonesia in maintaining and upholding freedom of navigation, commitment to the rule of law in settling maritime disputes, enhancing cooperation on cybersecurity, international terrorism, and transnational crimes, and building enforcement capability at sea. Japan has committed to providing the necessary equipment to build a cybersecurity system in Cambodia and the provision of equipment necessary for clearing unexploded ordnance in Laos (MOFA 2023b).

Japan is considered the largest ODA donor to Southeast Asia from 2015 to 2021, with an average of 31.4 per cent, maintaining a significant lead over other multilateral organisations or donor countries such as the World Bank, the United States, Germany, China, and France (Tan 2024).

5. Japan's Approach to Development Diplomacy

The use of foreign aid from the perspective of neo-colonialism always maintains the power imbalance between donor countries and recipient countries (Prabhu/Basu 2024). The influence of donor countries on recipient countries is exerted in various ways with a carrot-and-stick approach in the realm of political economy, as Salami (2020) observes that "aid by the donor countries is a double-edged sword because of the conditionalities often attached; you agree to our terms, you get our aid; if not, you do not." This remark is not entirely accurate as Japan, in its capacity as an aid-giving country, has undergone changes in its approach to development diplomacy in line with the evolving international context and its relations with developing countries over time. Since World War II, Japan has consistently demonstrated a strategy of implementing foreign aid not as vertical aid from rich countries to poor countries but as horizontal cooperation between equal nations, respecting the sovereignty of the recipient country, and not interfering in politics (Shiga 2023).

The 2015 Charter uses the term *development cooperation* instead of *development assistance* to emphasise Japan's shift in approach to foreign aid. Trinidad (2018) observes

> "Foreign aid as development assistance connotes gift-giving that obligates the recipient to be grateful to the generous giver (i.e. aid-donor). On the contrary, development cooperation connotes partnership, collaboration and mutual benefits between cooperators."

As a member of the DAC-OECD, Japan adheres to the principles of funding in North-South cooperation, while also skilfully integrating the approaches of South-South development cooperation in Southeast Asia. The uniqueness in Japan's ODA approach lies in reducing the *donor* aspect of traditional North-South relations and incorporating the *partner* aspect in South-South Development Cooperation, while maintaining the principle of non-political and non-military cooperation in the distribution of foreign aid. Japan hopes to create a co-creative relationship and collaborate to attract additional financial resources beyond ODA to enhance effective support for developing countries. MOFA (2023a) states that

> "Japan's ODA represent the characteristics of Japan development assistance, which respects the ownership of partner countries based on Japan's experience and knowledge, in order to provide support that is suitable for the actual situation and needs of partner countries."

Thanks to the effective implementation of high-quality and diverse projects aimed at development goals in recipient countries, Japan has gained the public's trust regarding its commitments to foreign aid. In addition to the strategy of using aid for security purposes and ensuring regional peace, foreign aid for development can enhance Japan's prestige and position as a responsible international nation in contributing to the achievement of MDGs and SDGs.

Human security is one of the three pillars of Japan's foreign aid policies. Healthcare projects, COVID-19 vaccine support, and educational scholarships for students from developing countries in the region studying at Japanese universities, as well as scholarships from Japanese investment corporations for students from their home countries, aim to promote foreign public awareness of the universal values of foreign aid as well as the values of Japanese work ethics, enthusiasm for working, morals, and management skills that Japan is bringing to them (MOFA 2023a).

The 2023 Charter clearly acknowledges that "development cooperation plays an extremely important role in Japan's diplomatic efforts." (MOFA 2023c) To date, Japan has supported up to 190 countries and regions through its ODA. Especially, with close political and economic relations, Japan considers the Asian region as its top priority for ODA and has provided a significant amount of ODA to this region. In the *Opinion Poll on Japan in Seven ASEAN Countries* conducted in 2014, about 90 per cent of the people stated that the economic and technical cooperation provided by the Japanese Government had helped develop their country (MOFA 2024).

6. The Method of Building Japan's Soft Power through Development Diplomacy

As Ney (2008) previously argued, soft power avoids traditional foreign policies like the stick and carrot approach; instead, it relies on the appeal of a nation's organisations, institutions, culture, politics, and diplomatic policies to shape the preferences of others. Japan wants to demonstrate itself as a peace-loving nation and a responsible member of the international community through ODA to support developing countries in addressing global challenges. In addition, ODA is also a channel for Japan to seek greater public understanding both domestically and internationally regarding Japan's foreign aid, promoting friendly relations between countries. From there, Japan can strengthen its position on the international stage (MOFA 2003).

At the meeting between Japanese Prime Minister Kishida Fumio and Vietnamese Prime Minister Phạm Minh Chính in November 2021, Vietnam acknowledged Japan's role as a long-term and important partner of Vietnam. The Prime Minister of Vietnam thanked the Japanese Government and people for their international support through ODA, which has helped Vietnam's socio-economic development and poverty reduction over the past 30 years, and more broadly, the entire Mekong region. On the contrary, Prime Minister Kishida Fumio also affirmed that Vietnam and ASEAN are important partners, and Japan is ready to support and cooperate with ASEAN countries in implementing the ASEAN Outlook on the Indo-Pacific. Additionally, what Japan received was the affirmation from Prime Minister Phạm Minh Chính that Vietnam supports Japan's candidacy for the non-permanent member position on the United Nations Security Council for the 2023–2024 term (Government 2021). Clearly, the soft power that Japan has built is the mutual trust and support between partner states in Southeast Asia and Japan.

Figure 1: Opinion poll on Japan conducted in ASEAN

Issues	2019	2021	2023
Friendly Relations with Japan	93%	93%	91%
Japan as Reliable Friend	93%	92%	91%
Japan as a Peace-Loving Nation	90%	88%	88%
Role of Japan in Stabilization and Growth of World Economy	87%	90%	88%
Japan's Contribution to Maintaining Global Peace and Establishment of International Order	92%	91%	91%
Japan as an Important Partner in the Future	51%	43%	43%
The Most Reliable Friend	N/A	N/A	17%

Source: Aggregated by the author from opinion polls on Japan, 2019–2023, MOFA 2024b. Countries: Brunei Darussalam, Cambodia, Indonesia, Laos, Malaysia, Myanmar, Philippines, Singapore, Thailand, and Vietnam

The above indicators show that Japan has successfully implemented public diplomacy, receiving very high evaluations and no significant changes in public opinion in ten ASEAN countries over three years of surveys. Japan's development diplomacy policy has made significant contributions to the perception of the ASEAN public, with 31 per cent of respondents noted that Japan provides development cooperation in the international community, including official development. Additionally, 24 per cent of respondents recognised Japan's contributions to addressing to global issues such as the environment, climate change, infectious diseases, population, poverty, etc. (MOFA 2024b). The first evaluation of Japan as *The Most Reliable Friend* was positively assessed whereas it is ranked second, following ASEAN and preceding China, the USA, Saudi Arabia, Russia, and others.

Figure 2: Assessment of soft power index in the Southeast Asia region

Soft Power					
	Cambodia	Indonesia	Philip-pines	Vietnam	Thailand
Japan	10	8.00	10.00	8.50	9.75
U.S.	8.6	9.00	9.00	8.75	8.75
Australia	8.4	8.00	8.00	4.25	4.50
India	7.8	7.00	7.00	4.5	6.25
EU	6.4	8.00	8.00	7.00	7.25

Source: Shigenoi 2022, 2

The survey on soft power conducted independently by Shigenoi is based on interviews with policymakers and experts in five countries: Cambodia, Indonesia, the Philippines, Vietnam, and Thailand. The soft power index of Japan was evaluated from 8.00 to 10 points which was higher than that of the US, EU, Australia, and India. Additionally, Shigenoi also took interviews on geopolitical significance, geoeconomic significance, and geotechnical significance. The result indicates that Japan always ranks first with scores respectively ranging from 6.75–9.60; 8.00–9.20; and 8.00–10.00 compared to the other four countries. This result proves that policymakers and experts in five countries hold a positive perception of Japan across multiple dimensions, recognising it as a favoured partner. The above surveys indicate that ASEAN countries acknowledge Japan's development partnership success in three primary domains:

Firstly, Japan is increasing ODA and economic cooperation to attract private sector investment in Southeast Asia. This effort develops transportation, energy, education, healthcare, green growth, and human security infrastructure in this region. Japan has signed various bilateral agreements with ASEAN countries to provide foreign aid that coincides with their development plans and ASEAN agreements, notably the Regional Comprehensive Economic Partnership. Development assistance and economic relations are the main factors increasing Japan's trust in the region (Shigenoi 2022, 4).

Secondly, the unique nature of Japanese ODA is characterised by its *value-oriented diplomacy* approach, which emphasises rule of law, human rights, promotion of democracy and good governance, and market economy. The approach diverges to some extent from that of traditional DAC-OECD donors, who provide tied aid linked to institutional and democratic reforms, while resembling China's non-interventionist political stance. But Japan's ODA continues to prioritise the implementation of the MDGs and SDGs. The 2023 Charter clearly acknowledges that "development cooperation has an exceptionally vital role to play in Japan's diplomatic efforts." (MOFA 2023c)

Thirdly, the declaration that Japan is "a peace-loving nation and responsible major power and is in a position to lead such international cooperation based on the concept of human security" (MOFA 2023c) suggests that recipient countries trust and rely on Japan. It has established comprehensive strategic partnerships with several Southeast Asian countries and India as well. This highlights Japan's important role in Southeast Asia and the broader Indo-Pacific context. Development diplomacy is becoming a key strategy for Japan to influence regional developing countries' economic and social growth under FOIP vision. In contrast, Japan may use its economic and cultural influence "to play a hedging role against deepened economic dependence on China." (Shigenoi 2022, 6) In fact, Japan has used development diplomacy as Prabu and Basu (2024) remarked that "the use of aid is not a neutral act; it carries the weight of political intentions and often reflects a country's ambition to project its soft power."

From a development perspective, Japan uses development cooperation as a diplomatic tool to support Southeast Asian countries in achieving MDGs and SDGs. The purpose of Japan's foreign aid is to promote self-reliance by supporting the self-help efforts of developing countries. The MOFA (1994) stated:

> "The significance of ODA loans is to meet the demand for large-scale capital and impose repayment obligations, thereby supporting developing countries in their efforts to become economically independent."

From a diplomatic perspective, Japan strives to maintain a balance between upholding universal values in its ODA policy and avoiding debt burdens for recipient countries. Shiga (2023) observes that:

> "This balance is achieved by shifting the focus of support away from issues of democracy and human rights in each country towards the rule of law in international relations. This serves Japan's security interests by allowing the country to engage in security cooperation with nations that have questionable internal governance records."

Some countries in the region receiving development aid from China are apprehensive and wish to seek Japan's foreign aid to balance and avoid economic and international relations dependence. Hedging and balancing is a common diplomatic technique in the region in responding with the US-China trade war. China's *debt trap* in development cooperation has taught Vietnam and Indonesia, Malaysia, and the Philippines to carefully review projects signed with China to ensure favourable conditions, effective implementation, and to avoid excessive dependence on China. A proposal for Japan to enhance its ODA and engage Japanese investors in high-quality infrastructure and green transition projects is regarded as a viable risk mitigation strategy for Southeast Asian countries. But in certain cases, Shigenoi (2022, 6) suspects that some countries may refuse Japanese ODA if it comes with conditions related to democracy and human rights, despite maintaining their trust in Japan. Alternatively, they may be more inclined to accept China's ODA due to its non-interference policy.

7. Conclusion

Japanese ODA in Southeast Asia extends beyond mere development assistance. It represents a strategic investment in partnerships aimed at strengthening bilateral cooperation and augmenting Japan's influence through development diplomacy. The *win-win* approach to generating mutual benefits for all stakeholders is garnering significant interest from governments and the public in various countries regarding Japan's development cooperation. This result provides the Japanese government with a foundation to persuade the populace regarding the efficacy of aid and development, illustrating how development diplomacy can advance Japan's domestic objectives and soft power from abroad. Japan aims to illustrate its position as an equal partner to developing nations in collaborative efforts to tackle challenges confronting the international community. Japan has consistently endeavoured to earn the respect and trust of ASEAN governments and their populations over the years. Japan is expected to assume a proactive role and enhance its contributions to the peace, stability, and prosperity of the international community in alignment with its national capabilities.

8. References

Abe, Shinzo (2007, August 22): Confluence of the Two Seas (Speech at Parliament of the Republic of India). https://www.mofa.go.jp/region/asia-paci/pmv0708/speech-2.

Alesina, A./Dollar. D. (2000): Who Gives Foreign Aid to Whom and Why? In: Journal of Economic Growth, 5(1), 33–63. doi:10.1023/A:1009874203400.

ASEAN (2019, June 23): ASEAN Outlook on the Indo-Pacific. https://asean.org/asean-outlook-on-the-indo-pacific/.

ASJA (nd): Fukuda Doctrine. https://asja.gr.jp/en/asja/fukuda.html.

Cárdenas, E. J. (1995): The Change Aid Environment: Perspectives on the Official Development Assistance Debate. In: ISLA Journal of Int'l & Comparative Law, Vol 2, 189–201.

Daimon-Sato, T. (2020): Sino-Japanese Competition over the Aid Market in ASEAN: Political Tensions and Consequences. In: Foreign Policy Review, 13, 58–73.

Erudera News (2024, March 4): Stats Show Decline in International Student Enrolment in Japan. https://erudera.com/news/stats-show-decline-in-international-student-enrollment-in-japan/.

Government (2021, November 24): Joint Statement Vietnam-Japan: Towards a New Phase of the Extensive Strategic Partnership for Peace and Prosperity in Asia (Chính phủ. 2021. Tuyên bố chung Việt Nam – Nhật Bản: Hướng tới một giai đoạn mới của quan hệ Đối tác Chiến lược sâu rộng vì hoà bình và thịnh vượng ở châu Á). https://baochinhphu.vn/tuyen-bo-chung-viet-nam-nhat-ban-huong-toi-mot-giai-doan-moi-cua-quan-he-doi-tac-chien-luoc-sau-rong-vi-hoa-binh-va-thinh-vuong-o-chau-a-102304428.htm.

Gulrajani, N. (et al.) (2020, February): Report: The New Development Diplomacy in Middle-Income Countries. The Changing Role of Traditional Donors in India. https://cdn.odi.org/media/documents/the_new_development_v5.pdf.

ISEAS (2022): The State of Southeast Asia 2022 Survey Report. https://www.iseas.edu.sg/wp-content/uploads/2022/02/The-State-of-SEA-2022_FA_Digital_FINAL.pdf.

Kayashima, N. (2022): Japan's ODA for the Development of Higher Education Institutions in Developing Countries: Supporting Leading Universities for Human Resource Development and Knowledge Creation and Diffusion. In: Kayashima, N./Kuroda, K./Kitamura, Y. (eds.): Japan's International Cooperation in Education. Education in the Asia-Pacific Region: Issues, Concerns and Prospects, vol 63. Springer, Singapore. https://doi.org/10.1007/978-981-16-6815-9_9.

Koga, K. (2024, May): Strategic Dynamic: 50th Anniversary of Relations and New Security Ties. Comparative Connections, Vol. 26, No. 1, 191–200. https://cc.pacforum.org/2024/05/strategic-dynamism-50th-anniversary-of-relations-and-new-security-ties.

Lancaster, C. (2027): Foreign Aid: Diplomacy, Development, Domestic Politics. The University of Chicago Press, London.

MLIT (Ministry of Land, Infrastructure, Transport and Tourism) (2019): White Paper on Land, Infrastructure, Transport and Tourism, p214, https://www.mlit.go.jp/common/001325161.pdf.

MOFA (Ministry of Foreign Affairs of Japan) (1994): Japan's ODA: Annual Report (Summary). https://www.mofa.go.jp/policy/oda/summary/1994/index.html.

MOFA (1994): Japan's ODA: Annual Report (Summary). https://www.mofa.go.jp/policy/oda/summary/1994/index.html.

MOFA (2002, January 14): Speech by Prime Minister of Japan Junichiro Koizumi. Japan and ASEAN in East Asia – A Sincere and Open Partnership. https://www.mofa.go.jp/region/asia-paci/pmv0201/speech.html.

MOFA (2003): Revision of Japan's Official Development Cooperation Charter. https://www.mofa.go.jp/policy/oda/reform/revision0308.pdf.

MOFA (2015): The Development Cooperation Charter. https://www.mofa.go.jp/files/000067701.pdf.

MOFA (2022 May 12): Japan White Paper on Development Cooperation 2020. https://www.mofa.go.jp/policy/oda/page22_001470.html.

MOFA (2023a, April 28): Japan White Paper on Development Cooperation 2021. https://www.mofa.go.jp/policy/oda/page22e_001039.html.

MOFA (2023b, April 28): Japan White Paper on Development Cooperation 2022. https://www.mofa.go.jp/policy/oda/page22e_001039.html.

MOFA (2023c): The Development Cooperation Charter (revision). https://www.mofa.go.jp/files/100514705.pdf (accessed 20 July 2024).

MOFA (2023d, June 5): ODA by Region East Asia. https://www.mofa.go.jp/policy/oda/page_000008.html#malaysia.

MOFA (2024a, June 3): History of ODA. https://www.mofa.go.jp/policy/oda/page22_001434.html.

MOFA (2024b, March 15): Opinion Poll on Japan. https://www.mofa.go.jp/policy/culture/pr/index.html.

MOFA (1992, June 30): Japan's Official Development Cooperation Charter 1992. https://www.mofa.go.jp/policy/oda/summary/1999/ref1.html.

Morgenthau, H. (1962): A Political Theory of Foreign Aid. In: The American Political Science Review. Vol. 56, No. 2. 301–308.

Nikkei Asia (2024, March 30): Japan's Labor-Starved Companies Welcome Expanded Foreign Worker Program. https://asia.nikkei.com/Spotlight/Japan-immigration/Japan-s-labor-starved-companies-welcome-expanded-foreign-worker-program.

Ney, J. (2008): Public Diplomacy and Soft Power. In: Annals of American Academy of Political and Social Sciences. 616, 94–109.

Ney, J. (2011): The Future of Power. New York. OECD (1996, May 30): Shaping the 21st Century: The Contribution of Development Co-operation, OECD Publishing, Paris. https://doi.org/10.1787/da2d4165-en.

Padhikari, B. (2019): Power Politics and Foreign Aid Delivery Tactics. In: Social Science Quarterly. doi:10.1111/ssqu.12653.

Prabhu, S./Basu, P. (2024, April 3): Navigating the Indo-Pacific: Development Cooperation as a Diplomatic Tool. ORF Issue Brief No.703. https://www.orfonline.org/research/navigating-the-indo-pacific-development-cooperation-as-a-diplomatic-tool.

Salami, Y. O. (2020): The Political Economy of Foreign Aid: An Overview of the Carrot and Stick. In: Cross- Cultural Communication, Vol 16 (2), 85–93.

Shiga, H. (2023): The dynamics of Japan's Official Development Assistance in an Era of Great Power Competition. In: Journal of Contemporary East Asia Studies, 12:1. 249–263. doi.org/10.1080/24761028.2023.2292438.

Shigenoi, K. (2022, May 22): Japan's Role for Southeast Asia Amidst the Great Power Competition. https://kas-japan.or.jp/en/pub/japan-asean-study-japans-role-for-southeast-asia-amidst-the-great-power-competition-and-its-implications-for-the-eu-japan-partnership.

Tan, E. (2024, April 29): Rightsizing Japan's Economic Influence in Southeast Asia. https://fulcrum.sg/rightsizing-japans-economic-influence-in-southeast-asia/.

The Colombo Plan Secretariat (nd): The Colombo Plan – A Brief History. https://colombo-plan.org/who-we-are/.

Trinidad, D. (2018): What Strategic Partnerships with ASEAN Mean for Japan's Foreign Aid? In: Journal of Asian Security and International Affairs 5(3), 1–28. doi.org/10.1177/2347797018798996.

van der Veen, A. Maurits (2011): Ideas, Interests and Foreign Aid. Cambridge University Press

Yoshikawa, Yusaku (2023, June 2): Reimaging Japan's Relations with Foreign Workers. https://eastasiaforum.org/2023/06/02/reimaging-japans-relations-with-foreign-workers.

Zielinska, K. (2016): Development Diplomacy. Development Aid as a Part of Public Diplomacy in the Pursuit of Foreign Policy Aims: Theoretical and Practical Considerations. In: Historia i Polityka, 16 (23), 9–16. http://dx.doi.org/10.12775/HiP.2016.009.

About the Authors

Vu Thi Anh Thu (Dr.) serves as Vice Dean of Faculty of International Studies, VNU University of Social Sciences and Humanities, Hanoi. Thu holds a master's degree in law and a PhD in International Relations from the VNU-USSH that she is working at. Thu's research interest is in the areas of international organizations and non-government organizations, international development cooperation, public diplomacy, and public governance. ORCID 0000-0001-5187-2069.

Nguyen Thi Thuy Trang is a faculty member at the Faculty of International Studies, University of Social Sciences and Humanities, Vietnam National University, Hanoi. She holds a PhD from the same university and an M.A. from Waseda University, Tokyo. Her research focuses primarily on international relations in the Asia-Pacific region, non-traditional security and development issues in Southeast Asia.

Philippe Le Prestre is retired Professor of Political Science at Laval University (Quebec, Canada) and a visiting lecturer at the Diplomatic Academy of Vietnam (Hanoi). With a PhD in Political Science from Indiana University (Bloomington, USA) as well as graduate degrees in Ecology from the University of Paris Cité, his research has mostly focused on international environmental politics and foreign policy analysis. He is currently working on a book on the development of a complex systems approach to International Relations.

Vu Van Anh is a lecturer of the Division of International Relations, the Faculty of International Studies, VNU University of Social Sciences and Humanities in Hanoi. She received her doctoral degree in International Relations at the Diplomatic Academy of Vietnam (DAV) in 2018. Vu Van Anh has teaching experiences on IR theories, international conflicts, and foreign policy analysis. Power in IR, interstate rivalries and conflicts, and foreign policy behaviours of small states in Asia-Pacific are currently among her research areas of interest.

Nghiem Tuan Hung received his Bachelor's, Master's, and Doctoral degrees from the VNU University of Social Sciences and Humanities, specialising in international studies. Since joining the Institute of World Economics and Politics (IWEP) under the Vietnam Academy of Social Sciences in 2009, he has held various research and leadership positions. He is currently a senior researcher and serves as Head of the IWEP International Politics and Security Division. His academic interests focus on strategic studies, security issues, and US foreign policy in a changing global order.

Nguyen Thi Nhu Quynh is currently a master's student at the Faculty of International Studies, VNU University of Social Sciences and Humanities. Since 2022, she has participated in various research projects at the VASS Institute of World Economics and Politics. Her research focuses on regional structures and driving dynamics in the Asia-Pacific, with particular interest in geopolitical competition, regionalism, and strategic alignments in a shifting global context.

Detlef Briesen, PD Dr. phil. Dr. hon., works at Justus-Liebig University Giessen. In addition to teaching international development, he has carried out several European and international research projects for various governmental and non-governmental organisations. In recent years, one of his academic focuses has shifted to Vietnam. There he works, supported by DAAD, on the reorganisation of the higher education system and promotes scientific and publication projects – most recently on social development, socio-political issues, implementation research, administrative reform and environmental issues.

Bui Thanh Nam is an Associate Professor of Political Science and a Doctor of Political Economy at the University of Social Sciences and Humanities, Vietnam National University, Hanoi. Dr. Nam's main areas of expertise are international political economy, American studies and Vietnamese economy.

Pham Thi Thu Huyen is a lecturer of the European-American Department at the Faculty of International Studies, University of Social Sciences and Humanities, Vietnam National University, Hanoi. She holds a master's degree in law and a doctorate in political science. She is currently interested in political science, law and international studies for her teaching and training major.

Bui Hong Hanh is an Assoc. Professor of Political Sciences at University of Social Sciences and Humanities, Vietnam National University, Hanoi. Dr. Hanh holds a PhD in World History from USSH and a master's degree in development management from Ruhr University, Bochum, Germany. Dr. Hanh's research focuses on European studies, international politics and international organizations.

Nguyen Van Dap holds a doctoral degree in International Relations from Vietnam National University (VNU), Hanoi in 2020. Now he is working as a lecturer, with more than ten years- experience, at VNU University of Social Sciences and Humanities, Hanoi. His research includes Americas Studies, History of International Relations and the Issues of Sustainable Development.

Ho Thu Thao is a lecturer at the Faculty of International Studies, University of Social Sciences and Humanities, Vietnam National University, Hanoi. She completed a master's degree in international trade and economic law at the University of the West of England in 2015. In 2017, she began her academic career as a researcher and a lecturer at University of Social Sciences and Humanities, where she earned her PhD in international relations, with a focus on the European External Action Service. Her research mainly focuses on European politics.

Nguyen Thi Thanh Thuy is Associate Professor of Political Science and International Relations. She holds an M.A. degree in Asian Studies, conferred by Cornell University, and a PhD degree in world history, conferred by Vietnam National University (VNU-Hanoi). She is a former Deputy Dean and a former Head of Division of Americas Studies of the Faculty of International Studies, University of Social Sciences and Humanities, which is a member of VNU-Hanoi. She retired in January 2020. Dr. Thuy is the author of more than sixty papers published in either academic journals or workshop proceedings, four book-chapters, co-author and author of three books. Her works are on aspects of US foreign policy and relations, ASEAN issues, Canada's and Vietnam's external relations.

Tu Anh Tuan (M.A., PhD Student) is Acting Director at the Centre for Security and Development Research, Institute for Foreign Policy and Strategic Studies (IFPSS) of the Diplomatic Academy of Viet Nam, Ministry of Foreign Affairs. He has authored several articles and publications in both Vietnamese and English, focusing on the Belt and Road Initiative (BRI), BRICS, the Global South, Mekong, Artificial Intelligence (from an IR perspective), and Viet Nam's diplomatic strategies.

Tran My Hai Loc is a PhD Candidate at the University of Social Sciences and Humanities, Vietnam National University, Hanoi. He is also a Visiting Scholar at Tamkang University, Taiwan, as part of the 2025 Ministry of Foreign Affairs Taiwan Fellowship, and a 2025 Kautilya Fellow at India Foundation. He graduated with a bachelor's degree in international studies in 2014 and a master's degree in International Relations from the University of Social Sciences and Humanities, Vietnam National University Ho Chi Minh City, in 2017. His research focuses on India's foreign policy, defence cooperation, non-traditional security, geopolitics, and Indo-Pacific strategies.

Nguyen Van Duong (Dr.) is a Senior Lecturer at the Ho Chi Minh National Academy of Politics. He graduated with a bachelor's degree in International Relations in 2002; obtained a master's degree in International Studies, specializing in International Relations from the University of Social Sciences and Humanities, Hanoi National University in 2008; and earned a PhD in the field of History of the Communist Movement, International Workers' Movement, and the National Liberation Movement from the Ho Chi Minh National Academy of Politics in 2017. His main research areas include Vietnam's foreign policy and strategy, foreign policies of the United States, Russia, India, Japan, South Korea, Cambodia, Laos; international organizations; and multilateral diplomacy.

Tran Thi Thuy is a Lecturer at the Academy of Construction Strategy and Cadres Training. She graduated with a bachelor's degree in English Language from the University of Foreign Languages, Hanoi National University in 2002; obtained a master's degree in international studies, specializing in International Relations from the University of Social Sciences and Humanities, Hanoi National University (VNU-USSH) in 2016, and is currently a PhD candidate in International Relations at VNU-USSH. Her main research areas include Vietnam's foreign policy and strategy, foreign policies of Russia, India, the United States, Cambodia, and the global situation.

Nguyen Anh Cuong is an Associate Professor at the University of Social Sciences and Humanities, Vietnam National University, Hanoi, specializing in political science, international relations, and Vietnamese history. With a PhD in History (2012) and postdoctoral studies in political science from Seoul National University, he has authored numerous books and articles on democracy, human rights, and foreign policy. His research spans US-Vietnam relations, political thought, and regional security.

Nguyen Thi My Hanh holds a PhD in World History from University of Social Sciences and Humanities, Vietnam National University, Hanoi. Her research focuses on Vietnam's foreign relations.

Ngo Tuan Thang (Dr.) is currently the Vice Dean of the Faculty of International Studies at VNU-University of Social Sciences and Humanities, Hanoi (VNU-USSH, Hanoi). He was educated at VNU-USSH, Hanoi. He completed his BA (2008), MA (2012), and PhD in International Studies, specializing in International Relations (2018), at VNU-USSH in Hanoi. With regard to contemporary issues, Dr. Thang's research interests focus on the political institutions, public diplomacy (including its nature, mechanisms, and sources). His major areas of research also include Vietnamese politics and foreign relations, Chinese foreign relations, bilateral and multilateral cooperation in general.

Hoang Hue Anh (Dr.) serves as Director of the Centre for Chinese Studies, Institute of Asia-Pacific Studies, Vietnam Academy of Social Sciences (VASS). With a PhD in International Politics from the Renmin University of China (Beijing, China) as well as a graduate degree in Modern history of China from the Renmin University of China, her research has mostly focused on international politics, Chinese foreign and security policy, major-country relations, domestic politics of China and the Chinese Communist Party.

Pham Thao Nguyen (MBA) is an independent researcher specializing in Chinese politics and economy. He holds a degree in International Master of Business Administration from National Central University (Taoyuan, Taiwan).

Nguyen Thu Hang (Dr.) is a lecturer of the Faculty of International Studies, VNU University of Social Sciences and Humanities (VNU-USSH), Hanoi. She holds a master's degree in Asian Studies from VNU-USSH, where she is currently employed. Her primary research interests include Northeast Asian Studies, Japanese Studies.

Nguyen Vo Huyen Dung (Dr.) currently serves as Vice Dean of the Faculty of International Studies at University of Foreign Language Studies, The University of Danang. Dr. Dung holds a bachelor's degree in Asia Pacific Studies and a master's degree in International Cooperation Policy, both awarded by Ritsumeikan Asia Pacific University in Japan. Her research interests focus on international relations, with particular specialization in Northeast Asia, Japanese studies and theories of international cooperation.